Exam Number	MCSE Course Title	Course Number	MCSE Study Series Title	Required or Elective?
70-59	Internetworking with Microsoft TCP/IP on Windows NT 4.0	688	TCP/IP MCSE Study Guide Bulette, 0-7645-3112-3	E
70-14	Supporting Microsoft System Management Server 1.2	732	SMS 1.2 MCSE Study Guide Bulette, 0-7645-3163-8	E
70-87	Implementing and Supporting Microsoft Internet Information Server 4.0	936	IIS 4.0 MCSE Study Guide Dillon, Linthicum, 0-7645-3118-2	E
70-81	Implementing and Supporting Microsoft Exchange Server 5.5	771	Exchange Server 5.5 MCSE Study Guide Robichaux and Glenn, 0-7645-3111-5	E

Microsoft® Proxy Server 2.0 MCSE Study System

Microsoft® Proxy Server 2.0 MCSE Study System

Curt Simmons

IDG Books Worldwide, Inc
An International Data Group Company
Foster City, CA • Chicago, IL • Indianapolis, IN • New York, NY

Microsoft® Proxy Server 2.0 MCSE Study System

Published by
IDG Books Worldwide, Inc.
An International Data Group Company
919 E. Hillsdale Blvd., Suite 400
Foster City, CA 94404
www.idgbooks.com (IDG Books Worldwide Web site)

Library of Congress Catalog Card Number: 99-18441

ISBN: 0-7645-3336-3

Printed in the United States of America

10 9 8 7 6 5 4 3 2 1

1P/QV/QV/ZZ/FC

Distributed in the United States by IDG Books Worldwide, Inc.

Distributed by Macmillan Canada for Canada; by Transworld Publishers Limited in the United Kingdom; by IDG Norge Books for Norway; by IDG Sweden Books for Sweden; by Woodslane Pty. Ltd. for Australia; by Woodslane (NZ) Ltd. for New Zealand; by Addison Wesley Longman Singapore Pte Ltd. for Singapore, Malaysia, Thailand, and Indonesia; by Norma Comunicaciones S.A. for Colombia; by Intersoft for South Africa; by International Thomson Publishing for Germany, Austria and Switzerland; by Distribuidora Cuspide for Argentina; by Livraria Cultura for Brazil; by Ediciencia S.A. for Ecuador; by Ediciones ZETA S.C.R. Ltda. for Peru; by WS Computer Publishing Corporation, Inc., for the Philippines; by Contemporanea de Ediciones for Venezuela; by Express Computer Distributors for the Caribbean and West Indies; by Micronesia Media Distributor, Inc. for Micronesia; by Grupo Editorial Norma S.A. for Guatemala; by Chips Computadoras S.A. de C.V. for Mexico; by Editorial Norma de Panama S.A. for Panama; by Wouters Import for Belgium; by American Bookshops for Finland. Authorized Sales Agent: Anthony Rudkin Associates for the Middle East and North Africa.

For general information on IDG Books Worldwide's books in the U.S., please call our Consumer Customer Service department at 800-762-2974. For reseller information, including discounts and premium sales, please call our Reseller Customer Service department at 800-434-3422.

For information on where to purchase IDG Books Worldwide's books outside the U.S., please contact our International Sales department at 317-596-5530 or fax 317-596-5692.

For consumer information on foreign language translations, please contact our Customer Service department at 800-434-3422, fax 317-596-5692, or e-mail rights@idgbooks.com.

For information on licensing foreign or domestic rights, please phone +1-650-655-3109.

For sales inquiries and special prices for bulk quantities, please contact our Sales department at 650-655-3200 or write to the address above.

For information on using IDG Books Worldwide's books in the classroom or for ordering examination copies, please contact our Educational Sales department at 800-434-2086 or fax 317-596-5499.

For press review copies, author interviews, or other publicity information, please contact our Public Relations department at 650-655-3000 or fax 650-655-3299.

ABOUT IDG BOOKS WORLDWIDE

Welcome to the world of IDG Books Worldwide.

IDG Books Worldwide, Inc., is a subsidiary of International Data Group, the world's largest publisher of computer-related information and the leading global provider of information services on information technology. IDG was founded more than 30 years ago by Patrick J. McGovern and now employs more than 9,000 people worldwide. IDG publishes more than 290 computer publications in over 75 countries. More than 90 million people read one or more IDG publications each month.

Launched in 1990, IDG Books Worldwide is today the #1 publisher of best-selling computer books in the United States. We are proud to have received eight awards from the Computer Press Association in recognition of editorial excellence and three from Computer Currents' First Annual Readers' Choice Awards. Our best-selling *...For Dummies®* series has more than 50 million copies in print with translations in 31 languages. IDG Books Worldwide, through a joint venture with IDG's Hi-Tech Beijing, became the first U.S. publisher to publish a computer book in the People's Republic of China. In record time, IDG Books Worldwide has become the first choice for millions of readers around the world who want to learn how to better manage their businesses.

Our mission is simple: Every one of our books is designed to bring extra value and skill-building instructions to the reader. Our books are written by experts who understand and care about our readers. The knowledge base of our editorial staff comes from years of experience in publishing, education, and journalism — experience we use to produce books to carry us into the new millennium. In short, we care about books, so we attract the best people. We devote special attention to details such as audience, interior design, use of icons, and illustrations. And because we use an efficient process of authoring, editing, and desktop publishing our books electronically, we can spend more time ensuring superior content and less time on the technicalities of making books.

You can count on our commitment to deliver high-quality books at competitive prices on topics you want to read about. At IDG Books Worldwide, we continue in the IDG tradition of delivering quality for more than 30 years. You'll find no better book on a subject than one from IDG Books Worldwide.

John Kilcullen
Chairman and CEO
IDG Books Worldwide, Inc.

Steven Berkowitz
President and Publisher
IDG Books Worldwide, Inc.

Eighth Annual Computer Press Awards ≥1992

Ninth Annual Computer Press Awards ≥1993

Tenth Annual Computer Press Awards ≥1994

Eleventh Annual Computer Press Awards ≥1995

IDG is the world's leading IT media, research and exposition company. Founded in 1964, IDG had 1997 revenues of $2.05 billion and has more than 9,000 employees worldwide. IDG offers the widest range of media options that reach IT buyers in 75 countries representing 95% of worldwide IT spending. IDG's diverse product and services portfolio spans six key areas including print publishing, online publishing, expositions and conferences, market research, education and training, and global marketing services. More than 90 million people read one or more of IDG's 290 magazines and newspapers, including IDG's leading global brands — Computerworld, PC World, Network World, Macworld and the Channel World family of publications. IDG Books Worldwide is one of the fastest-growing computer book publishers in the world, with more than 700 titles in 36 languages. The "...For Dummies®" series alone has more than 50 million copies in print. IDG offers online users the largest network of technology-specific Web sites around the world through IDG.net (http://www.idg.net), which comprises more than 225 targeted Web sites in 55 countries worldwide. International Data Corporation (IDC) is the world's largest provider of information technology data, analysis and consulting, with research centers in over 41 countries and more than 400 research analysts worldwide. IDG World Expo is a leading producer of more than 168 globally branded conferences and expositions in 35 countries including E3 (Electronic Entertainment Expo), Macworld Expo, ComNet, Windows World Expo, ICE (Internet Commerce Expo), Agenda, DEMO, and Spotlight. IDG's training subsidiary, ExecuTrain, is the world's largest computer training company, with more than 230 locations worldwide and 785 training courses. IDG Marketing Services helps industry-leading IT companies build international brand recognition by developing global integrated marketing programs via IDG's print, online and exposition products worldwide. Further information about the company can be found at www.idg.com.

1/24/99

The Value of Microsoft Certification

As a computer professional, your opportunities have never been greater. Yet you know better than anyone that today's complex computing environment has never been more challenging.

Microsoft certification keeps computer professionals on top of evolving information technologies. Training and certification let you maximize the potential of Microsoft Windows desktop operating systems; server technologies, such as the Internet Information Server, Microsoft Windows NT, and Microsoft BackOffice; and Microsoft development tools. In short, Microsoft training and certification provide you with the knowledge and skills necessary to become an expert on Microsoft products and technologies — and to provide the key competitive advantage that every business is seeking.

Microsoft offers you the most comprehensive program for assessing and maintaining your skills with our products. When you become a Microsoft Certified Professional (MCP), you are recognized as an expert and are sought by employers industry-wide. Technical managers recognize the MCP designation as a mark of quality — one that ensures that an employee or consultant has proven experience with Microsoft products and meets the high technical proficiency standards of Microsoft products.

As an MCP, you receive many benefits, such as direct access to technical information from Microsoft; the official MCP logo and other materials to identify your status to colleagues and clients; invitations to Microsoft conferences, technical training sessions and special events; and exclusive publications with news about the MCP program.

Research shows that organizations employing MCPs also receive many benefits:

- A standard method of determining training needs and measuring results — an excellent return on training and certification investments
- Increased customer satisfaction and decreased support costs through improved service, increased productivity, and greater technical self-sufficiency
- A reliable benchmark for hiring, promoting, and career planning

- Recognition and rewards for productive employees by validating their expertise
- Retraining options for existing employees, so they can work effectively with new technologies
- Assurance of quality when outsourcing computer services

Through your study, experience, and achievement of Microsoft certification, you will enjoy these same benefits, too, as you meet the industry's challenges.

Nancy Lewis
General Manager
Microsoft Training and Certification

Foreword to the MCSE Series

Certifications are an effective way of "selling your skills" to prospective employers, since they represent a consistent measurement of knowledge about specific software or hardware products. Because of their expansive product line and tremendous marketing efforts, Microsoft certifications have become the gold standard in the exploding certification industry. As a Microsoft Certified Professional, you are recognized as a "Subject Matter Expert" as defined by objective standards. As a training organization, we recognize the value of offering certification-level training. In fact, approximately 55 percent of students in our Microsoft classes are working toward certification, and I expect that number to continue to rise.

Studies have been conducted that show increased productivity among Microsoft Certified Solutions Developers versus noncertified programmers. Additionally, compensation for Microsoft Certified Systems Engineers and Microsoft Certified Solutions Developers averages higher than for those without certification. For individuals looking for a career in these areas, there is no better metric of legitimacy that can be placed on a resume than Microsoft certification credentials.

Information Systems/Information Technology (IS/IT) decision makers for ExecuTrain clients worldwide increasingly require certifications for their IS employees. Often, individuals are required to be certified or find that certification was their competitive edge in landing the job. Conventional wisdom and every study you read indicates these trends will continue as technologies become more a part of daily business in corporations.

Microsoft recently certified the 100,000th Microsoft Certified Professional. I expect this number to balloon as corporations make certification part of IS staff job descriptions. I predict certified candidates can expect better-paying jobs and positions with more technical responsibility to match their hard-won certification. Although the number of MCPs rises daily, that population is eclipsed by the more than 200,000 open IT positions reported today. Microsoft tracks these open positions and would like to fill each of them with an MCP. My bet is that if anyone can make the math work, they can.

Kevin Brice
Vice President/General Manager
Technical Training
ExecuTrain Corporation

Credits

ACQUISITIONS EDITOR
Ann Lush

DEVELOPMENT EDITORS
Diane Puri, MCP+I, MCT
Jennifer Rowe

TECHNICAL EDITOR
Dennis A. Jones, BSMIS, MCSE

COPY EDITORS
Brian MacDonald
Adam Newton
Dennis Weaver

BOOK DESIGNER
Kurt Krames

PRODUCTION
Foster City Production Department

PROOFREADING AND INDEXING
York Production Services

About the Author

Curt Simmons is a freelance writer and technical trainer. He is a Microsoft Certified Systems Engineer and a Microsoft Certified Trainer, and is most interested in Microsoft operating systems and Internet technologies and solutions. He is the author of several books, including *MCSE Windows 98 Ace It!* (IDG Books Worldwide, 1998) and *MCSE Study Tips For Dummies* (IDG Books Worldwide, 1998). Curt lives and works in Dallas, Texas. Visit Curt on the Internet at `http://curtsimmons.hypermart.net`.

To Todd Tabor, my first teacher

PREFACE

Welcome to *Microsoft Proxy Server 2.0 MCSE Study System*. This book is all you need to prepare for exam 70-88, Implementing and Supporting Microsoft Proxy Server 2.0.

Proxy Server 2.0 counts as an elective exam for the MCSE certification and counts as an MCP exam. Proxy Server 2.0 is also one of the major electives offered for the new MCSE + Internet certification.

This book is designed to give you an in-depth, well-rounded exploration of Proxy Server 2.0. The book prepares you for the exam, but it also gives you a look at real-world issues and problems while providing a hands-on approach to learning the product. Once you complete this study, you will be able to install, configure, and optimize Proxy Server and various network configurations to support Proxy Server.

As the Internet continues to grow and becomes more pervasive in business and organizations, you will be one of those individuals uniquely qualified to support Proxy Server and Internet access solutions.

HOW THIS BOOK IS ORGANIZED

This book is organized into four parts to help you keep your studies on track. In each chapter, you are presented with the chapter content, and then you have a chance to practice what you learn. At the end of each chapter, there is an Exam Preparation Summary, where I point out the major exam facts you should focus on, followed by a Key Point Summary to help you review. Then you can check your mastery of the chapter's content with Instant Assessment Questions and a few Critical Thinking Labs. Following that is an opportunity to practice some Hands-on Labs with your computer. The Hands-on Labs help you see how the software actually functions and increase your chance for success on the exam. The Resources section at the end of the book contains a number of sections that further your knowledge of Proxy Server and help you as you study.

Part I: Introduction to Proxy Server 2.0

Part I is an introduction to the purposes and functions of Proxy Server 2.0, as well as an overview of the TCP/IP protocol. You can use this part to make sure you have a solid knowledge base before beginning your study.

Part II: Installation

Part II gets you ready for installation and then walks you through the actual installation of Proxy Server 2.0. You learn about Internet Information Server (IIS), how Proxy Server uses IIS, installation of IIS, and then the installation of Proxy Server.

Part III: Configuring Proxy Server

Part III explores the configuration options for Proxy Server. In this part, you learn about Proxy Server's architecture, managing the interface, configuring security, and configuring caching functions. You also learn how to configure client computers to use the various services provided by Proxy Server. I also explain WAN solutions where you can use multiple Proxy Servers, and how to configure Proxy Server to work with other BackOffice products, such as Exchange Server.

Part IV: Optimizing Proxy Server

Part IV teaches you how to maximize Proxy Server's performance by using Proxy Server Performance Monitor counters to monitor Proxy Server. You also learn about troubleshooting Proxy Server.

Resources

The Resources section at the back of the book contains a wealth of information. In addition to a detailed glossary and thorough index, you'll find the exam objectives for the Proxy Server 2.0 exam, a detailed Exam Objectives cross-reference chart for study purposes, exam preparation tips, answers to the chapter Instant Assessment questions and Critical Thinking labs, a Mini-Lab Manual that features all the labs in the book, and a description of the CD-ROM contents.

CD-ROM

The accompanying CD-ROM contains the following materials:

- An electronic version of this book in Adobe Acrobat format
- Adobe Acrobat Reader
- BeachFront Quizzer test simulation software

- Microsoft Internet Explorer
- *Micro House Technical Library* (evaluation copy)
- Microsoft TechNet (trial version)
- Microsoft Proxy Server 2.0 30-day trial

How to Use This Book

This book can be used in a classroom setting, or as a personal study guide. It is designed to teach you how to install, implement, configure, and support Microsoft Proxy Server 2.0. Although this book focuses on preparing you for the exam, it is designed to teach you how to support the product. The best approach for success with the exam and in the workplace is to work through this book chapter-by-chapter. I don't recommend that you skip around as you read and study. It is best to start at the beginning of the book and work through to the end.

In each chapter, you are presented with detailed content as well as a number of tips. Don't be afraid to break out your highlighter and use the book as a study manual. After you study each chapter, practice the Instant Assessment questions and the Critical Thinking labs. These exercises test your knowledge of the content of the chapter. Make sure you master each chapter's content before moving on to the next chapter.

Also, most chapters contain hands-on labs that enable you to practice various skills you learn in the chapter. You should complete each lab, and don't hesitate to repeat labs on content that is very unfamiliar to you. All the labs can also be found in Appendix C.

Prerequisites

This book is primarily composed of advanced concepts, and the Proxy Server 2.0 exam expects you to have a broad technical knowledge. In order to prepare for the exam, you should meet these prerequisites before beginning your study:

- You should pass the exam 70-58, Networking Essentials, or at least have solid networking knowledge.
- You should have an in-depth knowledge of Windows NT Server and a working knowledge of client computers such as Windows NT Workstation, Windows 95, and Windows 98.

- You should have a working knowledge of protocols, especially TCP/IP.

If you meet these prerequisites, you're ready to begin this book.

Determining What You Should Study

Regardless of your goals or skills, you should study this book to make certain you have the skills necessary to pass the Proxy Server 2.0 exam. Even if you have a solid knowledge of some of the concepts presented in the book, you should review those chapters as well.

System Requirements for Proxy Server 2.0

- Pentium processor or higher
- At least 32MB of RAM
- CD-ROM drive
- VGA monitor and graphics card
- Two network adapters and cabling, or a network adapter and a modem.

System Requirements for Proxy Server Client

- 486 Processor or higher
- 16MB of RAM or higher
- Network adapter and cabling

Software Requirements for Proxy Server 2.0

- Microsoft Windows NT 4.0 Server with Service Pack 3
- Internet Information Server 3.0 or higher (downloadable from `www.microsoft.com`)
- Proxy Server 2.0 software (evaluation version downloadable from `www.microsoft.com`)
- Internet Explorer 4.01 or higher

Software Requirements for Proxy Server Client

- Windows 3.x, Windows NT workstation, Windows 95, Windows 98, or Macintosh
- CERN-complaint browser such as Internet Explorer or Netscape Navigator

Icons Used in This Book

Several different icons used throughout this book draw your attention to matters that deserve a closer look:

This icon points you to another place in this book (or to another resource) for more coverage on a given topic. It may point you to a previous chapter where important material has already been covered, or it may point you ahead to let you know that a concept will be covered in more detail later.

This icon points out information that can prevent system problems.

This icon identifies important advice for those studying to pass the Proxy Server 2.0 exam.

I know this will be hard for you to believe, but sometimes things work differently in the real world than books or software documentation say they do. This icon draws your attention to the author's real world experiences, which will hopefully help you on the job, if not on the Microsoft Certified Professional exams.

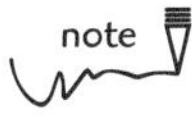

This icon points out an interesting or helpful fact, or some other comment that deserves emphasis.

Here's a little piece of friendly advice, or a shortcut, or a bit of personal experience that might be of use to you.

That should be enough to get you started. Good luck as you study this book and prepare for the Proxy Server 2.0 exam!

Acknowledgments

I would like to thank everyone at IDG Books Worldwide for their support and encouragement as I wrote this book. I would particularly like to thank Ann Lush for her confidence in me, and Diane Puri for her tireless efforts during this book's development. I also owe a huge debt to my agent, Margot Maley, for her constant work and support.

Contents at a Glance

Contents

PART

Introduction to Proxy Server

I

Part I gets your study of Proxy Server 2.0 started by introducing you to Proxy Server 2.0 and related concepts you need to know. In Chapter 1, you learn the basic services and functions of Proxy Server, and how Proxy Server can be beneficial in most network environments.

In Chapter 2, you get an overview of the TCP/IP protocol. You need to have a good understanding of TCP/IP to work with Proxy Server 2.0 and pass the Proxy Server exam. This chapter gives you all the fundamentals you need to know.

Both of the chapters in Part One are stepping stones to the content you learn in later chapters, so make certain you read and review Part I carefully.

CHAPTER

1

Introduction to Proxy Server 2.0

About Chapter 1

This chapter begins your study of Microsoft Proxy Server 2.0. This chapter provides a high-level overview by introducing the functions of Proxy Server, the services it provides, and the benefits it offers to organizations. Chapter 1 also gives you the background you need to begin your study of Proxy Server components explored in later chapters.

What Is a Proxy?

If you ask an ordinary user at a typical company if they use a proxy server, you more than likely will get a raised eyebrow. The functions and services a proxy server provides to an organization are often not readily apparent — and this is by design, as this book explains. In fact, a proxy server that is working well will be transparent to end users. Users often have no idea what a proxy server is. As an IT professional, however, you need to understand not only the purposes and functions of a proxy server, but how to configure and optimize one as well. So, let's begin with a basic question: What is a *proxy,* anyway?

A *proxy* is generally defined as "a person or agency that is authorized to act in the place of another." Historically, the term *proxy* has been used in conjunction with voting, which is probably how you are familiar with the term. In a *proxy vote,* a particular person is authorized to vote for another. In the case where someone is physically unable to appear at the voting booth and do the job himself, a proxy can stand in the place of that person and vote for him. You can also think of a proxy as an agent or intermediary. The idea is that someone or something can stand in the place of another and perform some job or action.

A proxy represents someone else and has the authority to act on that person's behalf. A proxy server, then, is a server that represents other computers and has the authority to act and perform on their behalf.

What Is Microsoft Proxy Server 2.0?

Microsoft Proxy Server 2.0 is Microsoft's answer to the needs of organizations that use the Internet. You can think of Proxy Sever as a hybrid piece of server software that integrates with Windows NT Server. Proxy Server performs several functions originally provided by individual pieces of software: it provides Internet security while improving network response time and efficiency. In other words, Proxy Server is a gateway between the local area network (LAN) and the Internet. These functions give Proxy Server a robustness that is unmatched by other vendors.

Just a few years ago, organizations and businesses were isolated islands. They had little need for Internet connectivity. Businesses today that do not have a place on the World Wide Web find themselves at a distinct disadvantage. E-mail, sales, information, advertising, you name it, it's on the Web. In most medium or large LANs, client computers now have Internet access.

This, however, brings it own set of problems. The LAN is no longer an isolated island, but now has a huge highway going in and out of it. This greatly increases security problems and issues because the LAN is now susceptible to outside attacks. A proxy server can greatly reduce security problems and issues through reduced bandwidth by providing one outlet to the Internet instead of multiple connections throughout the LAN. A proxy server's job, then, is to stand in the place of the computers on the LAN, as shown in Figure 1-1.

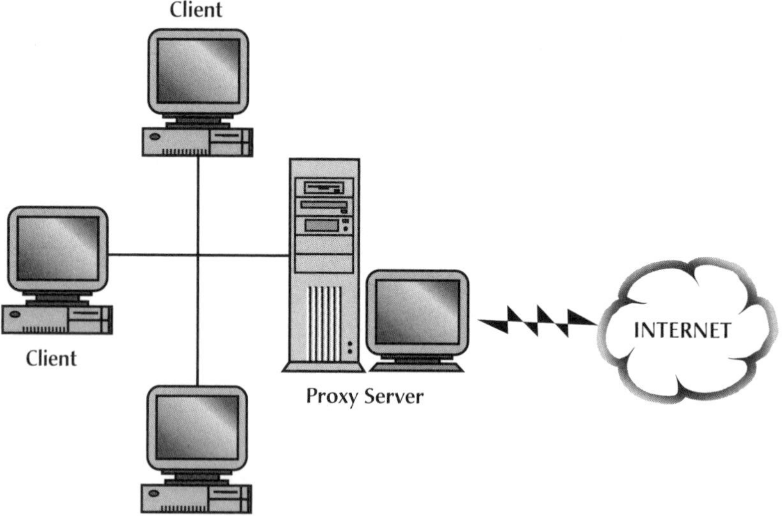

FIGURE 1-1 Proxy Server's place on the network

When a computer makes a request to the Internet, the proxy server takes the request, retrieves the information, and provides the information to the client. In the meantime, the proxy server also keeps unauthorized users out of the LAN and watches for potential attacks. Proxy Server can also be configured to restrict access to certain sites or domains. You can think of this relationship as similar to that between a parent and a child. In essence, I am the proxy server at my house. As long as my daughter is inside the house, she is protected. I keep unauthorized people out so the house is safe. If my daughter wants to go outside and play, I will permit her to go. However, I will restrict her access to certain areas, because she is not allowed to play in the street. Proxy Server provides this functionality by enabling system administrators to control Internet access from one central point, which greatly reduces the likelihood of a security breach from the Internet.

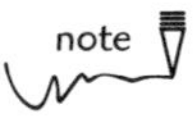

Third-party products, such as Site Blocker from CSM, can be used in conjunction with Proxy Server 2.0 to gain additional security and site restriction options.

Proxy Server Grows Up

As I mentioned previously, Proxy Server 2.0 is a hybrid of sorts. It provides a number of functions that were originally available in individual products from different vendors. If you are familiar with Proxy Server 1.0, you will find that the changes in version 2.0 are significant. For the most part, Proxy Server 1.0 did not provide firewall and security support, but Microsoft combined these features and a number of new features into one product with the release of version 2.0. The following is a brief look at some of the major features of Proxy Server 2.0, which are covered in detail in later chapters.

- Firewall protection
- Content caching
- Security alerts and logging
- Reverse proxy
- Reverse hosting
- Server proxying
- Additional features:
  - Support for HTTP1.1, FTP caching, cache array routing protocol (CARP), and virtual private networks (VPNs)
  - Integration with Netscape Navigator, FTP, and RealAudio

Firewall Protection

When organizations began using the Internet for their business, it became obvious that security was an issue. With Internet connectivity, the LAN became open to security attacks from the Internet. One of the first answers to this problem was a *firewall*. A firewall is a piece of software or hardware that restricts access to the network, usually where it connects to the Internet. A firewall works by using assorted packet filtering schemes, which address traffic at the data-link layer of the Open Systems Interconnection (OSI) model.

A review of the data-link layer and the OSI model is provided in Chapter 2.

Firewalls were difficult to manage and unreliable at first, but with the huge growth of the Internet, firewalls have grown as well. Proxy Server 2 provides full firewall features to restrict and control access to the LAN from the Internet.

Content Caching

The main reason Proxy Server is called a hybrid is because of its firewall and content caching functionality. Proxy Server doesn't only provide security; it provides caching services as well. A *cache* is a temporary storage location, and the concept of content caching has become popular as more and more organizations depend on the Internet for access to resources. The idea of content caching gave proxy servers their name — the proxy server is the intermediary for the computer requesting the resource. The proxy server can retrieve that information from the Internet, but it can also store popular requests in a cache, as shown in Figure 1-2. This is useful because it reduces network traffic to the Internet and provides content to users more quickly.

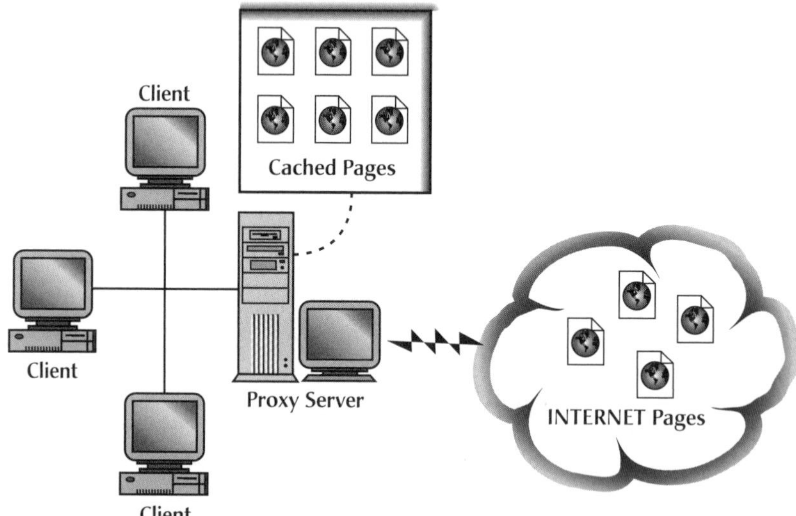

FIGURE 1-2 Proxy Server Cache

There are many configuration options with caching. For example, the administrator can set time to live (TTL) values. A TTL assigns an expiration time to cached material. This way, an administrator can control how long the Internet content remains available in the cache. The administrator can also force certain sites to be updated at certain intervals — whatever the Internet needs of the organization, Proxy Server can help manage it so users get the content faster. All of this is invisible to the user, who feels as though he or she is using the Internet as if there were no proxy server.

Filtering

Proxy Server can also *filter*, or restrict, access to sites, IP addresses, or even domains. For example, you can restrict any site in the `.edu` domain if you want, or you can restrict access to a specific IP address or even a Uniform Resource Locator (URL), such as `http://www.infoseek.com`. This site-filtering function of Proxy Server gives administrators more control over what employees view and use while on the Internet.

Security Alerts and Logging

Proxy Server 2.0 provides a number of security alerts. The alerts for Proxy Server work in conjunction with Windows NT's alerts, and can notify administrators of rejected packets and other indicators that the network could be under attack from the Internet. The alerts are *real time*, meaning that the server can send an e-mail message to the administrator as the event is taking place. Proxy Server also provides various logging capabilities to give administrators a written record of events. Log files can be stored in standard form, Open Database Connectivity (ODBC) format, or structured query language (SQL).

Reverse Proxy

Proxy Server 2.0 also provides a unique function known as *reverse proxy*. Reverse proxy enables a company or organization to publish a Web site on the Internet. The reverse proxy permits traffic from the Internet to access the computer hosting the site, but keeps Internet traffic out of other parts of the network, as shown in Figure 1-3. As you can imagine, this functionality requires some planning to ensure network security.

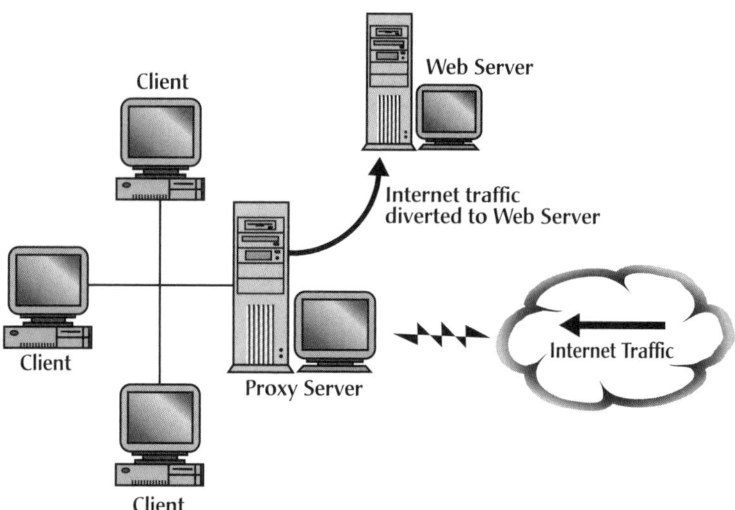

FIGURE 1-3 Reverse proxy

Reverse Hosting

Reverse hosting works with reverse proxy to enable multiple servers on your network to host your Web site. This process makes the multiple servers appear as one Web site to viewers on the Internet while still providing tight security for your network.

Server Proxying

The server proxying service enables Proxy Server to detect the destination of certain packets and send them on to a specified server. This function enables you to have an Exchange Server on your network to send and receive Internet mail. Even though the Exchange Server is located behind the Proxy Server, server proxying still maintains security by keeping these specialized packets on the right track and away from other parts of the network.

Additional Features

There are a number of additional features in Proxy Server 2.0. This latest version supports HTTP1.1, FTP caching, CARP, and VPN support, as well as a number of design options that increase performance. Proxy Server 2.0 also integrates well with other vendors' products, such as Netscape Navigator, FTP, and RealAudio.

Proxy Server even supports streaming, so users can watch live video or hear an audio feed over the Internet.

Services Provided by Proxy Server 2.0

At its core, Proxy Server 2.0 is made up of three different services that support various functions. The Web Proxy Service, the Winsock Proxy Service, and the SOCKS Proxy Service are considered core services. The following is a general overview of each, but I explore them in detail in later chapters.

Web Proxy Service

The Web Proxy Service provides services for the World Wide Web, as you can probably imagine. The Web Proxy Service fully supports Internet protocols such as HTTP, Gopher, FTP, and TCP/IP.

Chapter 2 explains how communication takes place on the Internet with TCP/IP.

For the most part, the Web Proxy Service enables users on a local area network (LAN) to do what one would normally do on the Internet: read Web pages, submit on-line registrations, retrieve documents, and so forth. Proxy Server supports most popular browsers, and can be used by any client computers in an NT domain, such as Windows NT, Windows 98, Windows 95, Macintosh, and NetWare.

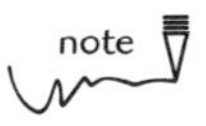

Some configuration options vary depending on what browser you choose to use. These issues are explored later in the book.

Winsock Proxy Service

The Winsock Proxy Service is provided to support client applications that were designed using the Windows Sockets Application Programming Interface (API). The Windows Sockets API is a set of standards that enable applications to communicate with each other. A *socket* is a combination of a port and IP address. Winsock works by using sockets to communicate, and the Winsock Proxy Service provides support for this socket communication. Telnet and WS-FTP are good examples of Winsock applications.

SOCKS Proxy Service

SOCKS Proxy Service provides support for SOCKS 4.3 for non-Windows or non-Winsock clients. The SOCKS standards provide for a secure communication link between a client and a server. Macintosh and Novell clients make use of SOCKS for HTTP, FTP, Gopher, and Telnet. SOCKS does not support User Datagram Protocol (UDP), so any applications that use UDP, such as RealAudio, are not supported under SOCKS Proxy.

What Was That Again?

The Web, Winsock, and SOCKS proxy services are often confusing for those new to Microsoft Proxy Server. I discuss each of these in detail later in the book, but the important thing to understand for the moment is that these services are available to provide support for various services and operating systems. This enables Proxy Server to be valuable in any networking environment, regardless of the services or operating systems used. Table 1-1 gives you an overview of what operating systems use what services.

TABLE 1-1 SERVICES AND PLATFORMS

Service	*Platform*
Web Proxy Service	Windows, Macintosh, Novell, UNIX
Winsock Proxy Service	Windows
SOCKS Proxy Service	Macintosh, UNIX

Benefits of Proxy Server 2.0

Why use a Microsoft Proxy Server 2.0? You can probably see the benefits from what you have learned so far, but I'll take a look at the overall benefits Proxy Server 2.0 provides. These sections outline Proxy Server's value to the industry as well as introduce a few key concepts that I spend more time on later.

Reliability

A great benefit of Proxy Server 2.0 is not only the reliability of the product itself, but the reliability it brings to an organization's Internet connectivity. Imagine a network that accesses the Internet as shown in Figure 1-4.

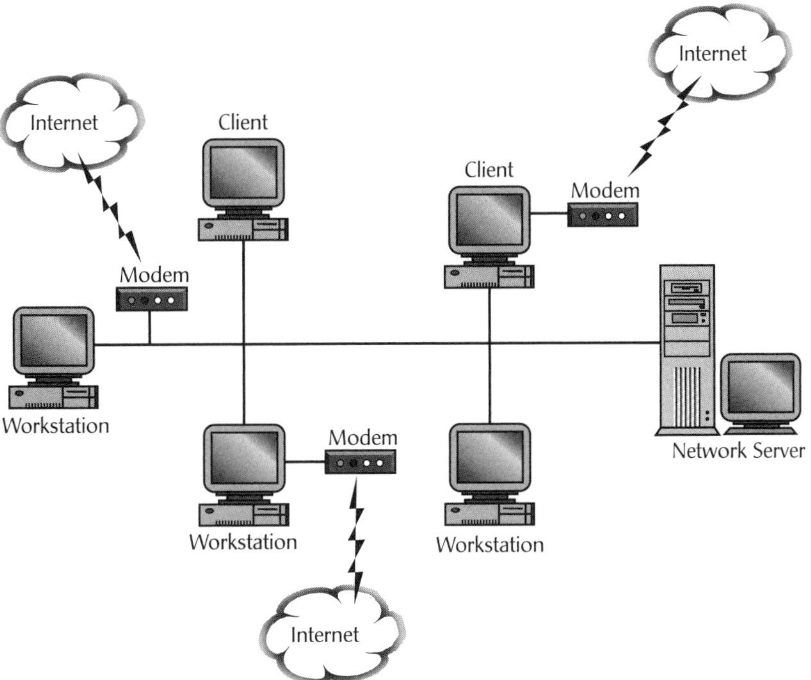

FIGURE 1-4 Dial-up configuration

With individual computers each using their own modem or even sharing modems, connectivity is on a first-come, first-served basis. Depending on modem availability or the traffic the Internet Service Provider (ISP) is experiencing, some computers may have connectivity while others may not. This method of Internet usage is impractical for a productive business that uses the Internet on a daily basis — not to mention slow.

Proxy Server removes this problem by channeling all Internet requests through one dedicated link. This way, all computers on the network have equal, reliable Internet access on a daily basis. This process is transparent to the users, who can use the Internet as if they were connected directly. The reliability of Proxy Server increases the productivity of the whole office.

Performance

Proxy Server provides superior performance in addition to reliability. Through caching, Internet resources can be retrieved immediately, without waiting for downloading or busy servers. When connecting to the Internet from a client machine using a modem, the computer requests data from the site, and the site then returns the request while the user waits and watches the modem lights blink. This process can be time-consuming, as you are probably well aware. As mentioned earlier, caching enables Proxy Server to store popular or frequently accessed sites on an NTFS volume on the Proxy Server. These options can be configured as desired so that the cache is updated at regular intervals. This way, when Internet requests are made from a client, Proxy Server first checks its cache. If the material is there, it returns the cached data to the client. The speed of retrieval is just as fast as other network functions.

If the request is not in the cache, Proxy Server will retrieve the information from the Internet. For sites that change constantly, Proxy Server can be configured to never cache those sites, so the content retrieved is always the most current. For the most part, Internet sites do not change on an hourly (or even daily) basis. This content can be cached so that retrieval on the client end is almost immediate.

The disk space allocated for the cache has to be able to handle the workload. I examine this issue in more detail later.

Scalability

The term *scalability* has become a buzzword when used in reference to computers, especially servers. Basically, the term means that a piece of software or hardware can rise to meet the demand placed on it by the network. Software and hardware that is too restrictive in the number of users who can be serviced quickly is not scalable. For example, a scalable server can quickly handle requests from 5 clients or 500 — it can meet the demand as an organization grows. Proxy Server is a scalable product. When configured appropriately, Proxy Server can handle client requests from a handful of clients up to about 2,000 per server. Proxy Server even extends it scalability further by being a *cooperative* server. This means that multiple Proxy Servers can be configured to work together in a variety of configurations, such as chains and arrays, to meet high traffic demands on a large LAN or WAN. These scalability solutions are explored in detail in later chapters.

Proxy chains and arrays provide unmatched performance, but they should only be implemented after careful planning.

Security

The security features of Proxy Server are among its most important. As I mentioned earlier, an isolated LAN, an island if you will, is in no danger of security breaches from the outside world. If there is no way in, there is no danger. The Internet changes this. Because the Internet enables communication with millions of sites and people around the world, it also opens the door to attack from the outside world. Most businesses today depend on the security and even the secrecy of their data for them to be competitive in the marketplace. An open door to the outside world is a serious concern.

Proxy Server is fully equipped to permit the Internet access for the LAN or WAN while keeping unwanted people out. Because Proxy Server can read and deny access to data at the packet level of communication, its security is difficult to breach. Even sniper-type programs, which are often available on the Internet for free, have great difficult breaching Proxy Server security. This is because the packet level security can determine which kinds of packets are permitted, in the network as well as out. Proxy Server also contains *circuit-layer* security to provide various functions available for Winsock and SOCKS services, such as data streaming and even Internet Relay Chat (IRC). Proxy Server can support this functionality through circuit-layer security while still providing the needed security for the network. Proxy Server supports secure protocols, such as SHTTP and NT Challenge-Response.

There are a lot of options for system administrators to configure security on Proxy Server. I explore all of these options in later chapters.

Internet Access Control

Another great benefit of Proxy Server is the ability to control access to Internet resources. The Internet is able to provide a virtually unlimited and uncensored amount of information — and that asset is also one of the Internet's greatest problems and challenges. Certain content is not desirable. As the debate rages on about how to control pornography and violent content on the Internet, the fact is that almost anything is available. This is a great concern for parents who have computers, but it is also a concern for businesses and organizations. Through various filtering options, Proxy Server can be configured to deny access to certain sites or domains. This functionality helps administrators keep users away from undesirable or inappropriate content.

LAN Support

Proxy Server does not exist on its own. Its purpose is to provide a variety of services to the LAN or WAN so that Internet connectivity can take place. With that in mind, Proxy Server provides a number of features that are beneficial to existing LANs.

- Proxy Server isn't picky about NIC cards or hardware requirements. Anything that Windows NT 4.0 can use, Proxy Server can use. It is not necessary for network administrators to buy a lot of new hardware just to use Proxy Server.
- Proxy Server provides backup and restore options so that content can be restored in case of a system failure.
- Proxy Server supports a number of configuration options, including Remote Access Service (RAS) and auto-dial, if a modem is used, as well as backup routes in case the main link fails.
- Proxy Service provides unique gateway services. A LAN no longer has to use TCP/IP in order to use the Internet. Proxy Server is able to perform IPX to IP conversion so networks who use NetWare's IPX/SPX protocol can still use the Internet (which only uses TCP/IP). This functionality is a huge plus for NetWare environments.
- Finally, Proxy Server is easy! Proxy Server provides a graphical user interface (GUI) for all configurations and functions, as well at HTML and command-line support, even for complicated configuration options.

From an administrator's point of view, one of the biggest benefits of Proxy Server is that it takes care of itself. Once Proxy Server has been configured properly for the needs of the network, it rarely requires intervention from the administrator.

Exam Preparation Summary

This chapter serves as an overview of the functions, purpose, and benefits of Microsoft Proxy Server 2.0. You will be expected to understand the functions and benefits of Proxy Server for the certification exam, but in more detail than is provided in this chapter. The remaining chapters in the book explore these details and give you tips to prepare you for the exam. As far as the content in this chapter is concerned, make sure you understand the benefits of Proxy Server, such as security and reliability, the services it provides (Web, Winsock, and SOCKS services), and the overall functionality of the product.

Key Point Summary

This chapter provided an overview of Microsoft Proxy Server 2.0. The major topics covered were the functions, services, and benefits of Proxy Server.

- Proxy Server 2.0 is considered a hybrid product that provides firewall and caching functions and is an add-on component to Windows NT Server.
- A *firewall* is a piece of software or hardware that restricts Internet users' access to a LAN or WAN.
- A *cache* is a temporary storage. Proxy Server provides content caching to make retrieval of Internet resources faster for the clients.
- Proxy Server 2.0 provides a number security and logging features, such as administrative alerts and logging to various database formats, such as SQL.
- Proxy Server 2.0 also provides reverse proxy and reverse hosting services. These services enable a company to publish a Web site Internet users can access, but keeps the Internet users out of the actual LAN or WAN.
- Server proxying is also provided. This functionality sends certain kinds of packets to certain servers so a company can use Microsoft Exchange for Internet mail without violating network integrity.
- Proxy Server 2.0 also supports a number of additional features and technologies, such as HTTP 1.1, RealAudio, audio and video streaming, and VPNs.

- Security technology ,such as SHTTP and NT Challenge Response, is supported in Proxy Server.
- The Web proxy service provides World Wide Web support for Internet protocols and functionality.
- The Winsock proxy service provides support for the Windows Sockets API.
- The SOCKS proxy service provides support for systems, such as Macintosh and UNIX, that use SOCKS 4.3
- Proxy Server has a number of benefits for organizations. Some of the most apparent ones are reliability, scalability, performance, security, and site restriction.

Applying What You've Learned

The following review questions give you a chance to test your knowledge of the content in this chapter. Should you miss some, review the appropriate portions of the chapter. The answers to the Instant Assessment questions can be found in Appendix C.

Instant Assessment

1. What are the two main functions of Proxy Server? (Choose two.)

   A. Security

   B. Caching

   C. Application Server

   D. User authentication

2. What is a piece of software or hardware that is meant to protect a network against intruders from the Internet?

   A. Caching Server

   B. Application Server

   C. Security Wall

   D. Firewall

3. What is meant by *content caching*?
   - **A.** Local storage of Internet objects
   - **B.** Remote storage of Internet objects
   - **C.** Security
   - **D.** Web page hosting
4. What is the primary benefit of content caching?
   - **A.** Filtering
   - **B.** Security
   - **C.** Performance
   - **D.** Access
5. What does the Web proxy service provide?
   - **A.** Security
   - **B.** Typical WWW services
   - **C.** Winsock support
   - **D.** SOCKS support
6. What does the Winsock proxy service provide?
   - **A.** WWW services
   - **B.** SOCKS services
   - **C.** Winsock application service
   - **D.** Winsock development
7. What is an example of an application at uses Winsock?
   - **A.** WS-FTP
   - **B.** Internet Explorer
   - **C.** Microsoft Word
   - **D.** Netscape Navigator
8. What does the SOCKS proxy service provide?
   - **A.** WWW service
   - **B.** SOCKS client support
   - **C.** SOCKS application development
   - **D.** Security

9. When Proxy Server redirects Internet traffic to an internal Web server, this service is called?

   A. Reverse hosting

   B. Reverse proxying

   C. SOCKS

   D. Winsock

10. How can you restrict the Internet sites users access?

    A. Packet security

    B. Site filtering

    C. Packet filtering

    D. Winsock

CHAPTER

TCP/IP: The Language of the Internet

2

About Chapter 2

This chapter explores the fundamental concepts of the **Transmission Control Protocol/Internet Protocol** (TCP/IP) that you need to understand in order to support and implement Microsoft Proxy Server 2.0. This chapter explains the foundations of the TCP/IP protocol suite, IP addresses and class schemes, TCP/IP name resolution strategies, and TCP/IP utilities. This chapter has both critical thinking and hands-on labs. In the Critical Thinking Labs, you are given three analysis questions to consider, and in the Hands-on Lab, you will install and configure TCP/IP on your computer.

TCP/IP Overview

Network communication, as well as communication on the World Wide Web, has become so commonplace that we seldom give thought to the process. Yet, this global communication is no small feat, and it has been only in recent years that a computer in Dallas and a computer in Tokyo could talk to each other. This ability to communicate through the Internet has changed the way the world works and plays.

To begin a discussion of TCP/IP, it is a good idea to understand how it actually developed, so I will begin with a quick history lesson. TCP/IP and the concept of the Internet originally began with the Department of Defense in the late 1960s. The idea was simply that government agencies and educational research institutions would benefit if their independent computers could communicate with each other. The Advanced Research Projects Agency (ARPA) developed this idea until the Internet Protocol (IP) was developed. This *protocol,* or rule of behavior, provided a standard for each computer to communicate on the network through a packet-switched environment.

With the success of IP, additional protocols were developed to assist IP with file transfers, printing, e-mail, terminal emulation, network management, and others. In 1969, four sites were finally connected, which signaled the beginning of the Internet.

Over the next several years, the number of connected sites grew as other universities and the National Science Foundation began using the technology. At that time, the development of the World Wide Web (WWW), Hypertext Transfer Protocol (HTTP), and Hypertext Markup Language (HTML) once again revolutionized the way computers could communicate with each other. Although it was simple compared to today's complex Web sites, this was the official beginning of the Internet we all know. In the mid-1980s, the National Science Foundation bowed out, leaving the Internet as public domain, because the Department of Defense originally developed it. The rest, as they say, is history!

What Is TCP/IP?

At its core, TCP/IP is simply a standard of rules computers must follow to communicate on the Internet. Just as two humans have to speak the same language to communicate, different operating systems on different network topologies must use a common protocol to communicate with each other. TCP/IP is considered to be a *suite* of protocols, which means there are a number of independent protocols that make up the TCP/IP suite. This is necessary because there are so many different things you can do on the Internet. From browsing, to file transfer, to e-mail, to chat, TCP/IP must be able to accommodate all of these different functions of communication through a variety of protocols. In fact, there are over 100 different protocols combined with TCP/IP. These different protocols provide the vast functionality now available on the Internet. Table 2-1 provides an overview of some of major protocols in the TCP/IP protocol suite.

TABLE 2-1 TCP/IP PROTOCOLS

Protocol	*Description*
Transmission Control Protocol (TCP)	TCP is responsible for managing transmission, error control, and ensuring that data arrives intact. TCP is considered a connection-oriented protocol.
Internet Protocol (IP)	IP manages routing and traffic issues.
Simple Mail Transport Protocol (SMTP)	SMTP provides messaging services.
File Transfer Protocol (FTP)	FTP is used for file transfers as well as directory additions or deletions.
Hypertext Transfer Protocol (HTTP)	HTTP is the de facto standard for Internet delivery of HTML documents.
Simple Network Management Protocol (SNMP)	SNMP is used to manage network devices and monitor network events.
Routing Information Protocol (RIP)	RIP maintains and disseminates routing information for the network by using a distance vector algorithm.
Address Resolution Protocol (ARP)	ARP assists in translation of IP addresses to MAC (Media Access Control) addresses.
Internet Control Message Protocol (ICMP)	ICMP is used by TCP/IP utilities to request certain responses from network components.
User Datagram Protocol (UDP)	UDP provides connectionless communication similar to TCP.
BootP	BootP is normally used by diskless workstations to obtain a boot program from the server.

PROTOCOL	DESCRIPTION
X Window	X Window is used to define a protocol for the writing of graphical client/server applications.
Telnet	Telnet provides terminal emulation for remote connections.

All these protocols work together to provide the various and assorted functionality found on the Internet. The functions of the protocols in the TCP/IP suite are generally divided into three sections: application protocols, transport protocols, and network protocols. These divisions help define the functions of the protocols and how they relate to the Open Systems Interconnect (OSI) model. Before continuing, take a quick look at OSI.

OSI: The Network Communication Standard

If you have spent any time studying networking, the odds are pretty good you know a thing or two about the OSI model. In fact, if you have taken any of the Microsoft certification exams, you have probably memorized it. The OSI model is referred to as a standard for network communication. Originally developed by the International Standards Organization (ISO) in 1978 and later revised in 1984, it has become the standard for different vendors to create network hardware and software that work together to communicate. This way, network environments can communicate without having to use the same operating system with the same hardware.

The OSI model consists of seven different layers with various network functions defined at each layer. Operating systems, network devices, and protocols all use this model to define their various functions and places in the network. Just as different human languages have rules, syntax, and structure that enable people to create understandable messages, the OSI model provides a layered approach to ensuring accurate and error-free communication among network nodes. Figure 2-1 is a graphical representation of the OSI Model.

FIGURE 2-1 The OSI model

The model functions with the application layer at the top, and the lowest layer, the physical layer, represents the physical hardware, such as a network interface card. Packets of data travel down the OSI model, with each layer performing calculations and adding networking data until it is sent over the physical wire to the receiving computer. At the receiving computer, the data is passed up through the OSI model with each layer removing the networking data and performing calculations to ensure that corruption has not taken place. Figure 2-2 is a graphical representation of this process. You can remember the OSI model with the mnemonic phrase, "All People Seem To Need Data Processing." Or the reverse, "Please Do Not Throw Sausage Pizza Away."

Communication between two computers is made possible by a variety of network devices and protocols that adhere to the conventions of the OSI model.

The great thing about the OSI model is the standard it provides for networking components. This means that a network can use network adapter cards, routers, and even operating systems all made by different vendors. This functionality saves money by letting network administrators work with what they already have while slowly phasing in new hardware and software as needed.

Because the OSI model is a layered architecture, each layer builds on what was done by the previous layer. The function of each layer also corresponds to what is done in the same layer of the other computer you are communicating with. Here is a quick look at the basic jobs each layer performs.

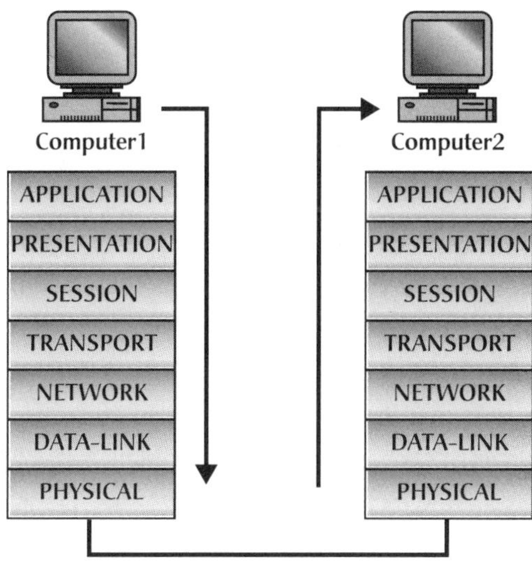

FIGURE 2-2 Communication between nodes

- **Application:** The application layer serves a window for applications and processes to use network services. This layer handles network access, error and flow control, and enables end-user applications, such as e-mail, to use the network.
- **Presentation:** The presentation layer takes data and makes it "presentable" to the network. It strips away application-specific information and puts the data in a plain, intermediate format. You can think of the presentation layer as the network's translator. The presentation layer is responsible for data encryption, data compression, and character-set conversion.
- **Session:** The session layer creates a virtual *session* between two network nodes. NetBIOS functions at this layer, so this layer performs name-recognition functions. The session layer also places checkpoints in the data stream to assist in data synchronization.
- **Transport:** The transport layer sorts and packs data for transmission. You can think of the transport layer as packing a suitcase for a trip. The Transport layer organizes data, ensures that there are no errors or duplications, and places packets together in organized packages.

- **Network:** The network layer prepares the data for transmission on the network. The network layer is like planning for a trip by reading a road map and making decisions about the route. The network layer plans the trip for the data by making decisions about routing and avoiding congested or troublesome network areas.
- **Data-link:** The data-link layer adds additional header information to each data frame, or grouping of packets. It adds a destination address and an origination address, much the same as you would address an envelope to send mail in. It also adds a cyclical redundancy check (CRC) to the end of the data, which is used by the receiving computer to verify that there is no error in the data. The data-link layer is made up of two sublayers, the logical link control (LLC) and the media access control (MAC). The LLC manages data-link communication and defines logical interface points, whereas the MAC manages access methods and the translation of the IP address to the hard coded MAC address that is factory-burned into the ROM of every network interface card.
- **Physical:** The last layer of the OSI model is the physical transmission of data from the data-link layer to the network interface card, and then onto the network cable.

How TCP/IP Is Placed in the OSI Model

As I mentioned earlier, all networking components adhere to the OSI model to provide interoperability, and TCP/IP is no exception. Because TCP/IP is a suite of protocols, the individual protocols work at various layers throughout the OSI model, but they are generally defined as application, network, and transport protocols. The point is that all protocols in the TCP/IP protocol suite adhere to the standards of the OSI model. Figure 2-3 shows where some of the major TCP/IP protocols fit into the OSI model.

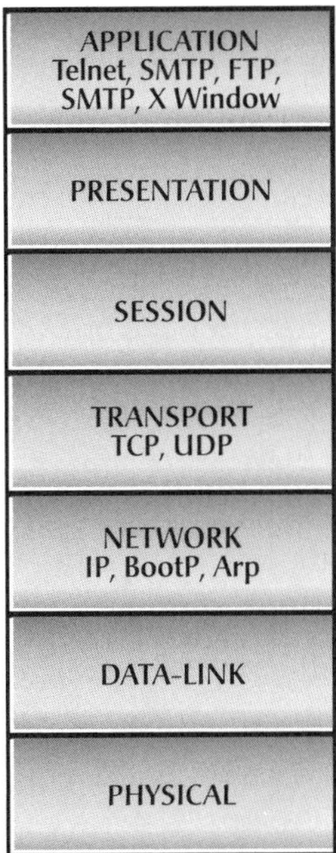

FIGURE 2-3 TCP/IP protocols in the OSI model

How TCP/IP Works

Now that you have taken a look at the background and organizational structure of TCP/IP, you need to know how TCP/IP actually works, starting with a look at TCP/IP ports. TCP is a *connection-oriented protocol*. This means that TCP/IP makes *logical connections* to verify that data arrives at the receiving end. To use a post office metaphor, TCP/IP is a lot like a certified letter — it makes certain that the data arrives at the receiving computer. To establish these connections through the various protocols in the suite, TCP uses ports to create logical connections. Most TCP/IP protocols have an assigned port. Proxy Server can use these ports to establish filters (which are explained in later chapters) so the administrator can grant or restrict access to certain TCP/IP protocols. TCP/IP ports 0 through 1023 are called *well-known ports* and are assigned by the Internet Assigned Numbers Authority (IANA) Table 2-2 is a list of some of the most common well-known ports, and you can find a complete list of well-known ports in Appendix E.

You will see port numbers appear in both questions and answer responses. You should memorize Table 2-2 to prepare you for these questions.

TABLE 2-2 TCP/IP PORTS

PROTOCOL	*PORT*
FTP	20
Telnet	23
SMTP	25
HTTP / WWW	80
POP3	110
NetBIOS Name Service	137
SNMP	161
NNTP	532

At its core, there are three components of TCP/IP: the IP address, the subnet mask, and the default gateway, as you can see in the TCP/IP Properties sheet in Figure 2-4.

These three components provide communication on a small LAN or even the mammoth network of the Internet. The following sections explore each of these three components in more detail.

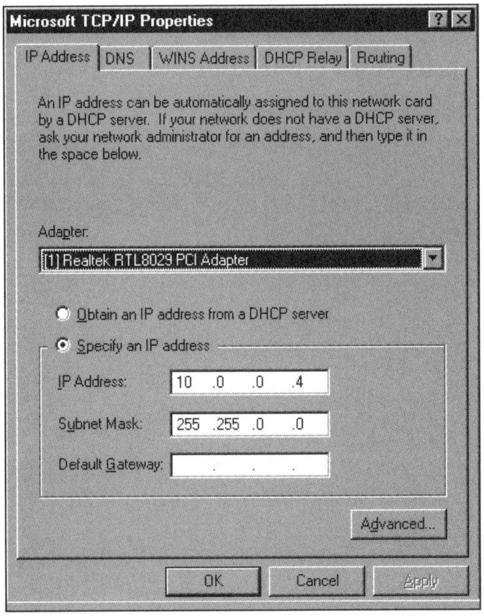

FIGURE 2-4 TCP/IP properties sheet

IP Addresses

Each IP address is 32 bits long, represented as 4 bytes, and usually referred to as an *octet*. Unfortunately, to understand IP addressing, you have to begin thinking in binary math terms, which is painful for most people. Remember that binary math is made up of ones and zeros, where a 1 equals "on" and a 0 equals "off." Binary numbers are calculated by counting from right to left. Each bit counts twice the value of the previous bit. The first bit on the right represents either a 1 or a 0 in base 10, the second bit represents either 2 or 0, the third bit represents either 4 or 0, and so on, up to the eighth bit in the octet, which represents either 255 or 0. So, a binary representation of the decimal value 0 is 00000000 because all of the bits are turned off. The binary representation of the decimal value 255 in binary is 11111111. Using the binary method, you can represent any number from 0 to 255 in an octet.

Here's an example. How do you represent the number 10 in binary? Remember, the binary ones and zeros refer to on and off. Because you start counting at the right, and each bit is worth twice value of the previous bit, you have to find the right combination of bits to set "on" and "off" to equal the decimal value of 10. In this case, you want the bit with a value of 2 and the bit with a value of 8 to be on, because these equal 10 when added together. So, the binary representation would look like this:

```
00001010
```

Remember that each bit value is added to the next to determine the total value. In decimal terms, 00001010 equals 0+0+0+0+8+0+2+0, which equals 10.

Here's one more example. What is the binary value for 255? As mentioned earlier, 255 is a binary octet of all ones. How does this translate to decimal? Because all of the bits are on, and each bit is worth twice the value of the previous bit, the decimal format looks like this:

```
128+64+32+16+8+4+2+1 = 255
```

An IP address is composed of four octets, separated by periods (called a dotted-decimal format). So, the decimal representation of a typical IP address looks like this: 10.2.0.4. In binary form, 10.2.0.4 looks like this:

```
00001010 00000010 00000000 00000100
```

note **When setting up Internet connectivity on a LAN, the network administrator cannot assign whatever IP address he or she desires. Because all IP addresses on the Internet must be unique, an organization called the InterNIC performs the task of assigning IP addresses for use. Companies or individuals must apply and pay a fee to the InterNIC to be issued an IP address. This can be done through an Internet service provider (ISP), or directly at** `www.internic.net`.

Address classes

In each IP address, part of the address identifies the network the computer is on, and part of the address identifies the actual computer. It's a lot like the postal mail. Part of your address identifies your country, state, and city, part identifies your street, and part identifies you. The same is true with an IP address — the part of the address that identifies the network is called the *network ID,* and the part that identifies the actual computer (or node, such as a router), is called the *host ID.* IP addresses are divided into three major groupings: *Class A, Class B,* and *Class C.* The three classes break down an IP address to identify which parts of the address belong to the network and which parts belong to the host.

- **Class A:** In Class A addresses, the first octet is assigned by the InterNIC and the other three octets are assigned by the administrator. Class A addresses use the numbers 1 through 126 for the first octet. They were originally developed for large networks, and getting your hands on a Class A address today is very difficult! A single Class A address can support up to 16,387,064 hosts.
- **Class B:** In Class B addresses, the first two octets are assigned by the InterNIC and the other two are assigned by the administrator. Class B addresses use the numbers 128 through 191 for the first octet. Class B addresses can support 64,516 hosts.
- **Class C**: In Class C addresses, the first three octets are assigned by the InterNIC and the last one is assigned by the administrator. Class C addresses use the numbers 192 through 255 for the first octet. Class C addresses can only support 254 hosts.

Did you notice that the number 127 is missing from the classes? No one ever expected an IP shortage (or the tremendous growth of the Internet), so 127 is reserved for loop-back tests, which are discussed later in the chapter. A whole upper-class address is reserved just for connectivity testing!

Subnet Mask

The second part of understanding IP addressing fundamentals is the *subnet mask.* Understanding and calculating the subnet mask for a network is often a source of great headaches for system administrators. As I mentioned, part of the IP address denotes the network and part denotes the host. But which part is which? This is where a subnet mask comes into play. A subnet mask hides, or *masks,* part of the IP address to keep the network ID and host ID separated.

Because the subnet mask hides part of the IP address, the default values are based on the class system. The computer can identify which parts of the IP address are the network ID and which are the host ID by determining which bits are on or off in the subnet mask. Table 2-3 shows how it breaks down:

TABLE 2-3 DEFAULT SUBNET MASKS FOR EACH CLASS

CLASS	SUBNET MASK (BASE 10)	SUBNET MASK (BINARY)
A	255.0.0.0	11111111 00000000 00000000 00000000
B	255.255.0.0	11111111 11111111 00000000 00000000
C	255.255.255.0	11111111 11111111 11111111 00000000

This seems easy enough, But subnets masks become difficult as you break down your network into smaller subnets. When this occurs, a subnet masking scheme is necessary to give each subnet its own subnet mask. Using smaller subnets is often a good idea to reduce traffic on all major segments, and to reduce the number of computers on each segment. Also, subnetting provides more network growth with fewer growing pains. Often you will see a Class B address using a Class C subnet mask, because this enables administrators to break the network down into manageable pieces.

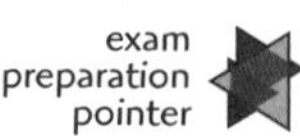

You will probably not be tested on subnet masking on the Proxy Server 2.0 exam. If you want to learn more about the intricacies of subnet masking, however, check out *TCP/IP MCSE Study Guide* by Greg Bulette (IDG Books Worldwide).

Default Gateway

The final portion of an IP address is the *default gateway*. A default gateway is a server or a router that knows the path packets should take to get off the local subnet and be routed to a remote subnet. In other words, the gateway knows that path that leads out of town. For packets to get out of the local subnet, they have to know the address of the default gateway that can send them on their way.

TCP/IP Resolution Strategies

The computer world would be much simpler if humans would simply learn to speak and think in binary math as computers do. Yet, no matter how mathematical we may be, humans are language-based creatures — we speak and think in terms of language. Computers, however, perform calculations in terms of binary math. The TCP/IP protocol is no exception to the rule. If computers could communicate and perform the actions we need them to without intervention from humans, there would be no problem, but we need to work with our computers and interface with the TCP/IP environment.

As I mentioned earlier, computers in a TCP/IP network recognize and communicate with each other by an IP address. This address is essentially each computer's name. But humans have a hard time remembering the IP addresses of every computer on the network. To make both the local network and the Internet user-friendly, computers are recognized by friendly NetBIOS names such as `Server1`, on the local network, and by domain names such as `microsoft.com`, on the Internet. These friendly, language-based names enable you to easily navigate on the network.

Computers, however, do not understand these language-based, friendly names, so the names must be resolved to IP addresses. In essence, computers on the network have to understand that `Server1` really equals IP address 131.107.2.200. To accomplish this resolution, a number of name resolution strategies have been developed to work with TCP/IP. This section examines each of these.

Dynamic Host Configuration Protocol

The *Dynamic Host Configuration Protocol* (DHCP) provides automatic assignment of the IP addresses to computers. DHCP was a revolutionary development in and of itself because it removed the labor-intensive task of manually assigning IP addresses to computers. In larger networks, this is particularly useful. Because each computer on a network must have a unique IP address to communicate, manual assignment is difficult and a simple keystroke error can leave a computer with no connectivity. Troubleshooting was also difficult. With the threats of both administrative and user error, TCP/IP gained the reputation of being difficult to manage and having a high overhead.

DHCP changed all this because of its dynamic ability to lease an IP address to a computer. This eliminates the duplication of IP addresses and greatly reduces the administrative overhead required. DCHP originated from the Bootstrap protocol, which provided IP addresses to diskless workstations. DHCP, however, can be configured to provide not only an IP address and subnet mask, but also the default gateway, the address of the WINS server, and the address of the DNS server.

Any TCP/IP client can be configured to use a DHCP server by selecting the Obtain IP address automatically radio button in the TCP/IP properties sheet, as shown in Figure 2-5.

When a computer comes online in a network, it sends a broadcast request packet to the DHCP server. This packet asks the DHCP server to provide an IP address to use on the network. The DHCP server leases an IP address to computer for a period of time specified by the network administrator. Once half of the lease time has expired, the client requests a lease renewal from the DHCP server. If the DHCP server renews the lease, this process repeats. If the DHCP server is offline, the client computer waits until 87.5 percent of the lease time has expired, and then make another renewal request. If the DHCP server is still unavailable, or if it sends a negative acknowledgement, the client computer issues a new request with a broadcast request packet.

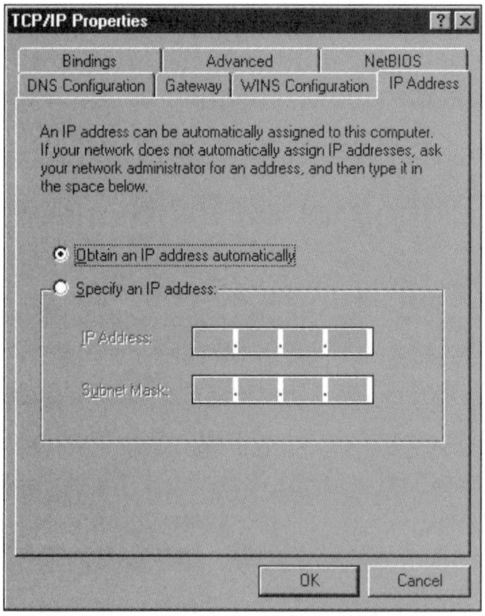

FIGURE 2-5 TCP/IP Properties Sheet

Windows Internet Naming Service

The *Windows Internet Naming Service* (WINS) maps NetBIOS names to IP addresses. WINS enables computer users to call servers and clients by a friendly computer name, such as `Server 1` or Joe's Computer in a TCP/IP network. By using NetBIOS names, you can easily locate the server or client you need to connect to with the friendly name rather than having to keep track of its IP address. Once again, however, computers do not understand NetBIOS names for network communication in TCP/IP, so the friendly name has to be resolved to the computer's IP address, which is then resolved to the MAC address for network communication.

For more information about the MAC address, see the OSI Model section earlier in this chapter.

Networks that do not use WINS use the broadcast method to resolve NetBIOS names, but instead broadcast messages for name resolution, which greatly increases network traffic. When using WINS on an NT Server, the WINS server keeps track of the all NetBIOS names and IP addresses, thus eliminating the need for broadcast messages.

Domain Name System

The *Domain Name System* (DNS) is a static mapping that resolves domain names to IP addresses. Just as NetBIOS names must be resolved to IP addresses for network communication to take place, Internet domain names, such `www.microsoft.com`, must be resolved to IP addresses for Internet communication to occur. As with WINS, DNS enables you to use friendly domain names instead of having to remember the IP address for every site you want to visit.

DNS provides the service of looking up the domain name to the IP address. It does this by first finding the top-level domain. All fully qualified domain names end in a domain extension, such as `.com` or `.net`. Table 2-4 is a list of some of the most common top-level domains.

TABLE 2-4 COMMON TOP-LEVEL DOMAINS

DOMAIN	DESCRIPTION
`.com`	Stands for commercial.
`.net`	Stands for network.
`.edu`	Stands for education.
`.gov`	Stands for government.
`.mil`	Stands for military.
`.org`	Stands for organization.
`.int`	Stands for international.

There are a number of other domains that exist to identify foreign countries, such as `.au` for Australia, `.jp` for Japan, and so forth. DNS resolves Internet names using what is often called the Domain Name Space. With this tree-like structure, resolution occurs by first resolving the domain, such as `.com`, to the appropriate IP address, then moving to left to resolve the next level, such as `microsoft`, and finally resolving of the lowest part of the tree, such as `www` or `ftp`.

For resolution of Internet domain names, a number of Internet servers are usually involved in the process, and as you can imagine, the list is very long. Windows NT includes services for DNS, which can also be used with WINS to achieve both NetBIOS and domain name resolution.

HOSTS and LMHOSTS Files

HOSTS and LMHOSTS files provide the same services as WINS and DNS. A HOSTS file is a file on the local machine containing domain name mappings to IP addresses. The LMHOSTS file is a file on the local machine that maps NetBIOS names to IP addresses. Although these files are still useful in some circumstances today, WINS and DNS have replaced them in most cases. Because these files have to be manually configured at the local machine, you can imagine why!

TCP/IP Utilities

Troubleshooting TCP/IP connectivity problems can be difficult, but fortunately, a number of utilities are available to provide information about IP configuration and connectivity. As a Proxy Server administrator, you will find these tools invaluable for troubleshooting purposes. The following sections list some of the major utilities available with TCP/IP.

Ping

Ping is a popular utility used to test connectivity to another node or even to perform a self-test to see if the network interface card is functioning properly. When you are troubleshooting network or Internet connectivity, you should use Ping first.

First, Ping can be used to perform a self-test. As mentioned earlier in the chapter, a whole Class-A address (127) is reserved for loop back functions. You can test the operation of your network interface card by following these steps:

1. Choose Start ⇒ Run, and type **command** in the dialog box. An MS-DOS dialog box appears.
2. Type **ping 127.0.0.1** at the command line and press Enter.

If your loop-back test is successful, you will get a reply message, as shown in Figure 2-6. This tells you that your network interface card is functioning correctly and is connected to the network.

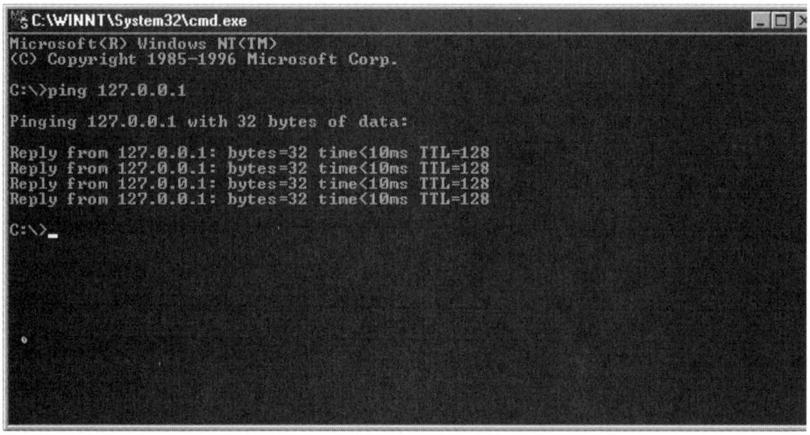

```
C:\WINNT\System32\cmd.exe
Microsoft(R) Windows NT(TM)
(C) Copyright 1985-1996 Microsoft Corp.

C:\>ping 127.0.0.1

Pinging 127.0.0.1 with 32 bytes of data:

Reply from 127.0.0.1: bytes=32 time<10ms TTL=128
Reply from 127.0.0.1: bytes=32 time<10ms TTL=128
Reply from 127.0.0.1: bytes=32 time<10ms TTL=128
Reply from 127.0.0.1: bytes=32 time<10ms TTL=128

C:\>_
```

FIGURE 2-6 A successful loop-back test

The loop-back test is usually the first test you should perform if you are having connectivity problems. This tells you right away if your computer is the problem or not. If the loop-back test fails, you will get a time-out message. Once you have determined that your computer has connectivity, you can ping the IP address of computer you are trying to reach, or the address of another network node, such as a router. You can type **ping** followed by the IP address, such as **ping 131.107. 2.200,** or you can use the NetBIOS name if WINS is enabled, such as **ping server1**. You can also ping sites on the Internet via an IP address, or though the domain name by DNS, such as **ping www.idgbooks.com**. Again, if the ping is successful, you will get a reply message, or if it is unsuccessful, you will get a time-out message. This success or failure gives you your first clues about connectivity problems or issues.

Netstat

Netstat is a utility that provides TCP/IP statistics and current connections. This utility is useful to get a snapshot of your current connections as well as find clues about potential problems. Typing **netstat** at the command line gives you a general connections screen, as shown in Figure 2-7.

Netstat also comes with a number of switches that provide more detailed information about your current settings. The switches are outlined for you in Table 2-5, or you can view them by typing **netstat ?** at the command prompt.

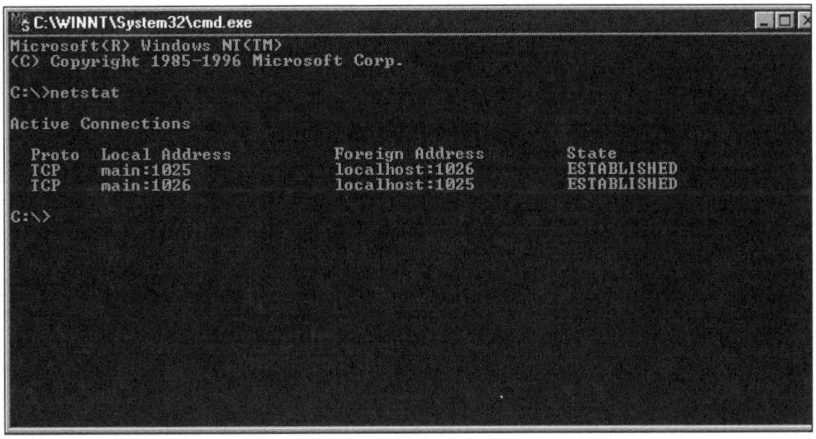

```
C:\WINNT\System32\cmd.exe
Microsoft(R) Windows NT(TM)
(C) Copyright 1985-1996 Microsoft Corp.

C:\>netstat

Active Connections

  Proto  Local Address          Foreign Address        State
  TCP    main:1025              localhost:1026         ESTABLISHED
  TCP    main:1026              localhost:1025         ESTABLISHED

C:\>
```

FIGURE 2-7 Netstat screen

TABLE 2-5 NETSTAT OPTION SWITCHES

NETSTAT SWITCH	*DESCRIPTION*
`netstat -a`	Displays all connections and listening ports.
`netstat -e`	Displays Ethernet statistics.
`netstat -n`	Displays addresses and port numbers in numerical form.
`netstat -p` *proto*	Shows the connections for the protocol specified by *proto,* for example, `netstat -p tcp`.
`netstat -r`	Displays the information in the routing table.
`netstat -s`	Displays statistics by protocol.
`netstat interval`	Redisplays statistics, pausing for intervals between each display.

Ipconfig

Ipconfig is similar to Netstat, but you can gain more information about current settings, such as the IP address of the WINS server, the DHCP server, your current DHCP lease and expiration information, and so forth. Type **ipconfig** at the command prompt, to get TCP/IP information for your machine. Most people use **ipconfig /all,** which gives you a full look at your TCP/IP settings. Figure 2-8 shows the information provided by **ipconfig.**

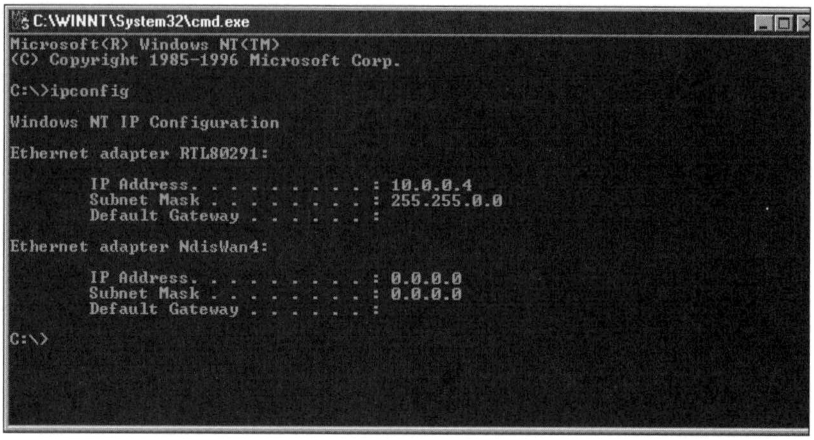

```
C:\WINNT\System32\cmd.exe
Microsoft(R) Windows NT(TM)
(C) Copyright 1985-1996 Microsoft Corp.

C:\>ipconfig

Windows NT IP Configuration

Ethernet adapter RTL80291:

        IP Address. . . . . . . . . : 10.0.0.4
        Subnet Mask . . . . . . . . : 255.255.0.0
        Default Gateway . . . . . . :

Ethernet adapter NdisWan4:

        IP Address. . . . . . . . . : 0.0.0.0
        Subnet Mask . . . . . . . . : 0.0.0.0
        Default Gateway . . . . . . :

C:\>
```

FIGURE 2-8 Ipconfig properties

There are also additional switches that give you more information. The options are listed in Table 2-6, or you can simply type **ipconfig** at the command prompt.

TABLE 2-6 IPCONFIG OPTION SWITCHES

IPCONFIG SWITCHES	*DESCRIPTION*
`Ipconfig /all`	Provides a detailed list of all TCP/IP settings, including DHCP lease and expiration.
`ipconfig /renew_all`	Renew all adapters.
`ipconfig /release_all`	Release all adapters.
`ipconfig /renew` *N*	Renew adapter *N*.
`ipconfig /release` *N*	Release adapter *N*.
`Ipconfig /batch`	Write to a file.

Nbtstat

Nbtstat is like Netstat in that it displays current TCP/IP settings, but Nbtstat displays current TCP/IP settings using NetBIOS over TCP/IP. You would use Nbtstat to find out more information concerning NetBIOS names. Nbtstat also has a number of switches, which are listed in Table 2-7, or you can type **nbtstat** at the command prompt.

TABLE 2-7 NBTSTAT OPTION SWITCHES

NBTSTAT SWITCH	*DESCRIPTION*
`nbtstat -a`	List the remote machine's name table, given its name.
`nbtstat -A`	Lists the remote machine's name table, given its IP address.
`nbtstat -c`	Lists the remote name cache, including the IP addresses.
`nbtstat -n`	Lists local NetBIOS names.
`nbtstat -r`	Lists names resolved by broadcasts and WINS.
`nbtstat -R`	Purges and reloads the remote name cache table.
`nbtstat -s`	Lists the sessions table with destination IP addresses.
`nbtstat -S`	Lists the sessions table converting destination IP addresses to host names using the HOSTS file.

Exam Preparation Summary

The details of TCP/IP do not comprise a large portion of the exam questions. You are expected to have a good understanding of TCP/IP to answer questions that indirectly relate to TCP/IP addressing for security purposes. These concepts are fully explained in later chapters. You should know the well-known ports listed in Table 2-2. You will see questions about port filtering options, and you will have to know what port 80 actually filters (HTTP) to answer the question correctly. This too is addressed in later chapters. You should have solid working definitions of DHCP, WINS, and DNS, and know the differences between the three. You may see some of the utilities, especially Ping, appear in troubleshooting questions, but you will not receive direct questions on these.

Key Point Summary

This chapter provided you with an overview of the TCP/IP protocol suite, including the fundamentals of IP addressing, name resolution, and troubleshooting tools.

- TCP/IP was originally developed by the Department of Defense as a way to network remote computers in government and research institutions. It later became the standard protocol for Internet communications.

- TCP/IP is a suite of protocols, made up of over one hundred individual protocols such as TCP, IP, SMTP, NNTP, Telnet, and many others.
- The TCP/IP protocols conform and map to the OSI model, the standard for network communication.
- TCP/IP is a connection-oriented protocol that uses ports for reliable connections. Ports 1 through 1024 are called well-known ports.
- TCP/IP configuration is made up of three components: the IP address, the subnet mask, and usually a default gateway. IP addresses fall into three Classes: A, B, and C, depending on numerical value of the first octet. The IP address is made up of four octets, which represent the binary IP address. The subnet mask is designed to hide, or mask, part of the IP address so the network ID and the host ID can be determined. The default gateway provides the path out of the local subnet so the data can travel to remote subnets.
- Three major name resolution strategies exist to make the use of TCP/IP easier for humans. DHCP automatically configures and leases IP addresses to network nodes, WINS provides NetBIOS name-to-IP address resolution, and DNS resolves domain names to IP addresses. HOSTS files reside on the local machine and can also provide domain name-to-IP address resolution, whereas LMHOSTS provide NetBIOS name-to-IP address resolution.
- A number of TCP/IP utilities are available for information and troubleshooting. Ping provides a connectivity test to another node or even a self-test. Netstat, Ipconfig, and Nbtstat all provide specific IP configuration information.

Applying What You've Learned

The following review questions give you a chance to test your knowledge of the content in this chapter. Should you miss some, review the appropriate portions of the chapter. The answers to the Instant Assessment questions can be found in Appendix C.

Instant Assessment

1. Who originally developed the TCP/IP protocol?

   A. Microsoft

   B. The Department of Justice

   C. ARPA

   D. The University of California

2. Why is TCP/IP referred to as a protocol suite?

   A. TCP/IP borrows protocols from other suites.

   B. TCP/IP contains multiple protocols.

   C. TCP/IP contains connectors for various additional protocols.

   D. No reason.

3. What are two protocols in the TCP/IP protocol suite?

   A. SMTP

   B. DLC

   C. IPX

   D. NNTP

4. What is a logical connection TCP/IP uses to communicate with individual protocols?

   A. TCP

   B. IP

   C. Port

   D. NNTP

5. What port is used by FTP?

   A. 7

   B. 19

   C. 20

   D. 48

6. What range of IP address are contained in Class B?

   A. 56–78

   B. 128–191

   C. 148–205

   D. 178–220

7. Which is a component usually needed to configure TCP/IP?

   A. Default gateway

   B. SNMP

   C. NNTP

   D. SMTP

8. What is the numerical value of 10000011 01101011 00000010 11001000?

   A. 131.128.2.150

   B. 141.107.2.178

   C. 131.107.2.200

   D. 141.128.2.200

9. What element of IP configuration is designed to hide the network portion of the octet?

   A. Default gateway

   B. Subnet mask

   C. IP address

   D. TCP

10. What is the default subnet mask for Class C networks?

    A. 255.0.0.0

    B. 255.255.0.0

    C. 255.255.255.0

    D. 0.255.255.0

11. What element of IP configuration directs traffic out of the local subnet?

    A. Default Gateway

    B. Subnet Mask

    C. IP address

    D. TCP

12. Which of the following provides dynamic resolution of NetBIOS names to IP addresses?

A. WINS

B. DHCP

C. DNS

D. Nbtstat

13. Which of the following resolves domain names to IP addresses?

A. WINS

B. DHCP

C. DNS

D. Nbtstat

14. What is the command syntax to perform a loop-back test?

A. ping *ipaddress*

B. ping 127.0.0.1

C. ping 128.0.0.1

D. ping *servername*

15. Which utility should be used to view NetBIOS over TCP/IP configuration?

A. Ping

B. Netstat

C. Nbtstat

D. Arp

16. Which Ipconfig switch can you use to get a full TCP/IP configuration listing?

A. `-n`

B. `/c`

C. `/a`

D. `/all`

Critical Thinking Labs

These labs present you with analysis problems to test your critical thinking skills with the content in this chapter.

Lab 2.1 *Connectivity tests*

You are having problems connecting to a server on your TCP/IP network. The server's name is `CorpServerD`, and you have WINS enabled on your network. What are two quick tests you can perform at your client computer to test connectivity?

Lab 2.2 *IP address classes*

A friend asks you to explain the differences between IP Classes A, B, and C, and the default subnet mask for each. How would you explain this?

Lab 2.3 *Subnet masks*

Some networks choose to use a subnet mask that differs from the IP class. For example, some Class B networks use a Class C subnet mask. What are the benefits of this?

Hands-on Labs

The Hands-on Labs give you an opportunity to practice skills you have learned in this chapter. Make sure you read the system requirements for each lab to make certain you have the correct configuration before beginning the lab.

Lab 2.4 *Installing TCP/IP*

For this lab, you need a computer running either Windows NT Workstation 4.0 or Windows NT Server 4.0 on which TCP/IP is *not* installed. It is not necessary that this computer reside on a network. In this lab, you will install and configure TCP/IP on your computer. Follow each step completely:

1. Right-click Network Neighborhood and choose Properties from the menu that appears.
2. The Network properties sheet appears. Click the Protocols tab.
3. Click the Add button.

4. NT builds a protocol list. Select TCP/IP from the list. You computer gives you a message asking if you would like NT to use a DHCP server. Click No. Your computer may ask you for the location of the setup files; you should either specify a directory or your CD-ROM drive.
5. The computer installs the protocol. Click the Close button on the Network properties sheet. The binding configuration is stored, and the TCP/IP properties sheet appears.
6. Because you do not want to use a DHCP server for this lab, you must input an IP address and a subnet mask manually. Assign this computer an IP address of 10.0.0.4 by entering the address in the IP Address section of the dialog box. You can accept the default subnet mask of 255.255.0.0, and you do not need to enter a default gateway. Click Apply, and then click OK.
7. You are asked to reboot the computer. Do so.
8. Once your computer has rebooted, you can verify the install by right-clicking Network Neighborhood, and selecting Properties from the list. When the Network property sheet appears, click the Protocols tab again, and you will see the TCP/IP protocol installed. That's all there is to it!

PART

II

Installation

Part II takes you through the installation of Proxy Server 2.0. Chapter 3 explores the planning stage of installation and covers the issues and potential problems you should examine carefully before beginning an installation.

Chapter 4 explores the functions and installation of Internet Information Server (IIS). Proxy Server 2.0 requires that IIS be installed, and this chapter guides you through that installation, and gives the basics of how IIS works and what services it can provide.

Chapter 5 walks you through a Proxy Server installation. In this chapter, you learn how to install Proxy Server and how to create a Local Address Table correctly.

There are a number of potential exam issues in this part, so study carefully. Also, if at all possible, practice the installation process on a computer.

CHAPTER

Before You Install Proxy Server

3

About Chapter 3

This chapter discusses the issues you should consider before you install Proxy Server 2.0. Planning is of utmost importance, and this chapter explores how to perform a needs analysis, how to prepare a local machine for a Proxy Server installation, how to assess the local network, and what types of Internet connections are available. This chapter has six labs, four critical thinking and two hands-on, to test your knowledge and the skills you gain from this chapter.

An Ounce of Prevention

"An ounce of prevention is worth a pound of cure." You're familiar with this old saying, and this life rule certainly applies in the world of computers and networking. One of the most important things you can do before installing any new software, hardware, or before making network changes, is to plan carefully — and a Proxy Server installation is no exception. There is nothing worse than installing new software that does not meet the needs of the organization, does not function properly, or fails completely. The key to avoiding all of these problems is to plan the installation and configuration carefully, and also know exactly what the deployment is intended to do for the organization. There are a number of logical steps to take before rolling out a Proxy Server installation, beginning with taking a look at the needs of the organization.

Needs Assessment

A needs assessment seems almost unnecessary in many circumstances. After all, new software and technology is always good, right? Software and hardware changes or upgrades are often necessary, but sometimes they simply are not cost-effective. In other words, the benefits to the organization do not justify the expense or the upheaval of a change. Before installing Proxy Server, the administrator should ask some basic questions: Why do we need Internet access? Why do we need Internet access via a proxy server? What are our security needs or concerns? How will Proxy Server benefit our organization? How will Proxy Server make our work easier and faster? Are we concerned about what sites our employees use on the Internet? Do we need a company presence on the World Wide Web? What kind of administrative burden will this product place on our network employees? How will this product pay for itself?

These questions help you take a close look at the needs of your organization and your return on investment (ROI) before you install Proxy Server. The following is a detailed look at each of these questions, which should help you understand the needs of your organization.

Why Do We Need Internet Access?

Online services have become so pervasive in our society that this question almost seems silly. However, not every organization realizes financial or productivity benefits by giving Internet access to its employees. This is especially true of smaller organizations whose business is concentrated in one geographical location. Internet access, though normally affordable, may be a resource drain for certain businesses. For example, supposed ABC Construction Company is considering providing Internet access. They have a small LAN of 30 workstations and one NT Server. Their main business, of course, is building homes. They have a stable name and are not interested in expanding out of their current location. They don't send Internet mail and have no need for Internet resources or a presence on the World Wide Web. Considering this company's business and direction, does it really need Internet access right now? Although Internet access and even a Web site may be nice to have, sound business practices dictate that you should have a need for this service, not just a desire for it. So, this simple question, "Do we really need Internet access?" is an important one that you should consider carefully.

Why Do We Need Internet Access via a Proxy Server?

If you determine that Internet access is a needed part of your business, this question analyzes your need for a proxy server. As I stated in Chapter One, a proxy server provides a single point of access for all network clients. That is, the proxy server acts on behalf of the client and the proxy server is the only way out and into the local network. To return to the example of the ABC Construction Company, suppose the two sales representatives have a need to send e-mail to various points of contact in town. Other than e-mail, they don't need the Internet for their business. In this case, the easiest and most least expensive method is to provide modems for these two sales reps so they can dial out to an ISP and connect that way. It's cheap, it's easy, and it meets the need. However, say that 20 of the clients on the LAN need to send e-mail and even access some Internet resources. Also, suppose the LAN contains sensitive documents. In this case, it's time for this company to begin using Proxy Server to avoid multiple modems and to provide security. The general rule is: If one or two clients need connectivity, a modem is probably your best choice. If most of the LAN needs connectivity and security may be an issue, then Proxy Server will be your best choice.

What Are Our Security Needs and Concerns?

If you have sensitive data on your network (which most companies do) and you are concerned about sabotage from the Internet, you certainly want to use Proxy Server. Proxy Server can control which LAN clients can use various Internet services, and it can also provide firewall services to keep unauthorized individuals out of the local LAN. Modems do not provide the security or centralized administration of Proxy Server, so when security is a concern, Proxy Server is your best choice for Internet connectivity.

You can purchase and use firewalls instead of Proxy Server to provide security. However, Proxy Server is normally a better choice because you get additional services, such as caching and filtering, combined with firewall functions.

How Will Proxy Server Benefit Our Organization?

Once you determine that you need Internet access, you should question whether or not Proxy Server will provide a benefit to the organization. This is an easy question to answer. If you need Internet connectivity, and you have a number of users who need this connectivity, Proxy Server provides a number of services that can benefit any organization. Again, Proxy Server provides security against attacks from the Internet, but with its caching functionality, Proxy Server can greatly speed up retrieval of Web content. Proxy Server also provides Internet mail while maintaining security, and it provides centralized administration so access and usage can be monitored and controlled if necessary.

How Will Proxy Server Make Our Work Easier and Faster?

Proxy Server provides one point of contact for network troubleshooting. This way, one network administrator in one location can troubleshoot connectivity problems, instead of dealing with multiple modem and configuration issues throughout the network. Also with modems, each client needs to establish an individual connection with an ISP. Proxy Server alleviates this problem by providing equal access. Proxy Server makes work faster through its caching functions. This way, Proxy Server can cache popular sites so they are returned to users more quickly. The caching functions are configurable, so Proxy Server can meet the caching needs of your organization. If easy troubleshooting and fast access are important, Proxy Sever is designed to meet these needs.

Are We Concerned About What Sites Our Employees Use on the Internet?

A lot of companies today are concerned about user productivity if Internet access is available. The fear is that employees will spend more time surfing the Web rather than working. There is also a lot of content available on the Internet that is not appropriate for the workplace. If what employees view on the Web is a concern, the first step is to establish clear, concise guidelines for Internet usage. Once employees understand what is expected of them, Proxy Server can also be used to restrict access to this content. You can block access to IP address, domain names, or even entire domains if desired. These filtering functions are explored in detail later in the book.

Do We Need a Company Presence on the World Wide Web?

Just a few years ago, company Internet sites were something extra, but were not considered necessary. Today however, many businesses would be crippled without a Web site. As the technology has grown in the past several years, Web sites have become more interactive. Companies can use them get input from customers, collect customer data, conduct surveys, advertise products, or even offer downloads such as drivers, patches, demonstrations, documents, and so forth. If you need a company Web presence, there are a couple of possibilities. You can hire contractors to develop, publish, and promote your Web site. This takes the burden off the organization, but it can be expensive. If you have one or more employees who can develop the site, you can purchase space from an ISP, publish your site on their server, and then market it yourself. The drawback to this solution is that you have to pay for the Web space. A third option is to develop and publish the site on one of your company servers and use Proxy Server to manage Internet traffic to and from your Web site. Proxy Server provides the functionality to direct Web traffic to the Web server, while keeping this traffic out of the LAN.

Staff is a key factor in determining the method for Web site development and publishing. Many companies find it impractical to employ a Webmaster who can develop and handle the site traffic and issues on a daily basis. Other organizations, however, employ a number of Webmasters to handle their Internet and intranet sites. This decision has a lot to do with the kind of business the organization conducts on the Web and how important that business is to them.

What Kind of Administrative Burden Will This Place on Our Network Employees?

Any time an organization is considering rolling out new network software, you have to ask what kind of burden the configuration and maintenance of the software will place on network administrators and engineers, who are usually overworked anyway. Proxy Server is no different from any other software: It requires careful configuration and occasional maintenance to keep it running at its peak. However, Proxy Server is designed to take care of itself. Once it is configured properly, it does not have to be checked every day. If you need Internet access, Proxy Server should reduce the overall administrative burden, especially in medium to large LANs or WANs.

How Will This Product Pay for Itself?

ROI data is always important for technological environments, because network and computer equipment is so expensive. Essentially, hardware and software must provide enough service to the company that they pay for themselves. Proxy Server provides return on investment quickly, if it is used efficiently. Because Proxy

Server can protect the LAN and provide caching functions, both of which speed the retrieval of information, it makes the user's job faster and easier, resulting in more productivity. Also, if your company wants to publish its own Web site on a local Web server, Proxy Server is necessary to control Internet traffic, which saves money by self-publishing.

After you perform a needs assessment, and determine that Proxy Server is a wise business decision for your organization, you should then assess your network and current equipment. Start by taking a look at the local machine where you plan to install Proxy Server.

Local Machine Requirements

Once you have determined that Proxy Server is a good choice for your organization, your next step is to determine which computer Proxy Server will be installed on and if that computer meets the requirements for installation. As you are probably aware, the minimum requirements published by Microsoft and the practical requirements for day-to-day functionality differ, so I present both in this section.

Processor

Microsoft recommends that you use a 133 MHz Pentium or faster. This processor speed is enough for small LANs that do not place a heavy burden of requests on the Proxy Server. However, for medium-size or larger LANs, you should use at least a 200 MHz Pentium to get the best speed for your network.

Larger LANs or WANs normally use several Proxy Servers in a chain or array. I look at this concept in detail in a later chapter.

Hard Disk Space

How much hard disk space you need depends on the number of network clients, and how you implement caching. Proxy Server itself requires about 10 MB for installation, but you need an NTFS volume for caching. To determine the amount of cache you need, use the following formula:

100MB + (Number of users × 0.5MB)

For example, if you have 150 clients who access the Internet via Proxy Server, the size of the cache should be 100MB + (150 × 0.5MB) = 175MB. For 600 clients, you would need 100MB + (600 × 0.5MB) = 400MB. It is also a good practice to round up your numbers slightly. For example, if you have 150, clients you will need 175MB, but it certainly doesn't hurt to have more space, such as 200MB or more. This gives you a little more room to grow instead of using an exact number. Also, if you end up with a megabyte size that is a fraction, such as 175.5 MB, you at least need to round to a whole number. It is important to determine the number of clients who will use the Proxy Server, so this cache size can be configured before installation.

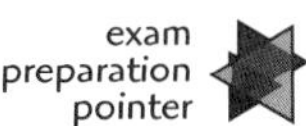

You will be expected to calculate the cache size for various installations on the exam, so make sure to memorize the cache size formula.

RAM

The more RAM you have installed on the proxy server, the better the performance, of course. Microsoft recommends that you have at least 32MB of RAM for a Proxy Server installation, but for satisfactory performance, you should have 64MB or more.

NTFS Volume

As I noted earlier, Proxy Server requires an NTFS volume for caching. The size of the volume should be large enough to handle the number of clients, as determined with the cache size formula. In reality, use as much storage space as you can spare. This will give you plenty of room for growth and avoid later problems with a cache that is too small. Proxy Server 1.0 could use a FAT volume instead of NTFS, so if you are upgrading to Proxy Server 2.0 and you currently use a FAT volume for caching, you must convert this volume to NTFS. This is easy to do, and you can convert without losing previously cached data.

Make sure the cache volume has been formatted with NTFS before beginning the Proxy Server installation.

Operating System

Proxy Server 2.0 requires NT Server 4.0 and Service Pack 3.

Multi-Homed Computer

Proxy Server must be installed on a multi-homed computer; that is, a computer that has two network interface cards (NICs). One NIC is connected to the local network and the other is tied to the Internet connection. This configuration ensures that the Internet is never directly connected to the network, and every piece of Internet communication, whether it is a Web page retrieval or Internet mail, must pass through the Proxy Server. If you want to use a dial-up connection with Proxy Server, you can use a modem or ISDN port. If you use a dial-up network connection, use at least a dedicated 56K or higher connection to retrieve Web content quickly.

I explore how Proxy Server interacts with Dial-Up Networking and how to configure it in a later chapter.

Internet Information Server

Proxy Server 2.0 requires Internet Information Server (IIS) 3.0. or later, which should be installed on the NT Server before beginning a Proxy Server installation.

Chapter Four gives provides overview of IIS and walks you through an IIS installation.

Those are the local machine requirements that you need to meet before installing Proxy Server. By checking these requirements carefully, you can avoid problems during the installation, or even an installation failure. Use Table 3-1 as a checklist for the local machine before you begin the installation process.

Can you install Proxy Server on your Primary Domain Controller (PDC)? This may be a common question. After all, this would save the use of another computer. The answer is yes, although it is usually not recommended. Because PDCs have a lot of work to do already, it is best to give the task of managing the Internet interface to a different server.

TABLE 3-1 LOCAL MACHINE REQUIREMENTS

COMPONENT	*REQUIREMENT*
Processor	At least a 133MHz Pentium (200MHz Pentium or greater recommended)
Hard disk space	10MB free for installation
Cache	NTFS volume using the formula 100MB + (number of users × 0.5MB)
RAM	At least 32MB (64MB or more recommended)
Operating System	NT Server 4.0 with Service Pack 3
NIC	Two NICs, or one NIC for the network connection and dial-up for a modem connection
IIS	IIS 3.0 or later

Examining Your Network

Before installing Proxy Server, you should take close look at your network. You need to gather some information to install Proxy Server, but there are also some network considerations before that.

Local Address Table

Before you install Proxy Server, you need to understand one of its components, and gather some information. The *Local Address Table* (LAT) is Proxy Server's storehouse of IP addresses for the local network. The LAT allows Proxy Server to understand which addresses are local, meaning that they reside on the LAN, and which are not. This tells Proxy Server who is a member of the LAN, and which IP addresses belong to the local network and not the Internet. When you install Proxy Server, you create the LAT and tell Proxy Server which IP addresses to include. You can manually add the IP address range or use an NT internal routing table to gather the information. You must also know the IP address range of the network. Before you install Proxy Server, it's best to gather this information before you install Proxy Server. If you are using a DHCP server, you need to include in the LAT the address range your DHCP server uses.

In Chapter 5, I explain how to construct the LAT in a step-by-step manner, but for now, you should gather IP address range information for your network to make the installation easier.

Network Traffic Considerations

As a part of examining your network, you should consider the traffic increase that Internet connectivity will bring. This is a point that is often overlooked. Internet service to clients will increase the traffic on the local network. As users begin accessing the Internet and services, this traffic will place an additional load on your network. Although Proxy Server speeds the retrieval of Web content by caching, it cannot aid with network traffic problems — this cached content still has to travel over the network to the client from the Proxy Server.

You can take a traffic assessment in a couple of ways. First, it is good idea to use Performance Monitor to watch the performance of the local machine where you will install Proxy Server. This will help you identify bottlenecks if any exist. A *bottleneck* is a network device, such as a NIC or processor, that cannot handle the number of service requests placed on it. If you follow the local machine requirements discussed earlier in the chapter, you should be in good shape, but you can use Performance Monitor to monitor the activity of your computer, as shown in Figure 3-1.

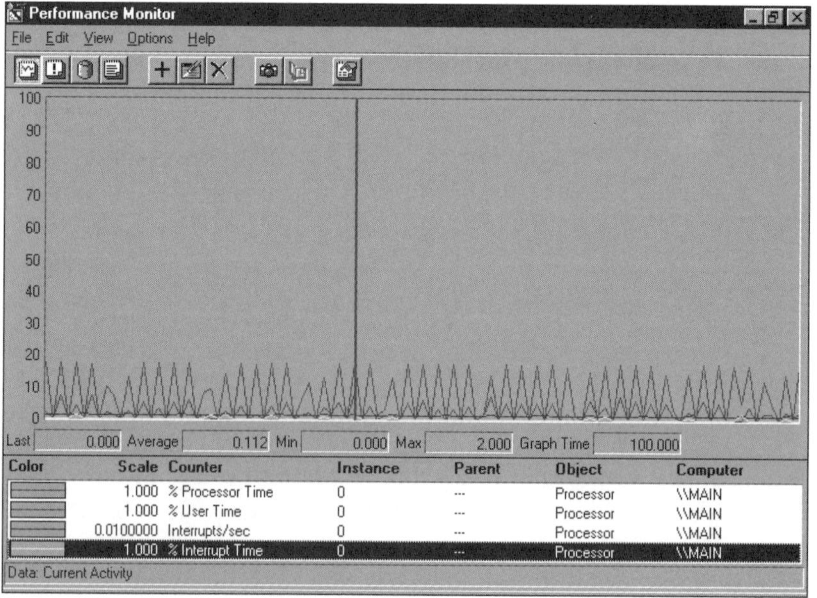

FIGURE 3-1 NT Server Performance Monitor

Performance Monitor enables you to view and record a variety of counters and statistical information about the performance of your computer, such as processor time, interrupts per second, user time, and so forth.

After you are satisfied with the performance of your local machine, you should then take into account the network performance. You can use Network Monitor in NT Server to view real-time statistics and packet capture to identify traffic or network utilization problems. Network Monitor is shown in Figure 3-2.

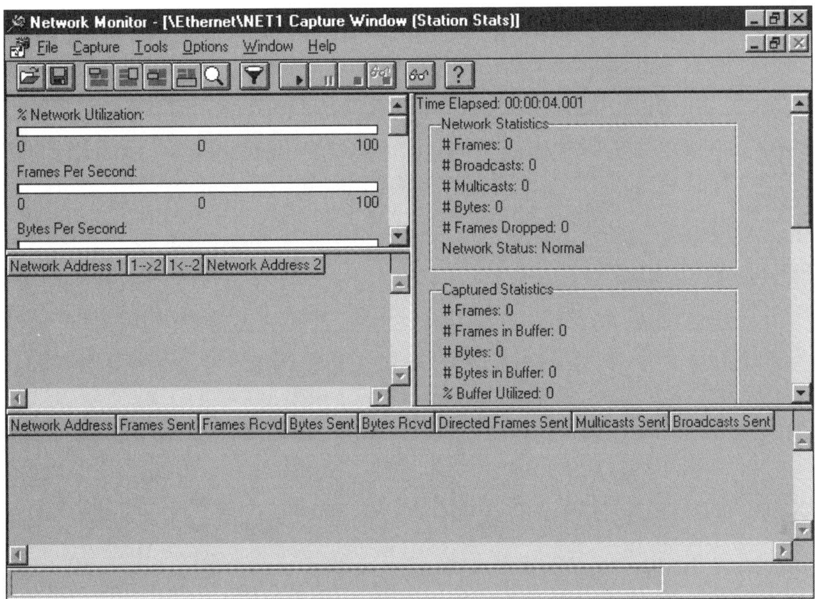

FIGURE 3-2 NT Server Network Monitor

You can compare the data from Network Monitor with the actual capacity of the hardware your network uses. Also, it is wise to establish a baseline of performance. A *baseline* is simply the average network traffic or utilization at a standard time during the day. Establish a baseline during normal working hours — not peak times or low utilization times, but during what is considered normal traffic time. A good baseline contains an average of three or four days of traffic taken from a normal traffic time. For example, you could gather network utilization statistics from 10 A.M. to 2 P.M. for three or four days, and then average the utilization data.

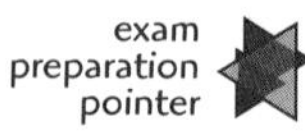

Keep in mind that a baseline of performance should be measured during normal utilization hours. This will give you an accurate measure of standard network utilization and performance.

After you establish the baseline, you will be able to see the standard utilization for your network. If your network is running consistently at 60 to 70 percent utilization, you will experience network problems when you add Internet traffic.

You should also keep in mind future growth. If you expect the network to grow significantly, your hardware must also grow to accommodate this new traffic load. If your network utilization is high, but you must provide Internet access, you can use Proxy Server to limit the kind of information users can access, which will help reduce Internet traffic and the load on the network. This is a temporary solution at best, however. The information you gain by using Network Monitor and establishing baselines will help you make decisions about future potential issues and problems so you can plan for them.

Connecting to the Internet

Once you decide to provide Internet access to your network, you must decide which kind of connection is best. This decision can be difficult, because it combines the factors of what you want, what you need, and what you can afford. Service in the price range you want may not provide the service you really need. The following is a look at the options and the advantages and disadvantages of each.

Standard ISP Accounts

The most common kind of connection to the Internet is through an ISP. When you use the term *ISP*, you're usually referring to a local ISP — that is, a company that has access points in your local area or perhaps a small extended area. Most ISPs do not provide services nationally or globally. The reality is that these ISPs purchase blocks of Internet access from wholesale providers who sell backbone access to smaller ISPs. This is a confusing structure, I admit.

Think of it this way: Large, wholesale ISPs own the backbone segments, which are capable of high bandwidth service. These wholesale ISPs normally do not sell dial-up services to individuals or businesses, unless the business is very large. The wholesale ISPs sell access to the backbone to local ISPs. The local ISPs then sell dial-up service to the customers. So, the local ISP is generally a middleman between the customer and the actual backbone, as shown in Figure 3-3. The distinction is fuzzy, however, because some local ISPs do sell direct backbone access to businesses and individuals.

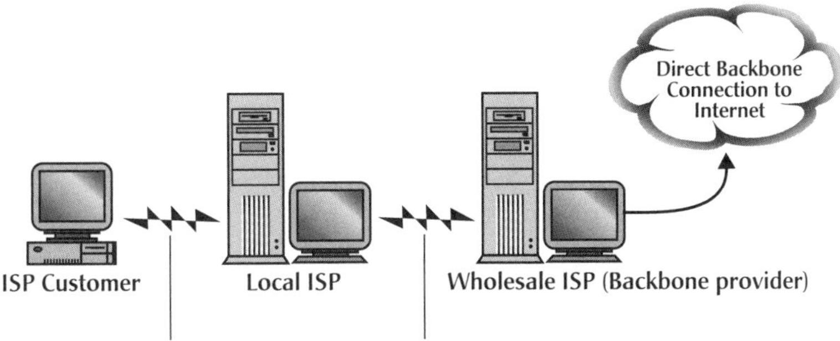

FIGURE 3-3 ISP connection design

When making an ISP selection, there are a few points you should keep in mind:

- **Connection time:** Does the ISP provide 24-hour unlimited access, or will you have to pay additional connectivity charges should you go over a certain amount of time? Most ISPs today sell unlimited connectivity for a flat rate.
- **Connection speed:** What kind of connection speed is available and how much does it cost? The speed and dedication of your connection is one of the most important questions — and the service varies greatly among ISPs.
- **Technical support:** Does the ISP provide round-the-clock customer support if you experience technical problems? Although this seems unusual, many ISPs do not provide free 24-hour technical support.
- **Payment:** How will your organization have to pay for connectivity charges? Can you pay on a monthly basis or do you have to pay for a yearly connection in advance? And if so, can you get your money back if you are unhappy with the service?

- **Reputation:** What does word of mouth say about the ISP? Are their services and connectivity generally reliable? Do they have enough modems to service their clients, or will you get a lot of busy signals?
- **Additional services:** Does the ISP provide additional services that may be of benefit to your organization in the future?

LAN connection options

One of the most important decisions you will make concerns the type of connection you choose to purchase. This will determine whether you will get the performance you want for your network. There are a number of types available; here's a look at the major ones.

Standard analog connections Standard analog connections are the most common. These are used by small business and individuals and provide a maximum bandwidth of 56Kbps, depending on the user's modem and traffic on the network. Standard analog connections are usually not *dedicated*. That is, you have to compete for a connection with other customers, although some ISPs are beginning to offer dedicated services at an additional cost. An analog connection is not a good choice for organizations that use a Proxy Server, because it cannot provide the necessary performance for the LAN. An analog connection, however, can be used as backup route, should the main connection fail.

Integrated Services Digital Network Integrated Services Digital Network (ISDN) is a digital connection that can communicate with other ISDN lines or standard analog lines. ISDN requires special connection equipment capable of digital communication. ISDN adapters are more comparable to NICs than modems, because modems translate digital signals from your computer to analog signals for the phone line, and vice versa., ISDN adapters do not translate data to analog form.

ISDN lines are available in either basic rate interface (BRI) or primary rate interface (PRI). BRI contains two 64Kbps channels and an additional 16Kbps for administrative call management. Combined, the maximum throughput is 128Kbps. PRI uses 24 channels along with one additional channel for administrative call management for a maximum throughput of 1.544Mbps.

T1 lines A T1 line is a digital link that provides a bandwidth of 1.54Mbps. A T1 line is considered a point-to-point dedicated link. T1 lines are made of 24 64Kbps wires. T1 lines are the standard for large organizations and provide highly reliable communication and service to the LAN. As you can imagine, they are expensive.

Fractional T1 Lines If a T1 line is too expensive for your organization, you can lease a *fractional T1*, or a fraction of a T1 line. The lease agreement normally allows you from 1 to 23 T1 wires at 64Kbps, depending on what you want and how much you want to pay. Most ISPs that offer T1 services have standard package offers for fractional T1 service.

What does all of this cost?

As you are aware, the cost of these services often drive which service you will use. The prices of these services vary from provider to provider, and it is always wise to do your homework and shop around. Table 3-2 gives the approximate cost of each kind of service, but do keep in mind that these prices vary depending on the local competition and from one geographical location to another. Keep in mind that these estimates do not include setup fees, which can range from $20 for a standard analog connection to over $1,000 for a T1 line.

TABLE 3-2 ISP Approximate Connectivity Prices

Service	Approximate Price per Month (Excluding Setup)
Standard analog connection (up to 56Kbps)	$15 – $30
128Kbps ISDN (not dedicated)	$30 – $45
128Kbps ISDN (dedicated)	$275 – $300
Fractional T1 (384Kbps)	$1300 – $1400
Full T1	$1900 – $2500

WAN connection options

There are some additional connectivity options available for WAN environments. These solutions are expensive and usually require expensive hardware to support them, but depending on the size of the WAN, they do offer superior communications performance. Here are three of the major ones.

T3 line The next step up from a T1 line is a T3. A T3 line equals 28 T1 lines, for a bandwidth of 44.736Mbps. You see T3 line used as backbones for large networks that require superior communications. As you can imagine, the expense is great. Most T3 lines cost in excess of $50,000 per month, which does not include equipment and installation.

Frame Relay Frame Relay is a digital packet-switching technology. It is a point-to-point system that uses private virtual circuits to transmit variable length frames. Bandwidth can be purchased on an as-needed basis, so it can handle virtually any kind of transmission, depending on how much you want to pay.

ATM Asynchronous Transfer Mode (ATM) offers speeds from 155Mbps to over 2Gbps, theoretically, although most ATM boards offer a speed of about 155Mbps or slightly less. ATM sends data in fixed-sized cells and is capable of transmitting voice, data, real-time video and audio, and other high-bandwidth transmissions.

Exam Preparation Summary

This chapter covers in part the planning objectives for the exam. Keep in mind that the best time to determine a baseline of performance is during normal network utilization times on normal days. Performance Monitor and Network Monitor are useful NT Server tools for assessing the performance of both the server and the network. You should keep in mind the requirements for a Proxy Server installation, especially an NTFS volume for the cache, IIS 3.0 or later, and two NICs. Also, remember the formula for calculating the disk space needed for the cache. You need to understand what the LAT does and how it works. I focus on the LAT in more detail later in the book. You will not see direct questions about ISDN, T1, T3, and so forth, but you should keep them in mind for troubleshooting questions and scenarios.

Key Point Summary

This chapter provided you with proper planning steps to ensure that a deployment of Proxy Server is successful in your network.

- A needs assessment should be carefully considered to determine if your network needs Internet access and if you should use Proxy Server for this access.
- Some of the determining factors when considering the need for Internet access and Proxy Server deployment are business need, expense, security, and network management.
- The minimum hardware requirements for a Proxy Server installation are at least a 133 MHz Pentium 133 processor, at least 32MB of RAM, and enough disk space for the installation (10MB) and caching.
- The Proxy Server cache requires an NTFS volume that is large enough to handle the caching needs of the network clients. This can be calculated by using the formula 100MB + (number of users × 0.5MB).
- Proxy Server must be installed on an NT Server with Service Pack 3.
- Proxy Server requires IIS 3.0 or later for installation.
- Proxy Server requires a multi-homed computer or a computer with one NIC and dial-up capability.
- The Local Address Table (LAT) is a Proxy Server component that is built during installation. The LAT contains the local IP addresses, which are not used for Internet communications.
- Network utilization should be considered before using Internet services. Internet traffic will increase network utilization, so the network must be able to handle the additional load.
- NT Server Performance Monitor and Network Monitor can be used to determine important network data concerning local machine bottlenecks and network traffic issues.
- A baseline of performance should be established during normal traffic times during a normal business day.
- ISPs provide a variety of service options other than normal analog connections. Some of the more common options are analog up to 56Kbps, ISDN, T1, and fractional T1.
- Additional WAN connectivity solutions are available. Some of the most common ones are T3, Frame Relay, and ATM.

Applying What You've Learned

The following review questions give you a chance to test your knowledge of the content in this chapter. Should you miss some, review the appropriate portions of the chapter. The answers to the Instant Assessment questions can be found in Appendix C.

Instant Assessment

1. What is the minimum processor recommended by Microsoft for a Proxy Server installation?

   A. 100MHz Pentium

   B. 133MHz Pentium

   C. 166MHz Pentium

   D. 266MHz Pentium

2. What is the minimum amount of RAM recommended by Microsoft for a Proxy Server installation?

   A. 16MB

   B. 32MB

   C. 64MB

   D. 128MB

3. How must the cache volume be formatted?

   A. FAT

   B. FAT32

   C. VFAT

   D. NTFS

4. Proxy Server requires a multi-homed computer. What does this mean?

   A. A computer with one NIC

   B. A computer with two NICs

   C. A computer with three NICs

   D. A computer with four NICs

5. If you have 475 clients who will use the Proxy Server, how much hard disk space should be used for caching?

   A. 337MB

   B. 400MB

   C. 632MB

   D. 783MB

6. What version of IIS must be used for Proxy Server 2?

   A. 2.0 or higher

   B. 3.0 or higher

   C. 4.0 or higher

   D. 5.0 or higher

7. What is the LAT?

   A. Local Access Table

   B. Local Address Table

   C. Local Alpha Team

   D. LAN Access Table

8. What IP addresses should be included in the LAT?

   A. Internal IP addresses only

   B. External IP addresses only

   C. Both internal and external IP addresses

   D. IP addresses are not included in the LAT

9. What Windows NT monitor should be used to gather statistics on the network utilization?

   A. Performance Monitor

   B. Network Monitor

   C. Client Monitor

   D. Proxy Monitor

10. What Windows NT monitor should be used to watch for bottlenecks on the local machine?

    A. Performance Monitor

    B. Network Monitor

    C. Client Monitor

    D. Proxy Monitor

11. When should a performance baseline be established?

    A. During peak traffic hours

    B. During slow traffic hours

    C. During normal traffic hours

    D. All of the above

12. What is the maximum modem speed that can be provided by analog dial-up accounts?

    A. 33Kbps

    B. 56Kbps

    C. 78Kbps

    D. 128Kbps

13. What is the bandwidth of an ISDN BRI line?

    A. 56Kbps

    B. 80Kbps

    C. 128Kbps

    D. 220Kbps

14. What is the bandwidth of a T1 line?

    A. 1.0Mbps

    B. 1.54Mbps

    C. 1.78Mbps

    D. 2.0Mbps

Critical Thinking Labs

These labs present you with analysis problems to test your critical thinking skills with the content in this chapter.

Lab 3.5 *Configuring the network*

Lewis Manufacturing Company has 1000 users on an NT network. They would like to provide Internet access to all of the users with Proxy Server. How much disk space should be allocated for the cache, and what type of ISP connection would be best for this amount of traffic?

Lab 3.6 *Internet connectivity*

As a consultant, you have been asked to outline the advantages and disadvantages of ISDN connectivity and T1 connectivity for a LAN of 600 users so management can make a decision about which one to purchase. What would you say?

Lab 3.7 *Establishing a baseline*

A friend has heard of establishing a baseline of performance, but doesn't understand the concept. How would you explain this to your friend, and what tools would you suggest to establish a network performance baseline?

Lab 3.8 *Needs assessment*

You have been hired by a small company that is considering adding Internet access to their LAN to perform a needs assessment. What are two major questions you should ask and why are those questions important?

Hands-on Labs

The Hands-on Labs give you an opportunity to practice skills you have learned in this chapter. Make sure you read the system requirements for each lab to be certain you have the correct configuration before beginning the lab.

Lab 3.9 *Local IP addresses using DHCP*

This lab assumes you are using NT Server 4.0 with TCP/IP installed on a TCP/IP network. In preparation for Proxy Server installation, it is a good idea to gather information about the TCP/IP address range of your network for the LAT construction during setup. This lab will guide you through a two-part process, depending on your network configuration.

To gather the IP address range for a network using DHCP Server, follow these steps:

1. In NT Server, click Start ⇛ Administrative Tools ⇛ DHCP Manager.
2. The DHCP Manager interface appears, as shown in Figure 3-4.

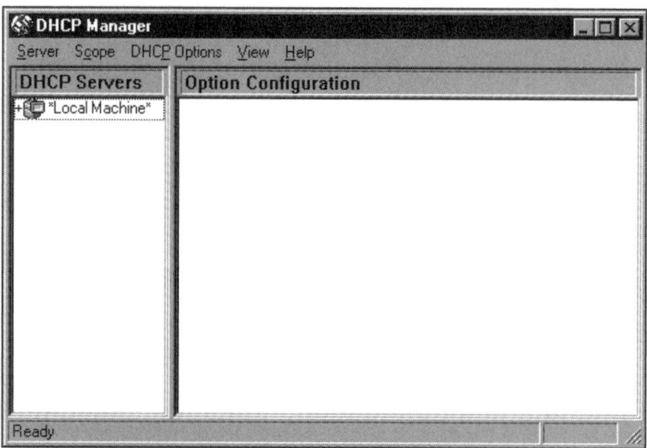

FIGURE 3-4 DHCP Manager

3. Click the Scope menu. You can view the scope properties and IP address range of your network. Note this address range should be noted and include it in the LAT. Make sure you include any reserved IP addresses as a part of the LAT.
4. If you are using a multi-homed computer, as recommended, make certain that the IP address of the NIC that is bound to the local network is included in the LAT. If the Server's IP address is assigned statically, view its IP address by right-clicking Network Neighborhood, choosing the Protocols tab, selecting TCP/IP Protocol, and clicking the "Properties" button. This page shows you the NIC and the IP address assigned to it.

Lab 3.10 *Local IP addresses without DHCP*

This lab assumes you use a network that does not have a DCHP Server, such as in a small workgroup or LAN.

1. If your workgroup or LAN does not use DHCP Server, you must note the IP address of each machine and network node manually.

2. First, find any documentation about the network. Hopefully, records have been kept for the network addresses that have been assigned to each node.
3. Whether a document exists or not, it is a good idea to go to each machine and check each IP address manually so you have an accurate range when you install Proxy Server.
4. To check the IP address of each NT machine, right-click Network Neighborhood, choose Properties, select the Protocol tab, select TCP/IP, and then click the Properties button. This gives you the IP address of the computer.
5. For Windows 95/98 computers, right-click Network Neighborhood, choose Properties, select TCP/IP Adapter, and then click the Properties button. This gives you the IP address of the computer.
6. If you are using Macintosh computers in your NT network, you can view the TCP/IP address of a Mac by opening control panel and double-clicking TCP/IP. This gives you the IP address of the computer.

CHAPTER

4

Internet Information Server Overview

About Chapter 4

This chapter gives you an overview of Internet Information Server (IIS). IIS is a separate component from Proxy Server, but it is required to install Proxy Server 2.0, so you need to know a thing or two about it.

This chapter provides an overview, explains the installation of IIS and related components, describes the features and core components of IIS, and explores the additional components that give IIS the functionality to work with the vast technologies and functions of the Internet.

What Is Internet Information Server?

IIS, at its core, does exactly what its name implies — it serves Web pages and related services to clients. The next logical question may be, "Why are you talking about IIS in a Proxy Server book?" The answer to that question is that IIS and Proxy Server 2.0 are closely tied together — in fact, IIS 3.0 or later is required to install Proxy Server 2.0 — even if you don't intend on hosting Web pages from your server.

IIS turns your server into a Web-hosting server. You can host Web sites using a wide variety of scripting options and functions, including FrontPage 98 Web sites. IIS includes many components that give your Web server additional functionality, such as Transaction Server, Index Server, Internet Connection Services for RAS, and a number of other services that I discuss in this chapter. IIS and Proxy Server 2.0 are close buddies — they work tightly together and are complementary products.

You don't have to be an IIS expert to use Proxy Server 2.0, but Proxy Server uses some of the services and functionality of IIS. From a certification point of view, the IIS and Proxy Server exams overlap to a degree, so you need to have a working knowledge of both for the Proxy Server exam and for implementing and supporting Proxy Server in the workplace.

How Can I Get IIS?

There are a couple of ways to obtain IIS. IIS 2.0 is available as an additional component on the Windows NT Server CD-ROM. You can upgrade IIS 2.0 to 3.0, and then move to IIS 4.0, which is the latest version. If you do not currently have any version of IIS installed, you will need to download IIS 4.0, which is available in the Windows NT Server 4.0 Option Pack. The option pack contains IIS 4.0 and a number of related components and services for Web hosting. In this chapter I focus on installing IIS 4.0 by using the NT Server 4.0 Option Pack.

The NT 4.0 Option pack is available in two major ways. First, it is included in TechNet. TechNet is Microsoft's premier technical network, which contains a huge knowledge base, service packs, patches, documentation, and the Option Pack. As you may be aware, service packs are updates to operating systems and BackOffice products. Service packs correct known issues or problems with the software after it has been released to the public. Also, patches provide solutions to certain technical problems in operating systems or software. Obviously, having the most current service pack, updates, and patches for your system is very important so you can avoid potential problems. MCSEs get a free one-year TechNet subscription once you complete all the certification tests, or you can subscribe for $300 per year at `www.microsoft.com/technet`. As a subscriber, you get a monthly release of CDs that is well worth the money for IT professionals.

The Option Pack is also downloadable for free at `http://www.microsoft.com/ntserver/nts/downloads/recommended/NT4OptPk/default.asp`. It's a large package, and even with a 56Kbps modem, it takes several hours to download. If you choose to do this, you should start the download at night and let the Web work for you while you sleep.

URLs change frequently and without notice. If you have problems locating the option pack or IIS at the noted locations, use the search engine at `www.microsoft.com`.

This chapter focuses on the installation and optional components that are available on the Option Pack, because these are the newest versions of the software components.

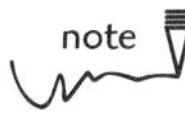

Proxy Server 2 requires at least IIS 3.0, so you need to download IIS 3.0 or secure a copy from the Option Pack, which includes IIS 4.0, to perform the labs in this chapter, and before you can install Proxy Server 2.0 in Chapter Five.

Installing IIS

I'll begin your study of IIS by taking a look at the installation requirements and process. Afterward, I'll explore its many components and its functionality.

Installation Requirements

IIS is designed to be a native component Windows NT Server, so if your computer meets the requirements for an NT Server installation, you can install IIS. As with most products, the more RAM you have installed, the better service you will get from IIS. For disk space, a plain IIS installation requires 188MB of disk space.

Each additional component you choose to install requires extra disk space, and the installation process will tell you how much space is required.

There are a few caveats for IIS installation. First, if you have been using a beta version of IIS 4, you need to uninstall versions prior to beta 3. Also, IIS requires that Service Pack 3 be installed on the NT Server. If you do not have Service Pack 3 applied to your server, the NT 4.0 Option Pack contains the service pack and will guide you through applying Service Pack 3 before it installs IIS. Finally, IIS requires Internet Explorer 4.01 or higher, which is also included in the NT 4.0 Option Pack. That's all there is to it. Table 4-1 is a summary of the installation requirements for IIS.

TABLE 4-1 IIS INSTALLATION REQUIREMENTS

Installation	*Requirement*
Operating system	Windows NT Server 4.0
RAM	At least 32MB
Disk space	188MB for IIS alone
Service Pack	Service Pack 3
Browser	Internet Explorer 4.01 or higher
IIS beta versions	IIS beta versions prior to beta 3 must be uninstalled.

Installation

This section will guide you through the installation process and options of the Option Pack. If you choose to install the Option Pack on your computer, it's a good idea to read this section and the rest of the chapter before beginning your own installation. Lab 4.15 gives you step-by-step instructions for installing the Option Pack.

The NT 4.0 Option Pack installation of IIS and additional components begins with an HTML welcome screen describing the overall functionality and services provided with the installation.

From this screen, you can select the action you want to take. As you can see in the left pane, you can select Learn About to review information about each of the components before you install the Option Pack. The Release Notes give you additional, up-to-date information about the product, such as documentation, known problems, feedback, and technical support. When you click the Install link, you are taken to a screen listing the steps you should complete before you begin the installation of the Option Pack, as shown in Figure 4-1.

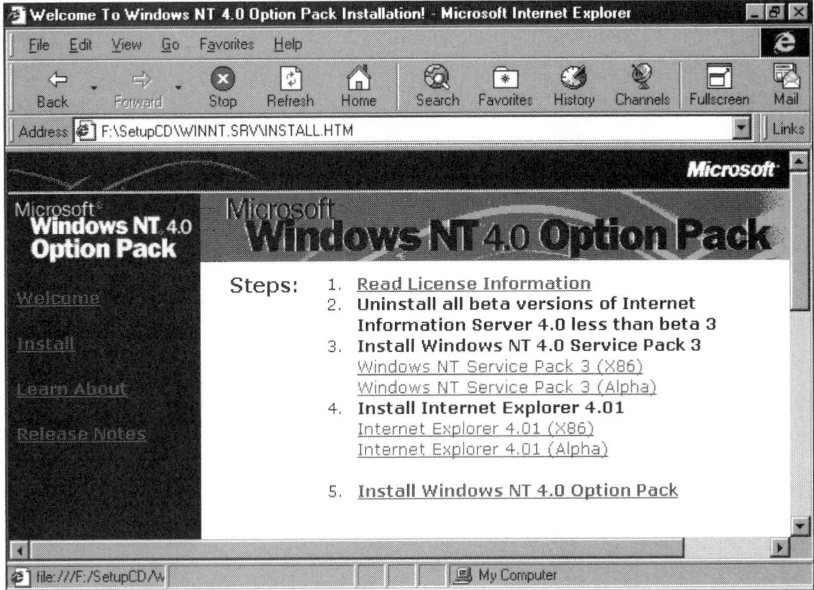

FIGURE 4-1 Option Pack installation screen

The first step asks you to read the licensing agreement, and the next instructs you to uninstall any beta versions of IIS 4 less than beta 3. If you need to do this, you will have to use Add/Remove Programs in the Control Panel. The next step is to install Service Pack 3 on your Windows NT Server if you have not already done so. If you need to install Service Pack 3, click the link marked X86. The final step before beginning the Option Pack installation is to upgrade Internet Explorer to at least version 4.01. Clicking the link installs IE 4.01 to your system. Once you have completed these steps, you are ready to install the NT 4.0 Option Pack. Click the link to begin the installation.

Once you click the installation link, setup initializes and brings you to the opening screen of installation.

This screen gives you a list of features that can be installed with the option pack. After you click the Next button, you are taken to the End User License Agreement page. You must click the Accept button to continue installation.

The next screen presents you with two options: Upgrade Only or Upgrade Plus.

If you have previously installed the Option Pack, you can click Upgrade Only to upgrade to the most current versions of the components. If you are installing the Option Pack for the first time, choose the Upgrade Plus option. This installs the newest versions of IIS and additional components that you can select. If you select the Upgrade Plus option, you are taken to the component selection screen.

From this section of Setup, you can choose which components to install with IIS. A short description of each component is included when the component is highlighted. Also, you can click the Show Subcomponents button, which will present you with the various subcomponents that can be selected or deselected, as shown in Figure 4-2.

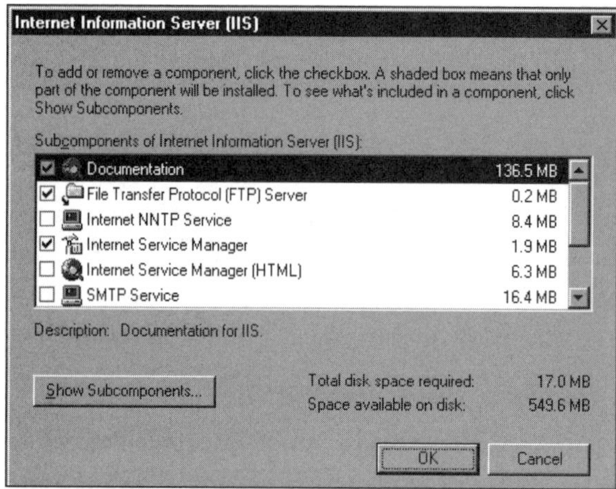

FIGURE 4-2 Subcomponent selection screen

As you can see in Figure 4-2, the subcomponents may even have subcomponents of their own, so it can get rather confusing. However, you can always return to the Option Pack and install additional subcomponents as needed, so selecting the right ones during the initial setup is not critical.

From the main selection screen you can select the following options (a more detailed explanation of each is included later in the chapter):

- **Certificate Server:** Used to create and read digital certificates.
- **FrontPage 98 Server Extensions:** Provides FrontPage 98 Web hosting.

- **Internet Connection Services for RAS:** Installs additional Remote Access Service components for dial-up administration purposes.
- **Internet Information Server:** The main application, which has a number of optional subcomponents available.
- **Microsoft Data Access Components 1.5:** Installs additional access components used by IIS.
- **Microsoft Index Server:** Enables users who browse your Web sites to perform full text searches.
- **Microsoft Management Console:** NT's premier management interface.
- **Microsoft Message Queue:** The MSMQ Server, controller or client.
- **Microsoft Script Debugger:** Services for debugging various Web scripts.
- **Microsoft Site Server Express 2.0:** The express version of Site Server, which provides site analysis, usage analysis, and other site management functions.
- **NT Option Pack Common Files:** Common program files used by multiple components.
- **Transaction Server:** Provides secure business transactions, such as credit card purchases or the transfer of financial records.
- **Visual InterDev RAD Remote Deployment Support:** Enables the remote deployment of applications on your Web server.
- **Windows Scripting Host:** Provides additional scripting functionality.

Each of these components gives the total disk space required for installation and the amount of space currently available on your computer. This is something you should take into account before installing too many of the options.

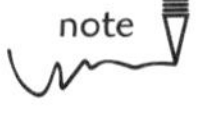

As with the subcomponents, you can always add and remove the main components at a later time, should you need to do so.

Once you select the components to install, you may see additional screens.

Once you complete these screens, Setup begins copying files and installing the Option Pack, as shown in Figure 4-3. At this point, further user intervention is not required.

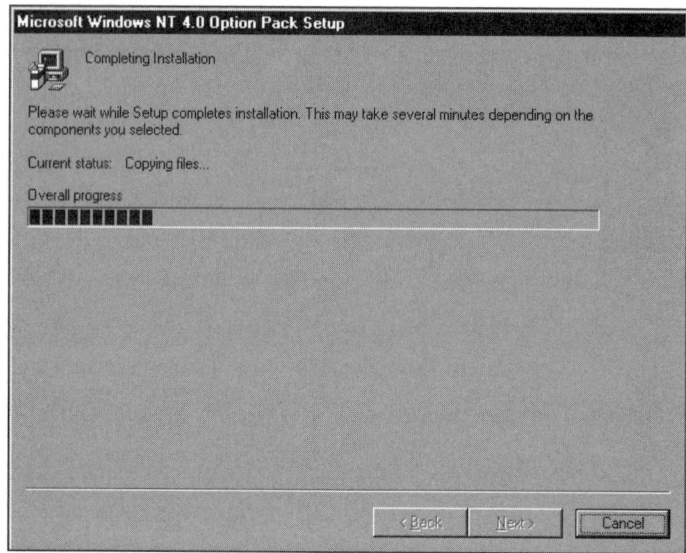

FIGURE 4-3 Automated Setup phase

When the installation is almost complete, you get a final screen that enables you to finish Setup. Once you click the Finish button, Setup is complete and you are prompted to reboot the computer.

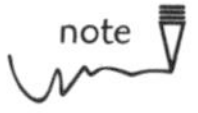

As a part of the installation, IIS installs a default user account for anonymous access named IUSR_<*server name*> and a default directory called Inetpub, which contains subdirectories of ftproot, wwwroot, and gophroot. These are used for FTP, WWW, and Gopher services, if all of those services are installed. Most companies that use IIS will use WWW services and also FTP services, if you make files available for download.

IIS Features

As I mentioned earlier, IIS is a full Web-hosting product that enables you to create, publish, and manage Web sites — whether they are small home pages or full company sites that offer a variety of services and features. As Internet technologies have grown, so has the work of server applications like IIS. A few years ago, people only used the Web to view HTML documents; they did not interact with them. Now, you can go out to your favorite music store on-line and buy a CD with a credit card. This interactivity requires a number of technologies to support it. Many of these technologies are considered core features of IIS, and several other add-on components give IIS the functionality needed in cyberspace today. The following sections provide a general look at the core features of IIS.

FrontPage Server Extensions

Microsoft FrontPage has become one of the most popular Web site building tools available today. It's easy, it's robust, and it is rather inexpensive (usually under $200) FrontPage enables users to build a Web site that contains graphics, frames, Web Bot components (interactive components such as hit counters), a variety of forms, discussion boards, chat services, and a number of other features. All of these can be built through wizards and a GUI interface. If you can use a word processing application, you can easily learn to use FrontPage. This functionality is very popular because it enables users to construct attractive and highly functional Web sites without knowing HTML.

FrontPage sites can be created on NT or Windows 95/98, but they must be published on a server that contains FrontPage Server Extensions, such as IIS. The server extensions interact with the FrontPage Web site to provide some of the functionality such as discussion boards, Web Bots, auto-submit forms, and so forth. The extensions perform the processing for these components, and FrontPage sites that are published to servers without the extensions will not have full functionality. FrontPage is the only Web building suite that is fully integrated with IIS. FrontPage and IIS fully support each other as well as NT authentication, such as NT Challenge Response (NTCR) and secure administration via Secure Sockets Layer (SSL).

Microsoft Index Server

Index Server is a powerful search engine that is integrated with IIS. FrontPage is fully integrated with IIS as well. Text searches from a FrontPage site work directly with Index Server to return the search information.

Index Server is essentially a indexing tool. It provides for keyword queries for sites stored locally as well as over the network or Internet. In essence, this enables FrontPage sites to contain a search engine to find key words on the Web for faster retrieval of desired information. Index server supports HTML and plain text, and is fully integrated with document types from Microsoft Office as well as Adobe PDF. Figure 4-4 shows the Index Server Interface displayed within the Microsoft Management Console (discussed later).

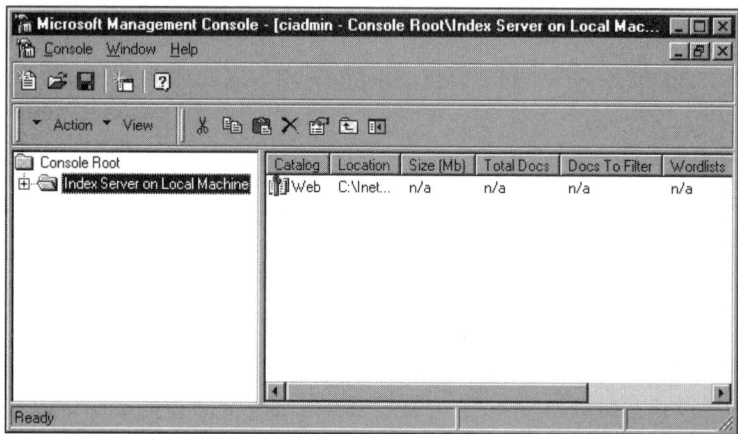

FIGURE 4-4 Index Server interface

Index Server is a dynamic system, because once you define the directories you want to index, the task is performed once, and automatically updated as changes are made to the directories. Each page is turned into a keyword directory that can used for any keyword search. Index Server enables organizations to also create custom search pages using a variety of other technologies such as Active Server Pages, ActiveX Data Objects, and structured query language (SQL).

Active Server Pages Support

Active Server Pages (ASP) enable plain HTML pages to be combined with other programming languages to create pages that are active in terms of the processes they do and how they interact with the user. ASP enables Web developers to integrate HTML with ActiveX scripts, Visual Basic scripts, Jscripts, and other programming. ASP is a built-in function of IIS and provides ASP development without additional tools or operating systems.

HTTP 1.1 Support

IIS 4.0 supports the new functionality of HTTP 1.1, while maintaining compatibility with HTTP 1.0. HTTP 1.1 provides a number of new features and improved performance. It is significantly faster than HTTP 1.0. IIS 4.0 supports the new HTTP 1.1 functions, such as:

- **Pipelining:** Pipelining enables the server to process multiple requests at one time. HTTP 1.0 processed only one request for a resource at a time, which forced the user to wait before the next request could be sent. HTTP 1.1 enables users to send multiple requests at the same time, which improves retrieval performance.
- **Persistent Connections:** Persistent Connections enable you to transfer multiple objects across a single connection. Originally, if an HTML document contained HTML and a JPEG photo, a connection would have to be established for the HTML transfer, and then a separate connection would have to be established for the JPEG photo.
- **Caching:** HTTP 1.1 contains caching information and technology built into the protocol, such as time of creation, expiration times, and so forth.

Bandwidth Throttling

IIS enables you to control how much bandwidth is allocated to a particular Web site through what IIS calls *bandwidth throttling*. This feature lets you give more bandwidth to high-traffic sites, or reduce bandwidth to sites that do not receive many hits per day. Bandwidth throttling should only be used after you research your site traffic so you do not give a site too little bandwidth, or too much to a site that does not need it.

TO VIEW THE TAB THAT ENABLES YOU TO CONFIGURE BANDWIDTH THROTTLING, FOLLOW THESE STEPS (ASSUMING IIS IS INSTALLED):

1. Click Start ⇒ Programs ⇒ IIS or NT 4 Option Pack, and select Internet Service Manager.
2. In the left pane, you see the Console Root and subdirectories of IIS and other applications you have installed, such as Transaction Server.

3. Expand IIS.
4. You see a computer icon and the name of your computer. Highlight it.
5. Click the Properties icon on the toolbar.
6. You are presented with a properties page, with a check box for Bandwidth Throttling where you can enable the feature and change the maximum network use default of 1,024Kbps.

Multiple Web Sites

IIS can be used to host multiple Web sites on multiple servers, and even supports browser-neutral host headers. If you use IIS 4.0 to host multiple Web sites, you can do so using a single IP address. IIS 4.0 can support this functionality for browsers that do not support host headers.

Discussion Groups and Mail

IIS supports the creation of local discussion groups using the Network News Transport Protocol (NNTP). IIS is also mail-enabled. This enables Web-based applications to send and receive mail. IIS can become a mail client using the Simple Mail Transfer Protocol (SMTP).

Microsoft Management Console

Microsoft Management Console (MMC) is Microsoft's way of providing one streamlined GUI interface for a variety of software. IIS uses the MMC as well as its components, as with Index Server. The MMC is a stripped-down GUI interface, as shown in Figure 4-5.

MMC provides one integrated interface, but the functionality of each application is provided via *snap-ins*. The snap-in works within the MMC to provide the functionality for whatever application you are using at the moment. Every IIS component can be managed using the MMC. MMC is Microsoft's version of streamlined administration, and you can expect to see it more fully integrated in Windows 2000.

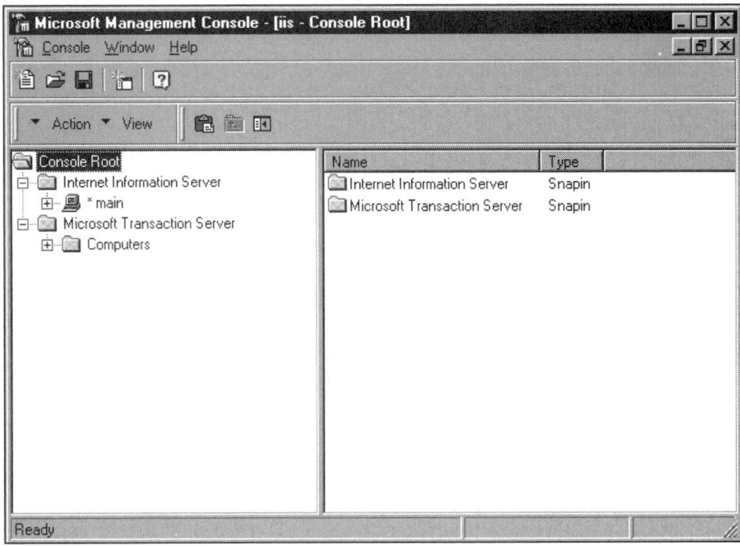

FIGURE 4-5 Microsoft Management Console

Web-based and Command Line Administration

IIS makes administration easy by providing administrators two major administrative methods: *Web-based Administration* and *Command Line Administration*. With Web-based Administration, an administrator can manage IIS remotely from any Web browser that supports frames and Jscript. Command Line Administration provides a variety of features, including task automation, virtual directories, and script writing.

Microsoft NetShow Support

NetShow enables you to transmit audio and video over the Internet in streaming and multicasting modes. NetShow, as well as NetMeeting, has become a popular mode of transporting classes, speeches, and other audiovisual files over the Internet. IIS fully supports NetShow and provides for control over bandwidth, performance, and transmission error correction mechanisms. NetShow includes full support for Windows ACM/VCM codec (Audio/Video Compression Modules encoder/decoder) which enables you to make virtually any media available on the network or from a Web site.

Crystal Reports

IIS supports Crystal Reports, a reporting tool from Seagate Software. This enables administrators to gather reports about the Web server's functionality and performance. Crystal Reports provides a variety of reporting functions, such as wizards and templates, to customize the reporting process. In addition, all information from Crystal Reports can be stored in Microsoft Access or Microsoft SQL Server databases.

Integrated Setup

IIS 4.0 gives administrators a number of options to either upgrade IIS or install it. IIS 4.0 upgrades previously installed versions of IIS 2.0, 3.0, or 4.0 beta 3, while maintaining the current configuration. This may not seem important at first glance, but because IIS 4.0 maintains the current configuration, Web servers do not have to be reconfigured, which saves administrators a lot of work time as well as downtime.

As you have already seen, IIS 4.0 provides all of the components through one Setup Wizard instead of requiring you to perform multiple installations to get all of the components you need.

IIS 4.0 provides selective Internet-based setup. This means that organizations can download and install various IIS components as they need them, instead of having to download one large package. This makes adding features faster and much easier.

IIS 4.0 also provides unattended setup features. Say you need to install IIS 4.0 on a number of servers at one time. You can use the unattended setup features to create a script that will install Windows NT Server 4.0, Service Pack 3, Internet Explorer 4.01, and whatever components in the Option Pack you want to install to whatever machines on the network you choose.

In larger network environments, unattended installations save a huge amount of time for network administrators, and are used as often as possible when rolling out installations on multiple computers.

Backup

IIS 4.0 gives administrators the ability to back up and restore Web server configuration settings. In case of a machine failure, the configuration can be restored more quickly, which gets the machine back on-line. IIS also contains a *roll back* feature. If changes are made to the Web server that later become undesirable or do not perform as planned, the administrator can roll back the settings to the previously saved state. This feature enables administrators to experiment with changes while preserving the current system settings.

Web Site Operators

Too many administrative duties? IIS makes administration easy by enabling administrators to assign individual operators to manage separate Web sites running on the same server. Suppose your company has three Web sites; the administrator can assign three different individuals to manage each Web site. This gives each person administrator privileges to his or her own Web site, but the other sites are off limits.

The Operators function works with Windows NT User Manager for Domains. You can assign any user administrator permissions for a particular Web site without giving that user administrative privileges to anything else, although most environments would only give this power to an administrator or backup operator.

Additional IIS Components

As I mentioned earlier, IIS contains a number of additional components — programs that work with IIS to make it more robust. You can add these components during the installation of IIS, or you can add them later if needed, though a few of them are required. For the labs in this book, you can simply accept the default selections, or you choose to add other components as well. There are several of them, so the following is a short description of each.

Certificate Server

Certificate Server is used to create and read *digital certificates*. Digital certificates are used to certify the identity of a Web site as well as the identity of users. The certificate provides a reliable assurance that a Web site is actually what it says it is and that users are actually who they say they are. For example, suppose you want to download an executable file from ABC Construction Company. The digital certificate ensures that the download is actually coming from ABC Construction — not from somewhere else that could be downloading a virus. Certificate Server gives IIS Web servers the ability to generate and process X.509 certificates.

Internet Connection Services for RAS

Internet Connection Services for Remote Access Service (RAS) installs additional RAS components for dial-up administration purposes. A number of services are added, mainly to centralize RAS functionality, such as network phone books, Remote Authentication Dial In User Service (RADIUS), and client dialers, as well as additional management tools. These functions give the administrator greater control over RAS usage, as well as dial-up administrative privileges. Internet Connection Services for RAS contains the Connection Manager Administration Kit.

This wizard enables you to customize the Connection Manager dialer according to the needs of your company. Once you have established your connection parameters, you can manage them through the Phone Book Administrator. From this utility, you can select various phone books, provide filters for them, and perform general administrative duties.

Microsoft Data Access Components 1.5

The Microsoft Data Access Components 1.5 installs additional access components used by IIS. The Data Access Components give you the ability to access many types of data throughout the enterprise, such as client/server applications deployed over a local network or the Internet. You can use the components to integrate information from numerous sources in relational and nonrelational databases.

Microsoft Message Queue

Microsoft Message Queue (MSMQ) enables applications to communicate with each other by providing a message *queue,* or holding area, such as a print job uses. This functionality provides communication between two applications, even if one is not available. The messages are stored, and the application can pick up its messages when available. It functions as a middleman between two applications. MSMQ provides tighter integration of IIS components, such as Transaction Server, and provides reliable communication between components.

Microsoft Script Debugger

The Microsoft Script Debugger provides services for debugging various Web scripts. This is a valuable tool for Web site developers who are writing custom scripts to use in a Web site. It works with any ActiveX-enabled scripting language, such as VB Script, Jscript, Java applets, and ActiveX components, as well as host-independent scripting languages such as REXX and Perl. The Script Debugger gives you a simple user interface to work from.

Microsoft Site Server Express 2.0

Microsoft Site Server Express 2.0 gives you a scaled-down version of Site Server that provides site analysis, usage analysis, and other site management functions. It contains a few tools that help you track what is happening with various Web sites:

- **Content Analyzer:** Content Analyzer enables you to explore the content of a Web site and create a Web map to track issues or problems with site construction.
- **Report Writer:** Report Writer translates IIS logs and provides information about a number of items, such as hit detail reports, bandwidth reports, and browser and operating system reports. These reports can be generated from the Report Writer Catalog and are provided in an easy GUI interface. Figure 4-6 shows a browser and operating system report.

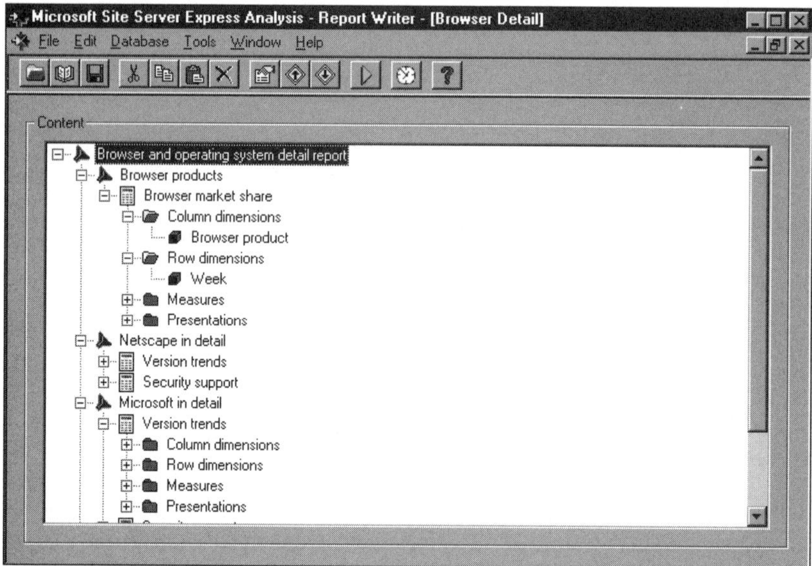

FIGURE 4-6 Site Server Express Report Writer

- **Usage Import:** Usage Import enables you to gather statistics and other information about Web site usage into a variety of file formats, such extended log file format, W3C extended log file format, NCSA log file format, and others. The full version of Site Server is available as a separate product, but the Express version contains some useful features for managing and gathering information about IIS Web sites.

NT Option Pack Common Files

The NT Option Pack Common files are installed by default and are a collection of common program files used by multiple components of IIS.

Transaction Server

Microsoft Transaction Server (MTS) provides secure business transactions over the Internet. Your company can offer products for sale and accept credit card orders from Internet users via MTS. However, MTS is not limited to financial transactions. It can be used to transfer information or even update databases.

Essentially, MTS provides a secure method for transferring any kind of sensitive data.

MTS functions by using an all-or-nothing approach. Transactions either complete fully or they fail entirely. This way, no partial data is transferred, and records cannot be partially changed. This protects the integrity of financial or database transactions, even when transmission problems interrupt the transaction.

MTS contains a Transaction Server Explorer, which is a snap-in to the MMC, as shown in Figure 4-7.

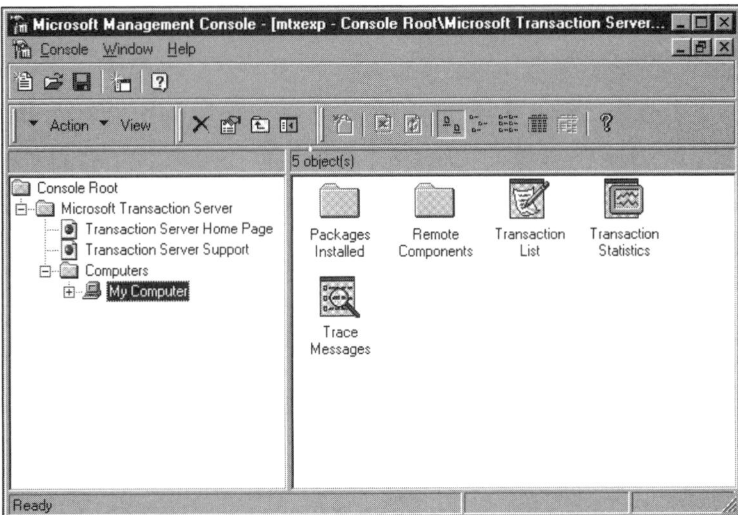

FIGURE 4-7 Transaction Server Explorer

Visual InterDev RAD Remote Deployment Support and Windows Scripting Host

Both these products provide additional support for hosting and maintaining custom Web sites. Visual InterDev RAD (Rapid Application Development) Remote Deployment Support enables the remote deployment of applications on your Web server, giving the administrator additional remote functionality. The Windows Scripting Host provides additional scripting functionality for IIS.

The IIS Interface

Now that you have examined the functionality of IIS 4.0 and its many components, have a look at IIS Interface. Most of the configuration management and administration takes place through the Internet Service Manager, but there is also the Key Manager and the FrontPage Server Administrator.

Internet Service Manager

The Internet Service Manager is the administrator's interface to managing the various services and functions of IIS. The site information is opened in the MMC and follows the format of Windows Explorer, as shown in Figure 4-8.

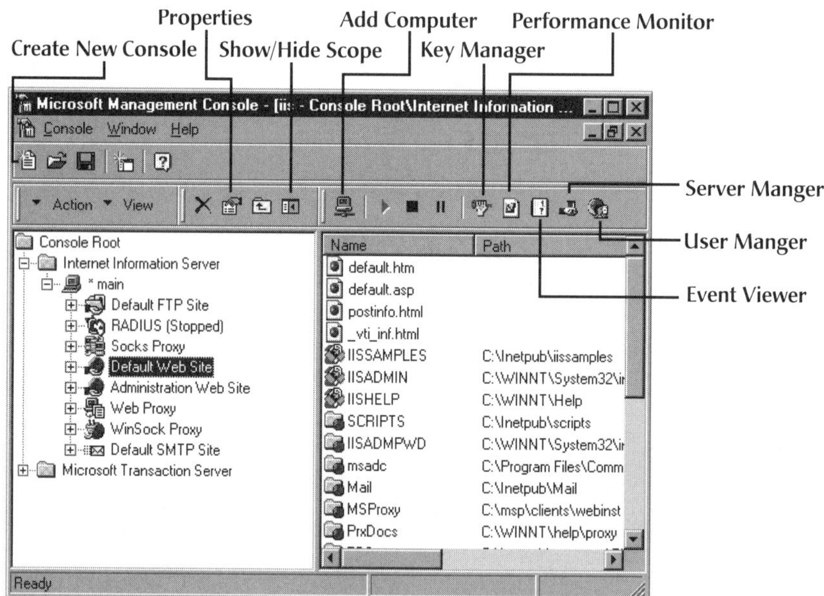

FIGURE 4-8 Internet Service Manager

From the Action menu shown in Figure 4-8, you can explore, browse, or stop and start a service, and perform a variety of other configuration options. The Internet Service Manager gives you several different views represented as icons on the toolbar.

Among these is Server Manager. This button brings up the Windows NT Server Manager, where you can monitor users, shares, what sites are currently in use, replication options, as well as configure administrative alters. Next to that is a button to bring up User Manager for Domains, which gives you quick access to NT User Manager. Event viewer and Performance Monitor are also available from the button toolbar.

IIS makes the administrator's work easy. Because these buttons are provided, you do not have to manually open User Manager for Domains or Event Viewer – these options are provided for the administrator directly.

With a directory selected in the left pane, you can click the Properties button on the toolbar. The Properties sheet gives you a number of tabs with information that can be configured. Figure 4-9 shows the properties of the Administration Web Site.

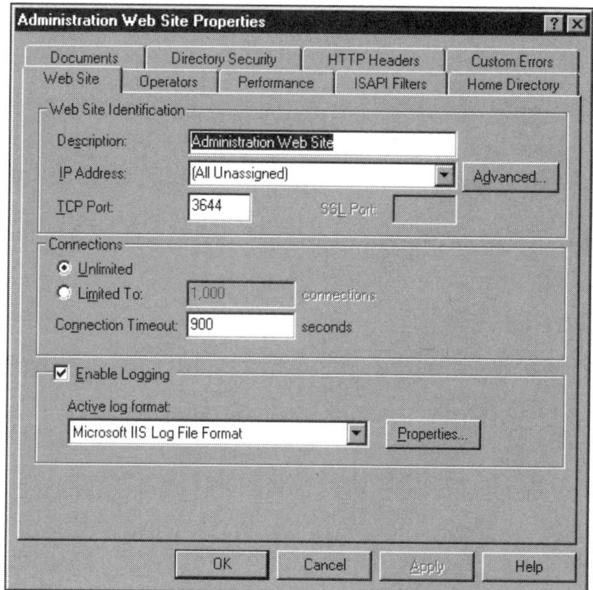

FIGURE 4-9 Administration Web Site properties

The Properties sheets for each directory enable you to control how the Web sites are administered. For example, in the Default Web Site Properties page, you can configure a number of options such as ISAPI (Internet Server Application Program Interface) filters, HTTP Headers, and user authentication, which is one of the most important features. IIS 4.0 provides three authentication methods, which can be selected, deselected, or edited by the administrator. The three methods are presented in Table 4-2.

TABLE 4-2 IIS AUTHENTICATION METHODS

ACCESS TYPE	*DESCRIPTION*
Allow Anonymous Access	No user name or password is required
Basic Authentication	User name and password are required, but they are sent as clear text
Windows NT Challenge/Response	User name and password are required. Client must support NT Challenge/Response.

You should know the differences between the three authentication methods for the Proxy Server 2 exam.

Labs 4.16 and 4.17 give you the opportunity to practice maneuvering through the Internet Service Manager once you have IIS installed.

Key Manager

Key Manager enables you to create and configure Secure Socket Layer (SSL) encryption to protect sensitive information on the Internet. Key Manager is available in Internet Service Manager as a toolbar button.

SSL provides security by using a combination of *public key cryptography* and *bulk data encryption*. If you are sending sensitive data, the data can be encrypted with the server's public key. The encrypted data is then sent to the server you are communicating with. The server you are communicating with must have the correct key to decode the encrypted data.

Key Manager is used to establish new keys and provides a wizard to guide you through the process. Overall, Key Manager makes data encryption easy and reliable.

You only need to have a general understanding of Key Manager for the exam. Don't worry about learning the entire process of key cryptography for the Proxy Server 2.0 exam.

It is not necessary to encrypt every piece of data that is sent over the Internet. Because of the administrative overhead of creating and managing keys, encryption should only be used for sensitive documents that must not be captured and read by other Internet users.

FrontPage Server Administrator

FrontPage Server Administrator is a simple utility for managing FrontPage Server Extensions. It can be accessed from the IIS directory in Windows Explorer. The Administrator provides one tab with a few options for configuring FrontPage Server Extensions, as shown in Figure 4-10.

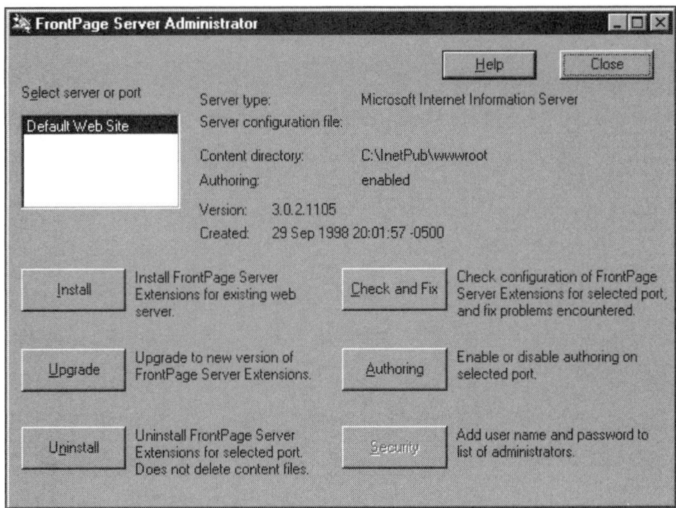

FIGURE 4-10 FrontPage Server Administrator

There are options to install, uninstall, and upgrade FrontPage Server Extensions. There is also an option to check and repair the server extensions for a selected port, as well as an option to enable or disable Web site authoring on a selected port.

The Big Picture

I have talked about a lot of IIS features and components in this chapter, and it is easy lose sight of the big picture. IIS 4.0 is a robust Web-hosting server. It enables you to publish and access both intranet and Internet sites. IIS contains a number of features, including native FrontPage support for FrontPage sites, full-text searches through Index Server, and support for the newest technology including HTTP 1.1, NNTP and SMTP. In addition, IIS provides Web hosting on single servers or across multiple servers, and easy administration through the MMC, Web browsers, and the command line. Setup and upgrading from previous versions of IIS is easy and usually trouble-free, and setup on multiple servers can be performed via unattended installations.

A number of additional components in the Option Pack give additional functionality for both services and administration. Transaction Server, Certificate Server, Internet Connection Services for RAS, and several others give IIS the robustness and versatility needed for today's complex Web sites and Internet technologies.

Exam Preparation Summary

You will not be tested extensively on the details of IIS on the Proxy Server 2 exam. You should keep in mind that at least IIS 3.0 is required for a Proxy Server installation, and you should know the requirements for installing IIS. IIS has a lot of components, as you have seen in this chapter. You will probably not be tested on these components, but they may appear in scenario-based questions on the exam. You will probably see a question or two about NT Challenge/Response, basic authentication, and anonymous authentication. You should know the differences between each of these, and I deal with the specifics of them later in the book. You should also remember the new functionality HTTP 1.1 brings to the Internet.

Key Point Summary

This chapter gave you an overview of installing IIS, its features, and its many components that make Web hosting robust and easy.

- IIS enables you to host sites using a wide variety of scripting options, including native support for FrontPage 98.
- IIS is available for download at Microsoft's Web site or through TechNet and other products, as well as through the NT 4.0 Option Pack.
- IIS installation requires NT Server 4.0, Service Pack 3, and Internet Explorer 4.01.
- Installation is performed through a wizard. If you are using the Option Pack, there are a variety of components that can be installed at the same time as IIS.
- FrontPage Server Extensions are included as a part of the IIS installation and required to host FrontPage sites.
- Index Server provides keyword queries and can perform exhaustive word searches.
- Active Server Pages enable developers to integrate HTML with various other scripts including VBScript and Jscript.
- HTTP 1.1 is fully supported in IIS. HTTP 1.1 adds improved transmission functionality such as Pipelining, Persistent Connections, and built-in caching features.
- IIS can provide both intranet and Internet sites, and also host Web sites on multiple servers using a single IP address.
- The Microsoft Management Console provides the GUI interface for IIS administration. The MMC provides a stripped-down GUI interface that works with various snap-ins that are application specific.
- IIS provides MMC, browser, and command-line administration.
- IIS setup supports unattended installations on multiple servers.
- IIS provides fault tolerance by providing configuration backup and roll back.
- IIS is fully integrated with Windows NT, and supports NT Challenge Response authentication, basic authentication, and anonymous authentication.
- IIS contains a number of additional components to provide further Web functionality and ease administrative burden, such as Certificate Server,

Transaction Server, Internet Connection Services for RAS, Script Debugger, and others.

- IIS is primarily managed through Internet Service Manager, which functions within the MMC.
- Key Manager enables the creation and administration of SSL encryption keys for secure transmissions.
- FrontPage Server Administrator enables you to add, remove, or check and upgrade FrontPage Server Extensions.

Applying What You've Learned

The following review questions give you a chance to test your knowledge of the content in this chapter. Should you miss some, review the appropriate portions of the chapter. The answers to the Instant Assessment questions can be found in Appendix C.

Instant Assessment

1. What browser is required to install IIS 4.0?

   A. Internet Explorer 3.0 or higher

   B. Internet Explorer 4.0 or higher

   C. Internet Explorer 4.01 or higher

   D. Netscape Communicator

2. Your company needs to send secure files over the Internet to another company. They would like to use IIS to help with this task. Which of the following can be used to generate authentic certificates to keep the security level high?

   A. Transaction Server

   B. Certificate Server

   C. Proxy Server

   D. Site Server

3. You want Internet guests who browse your company's Web site to be able to perform keyword searches. Which IIS component will enable you to do this?

   A. Transaction Server

   B. Certificate Server

   C. Index Server

   D. Site Server

4. Your company needs to send financial records to another company over the Internet. Also, your company would like to permit Internet users to purchase products online using a credit card. Which IIS component should you use?

   A. Transaction Server

   B. Certificate Server

   C. Proxy Server

   D. Site Server

5. Which console does IIS use?

   A. Proxy Server

   B. MMC

   C. MCM

   D. Site Server

6. What are two scripting languages ASP supports?

   A. ActiveX

   B. FORTRAN

   C. Jscript

   D. ASAPI

7. What is one service Site Server Express provides?

   A. Site Analyzer

   B. Content Analyzer

   C. Site filtering

   D. Site hosting

8. What is SSL?
   - A. Synthetic Sockets Layer
   - B. Secure Sockets Layer
   - C. Sockets Secure Layer
   - D. Sockets Synthetic Layer
9. You want to use the MMC to support not only IIS, but also other products such as Proxy Server and Systems Management Server. What enables you to integrate various applications into the MMC?
   - A. J-code
   - B. MMC Util
   - C. Snap-in
   - D. MMC Add-on
10. IIS installs three subdirectories called WWWROOT, FTPPUB, and GOPHPUB. What directory are they stored in by default?
    - A. IISPUB
    - B. INETWWW
    - C. INETFTP
    - D. INETPUB
11. What is the name of the user account installed by IIS for anonymous access?
    - A. IUSER
    - B. IUSER_*servername*
    - C. IUSER_*username*
    - D. IUSER_GUEST
12. What allows you to manage and create security keys?
    - A. Proxy Server
    - B. IIS Manager
    - C. Key Manager
    - D. Security Manager

Critical Thinking Labs

These labs present you with analysis problems to test your critical thinking skills with the content in this chapter.

Lab 4.11 *IIS features*

Your company is considering implementing IIS to host the company's new Web site and its forthcoming intranet site. You have been asked to give an overview of IIS's features and functions at a meeting. What are some of the things you will say?

Lab 4.12 *Securing transactions*

Your company uses IIS and needs to perform secure transfers of financial records over the Internet. As the administrator, you are asked how the company can do this so that no data is corrupted during transit. What IIS component should you use and why?

Lab 4.13 *Multiple administrators*

Your company is hosting a number of Web sites and the administrative load has become too much for you to handle. You would like for some other people within your company to have administrative privileges over these sites. How can you do this?

Lab 4.14 *Checking FrontPage Extensions*

There seems to be a problem with the FrontPage Server Extensions on your IIS server. What easy way can you check and repair errors to the Extensions?

Hands-on Labs

The Hands-on Labs give you an opportunity to practice skills you have learned in this chapter. Make sure you read the system requirements for each lab to be certain you have the correct configuration before beginning the lab.

Lab 4.15 *Installing the NT 4.0 Option Pack*

This lab assumes you are using an NT 4.0 operating system and have the NT 4.0 Option Pack. The Option Pack is available on CD through a TechNet subscription or it is downloadable from Microsoft at `http://www.microsoft.com/ntserver/nts/downloads/recommended/NT4OptPk/default.asp`

1. Open the option pack CD or launch Setup from the downloaded version. Internet Explorer opens and you are shown a Welcome Screen.
2. In left pane, click the Install link. This takes you to the installation page.
3. Follow the steps given on the installation screen. Begin by reading the licensing agreement.
4. Next, if you have beta releases of IIS 4.0 prior to beta 3 installed, you need to uninstall them. Go to Control Panel, select Add/Remove Programs, and select IIS from the list. Then click the Add/Remove button. The beta version of IIS is uninstalled and you may be required to reboot your system.
5. If you do not have Service Pack 3 installed on your NT 4.0 Server, choose the option to install the service pack. The Service Pack is installed, and you will have to reboot your computer.
6. If you are not using at least Internet Explorer 4.0, choose to upgrade to IE 4.01.
7. Once these steps are complete, you are ready to install the Option Pack. Click the Install Option Pack link. You are taken to a welcome screen. Click Next.
8. The next screen presents you with the End User License Agreement. You must accept the agreement for the installation to continue. Click Accept, and then click Next.
9. Next, you are asked to select either Update or Update Plus. Update Plus will install the core components and enable you to install additional components if you wish to do so. Choose the Update Plus option and click Next.
10. You are taken to a selection screen that enables you to choose the components you wish to install. Spend a few moments looking at the options and the subcomponents for each. Highlight the main component and click the Show Subcomponents button to view the subcomponents.
11. Select the components to install by clicking the check box beside each component. If you are unsure of what you need, simply accept the defaults and add components at a later time if you need them.
12. If you selected additional components, you may be presented with various screens asking for a local directory or additional information about administrative rights. Accept the defaults on these unless you know that you need to make specific changes.

13. Setup begins at this point by copying the files to your computer and beginning the installation process. A status bar is provided. This process usually takes from 10 to 15 minutes.
14. When the installation phase is complete, you are given a screen asking you to click Finish to finish the installation. Click Finish.
15. You are prompted to reboot your computer.

Lab 4.16 *The IIS interface*

This lab assumes you have installed IIS successfully in Lab 4.15. In this lab, you will explore the IIS interface.

1. Click Start ⇒ Programs ⇒ Windows NT Option Pack ⇒ Microsoft Internet Information Server, and then select Internet Service Manager.
2. The MMC launches and opens ISM. In the left pane, a Console Root with IIS is listed and perhaps other directories, depending on what you have installed.
3. Expand the IIS directory. You see the name of your computer with a computer icon, and perhaps others depending on your network configuration. Expand your computer.
4. You see a default Web site and default FTP site. Click the default Web site.
5. In the right pane, you see a listing of all of the files within the default Web site. Notice that new icons that have appeared on the toolbar. Click each one to see what they do, and then close the windows after you have seen them.
6. As you clicked on each icon, you are presented with NT's User Manager for Domains, NT's Server Manager, Event Viewer, Performance Monitor, and IIS's Key Manager.
7. Notice the computer icon on the toolbar. Click it. You see a dialog box, which enables you to connect to another server. Close the dialog box.
8. Also on the toolbar, you see an icon to Show/Hide Scope. If you click this button, it removes the left pane of MMC.
9. Notice the Action and View tabs. Click the Action tab. This enables you to explore, browse, start, stop, and pause various services, as well as to further configure the interface.
10. Click the View tab. In this tab, you can change the icon size, and also select list or detail.
11. At the top of the MMC screen, click the Console drop-down menu. Notice that you have several options here specific to the MMC. Click Add/Remove Snap-in.

12. You are presented with a screen to add new snap-ins to the Console root or to the other directories available. You would use this if you had additional snap-ins you wanted to use.
13. Close the snap-ins dialog box and close the MMC.

Lab 4.17 *Viewing properties*

This lab assumes you have successfully installed IIS in Lab 4.15. In this lab, you will view properties sheets within IIS.

1. Click Start ⇒ Programs ⇒ Windows NT Option Pack ⇒ Microsoft Internet Information Server, and then select Internet Service Manager.
2. MMC launches, and opens ISM. In the left pane, a Console Root with IIS is listed and perhaps other directories, depending on what you have installed.
3. Expand the IIS directory. You see the name of your computer with a computer icon, and perhaps others depending on your network configuration. Expand your computer.
4. You see a default Web site and a default FTP site. Click the default Web site.
5. On the toolbar, click the Properties icon.You are given a sheet of default Web site properties.
6. Take a moment to browse the various tabs.
7. Click the Operators tab. Notice that from this tab, you can give operator permissions to other users on the network.
8. Click the HTTP Headers tab. Notice that you can enable content expiration and configure expiration time. Notice also that there is a content rating section. Click the edit rating button. Notice that you can enable various ratings for the Web sites as needed. Close this tab.
9. Click Directory Security tab. Notice that there are three areas: Anonymous Access and Authentication Control, Secure Communications, and IP Address and Domain Name Restrictions. Click the Edit button for Anonymous Access and Authentication Control.
10. You see the authentication methods discussed in this chapter.
11. Click the Performance tab. Notice that there are several options to fine-tune the performance of your Web site, including bandwidth throttling.
12. Close the Properties window. Take a moment to look at the properties of the default FTP site and continue to look around the interface until you are comfortable with its content.

CHAPTER

5

Installing Proxy Server

About Chapter 5

This chapter explores the installation of Microsoft Proxy Server 2.0. I examine the installation process, the creation of the Local Address Table, and a number of installation issues. I also look at upgrading from Proxy Server 1.0 and uninstalling Proxy Server, and I provide a few troubleshooting tips. The labs in this chapter give you a chance to practice the installation process.

INSTALLING PROXY SERVER 2.0

If you have performed several installations of any kind, you probably have learned to do what most people do — hold your breath. Any number of software glitches and problems can arise during an installation, and there is always a feeling of trepidation, wondering if the installation will work the way it is supposed to or whether you will spend the rest of the day trying to recover.

Fortunately, Proxy Server is very forgiving. For the most part, administrator errors or problems encountered during Setup tend to be easy to recover from. This chapter walks you through the installation process, with step-by-step installation instructions in Lab 5.22, and I take a look at uninstalling Proxy Server, as well as troubleshooting the installation process.

Installation Requirements

In Chapter 3, I discuss performing a needs assessment and the requirements for installing Proxy Server. I explore the IIS component in detail in Chapter 4. Table 5-1 is a quick review of the installation requirements for installing Proxy Server.

TABLE 5-1 PROXY SERVER INSTALLATION REQUIREMENTS

Component	*Requirement*
Operating System	Windows NT Server 4.0
Service pack	Service Pack 3
RAM	32MB or greater
Processor	Pentium 133 or greater
IIS	IIS 3.0 or later
Cache drive	100MB plus 0.5MB per client minimum drive space

For the most part, if your system meets the requirements for a Windows NT Server installation, Proxy Server will install just fine. There are a few other factors you should keep in mind before installing Proxy Server, however.

- Before you begin installation, make sure you have established a location for caching storage. The drive or partition must be formatted using NTFS, and must have enough disk space to service the number of Proxy Server clients on your network. Remember to use the formula 100MB + (number of clients × 0.5MB).

To convert a drive to NTFS, use the `convert.exe` utility in Windows NT. If you have Proxy Server 1.0 installed and cached data on a FAT drive, the data will be preserved when you convert to NTFS.

- You must have administrative privileges on the machine you are installing Proxy Server on.
- Remember that Proxy Server requires a multi-homed computer — a computer with two NICs. If you are using Dial-Up Networking only, RAS and your modem (or ISDN adapter) must be configured with TCP/IP and working correctly.
- Make sure that TCP/IP is configured on at least the NIC that will serve as the external network interface. TCP/IP or NWLink can be used on the NIC that will serve as the internal network interface.
- The Server must be a domain controller or a member server.
- The Service Advertising Protocol (SAP) must be installed or you will get an error during setup. SAP enables servers to advertise their presence and services on the network.

TO INSTALL SAP ON YOUR SYSTEM, COMPLETE THE FOLLOWING STEPS:

1. Right-click Network Neighborhood and choose Properties.
2. Click the Services tab.
3. Click the Add button. A selection list appears.
4. Choose SAP Agent and click OK.
5. Setup needs to copy files to perform this operation. Choose the appropriate directory or the CD-ROM and click OK.
6. The SAP Agent is installed. Click Close and reboot the computer.

Proxy Server Licensing

The licensing requirements for Proxy Server are very simple. As with other additional Windows NT Server Components, Proxy Server requires a per-server license with no license requirements for the clients. Because Proxy Server must be installed on an NT server with IIS installed, licensing requirements for those products must be fulfilled to be in compliance with the Proxy licensing agreement. The Proxy Server license can be transferred between two systems, if Proxy is completely removed from the original system. In addition, you can sell your copy of Proxy Server to someone else, if you do not keep any copies in any form. Proxy Server cannot be shared, rented, or leased, as with similar products such as IIS. Proxy Server cannot be decompiled or re-engineered, and if you perform any kind of test on Proxy Server, all testing results must be submitted to Microsoft for approval before they are released to any third party.

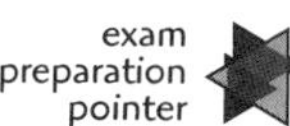

Keep in mind for the exam that only a per-server license is required. Proxy Server does not require client licenses.

Installation

Now you're ready to install Proxy Server. This section explains the installation procedure as it occurs through the Setup Wizard. Keep in mind that Lab 5.22 is a step-by-step walkthrough of the installation process .

When you insert the Proxy Server CD-ROM, `autorun.inf` starts the Installation Wizard. If this does not happen, you should run the Setup file on the CD-ROM. If you downloaded an evaluation version of Proxy Server, expand the download package, and run `setup.exe`. A welcome screen appears, as shown in Figure 5-1. The welcome screen instructs you to close any open applications before continuing with the installation. Note that the Internet Service Manager is stopped during the installation.

For instructions on installing the Microsoft Proxy Server 2.0 30-day Trial on the CD accompanying this book, see Appendix F.

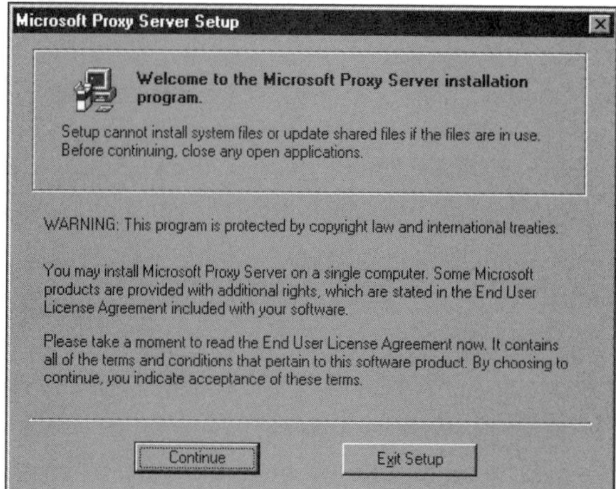

FIGURE 5-1 Welcome screen

The next screen asks you to enter the 10-digit CD Key, as shown in Figure 5-2. This key is found on the sticker on the back of the CD-ROM case. If you are using a downloaded evaluation version, the CD key screen does not appear. Installation will not continue without a valid CD Key.

Microsoft Proxy Server Setup

Locate your 10-digit "CD Key" number and enter it in the space below. You can find this number on the sticker on the back of your CD case.

CD Key:

OK

Exit Setup

FIGURE 5-2 CD Key screen

After you enter the key, the product identification box appears, as shown in Figure 5-3. Write down the product identification number for future reference, if you need to call Microsoft Technical Support.

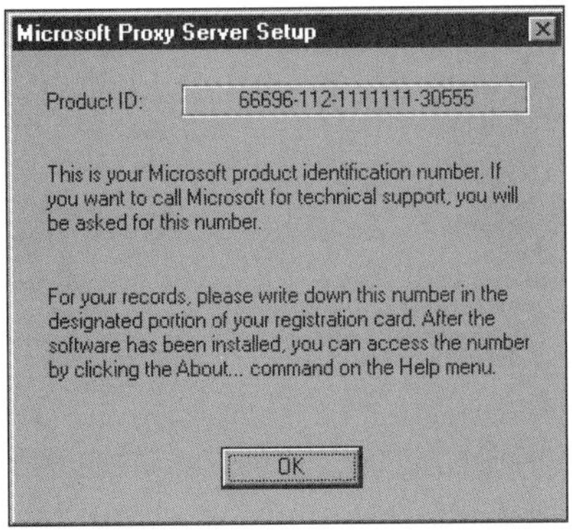

Microsoft Proxy Server Setup
Product ID:
66696-112-1111111-30555
This is your Microsoft product identification number. If you want to call Microsoft for technical support, you will be asked for this number.
For your records, please write down this number in the designated portion of your registration card. After the software has been installed, you can access the number by clicking the About... command on the Help menu.
OK

FIGURE 5-3 Product identification

At this point, the Proxy Server installation searches for any previously installed components, as shown in Figure 5-4. This may take several minutes, depending on the configuration of your system.

Setup is searching for installed components...

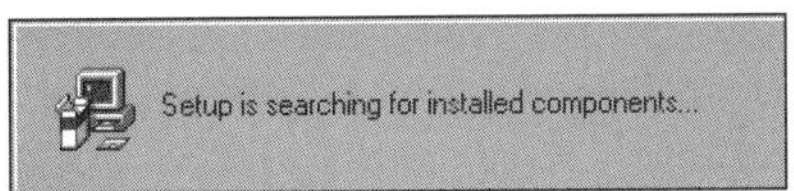

FIGURE 5-4 Setup search notice

The next screen displays a default directory destination. There is also a large Installation Options button, as shown in Figure 5-5.

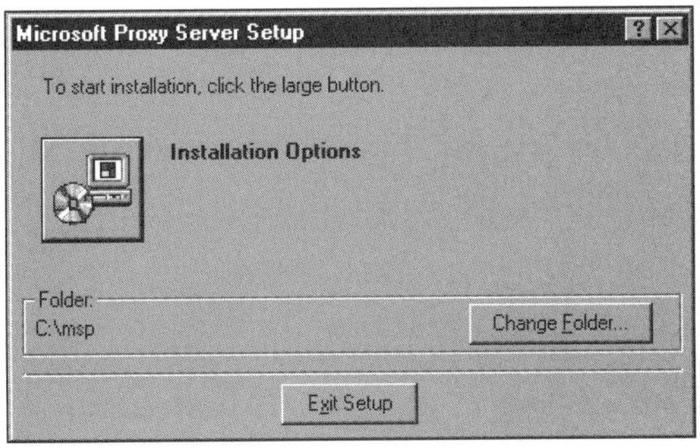

Microsoft Proxy Server Setup
To start installation, click the large button.
Installation Options
Folder:
C:\msp
Change Folder...
Exit Setup

FIGURE 5-5 Installation directory screen

You can accept this default directory or click the Change Folder button to specify a different directory, as shown in Figure 5-6.

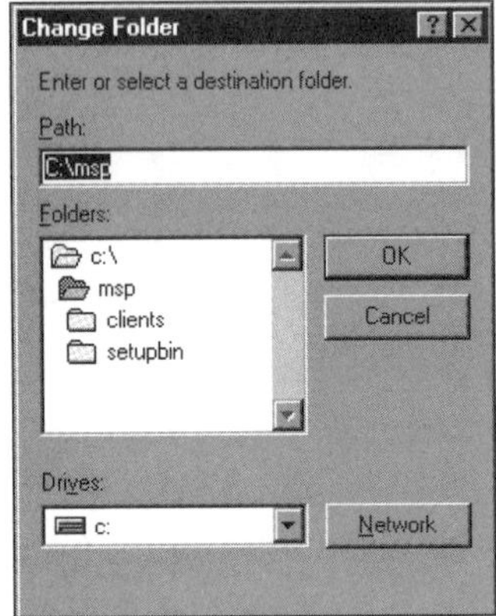

FIGURE 5-6 Change Folder screen

You can click the large button on the main screen to modify the Installation Options. The options box enables you to install Proxy Server, the Administrative Tools, or the documentation. All three options are selected by default, and you would normally want to install all three, as shown in Figure 5-7.

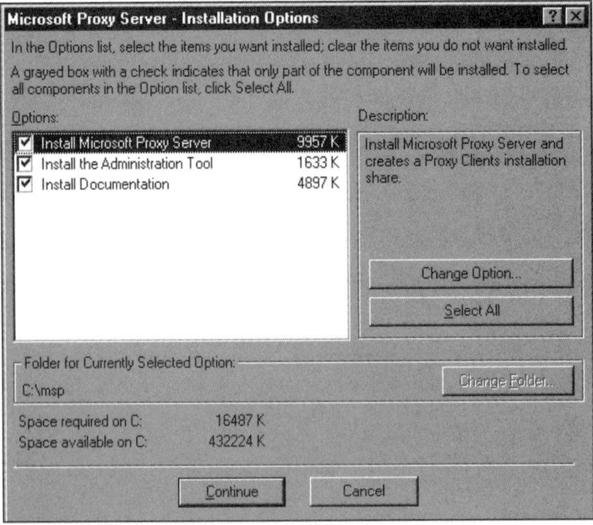

FIGURE 5-7 Installation Options screen

This screen is useful if you want to install only the Proxy Server documentation on another computer, without installing Proxy Server. The documentation is HTML-based, and can be used with any browser that supports frames, such as Internet Explorer 3.01 or higher. The documentation is divided into two panes, with the left pane containing links to the other areas of the documentation, and the right pane containing a help document, as shown in Figure 5-8.

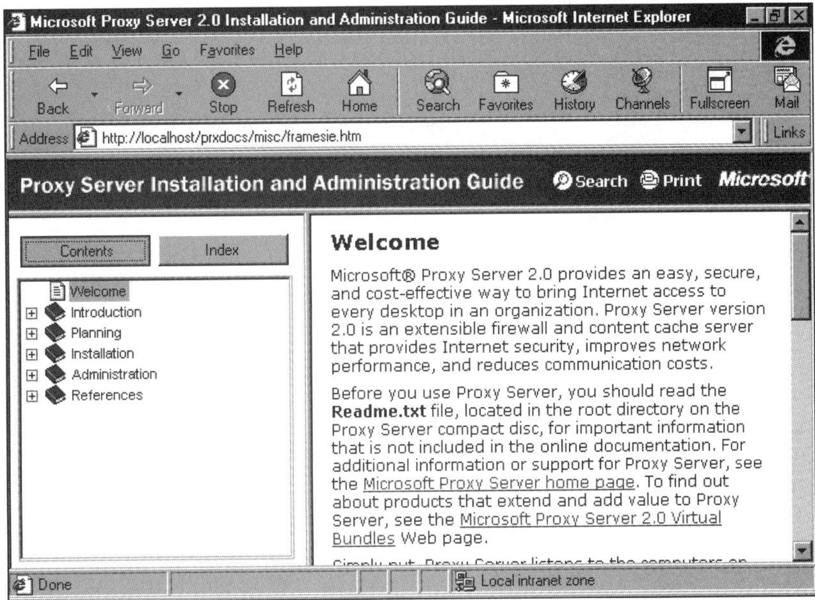

FIGURE 5-8 Proxy Server documentation

Administrators often find it useful to have online documentation on various network products on their personal computers for quick reference.

From the Installation Options screen, you can also click the Change Option button. This brings you to an additional option list that enables you to choose the type of client share to install, as shown in Figure 5-9.

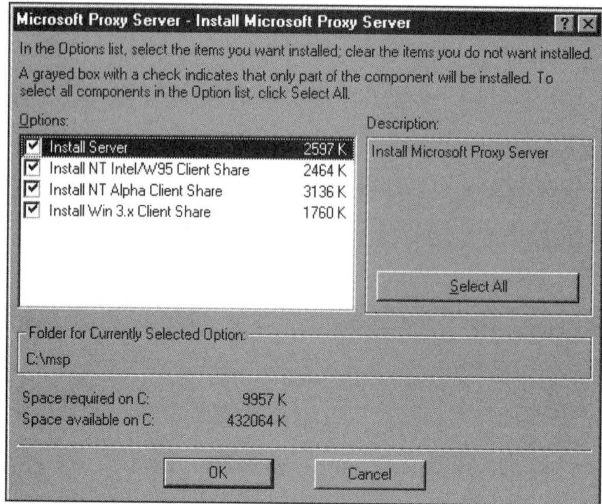

FIGURE 5-9 Options list

By default, all of the options are selected, but you can deselect some. For example, if you have no NT Alpha clients on your network and you are sure you will not have any in the future, you can choose not to install this option.

Once you accept the default settings or made the desired changes, click the Continue button. Setup then checks for necessary disk space. If there is not enough disk space for the installation, Setup gives you a message telling you to free more disk space before the installation can continue.

The Proxy Server Cache Drives dialog box appears next. Caching is enabled by default, and this dialog box asks you to select the drives that you want to use for caching. You must also enter an amount (in MB) in the Maximum Size field. Notice that only NTFS drives or partitions are available (FAT drives are grayed out), as shown in Figure 5-10.

The Maximum Size dialog box is where you enter the size of the cache. Determine the size from the number of clients, using the Proxy Server cache size formula. After you enter the cache size, click the Set button. If you want to use multiple drives to store the cache, continue this process until you have assigned all the drives.

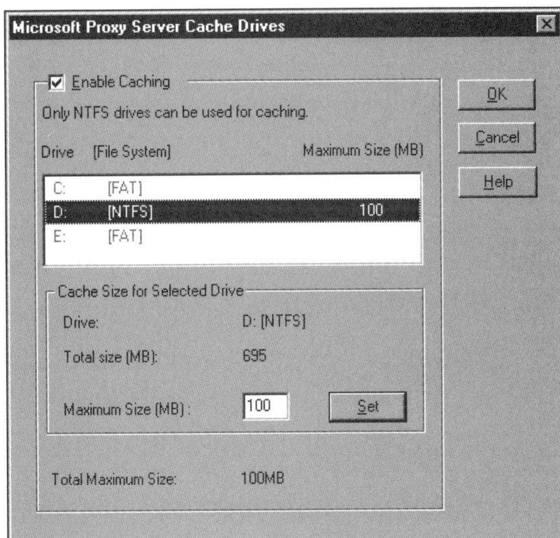

FIGURE 5-10 Cache Drives dialog box

The next step is to configure the Local Address Table (LAT). An empty LAT is shown in Figure 5-11.

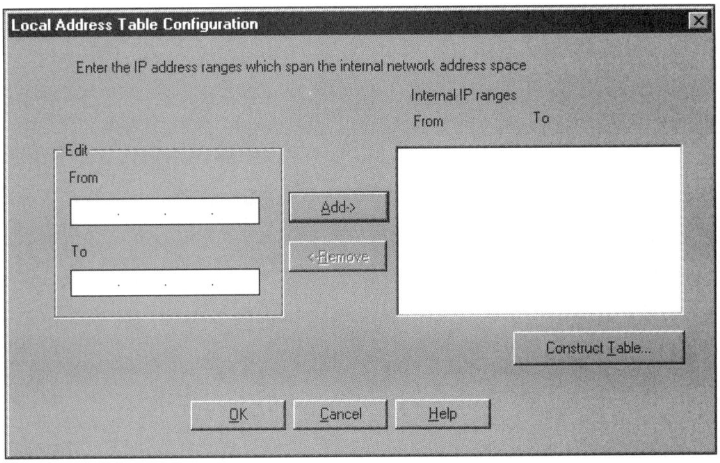

FIGURE 5-11 Empty LAT

Remember that the LAT stores the IP addresses that are local to your network. This is how Proxy Server knows if an IP address is on the local network or on the Internet. A copy of the LAT, called `msplat.txt`, is downloaded to the clients and stored in the MSPCLNT directory. This copy of the LAT on the client is updated on a regular basis so it is always current. Whenever a Winsock client attempts to make a connection, Proxy Server parses the LAT to determine if the requested IP address is local or not. If the address is local, Proxy Server makes a connection with that machine. If it is not local, the connection is made to the Internet through the Winsock Proxy Service.

There may be instances when clients need additional entries in the LAT for connections to other internal IP addresses not included in Proxy Server's LAT. In this case, a custom file called `locallat.txt` must be created and placed in the MSPCLNT directory. Because Proxy Server overwrites `msplat.txt` at regular intervals, the `locallat.txt` file is needed to keep Proxy Server from overwriting this additional addressing information.

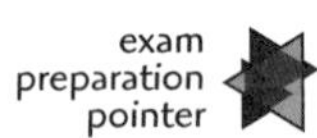

Make sure you remember the difference between `msplat.txt` and `locallat.txt`. The local LAT is local to the machine – it is not overwritten and updated by Proxy Server.

Although the Winsock Proxy Service briefly is mentioned briefly in Chapter 1, Chapter 6 is a detailed look at the Winsock Proxy Services and the other services offered by Proxy Server.

To begin the LAT construction, click the Construct Table button. This enables you to create the Local Address Table. As you can see in Figure 5-12, the selections enable you to include the private IP address ranges, and to load the addresses for all IP NICs from the NT internal routing table. You have two options in this section. You can load all known address ranges from all IP NICs, or you can load address ranges from a list that you select.

Construct Local Address Table

Select IP address ranges to load into Local Address Table

Add the private ranges 10.x.x.x, 192.168.x.x and 172.16.x.x - 172.31.x.x to the table.

Load from NT internal Routing Table

Load known address ranges from all IP interface cards

Load known address ranges from the following IP interface cards:

RTL80291(10.0.0.4)

OK Cancel Help

FIGURE 5-12 Construct Local Address Table dialog box

You can also add private ranges by clicking the Add Private Ranges radio button. These are private address ranges that are predetermined and assigned as private addresses by the InterNIC. This radio button enables you to enter the private addresses of the network so they will not be routed across the Internet. After either accepting the defaults or making changes to the table construction, you are given a dialog box, shown in Figure 5-13, asking you to verify the LAT and manually remove any external NIC addresses, if necessary.

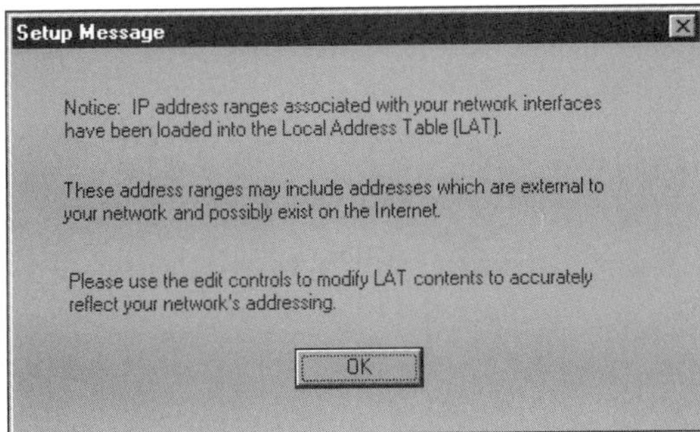

FIGURE 5-13 Verification message

Many companies choose to use Proxy Server with private address ranges to make administration easier. For example, Class A addresses beginning with 10 are reserved for private use, so it makes sense for private networks to use the private addresses.

Remember that the LAT is for local addresses only—addresses that are local to the network. Make sure you review the LAT carefully once it is constructed, although you can made additions or changes to the LAT after installation is complete. Once you complete the LAT construction and verify the table, it will look similar to the LAT shown in Figure 5-14.

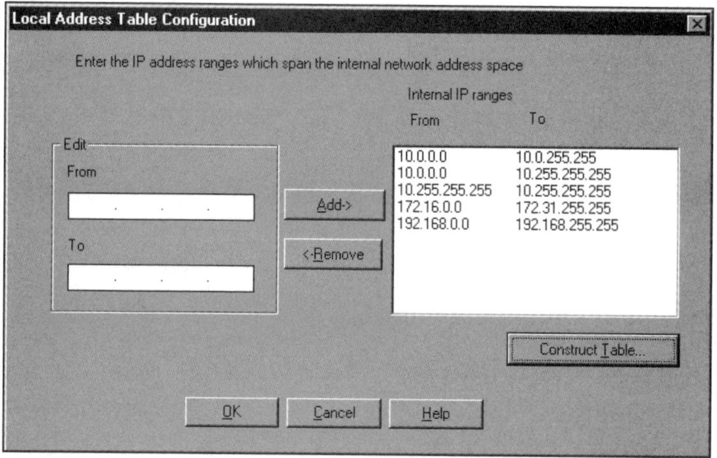

FIGURE 5-14 Completed LAT

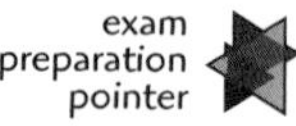

External NIC addresses may not be included in the LAT. This is a security breach and may open your network to intruders.

Once the LAT is complete, click OK, and you are taken to the Client Installation/Configuration screen, as shown in Figure 5-15.

You have a couple of options in this section. Notice that under the Winsock Proxy Client heading (which includes all your Windows computers), you have the option to connect to the Proxy Server via the server name or the IP address. The server name is selected by default. For NWLink clients, use the NetBIOS name rather than the host name.

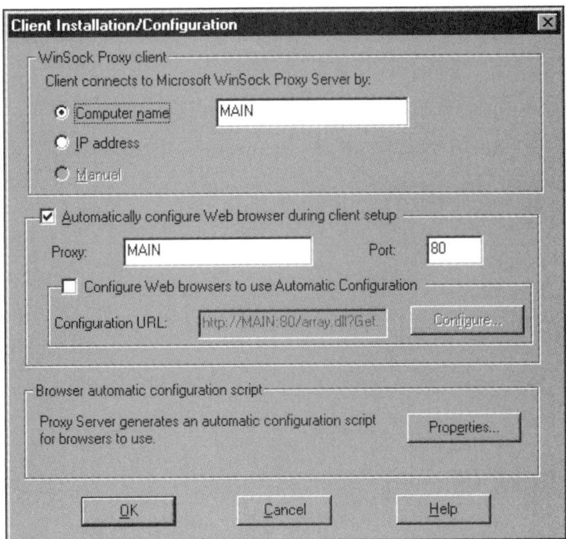

FIGURE 5-15 Client Installation/Configuration screen

In mixed Novell and Microsoft networks, it is not at all unusual for the protocol of choice to be NWLink, which is Microsoft's version of Novell's proprietary protocol, IPX/SPX. How can you use NWLink with a Proxy Server that must use TCP/IP to communicate on the Internet? It is actually quite easy. You can bind the proxy server's internal NIC to NWLink and its external NIC to TCP/IP. Proxy Server will handle the conversion between protocols for both inbound and outbound traffic. In fact, using NWLink on the internal network is a security benefit, because Internet traffic has to use TCP/IP.

There are a few details you should know about the client computer using NWLink, and I take a look at those in Chapter 8.

In the middle section of the screen, there is a check box that enables you to configure the Web browsers of the clients during client setup. You can see that the Proxy name and path point to the current Proxy Server. This option, which is not selected by default, lets the server automatically configure client browsers so they contact the Proxy Server for Internet communication instead of trying to reach the Internet on their own. The default script location is `http://`*`servername`*`:80/array.dll?Get`

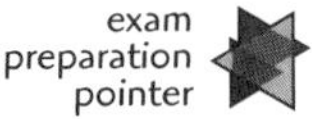

You should memorize the default script location when you prepare for the exam.

If you click the Configure button, you can provide a custom script, as shown in Figure 5-16. If you can write in JavaScript, you may find this option desirable because it enables you to customize the script to the needs of your environment.

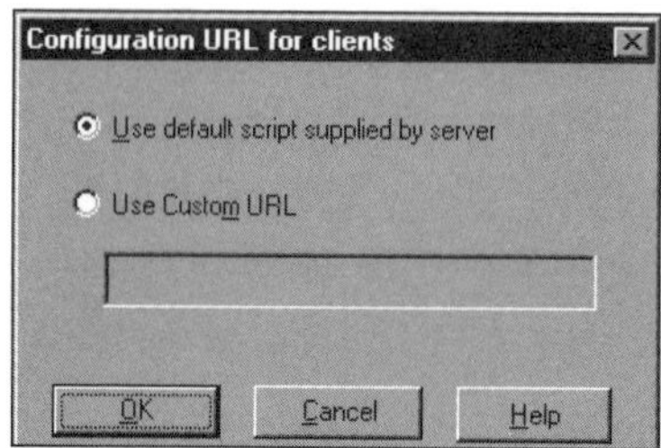

FIGURE 5-16 Custom Client Script dialog box

Client configuration is covered in detail in Chapter 8.

The bottom section of the Client Installation/Configuration Screen gives you the option to use the Browser Automatic Configuration script or use another script. If you click the Advanced button, a dialog box appears for further configuration options, as shown in Figure 5-17.

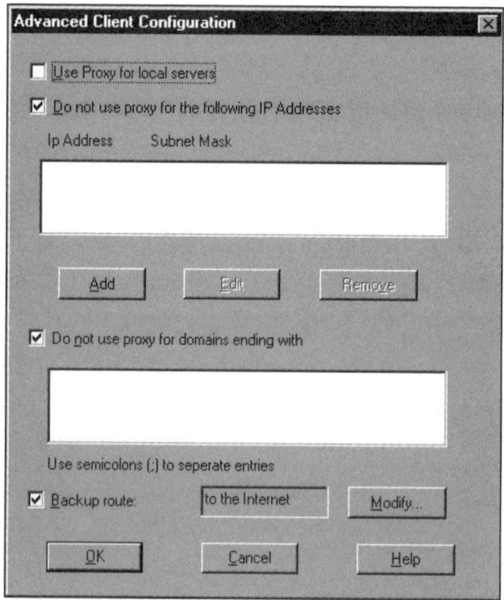

FIGURE 5-17 Browser Automatic Configuration Advanced dialog box

You can restrict access to certain Proxy Servers via IP address or domain. At the bottom of the screen, you have the option to configure a backup route should the Proxy Server's connection fail. This enables the Proxy Server to continue to serve the clients. If you click the Modify button, you get an additional dialog box, as shown in Figure 5-18.

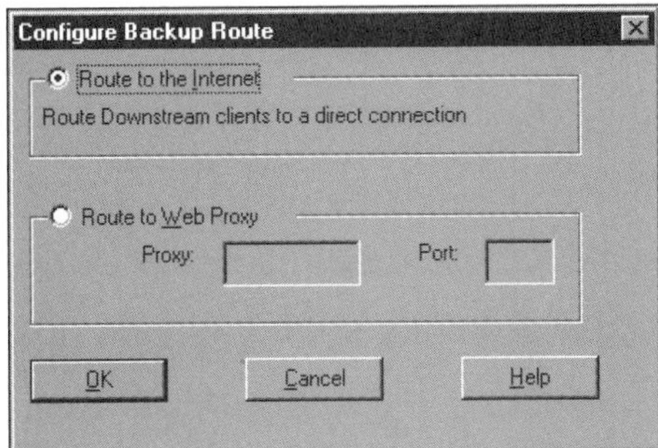

FIGURE 5-18 Configure Backup Route dialog box

This option enables you to route clients to another downstream Proxy Server or to configure a specific backup route.

Backup routes, downstream Proxy Servers, and additional multiple Proxy Server options are discussed in detail later in the book.

After you have made the desired selections in the Client Installation/ Configuration Screen, click OK to continue. The next screen enables you to set the access control for the Winsock and Web Proxy Services, as shown in Figure 5-19.

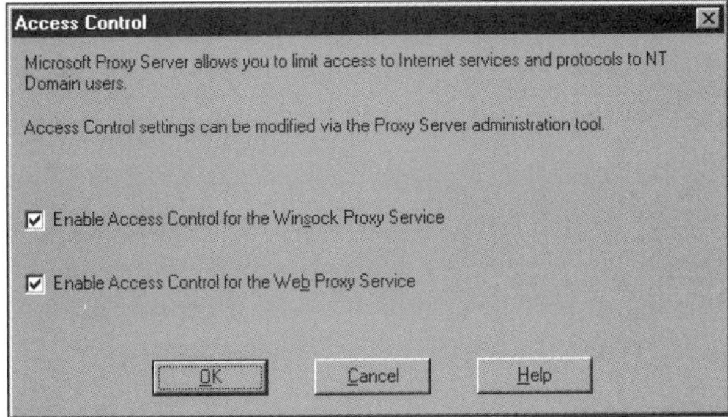

FIGURE 5-19 Access Control screen

Access control does just that — it controls the access of the clients and requires the administrator to give explicit rights to all clients. Each user must be added to a group or individually assigned rights to access services on the Internet. Notice that both the Winsock and Web Proxy Services are selected by default. If you deselect them, you disable access control, permitting clients to bypass security and use the Proxy Services, so you normally want to accept the defaults and keep access control enabled.

At this point, setup checks for necessary disk space for the options you have selected, and copies the files to your computer, as shown in Figure 5-20.

FIGURE 5-20 File copy process

Once the file copy process is complete, you receive a notification box about packet filtering security, as shown in Figure 5-21. Click OK.

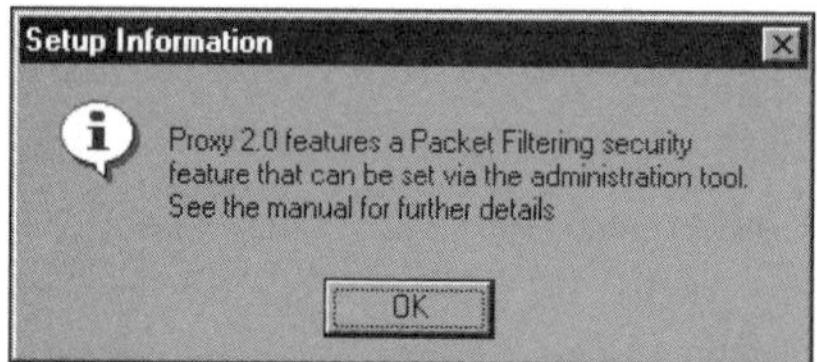

FIGURE 5-21 Packet filtering message

Setup completes and displays the final dialog box of the Wizard, as shown in Figure 5-22.

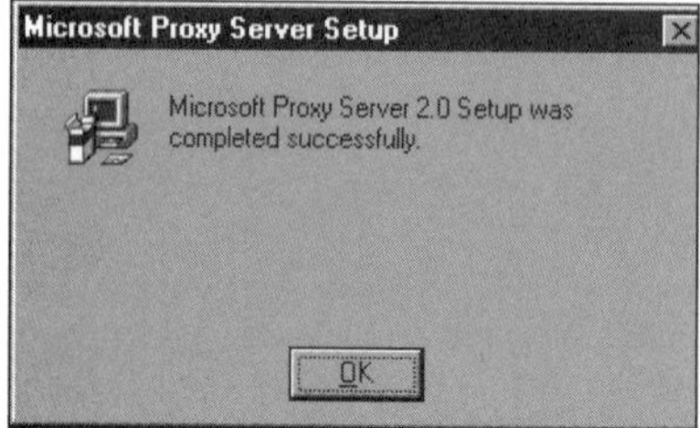

FIGURE 5-22 Setup completion

Setup is now complete, and you should have a functioning Proxy Server. In addition to the Proxy Server, its components, the LAT, and the documentation, Proxy Server also adds a directory to the server called MSPCLNT, which contains the Proxy Client installation software. Also, Proxy Server adds a Proxy Server Performance Monitor. I examine the additions and work with Performance Monitor later in the book, but you can take a look at the Performance Monitor after you install Proxy Server by clicking Start ⇛ Programs ⇛ Proxy Server ⇛ Monitor Microsoft Proxy Server Performance

Upgrading from Proxy Server 1.0

The upgrade path from Proxy Server 1.0 is very easy. At the beginning of the setup of Proxy Server 2.0, the installation program inspects your system for the presence of earlier versions of Proxy Server and upgrades them accordingly. Remember from Chapter 1 that Proxy Server 1.0 basically provided caching features; it did not provide the robust firewall protection and security of 2.0. There are two points to keep in mind before upgrading to Proxy Server 2.0:

- IIS 3.0 or higher must be installed before upgrading to Proxy Server 2.0.
- You need to install Internet Explorer 4.01 or higher.

Also, Proxy Server 1.0 permitted you to store the cache on a FAT partition. For Proxy Server 2.0, you must convert this partition to NTFS, if you choose to use the same partition for caching. This must be done before the upgrade begins.

Changing Installation Components and Uninstalling Proxy Server

Changing the configuration of a Proxy Server installation or uninstalling Proxy Server from the NT Server is a very simple process that works like most other Microsoft applications. You can perform either of these actions by inserting the CD-ROM and running Setup. You are presented with a screen enabling you to add or remove components, reinstall Proxy Server, or remove all the components of Proxy Server, as shown in Figure 5-23.

If you click Add/Remove, you are given some options to add or remove components, depending on your original installation. The other two buttons enable you to completely reinstall Proxy Server or completely remove Proxy Server from the system. If you choose to uninstall Proxy Server, you are given a dialog box to confirm your decision, and you are also prompted to delete the cache and the log files. The Web Service is stopped until the uninstallation is complete, and then restarted. Remember that if you uninstall the Proxy Server, each client will have to be reconfigured so it does not access the Proxy Server for Internet Connectivity.

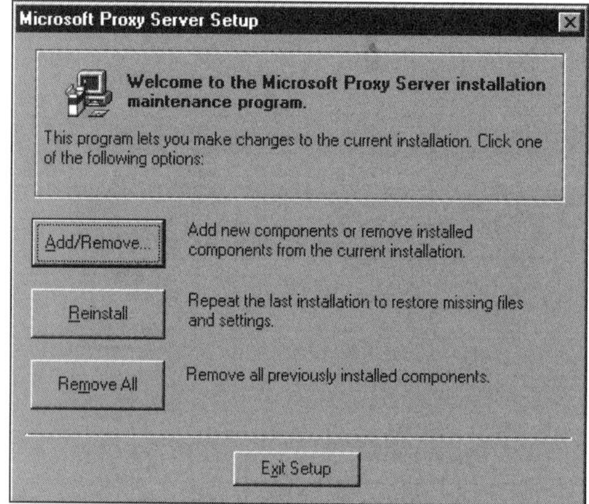

FIGURE 5-23 Configuration options screen

Changing or removing the client configuration is explored in more detail in Chapter 7.

Troubleshooting the Installation

Because Proxy Server is an additional server component that integrates with Windows NT Server and IIS, the installation of Proxy Server is usually trouble-free. That does not mean that no problems ever arise, but installation problems are normally few and easily remedied. The following is a list of the most common and the solution.

- **Minimum Requirement Failure:** Windows NT Server with Service Pack 3 and IIS 3.0 or later must be installed before Proxy Server installation. Also, you must have enough free disk space for the installation. Failing to meet the minimum requirements will cause the Proxy Server installation to fail.

- **Can't Select Cache Drives:** During installation, if the cache drives list is grayed out, the drives are formatted with FAT instead of NTFS. The drive(s) you want to use for caching must be converted to NTFS before you can configure caching.
- **SAP Setup Error:** SAP must be installed before you begin installation. If it is not, you will receive an error telling you install SAP, and then start the installation again.
- **General LAT Errors:** You may receive errors concerning the LAT configuration. This occurs because of mistakes in creating the LAT. A common error message states, "None of the Proxy Server's computer's addresses are internal." This error message is generated when the server's internal NIC IP address is not included in the LAT, which is required.

For troubleshooting tips and additional resource information, see Chapter 14.

Exam Preparation Summary

The Proxy Server installation is easy and usually trouble-free, and you probably will not see many detailed questions about installation. The bulk of the installation questions will concern the construction of the LAT. You may be given some scenario-based questions with information about the network configuration, and then asked which IP address ranges to include. These questions are not too difficult if you keep in mind that IP addresses from clients that will use the Proxy Server must be included in the LAT as well as the IP address of the Proxy Server's internal NIC.

Keep in mind that only a server license is required for Proxy Server — client licenses are not required. Also, you need to know the functions of and differences between Proxy Server directories and files, such as MSPCLNT, `msplat.txt`, and `locallat.txt`. Remember that `msplat.txt` is downloaded to the client from the proxy server and updated frequently, whereas `locallat.txt` is local to the client machine and is not overwritten by Proxy Server. These two files are stored in the MSPCLNT directory on the client. There is also an MSPCLNT directory on the proxy server that contains the installation files for the client.

A network can use NWLink as its protocol and still use Proxy Server. To accomplish this, the Proxy Server's internal NIC must be bound to NWLink, and the Proxy Server's external NIC must be bound to TCP/IP. Remember, the external NIC connects to the Internet and the internal NIC connects to the LAN. This multi-homed configuration ensures that all Internet traffic has to pass through the Proxy Server.

Key Point Summary

This chapter examined the installation of the Proxy Server 2.0. We focused on a number of specifics for the installation:

- The server you install Proxy Server on must meet both the hardware and software requirements for installation.
- Before installation, install SAP and format the drive or partition where you want the cache to be stored as NTFS.
- Proxy Server requires one license per server and no client licenses. You can sell Proxy Server, as long as you do not keep any copies, but you cannot rent or lease it. The licensing requirements for NT Server 4.0 and IIS must also be met to comply with Microsoft.
- The Proxy Server Installation Wizard provides an automated method for installation.
- You can choose if you want to install Proxy Server, the Administrative Tool, and the documentation. The documentation can also be installed on other machines without performing a full server installation.
- The Proxy Server documentation is HTML-based and can be read using any browser that supports frames.
- During installation, you must configure the size (in MB) of the cache using the cache size formula.
- The LAT must include all local network addresses that will use the Proxy Server, including the IP address of the internal NIC in the server. The external NIC must not be included in the LAT. This constitutes a security breach.

- A copy of the LAT, called `msplat.txt`, is downloaded to each client and stored in the MSPCLNT directory. Proxy Server periodically overwrites and updates this file.
- You must create a `locallat.txt` file if there are additional IP addresses you want to include in the LAT. These IP address, which are not included in Proxy Server's LAT, will be overwritten if you do not store them in `locallat.txt`.
- Private address ranges assigned by the InterNIC, such as 10.*XX*.*XX*.*XX*, can be automatically added to the LAT.
- Installation contains a default setup script for Proxy Server clients. This script can be replaced during setup by a custom JavaScript if desired.
- Access Control is enabled by default, but can be disabled for Winsock and Web Proxy Services during setup if desired, although this is usually not recommended.
- Upgrading from Proxy Server 1.0 is easy. Make sure that IIS 3.0 or later is installed and format the cache drive to NTFS. Proxy Server 1.0 permitted you to use a FAT drive for the cache, but this is not allowed in Proxy Server 2.0.
- You can add or remove components, reinstall Proxy Server, or uninstall Proxy Server easily via the CD-ROM or through the proxy server's directory.
- NWLink can be used as the network protocol with Proxy Server. The Proxy Server's internal NIC must be bound with NWLink and the external NIC must be bound with TCP/IP for this configuration. Proxy Server handles the protocol translation for both inbound and outbound traffic.

Applying What You've Learned

The following review questions give you a chance to test your knowledge of the content in this chapter. Should you miss some, review the appropriate portions of the chapter. The answers to the Instant Assessment questions can be found in Appendix C.

Instant Assessment

1. What is SAP?

   A. Service Address Protocol

   B. Service Address Packet

   C. Service Advertisement Protocol

   D. Service Advertisement Packet

2. How is the cache size (in megabytes) calculated?

   A. 120 × (number of users + 0.5MB)

   B. 100 + (number of users + 0.5MB)

   C. 100 + (number of users × 0.5MB)

   D. 100 × (number of users × 0.5MB)

3. What is contained in the LAT?

   A. IP addresses

   B. Internal IP addresses

   C. External IP addresses

   D. Internal and external IP addresses

4. What should not be included in the LAT?

   A. IP addresses

   B. Internal IP addresses

   C. External IP addresses

   D. Internal and external IP addresses

5. What is the Client Proxy directory called?

   A. MSP

   B. MSPPROXY

   C. MSPCLNT

   D. MSPCLNT.INI

6. Which file is copied to the clients and updated regularly by the Proxy Server?

   A. `msplat.txt`

   B. `msplat.ini`

C. `locallat.txt`

D. `locallat.ini`

7. Which file is stored on the client as is not updated by the Proxy Server?

A. `msplat.txt`

B. `msplat.ini`

C. `locallat.txt`

D. `locallat.ini`

8. What change should be made to cache drives before upgrade Proxy Server 1.0 to 2.0?

A. Format the drives with FAT.

B. Format the drives with NTFS.

C. Format the drives with FAT32.

D. Format the drives with VFAT.

9. If the cache drives are grayed out during setup, what is the problem?

A. The drives are full.

B. The drives are formatted as FAT.

C. The drives are formatted as NTFS.

D. The drives have failed.

Critical Thinking Labs

These labs present you with analysis problems to test your critical thinking skills with the content in this chapter.

Lab 5.18 *NWLink and Proxy*

Your company uses NWLink only, but wants to gain Internet access with a Proxy Server. Many people think they will have to change the network protocol to TCP/IP. What would you tell them?

Lab 5.19 *Building the LAT*

A friend is about to perform a Proxy Server installation, but doesn't understand the LAT and how to build one. How would you explain the LAT, its construction, and what warnings would you give?

Lab 5.20 *Troubleshooting Setup*

During Setup, a coworker receives the Proxy error message "None of the Proxy Server's computer's addresses are internal." What is most likely the cause of the problem?

Lab 5.21 *Proxy licensing*

Your company is considering using Proxy Server, but is concerned about the administration and expense of licensing. You have been asked to give an overview of Proxy Server licensing at an upcoming meeting. How would you explain?

Hands-on Labs

The Hands-on Labs give you an opportunity to practice skills you have learned in this chapter. Make sure you read the system requirements for each lab to be certain you have the correct configuration before beginning the lab.

Lab 5.22 *Installing Proxy Server*

This lab assumes you have a computer running Windows NT Server 4.0, Service Pack 3, and IIS 3.0 or greater, and that you have an NTFS drive to use for the cache. To install Proxy Server, follow these steps:

1. Insert the Proxy Server CD-ROM. `Autorun.inf` will initialize, or you can double-click Setup in the root directory of the CD-ROM to begin setup.
2. The Welcome Screen and End User License Agreement appears. Read the agreement and click Continue.
3. The CD key screen Enter the CD Key found on the CD-ROM case and click OK.
4. The Product Identification screen appears. Note the ID for future use. Click OK.
5. Setup searches the system for previously installed components, and then present an Installation Options screen. You can accept the default directory or change it if you wish. Start the installation by clicking the large button with a computer icon on it.
6. The Installation Options screen appears with the default options of installing Proxy Server, the Administrative Tool, and the documentation selected. If you click the Change Option button, you see additional client share options. Accept the defaults and click OK to return to the main screen.

7. Accept the defaults and click Continue.
8. Setup stops the WWW Services.
9. The Cache Drives dialog box appears. Select the drive you want to use for caching. Notice that any FAT drives are grayed out.
10. Next, you need to enter the cache size in the Maximum Size field. Use the cache size formula to calculate this. Enter the number and click the Set button. Click OK.
11. The LAT Configuration box appears. If you click the Construct Table button, you will be given some additional options that are selected by default. Click OK. You get a message telling you to make sure you edit out any external NIC addresses. Click OK.
12. Once you have configured the addresses you want to include in the LAT and made any editorial changes, click OK.
13. Next, you see the Client Installation/Configuration dialog box. Notice that if you enable the Configure Web browsers to use Automatic Configuration, you see the default Configuration URL. You can configure this by clicking the Configure button. Accept the default.
14. If you click the Properties button of the Browser automatic configuration script, you will see additional options for Client configuration. Click Cancel.
15. Click OK in the Client Installation/Configuration dialog box.
16. The Access Control dialog box appears. Access control for Winsock and Web Proxy Services are selected by default. Click OK to accept the default settings.
17. Proxy Server performs the installation.
18. You see a dialog box telling you that Packet Filtering can be set via the administration tool. Click OK. Setup updates the system and restarts the WWW services.
19. Once the WWW services are started, you see a dialog box telling you that Proxy Server setup was completed successfully. Click OK.

PART

Configuring Proxy Server

III

Part III takes you to the heart of the book, where you configure Proxy Server to provide the various kinds of services and functions that you need. In Chapter 6, you learn about Proxy Server architecture and the Web Proxy Service, the Winsock Proxy Service, and the SOCKS Proxy Service.

In Chapter 7, you take a tour around the Proxy Server interface. You see where the various services Proxy Server offers can be configured, and you take a look at the properties and tabs available.

In Chapter 8, you learn how to configure the client computers to use Proxy Server. In this chapter, you see how to configure the Winsock and SOCKS Proxy Services, and you also learn how configure browsers for use with Proxy Server.

Chapter 9 explores security issues and the security functions provided by Proxy Server. You learn how to configure various filters, and how to secure the LAN to protect it from Internet intruders.

In Chapter 10, you explore content caching and how to configure Proxy Server to cache or not cache various Web content. You learn how to create cache filters and how to manage the cache.

In Chapter 11, you take a look at Proxy Server in Enterprise environments. Here you learn how to configure and design large LAN and WAN solutions involving multiple sites and Proxy Servers.

Finally, in Chapter 12, you explore using a Proxy Server and Remote Access Service in Windows NT.

CHAPTER

6

Proxy Server Architecture

About Chapter 6

This chapter explores the architecture of Proxy Server 2.0, or how Proxy Server and its services work together to create a tightly integrated product. In this chapter, I take a look at an overview of architecture in general, and then explore the three Proxy Server services: the Web Proxy Service, the Winsock Proxy Service, and the SOCKS Proxy Service. The Critical Thinking Labs in this chapter give you a chance to test your knowledge of Proxy Server's architecture in real-world scenarios.

What Is Architecture?

If you have read any technical books before, you most likely have waded through a chapter on architecture — and possibly even dreaded the reading. Microsoft architecture can be dizzying at times, mostly because it has developed over the years as technology has changed and developed. At its core, *architecture* is the base on which a piece of software is built, whether it is an operating system or an application. The architecture is like a blueprint for building a house. The blueprint defines how the house should fit together; how different components, such as the plumbing and the electrical wiring, work together to create one product called a house. If something is added to the house later, such as another bedroom, the addition has to work within the architecture of the house.

Operating systems and software function in the same way. In reality, an operating system or application is simply lines of code that perform various tasks and functions. The architecture defines how these different tasks and functions work together to make up the whole product. The architecture defines how these processes work in terms of what they are permitted to do and what they are not permitted to do. This architecture creates a stable, robust operating system or application that can perform a wide variety of diverse functions while remaining a stable product. Without an architecture, the operating system or application would turn to chaos as various processes interfered with each other.

In a system such as Windows NT Server, the architecture defines how the system handles applications, how it provides various services, how it manages network functions and access, and how it communicates with other systems. Any additional components, such as IIS or Proxy Server, must function within the boundaries of NT's architecture.

You can learn more about the structure and components of Windows NT Server architecture from *Windows NT 4.0 MCSE Study Guide,* by Alan Carter (IDG Books Worldwide).

Proxy Server 2.0 Architecture

Windows NT Server is composed of a number of functions and services, which give it a robust and diverse functionality in virtually any network environment. Proxy Server follows this same path by providing various and assorted functions — a full plate of Internet, caching, and security operations. This diversity is created through a number of operations and services. In Chapter 1, I introduce the three core services of Proxy Server: the Web Proxy Service, the Winsock Proxy Service, and the SOCKS Proxy Service. These three services enable Proxy Server to be "all things to all people," providing full functionality across multiple platforms. Table 6-1 provides a brief definition of each, and I consider each in detail in this chapter.

TABLE 6-1. PROXY SERVER SERVICES OVERVIEW

Service	*Definition*
Web Proxy Service	Provides full Web cross-platform functionality for all CERN-compliant applications.
Winsock Proxy Service	Provides Winsock support for any Windows Sockets API functions.
SOCKS Proxy Service	Provides SOCKS support and functionality for Socket based processes.

Web Proxy Service

The Web Proxy Service, as you can imagine, provides services for the World Wide Web. This service is used by Web browsers and other CERN-compliant applications, and offers the full range of functions you normally think of when you discuss the World Wide Web. The following are a few of the main ones.

CERN Compliance

Users today take for granted the ability to launch any Web browser they choose from any operating system they choose, connect to the Internet, and use its services. This functionality did not happen by accident. As operating systems began using GUI interfaces, HTTP was developed to provide graphical retrieval of HTML documents. The Conseil Europeen pour la Recherche Nucleair (CERN), a Swedish company now called the European Laboratory for Particle Physics, developed HTTP. The CERN standard was developed to establish communication requirements for HTTP, and it became the accepted standard for HTTP communication. Most browsers today, such as Microsoft Internet Explorer and Netscape Navigator, are CERN-compliant. The Web Proxy Service is fully compliant with CERN.

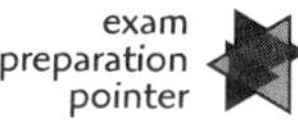

Any CERN-compliant browser can use Proxy Server's Web Proxy Service.

HTTP, FTP, and Gopher Support

The Web Proxy Service supports HTTP, FTP, and Gopher, as well as related protocols and technologies. All requests in the Web Proxy Service are sent in HTTP format. This allows the retrieval of Web documents as well as file transfer and Gopher requests. By definition, the function of HTTP is to transfer information from one place to another. This is accomplished with two major HTTP commands: `get` and `post`.

The `get` command enables HTTP to fetch a Web document for display on the user's computer. The `post` command enables the user to post information on a Web site, such as you would enter in an auto-submit form, discussion board, or something similar. These two commands enable you to get HTML documents and to post HTML on Web sites, as shown in Figure 6-1.

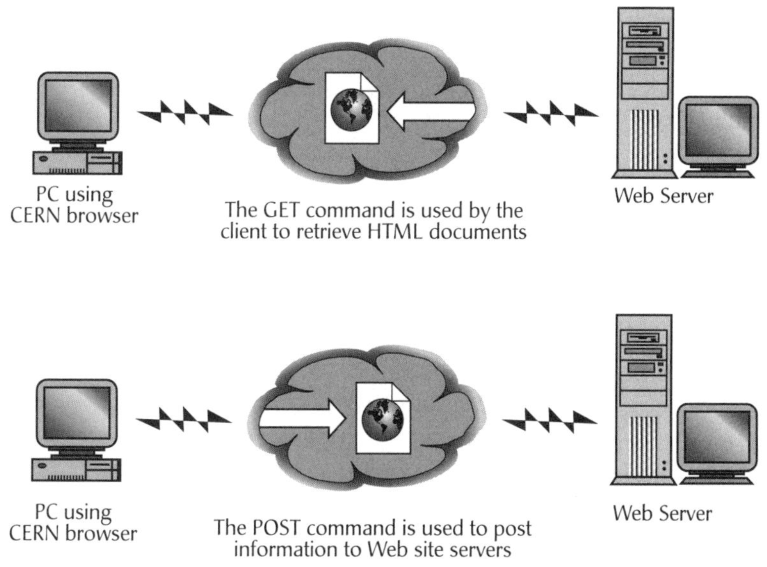

FIGURE 6-1 HTTP get and post commands

Internet Server Application Programming Interface

Internet Server Application Programming Interface (ISAPI) provides a standard API for the Internet Server component and for other HTTP servers that support ISAPI. ISAPI is made up of two applications; the ISAPI Filter and the ISAPI Application, which are actually dynamic link libraries (DLLs) written to the ISAPI interface. These two applications provide specific functions within Proxy Server and are a part of the `w3proxy.dll` file.

The ISAPI filter provides an extension to the IIS Web server, and is used whenever the server receives an HTTP request. An ISAPI filter can, in a sense, stand between events and the server. It can intercept specific server events before the server handles them. When a filter is loaded, it tells the server what sort of events it will handle. If these events occur, the filter can process the event, pass it on to another filter, or send it on to the sever.

Basically, the ISAPI filter looks at the kind of request being received. If it is a CERN proxy request, the ISAPI filter adds information to send the request to the ISAPI application. If the request is a standard HTTP request, it simply passes the request to the IIS server for processing. So in essence, the ISAPI filter does just what its name says — it filters ISAPI requests.

The ISAPI application takes the request from the filter and further processes it. Remember that ISAPI is a programming interface — it defines methods and processes for integrating Web components. You often see ISAPI used in Web sites where databases are used, or in dynamic HTML sites.

The ISAPI application checks the request in a number of ways, such as seeking authentication from the client, checking other filters to see if the request is permitted, or checking the cache to see if the request is current in the cache. If the request is current, the application returns the request to the client. If not, the application connects to the Internet site and retrieves the request for the client. For HTTP requests, the ISAPI application calls the Winsock API for processing of the request as well.

An important aspect of the ISAPI application is its ability to keep a connection active while the Proxy Server sends the data to the client. This is known as a *Keep Alive*. The Keep Alive function speeds the retrieval of additional information from that connection, if it is needed. Because browsers need to establish connections to retrieve information, the Keep Alive function keeps the line open for a period of time in case additional information is required.

Caching

As I mentioned before, *caching* is the ability to hold information in a storage location temporarily so it can be retrieved and used by clients without having to retrieve the information from the Internet. This functionality provides superior performance, and caching is a part of the Web Proxy Service. The Web Proxy Service within Proxy Server 2.0 supports two kinds of caching — passive caching and active caching.

Passive caching is the basic form of caching for Proxy Server, and is what you want to use in most circumstances. Passive caching means that Proxy Server checks the cache for a request. If the request is not there, it retrieves the request from the Internet, returns it to the client, puts the request in the cache, and assigns it a Time To Live (TTL). Future requests for this object are serviced from the cache until the TTL expires. After that, the object has to be retrieved from the Internet again and recached. At this point, as far as Proxy Server is concerned, the object is new, and it is given a new TTL. This process is illustrated in Figures 6-2 and 6-3. This method of caching is passive in that Proxy Server is not responsible for maintaining the object in the cache. Proxy Server checks the object's availability in the cache based on the TTL. The object simply has a TTL, and once that expires, the object is no longer available in the cache.

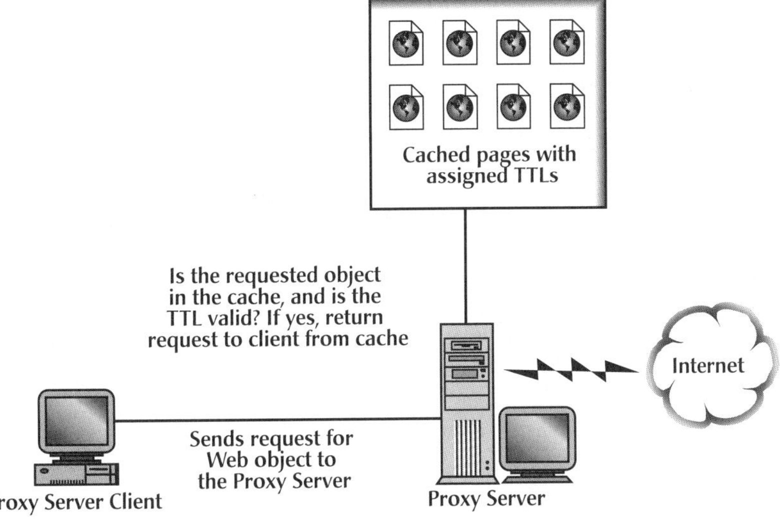

FIGURE 6-2 Passive caching object retrieval from cache

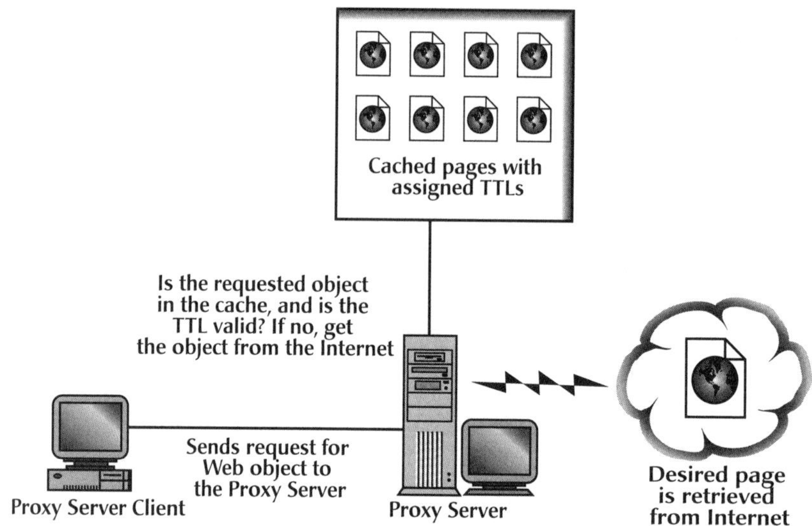

FIGURE 6-3 Passive caching object retrieval from the Internet

Active caching adds functionality to passive caching to increase the chances that the object will be in the cache when a request is made. This feature increases performance, but may require more disk space. Active caching looks at the TTL, the popularity of the object, and the server load. For example, if Proxy Server notices that a particular object in the cache is very popular, it begins updates and maintains this page in the cache. Proxy Server maintains the page by checking the Internet for changes to that page and updating the TTL. Proxy Server takes an active role in maintaining a cached object — it is not simply up to the TTL.

For example, suppose it's Election Day. News sites such as `cnn.com` and `abcnews.com` will receive a great number of hits (Internet requests). In a large company, many people will have their browsers pointed to these news sites so they can get election coverage updates, if this is permitted by the company. With active caching, Proxy Server notices that these sites are popular and begins updating and maintaining the cache as long as the objects remain popular, as shown in Figure 6-4.

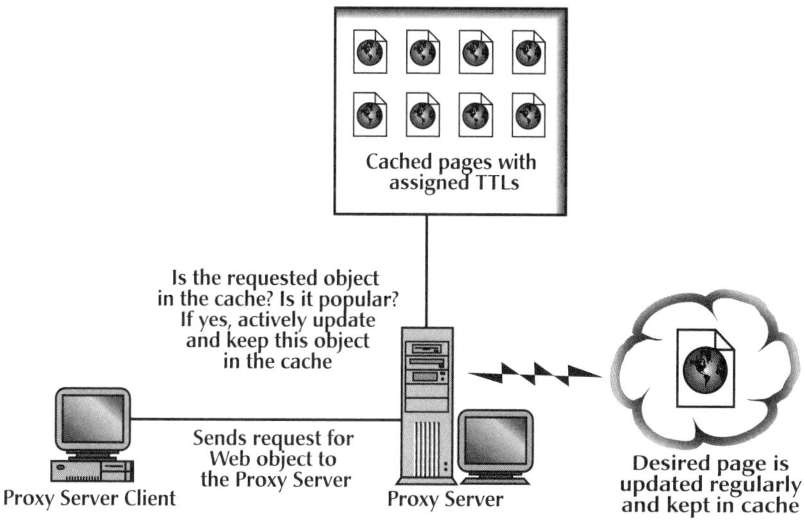

FIGURE 6-4 Active caching

Clients have the ability to bypass the cache and tell Proxy Server to directly retrieve the object from the Internet. Sometimes this is necessary for sites that change every few minutes when the most up-to-date information is needed. In Internet Explorer, you perform this action by pressing F5; in Netscape Navigator, you can do this by pressing the Reload button while holding down the Shift key.

I look at how to configure active and passive caching, as well as other cache options, later in the book.

Winsock Proxy Service

I have now looked at the Web Proxy Service and shown how it provides standard Web services, but there is more to TCP/IP than simple Web services. To provide these other communication functions, Proxy Server includes the Winsock Proxy Service, the second of the three services offered by Proxy Server. The following is an overview of Winsock and how Proxy Server uses this API.

Winsock API

Whenever you are learning about any architecture, it is easy to get overwhelmed. It is important to remember that various APIs did not develop overnight. Often, they began simply, for use with one system, and they evolved over time with other systems as the technology grew. Sockets and Winsock is no exception to this.

Like many technologies, particularly Internet and communication technologies, Sockets began with UNIX. The Socket connection provided a standard for communications technology — in other words, Sockets provided a standard set of rules an IP program followed to establish a connection. Socket technology has been refined and further developed and is still used by UNIX and NetWare. The Microsoft standard is known as *Windows Sockets*, or *Winsock*. These sockets provide a standard for connection, much the same way an electrical outlet in your home works. If you want to plug in a lamp, all you have to do is make the connection. You don't have worry about the wiring in your home or the technology that makes the lamp work; you just have to establish the connection.

How Sockets Work

Sockets and Winsock function by establishing a *socket connection*, which is composed of a TCP/IP address and a port number. I look at some of the major ports in Chapter 2, and you can also look at a list of socket ports on your NT Server in the `Winnt/System32/Drivers/Etc/Services` directory.

The IP address you use establishes the connection with the actual host that holds that IP address. The port number establishes a certain kind of application or service. For example, to establish a Telnet session, connect to the host through the IP address, and then connect to port 23 for Telnet. Notice that some ports are listed twice to provide both TCP and UDP functionality.

Remember from Chapter 2 that UDP is a connectionless protocol, and TCP is connection-oriented. In a UDP communication, the host and client do not communicate about the status of the transmission, just as you do not when you send a letter. You have no control about how the letter is sent or whether it gets to the intended recipient. UDP is usually used in audio and video transmissions, such as RealAudio.

Winsock Services

Winsock is an API that provides the establishment of socket connections. So what services does Winsock actually provide within Proxy Server? Table 6-2 provides a look at some of the more common ones.

TABLE 6-2 WINSOCK PROXY SERVICES

Winsock Service	*Description*
Support for additional protocols	Preconfigured support for RealAudio, NetShow, IRC, and UDP.
Access control	Provides both inbound and outbound access controls by port number and protocol, as well as by users or groups of users.
Protocol handling	Provides IP address translation and for IPX to IP gateway functions.
Site control	Provides site-specific denial via IP address, domain name, and subnet mask.
Security	Supports SSL and NT Challenge/Response, as well as network integrity by keeping Internet users out of the LAN.

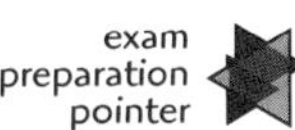

You need to remember the information in Table 6-2, especially that services such as RealAudio, IRC, SSL, and others are provided only through the Winsock Proxy Service.

Winsock Proxy Client

At its core, the Winsock Proxy Service enables Winsock application to function as if they were actually connected to the Internet instead of Proxy Server. This provides full Winsock functionality with various applications while providing access control and security via the Proxy Server. There are two Proxy DLLs that can be installed on the client that replace the standard non-proxy DLLs:

- `winsock.dll`: For 16-bit, Windows-based applications. Can be installed on Windows 3.*x*, Windows for Workgroups, or Windows 95/98.
- `wsock32.dll`: 32-bit Windows based applications. Can be installed on Windows 95/98 or Windows NT.

These DLLs take ownership of all Winsock calls and either process them locally on the network or pass them to the Winsock Proxy Service for processing. This process is transparent to the user, and the Winsock application functions as if it were directly connected to the Internet.

Control Channel

Proxy Server can use a *control channel* to manage the connection between the client and the server. The control channel adds overhead, so it should be used only when necessary. Essentially, the control channel helps facilitate the connection and reduce transmission problems associated with UDP. It performs four major functions:

1. It delivers the LAT to the client to determine whether or not the Winsock request is local to the network.
2. It establishes a TCP connection from the client to the server (remember that a TCP connection is a reliable connection). This connection is maintained while the Proxy Server attempts to connect to the remote host, as shown in Figure 6-5. Once the data begins transmitting, the control channel is not used.

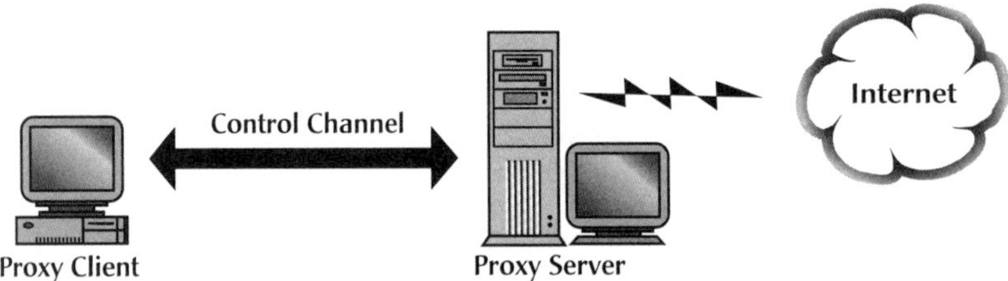

FIGURE 6-5 Winsock control channel

3. It manages UDP communications between the Winsock Proxy Client and the Winsock Proxy each time a new connection or remote peer transmits data. Once the session is established, the control channel is not used.
4. It handles requests for Winsock database information. It passes these requests to the appropriate resource and provides the response through the control channel.

The Control Channel uses UDP port 1745 in Proxy 2.0, but used port 9321 in Proxy Server 1.0.

SOCKS Proxy Service

The SOCKS Proxy Service is designed to support the needs of UNIX and Macintosh clients on a Proxy Server network. Windows can also use SOCKS, but because most applications use the Winsock API, the SOCKS functionality and purpose is primarily for UNIX and Macintosh.

For the most part, UNIX and Macintosh clients can have same functionality as Windows clients. They can use the Web Proxy Service, but the only drawback to the SOCKS Proxy Service is the lack of UDP connectivity. SOCKS only supports TCP or other connection-oriented communications. Socket clients cannot gain access to the Internet for UDP communications via Proxy Server. Connectionless applications do not function without modification.

The SOCKS Proxy Service functions by using two basic commands: `connect` and `bind`. To make a connection to the Internet, the SOCKS client sends a `connect` request, which contains the SOCKS protocol version number, command code, destination IP address, TCP port number, user ID, and additional addressing information. The request is either be granted by the server, or the request or fails or is rejected, in which case the connection is terminated and a failure notice is sent to the SOCKS client.

The `bind` command enables two applications to be bound to each other using the IP addressing and port information.

The Big Picture

As with any discussion of architecture, the big picture becomes fuzzy and confusing when you start talking about API and DLLs. The main point you should keep in mind with Proxy Server architecture is that Proxy provides three services: Web Proxy, Winsock Proxy, and SOCKS Proxy. These three services enable Proxy Server to be all things to all people, so a variety of services as well as client platforms are supported. This interoperability enables Proxy Server to provide a wide variety of services in both Microsoft and mixed environments.

Exam Preparation Summary

For the exam, you are expected to have a strong understanding of the differences between the Web Proxy Service, the Winsock Proxy Service, and the SOCKS Proxy Service. Keep in mind that CERN-compliant browsers, such as Microsoft Internet Explorer and Netscape Navigator, can use the Web Proxy Service regardless of the platform. You should have a general understanding of ISAPI and remember that it is a part of the `w3proxy.dll`. Keep in mind the differences between passive and active caching and remember that active caching requires more overhead and tends to take up more cache space.

Remember that the Winsock API supports Windows Sockets applications and is needed to additional Internet functionality, such as RealAudio and IRC, and provides additional security features such as SSL. For the Winsock client, there are two DLLs that are used to replace standard Winsock DLLs. `winsock.dll` supports 16-bit applications, whereas `wsock32.dll` supports 32-bit applications. The SOCKS Proxy Service supports clients that use SOCKS, such as UNIX and Macintosh.

Key Point Summary

The Proxy Server architecture integrates with Windows NT architecture and provides three major services for full Internet functionality.

- The Web Proxy Service supports all CERN-compliant browsers and applications and provides general Internet functionality regardless of platform.
- Passive caching is the most common form of caching. Internet objects are stored in the cache and given a TTL. Once the TTL has expired, the object must be recached from the Internet.
- Active caching is used to keep popular objects current. The Proxy Server determines the object's popularity and actively keeps the object updated and cached.

- ISAPI is composed of two DLLs — the filter and the application. This functionality provides additional security features and Keep Alive connection features.
- The Winsock Proxy Service supports Winsock applications to create socket connections.
- Socket connections function by using both the IP address of the host and a port number.
- UDP is normally used in audio and video transmission, such as RealAudio.
- The Winsock Proxy service is composed of the `winsock.dll` and `wsock32.dll`, which must installed on the client.
- The control channel creates a reliable connection between the client and the server and is often used for UDP requests.
- The SOCKS Proxy Service supports platforms that use Sockets, such as UNIX and Macintosh. UDP is not natively available through the SOCKS Proxy Service.

Applying What You've Learned

The following review questions give you a chance to test your knowledge of the content in this chapter. Should you miss some, review the appropriate portions of the chapter. The answers to the Instant Assessment questions can be found in Appendix C.

Instant Assessment

1. Your organization wants to use several different Web browsers with Proxy Server 2.0. What compliance must the browsers meet to use Proxy Server?

   A. Microsoft

   B. Netscape

   C. CERN

   D. CCITT

2. When you use your browser to retrieve an HTML document from the Internet, what command is used??

   A. `get`

   B. `post`

   C. `retrieve`

   D. `filter`

3. You use your Web browser to complete a registration form on a Web site. You then click a Submit button to send your information to the site. What command is used to place your information on the Web server?

   A. `get`

   B. `post`

   C. `retrieve`

   D. `filter`

4. Which of the following are the two components of ISAPI? (Choose two.)

   A. ISAPI Protocol

   B. ISAPI Filter

   C. ISAPI Application

   D. ISAPI Server

5. Your want your Proxy Server to react to client requests and update TTLs only if requested by clients. What kind of caching should you use to accomplish this?

   A. Active caching

   B. Passive caching

   C. Web caching

   D. Winsock caching

6. You want your Proxy Server to automatically cache popular sites and maintain the cached data as long as the site is popular. What kind of caching should you use?

   A. Active caching

   B. Passive caching

   C. Web caching

   D. Winsock caching

7. Where did the Winsock API originate?
   - **A.** Microsoft products
   - **B.** NetWare products
   - **C.** UNIX
   - **D.** Macintosh
8. Which of the following are two UDP transmissions common on the Internet? (Choose two.)
   - **A.** Chat
   - **B.** RealAudio
   - **C.** FTP
   - **D.** RealVideo
9. Which is one of the following DLLs designed for the Winsock Proxy Client?
   - **A.** `winsock32.dll`
   - **B.** `winsock16.dll`
   - **C.** `windowssock32.dll`
   - **D.** `windowssock16.dll`
10. What does Proxy Server use to control the connection between the client and the server?
    - **A.** Sockets
    - **B.** Winsock
    - **C.** `winsock16.dll`
    - **D.** Control channel

Critical Thinking Labs

These labs present you with analysis problems to test your critical thinking skills with the content in this chapter.

Lab 6.23 *Proxy Server clients*

Your company is migrating from Macintosh to Windows platforms. Currently about half of the client computers are Macintosh. You use an NT Server on the network. Your company is considering adding a proxy server, but is concerned about the connectivity options for Macintosh clients with Microsoft Proxy Server. What would you say to alleviate their concerns?

Lab 6.24 *Wsock32.dll file*

One of your coworkers doesn't understand why the `wsock32.dll` file is necessary for his Windows 98 computer. How would you explain this?

Lab 6.25 *Active and passive caching*

A friend asks you to explain the difference between active and passive caching. How would you explain this?

Lab 6.26 *Proxy Server services*

You have been asked to present an overview of the services provided by the three Proxy Server services and what functionality is provided by each service. How will you explain this?

CHAPTER

7

The Proxy Server Interface

About Chapter 7

This chapter takes you on a tour of the Proxy Server 2.0 interface. In this chapter, you learn how to configure various components of the Web Proxy Service, the Winsock Proxy Service, and the Socks Proxy Service. This chapter uses a hands-on approach to teach you the interface. You have seven labs at the end of the chapter to practice your critical thinking skills, and you gain hands-on experience with the configuration of Proxy Server's services.

The Interface

As you may have already guessed, Proxy Server and IIS work hand-in-hand in virtually every way, including the user interface. To manage Proxy Server, you use the Internet Service Manager that uses the MMC. I explore the Internet Service Manager in Chapter 4. It's important that you learn your way around the user interface to facilitate the work in this book, to succeed on the exam, and of course, to successfully administer your Proxy Server in the workplace. I configure some of the various options you see in this chapter, and take note of others that I return to in later chapters.

I have previously explored the three Proxy Server services: the Web Proxy Service, the Winsock Proxy Service, and the SOCKS Proxy Service. The Proxy Server user interface is designed around these three services as well.

You can access the Proxy Server interface through IIS, or by clicking Start ⇛ Programs ⇛ Microsoft Proxy Server ⇛ Microsoft Management Console. This brings you to the Console Root in Internet Service Manager as shown in Figure 7-1.

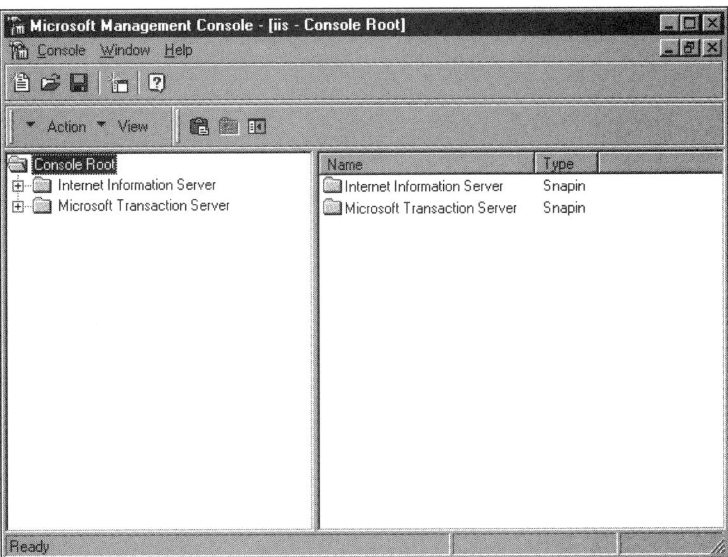

FIGURE 7-1 **The Console Root in Internet Service Manager**

When you expand the Internet Information Server directory and the server computer, as shown in Figure 7-2, you see that the Web Proxy Service, Winsock

Proxy Service, and the Socks Proxy Service have been added to the Internet Service Manager.

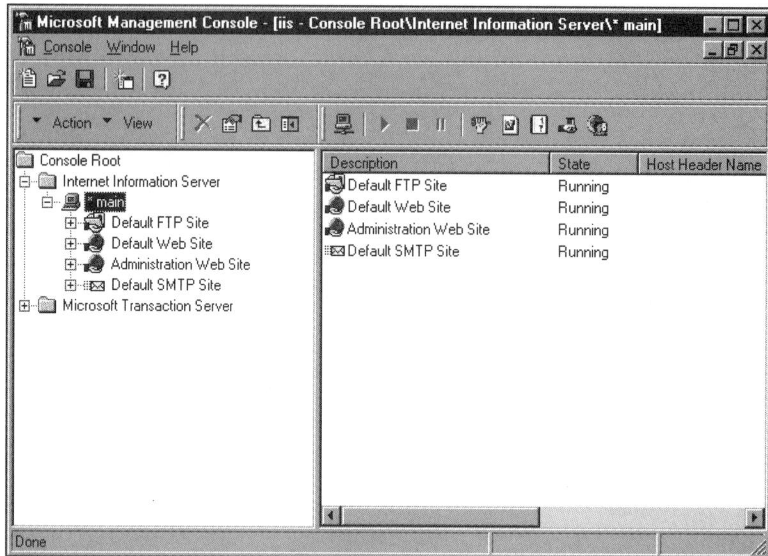

FIGURE 7-2 Proxy Services in Internet Service Manager

By selecting the desired service and clicking the Properties icon in the toolbar, or by right-clicking the service and clicking Properties, you can configure each service as needed. The following is a look at each of these services and the configuration options available.

The Web Proxy Service

The Web Proxy Service enables you to offer a variety of standard Web services for any CERN-compliant browser or application, regardless of the operating system platform.

You configure all of the options for the Web Proxy Service from the Internet Service Manager. By selecting Properties of the Web Proxy Service, you are taken to a page with six available tabs: Service, Permissions, Caching, Routing, Publishing, and Logging, as shown in Figure 7-3.

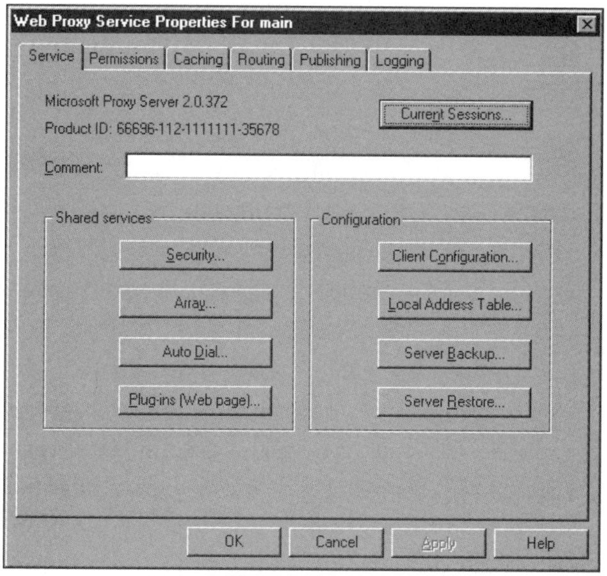

FIGURE 7-3 Web Proxy Service Properties for main

Service Tab

The Service tab gives you a number of configuration options from both a Shared Services and Configuration perspective. If you click Current Sessions on the right side of the tab, you can monitor the current Proxy Server sessions from any of the three services. By clicking the appropriate radio button, you can view the connected users and the duration of the connections for either the Web Proxy, Winsock Proxy, or Socks Proxy Services, as shown in Figure 7-4. Note that this is only a monitor — you cannot disconnect users.

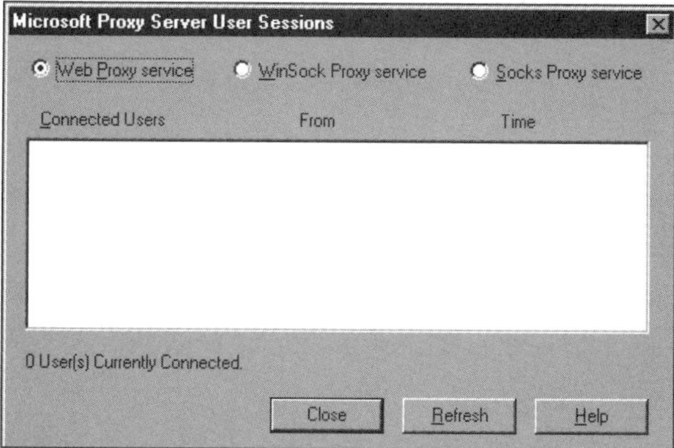

FIGURE 7-4 Microsoft Proxy Server User Sessions dialog box

In the Shared Services tab, you have four button selections: security, array, auto-dial, and plug-ins. As the tab name implies, these are services shared between all three Proxy Server services. I look at each of these in more detail in later chapters, so for now, here's a quick overview.

The Security button gives you some options to configure and manage packet filtering. This allows you to control what kinds of packets are allowed to enter your network. The Array button allows you to configure the Proxy Server to join another Proxy Server(s) to form a Proxy array. The Auto-dial button works with your RAS configuration to enable your Proxy Server to perform automatic dialing. This function is especially useful as a backup solution if your mail connection fails. The Plug-ins button allows you to configure various plug-ins for Web page use.

In the configuration section, you also have a number of options. When you click Client Configuration, you are taken to the dialog box shown in Figure 7-5.

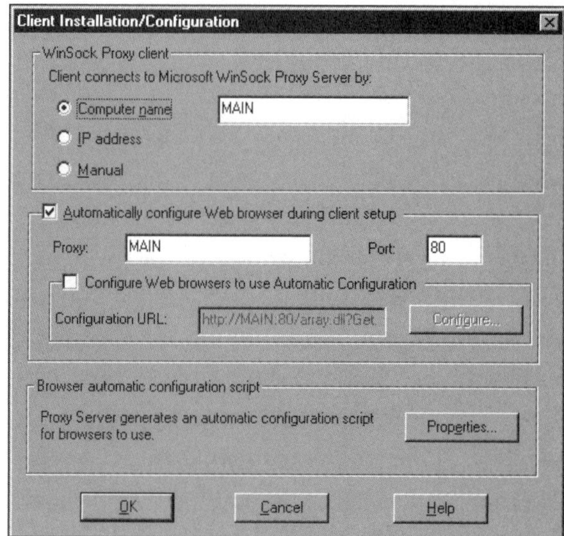

FIGURE 7-5 Client Installation/Configuration dialog box

Does this look familiar? This is the same dialog box you saw for client configuration during setup. The same is true for the next button, Local Address Table. This is why a Proxy Server installation is very forgiving — the interface permits you to come back and change some of the major pieces of the installation. This way, should you need to change the options and default installation file for clients, you can do so through this simple GUI. The same is true with the LAT. Network configuration may change, and thus, the IP address ranges of your network may need to change as well. This interface allows you to change the IP address ranges without having to reinstall Proxy Server.

The Server Backup and Restore buttons enable you to specify a directory to save a backup file. This is an especially useful action to perform before making significant configuration changes. The backup file is saved as `mspYYYYMMDD.mpc` where *YYYY* is the year, *MM* is the month, and *DD* is the day of the backup. For example, a typical backup file would read `msp19981012.mpc`.

The Restore button allows you to restore a previously backed-up configuration. You can choose to either partially restore or perform a full restoration from this dialog box. The Server Backup and Restore dialog boxes are shown in Figures 7-6 and 7-7.

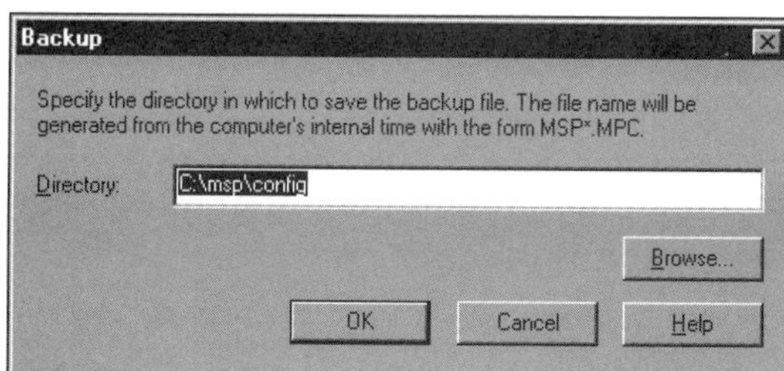

FIGURE 7-6 Backup dialog box

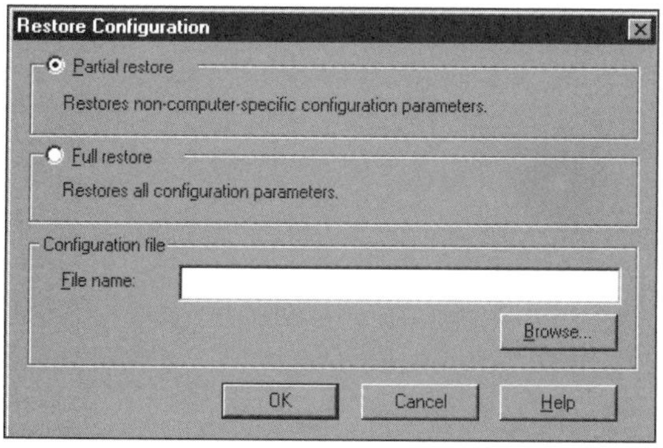

FIGURE 7-7 Restore Configuration dialog box

Permissions

When you click the Permissions tab, the Enable Access Control box is checked. You have a drop-down menu to choose protocols, such as FTP Read, WWW, and so forth. A box allows you to Grant Access To with the option to edit. Notice that no one is listed, as shown in Figure 7-8.

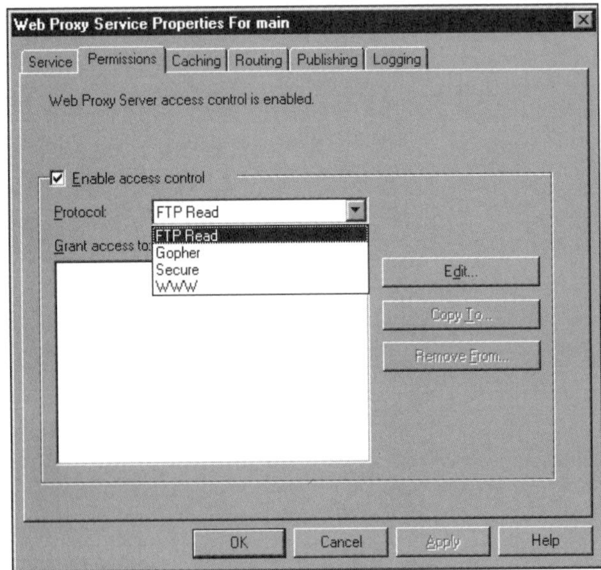

FIGURE 7-8 Web Proxy Service Properties For main Permissions tab

This is a security feature of Proxy Server. No one is given default permissions — the administrator has to specifically grant rights to individuals or groups.

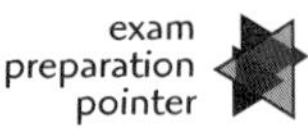

Keep in mind that without access control enabled, you, as the administrator, cannot control what the clients access on the Web.

To grant the needed rights to users, you first select the protocol for which you want to grant rights. Suppose you want to give WWW rights first. You select the WWW protocol from the drop-down menu, and then click Edit. The WWW Permissions dialog box shown in Figure 7-9 appears.

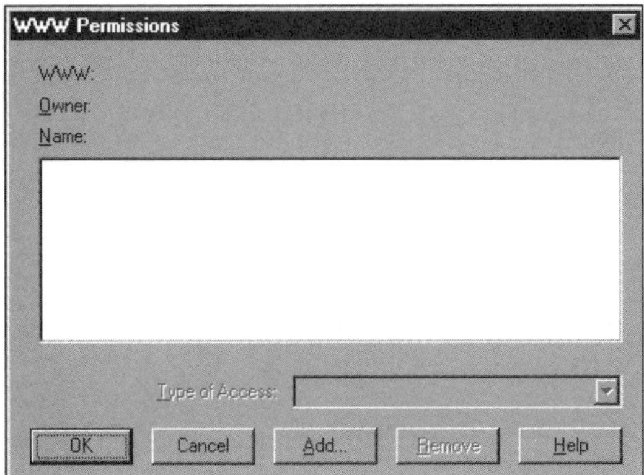

FIGURE 7-9 WWW Permissions dialog box

When you click Add, you are taken to the Add Users and Groups dialog box, which lists all the user and group entries, as shown in Figure 7-10.

FIGURE 7-10 Add Users and Groups dialog box

From this list, select the individual users or groups, then click Add to add the users or groups to the Add Names list box at the bottom of the dialog box. Once you have made your selections, click OK to return to the WWW Permissions dialog box.

Suppose you want to give everyone access to WWW. Select the Everyone group in the Add Users and Groups dialog box and click OK. In the WWW Permissions dialog box, confirm that Everyone has been added to the list box, as shown in Figure 7-11, and then click OK.

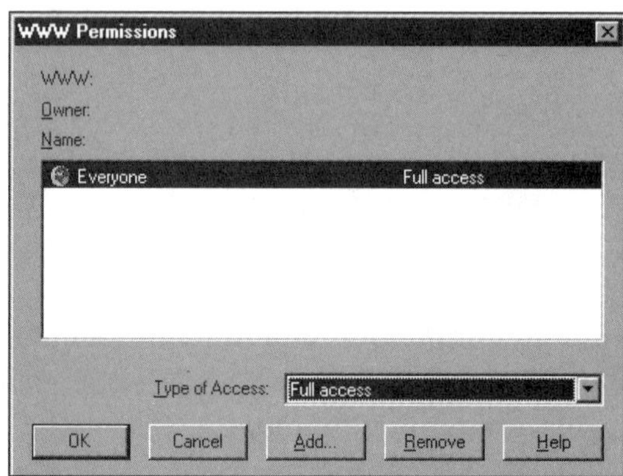

FIGURE 7-11 WWW Permissions dialog box

Now the Everyone group has permissions for the WWW protocol. If you want this group to have permissions for another protocol, such as FTP Read, you have to select the protocol from the drop-down menu and go through the same process again.

This process can be a daunting task if you look at the users on an individual basis. This is why it is wise to establish groups within User Manager for Domains. Proxy Server Permissions are easy to manage on a group-by-group basis.

Caching

The Caching tab is shown in Figure 7-12. Chapter 11 is solely devoted to caching and configuring cache options, so this section just offers a quick overview.

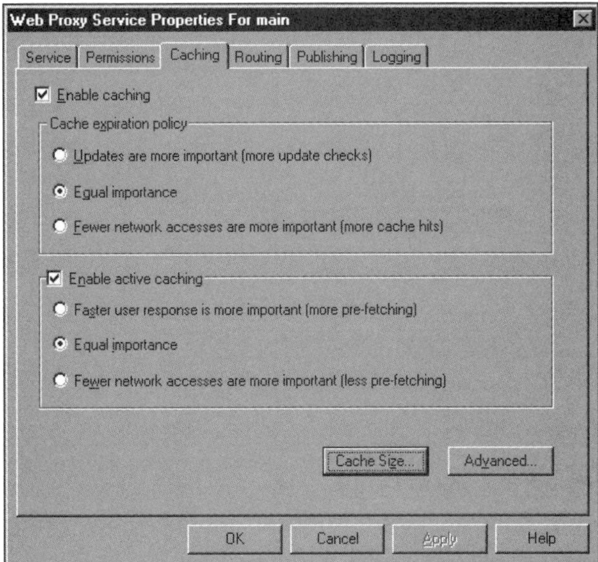

FIGURE 7-12 Web Proxy Service Properties For main Caching tab

Notice the Enable Caching check box has to be selected for caching to occur. You also have a section to enable active caching, with some rather confusing options I explore in Chapter 11. If you click Cache Size, you are taken to the same dialog box you configured during installation, as shown in Figure 7-13.

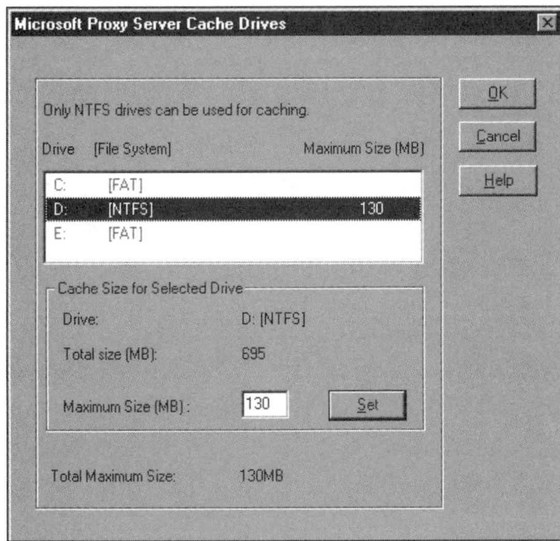

FIGURE 7-13 Microsoft Proxy Server Cache Drives dialog box

Again, this enables you to make configuration changes instead of having to reinstall Proxy Server. If your network suddenly grows by twenty users, you can adjust your cache size (using the cache size formula) easily to accommodate the new users, assuming you have enough disk space.

Clicking the Advanced button on the Caching tab takes you to the Advanced Cache Policy dialog box, shown in Figure 7-14, which enables you to set cache size options and time-to-live (TTL). I explore these options in detail in Chapter 11.

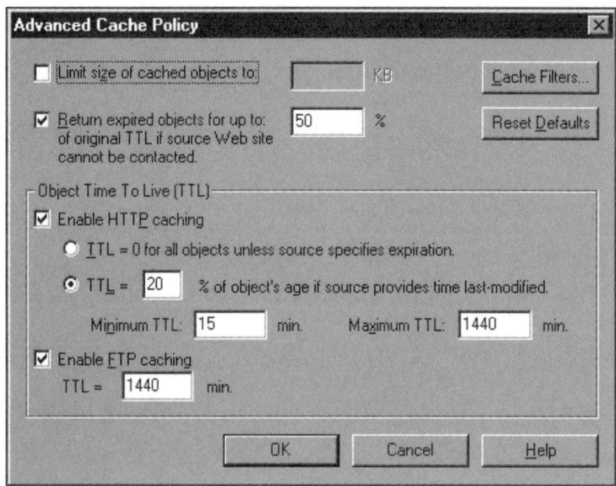

FIGURE 7-14 Advanced Cache Policy

Routing

If you click the Routing tab, you have some options to configure the Proxy Server's connections to other Proxy Servers, as shown in Figure 7-15.

At the top of the tab, you have the default server name to use as an HTTP header. You have options to configure Upstream Routing and a backup route. The options enable you to connect directly to another Proxy Server or to connect using Web Proxy Services or an array. Chapter 14 explores the use of multiple Proxy Servers and how to configure the backup routes and arrays. I take a look at detailed configuration options for routing in that chapter.

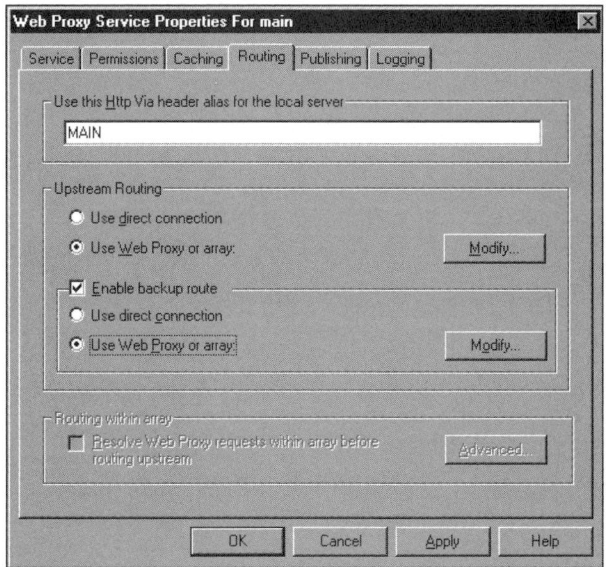

FIGURE 7-15 Web Proxy Service Properties For main Routing tab

Publishing

The Publishing tab has options to configure Web publishing, should you be offering Internet sites on your network. Notice in Figure 7-16 that incoming Web requests can be sent to the local Web server or to another Web server on your network. This function allows inbound Internet traffic to hit your Web server but keeps this traffic off the local network.

Specific configuration options for publishing are explored in detail in Chapter 10.

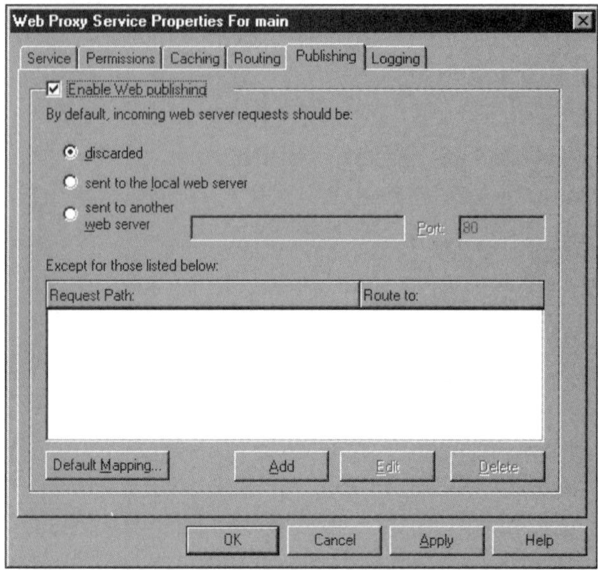

FIGURE 7-16 Web Proxy Service Properties Publishing tab

Logging

The final tab of the Web Proxy Service Properties page is Logging. As with the other tabs, I explore logging in a later chapter (Chapter 9), but this section gives you a quick look at the tab. Proxy Server enables a number of logging options with the ability to log selected intervals. Perhaps most important, Proxy Server also enables you to select the kind of log file you want to create, such as regular, verbose, or one that logs to a SQL or ODBC database. Figure 7-17 gives you look at this tab, and I explain the details later.

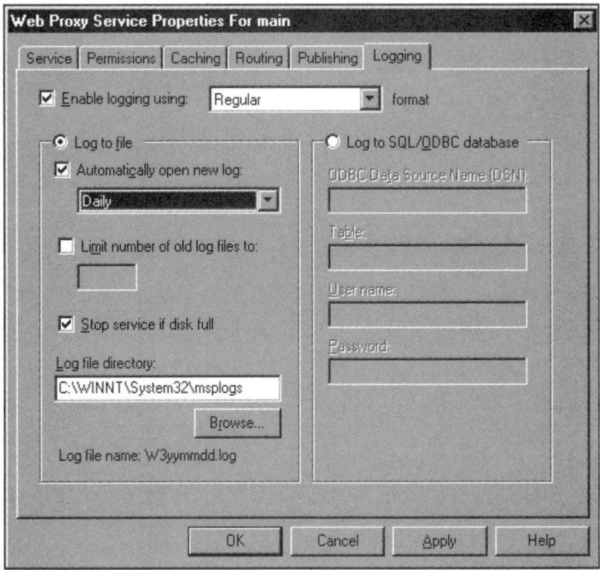

FIGURE 7-17 Web Proxy Service Properties Logging tab

The Winsock Proxy Service

The Winsock Proxy Service enables you to configure services for Winsock clients. The Properties sheet contains the following tabs: Service, Protocols, Permissions, and Logging. The Service and Logging tabs are the same for the Winsock Proxy Service as you saw in the Web Proxy Service, so this section focuses on the Protocols and Permissions tabs.

Protocols

The Protocols tab shown in Figure 7-18 enables you to add and remove protocols for Winsock. The protocols list in Figure 7-18 is a default list that is installed during the Proxy Server installation. Remember, the Winsock Service uses IP connections and ports to use various protocols. Each protocol defines a particular port the Winsock Service uses to provide that particular protocol communication. You can use the tab to add protocols or to remove particular ones from the list.

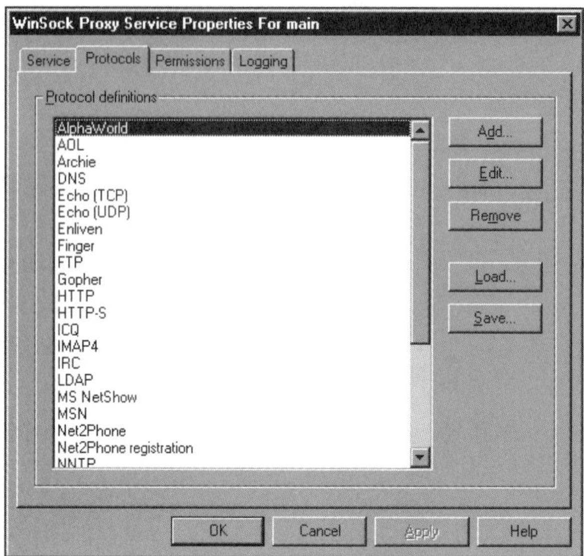

FIGURE 7-18 Web Proxy Service Properties For main Protocols tab

Click Add to add a protocol to the list, as shown in Figure 7-19. You have to specify the protocol name and the port. Using port 0 for inbound connections enables Proxy Server to use any port in the range from 1024 to 5000. The entire port range of Proxy Server is 0 to 65535. Also, you need to determine if the protocol is TCP or UDP and the direction (inbound or outbound) that will be used. If you add a protocol, remember that the users must be granted access permission to use the new protocol.

If you click Edit, you get the same dialog box as Protocol Definition, but you can make editorial changes to the protocol as needed.

You can also remove a protocol from the list. Why would you want to do this? For example, notice that IRC (Internet Relay Chat) protocol is installed by default. You have mostly Winsock clients on your network, and many of them have unlimited access. There is no reason employees should be using chat rooms at the office. The only way, then, to keep these users from hitting the chat rooms during work hours is to remove the protocol from the Protocol list. Once it is removed, chat services are not available, because there is not an available protocol for chat.

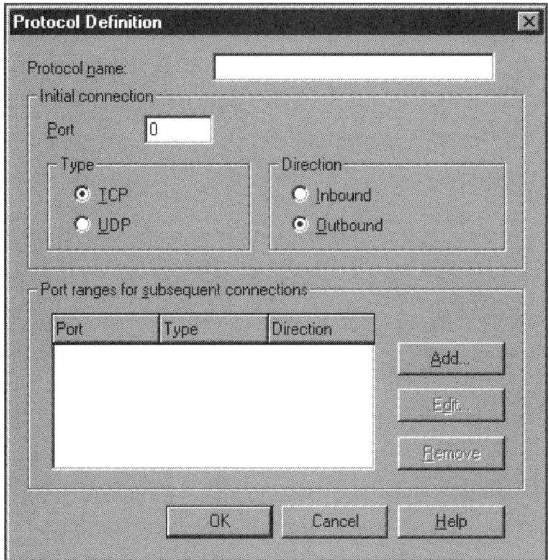

FIGURE 7-19 Protocol Definition dialog box

Permissions

At first glance, the Permissions tab appears the same as the Permissions tab in the Web Proxy Service Properties. It works the same way, but Protocol list contains the protocols from the Protocols tab.

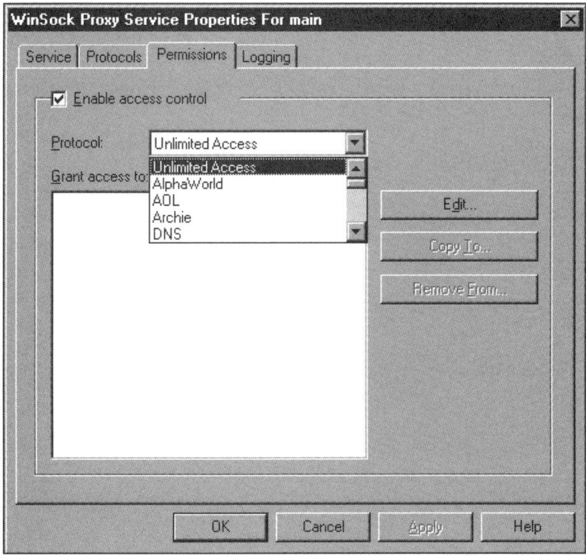

FIGURE 7-20 Web Proxy Service Properties For main Permissions tab

Notice that you have the option to permit Unlimited Access. This feature enables you to give full access to all Winsock Protocols, either to particular groups or to everyone if desired. This feature is useful because you may want most of your network users to have full access, while you may want to only permit specific protocols for a particular group.

If you want to permit particular protocols, you have a couple of options. You can individually assign these protocols to the groups through the Permissions tab, or you can remove all protocols you do not want used from the Protocols tab. If you do this, however, even the administrators will be restricted to only what protocols you have left in the Protocols tab.

What is done with Winsock Protocols has a lot to do with the regulations and rules of your network. Some networks simply give unlimited access to everyone and don't worry about what users might be doing on the Internet. Others are highly restrictive. This is why the regulations for Internet use must be carefully defined before the installation and configuration.

Socks Proxy Service

The Socks Proxy Service enables you to give additional services to Socks clients such as UNIX and Macintosh.

The Socks Proxy Service Properties sheet has three tabs: Service, Permissions, and Logging. The Service and Logging tabs are the same as the Web Proxy Service, so in this section I only look at the Permissions tab, which is significantly different from the Web Proxy and Winsock Proxy Services Permissions tabs.

Permissions

The Permissions tab for the Socks Service is defined according to the action you want to permit or deny to a Socks client. The entries contain an action, source, destination, and operation, as shown in Figure 7-21.

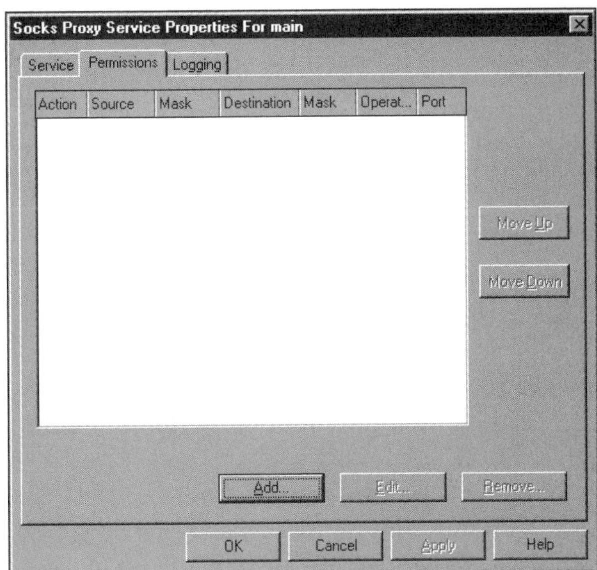

FIGURE 7-21 Socks Proxy Service Properties For main Socks Permissions tab.

Click Add to configure client access based on permit or deny, as shown in Figure 7-22.

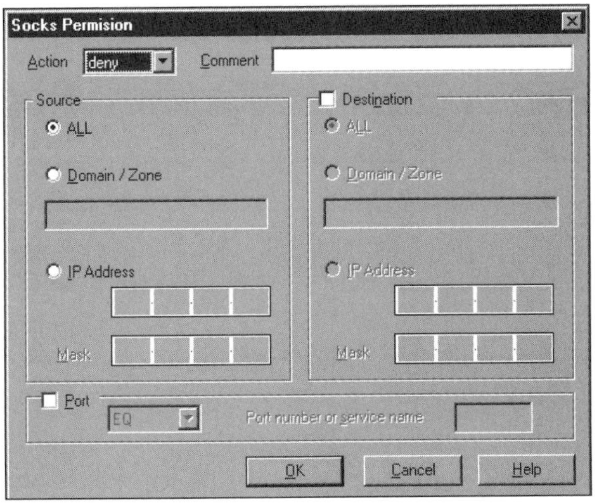

FIGURE 7-22 Socks Permission

Consider an example. If you have Macintosh clients on your network, you can choose to enable them to use the Socks Proxy Service by selecting All in the

Source section, and by using the Destination section to select All. This enables all Socks clients to use the Socks Service. You can also specify particular clients for certain kinds of access by identifying those clients by IP address in the Source section. Under the Port section at the bottom of the dialog box, you have a couple of options in the drop-down menu shown in Figure 7-23. Table 7-1 gives you a definition of each of these options.

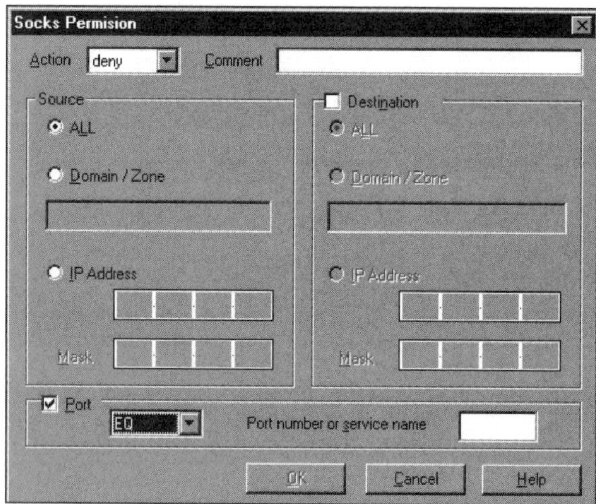

FIGURE 7-23 Socks port options

TABLE 7-1 PORT OPTIONS DESCRIPTION

Port Option	*Description*
EQ	Means *Equal To*. Permit access to the service that equals this port number.
NEQ	Means *Not Equal To*. Permit access to ports that are not equal to this port number.
GT	Means *Greater Than*. Permit access to ports that are greater than this port.
LT	Means *Less Than*. Permit access to ports that are less than this port.
GE	Means *Greater Than or Equal To*. Permit access to ports that are greater than or equal to this port number.
LE	Means *Less Than or Equal To*. Permit access to ports that are less than or equal to this port number.

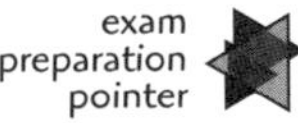

For the exam, keep the EQ option in mind. It is the most commonly used option.

Let's return to our IRC example. If you want to enable all the Macintosh clients to use chat, you specify the EQ option and enter a port number, which is 6667 for IRC, as shown in Figure 7-24. Now, all Macintosh clients on the network are permitted to use IRC chat.

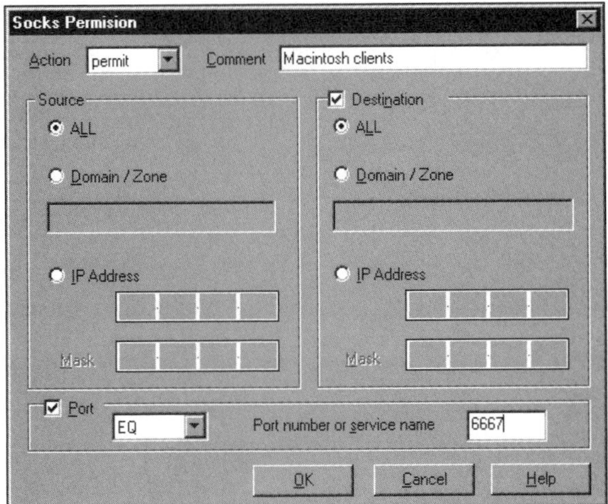

FIGURE 7-24 Socks chat permission configuration

In the same manner, you can use configuration to deny access to chat for all Macintosh clients, or even for a particular user. Suppose you have a user named Jerry, who you do not want using chat services. You can specify Jerry's Winsock client by IP address and deny access to chat using the EQ function and the port number for chat, as shown in Figure 7-25.

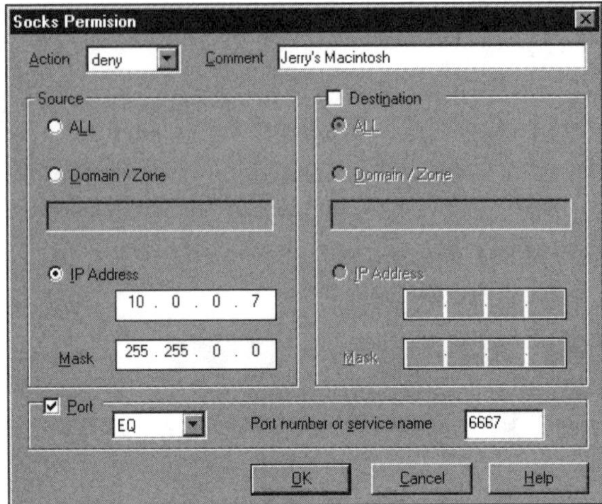

FIGURE 7-25 Socks individual denial of service

When permit or denials are added, they appear on the main Permissions tab, as shown in Figure 7-26.

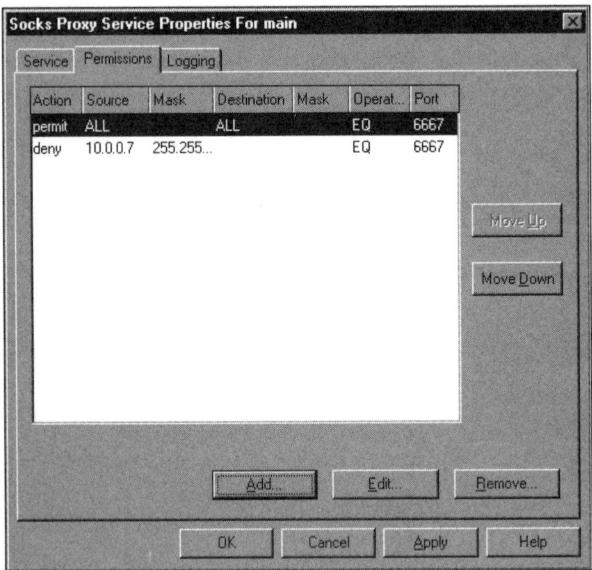

FIGURE 7-26 Socks Proxy Service Properties For main Permissions tab

You can make changes easily and at any time to the permissions you have granted or denied by clicking Edit, or you can remove a Permission altogether by clicking Remove. You can see that performing these actions is rather easy and does not require a lot of administrative time.

Exam Preparation Summary

The exam demands that you have a firm command of the user interface, as well as a detailed understanding of the configuration options of Proxy Server. The best advice to prepare for the exam is to continue to work with the user interface so that you learn where various configuration options reside. Keep in mind the following points:

- You can view user sessions from the Service tab, which is available in all three services.
- You can reconfigure client configuration and the LAT from the Service tab.
- You can configure auto-dial features from the Service tab.
- You can backup and restore Proxy configuration from the Services tab. The backup file is saved as `msp`*`YYYYMMDD`*`.mpc`.
- Keep in mind that access control must be selected to configure which users can perform which operations via Proxy Server.
- In the Winsock Proxy Service, you can add and remove Winsock protocols on the Protocols tab.
- The Socks service functions by assigning either permit or deny features in the Socks Permissions tab.
- Learn the port symbols such as EQ, GE, NEQ, and so forth (see Table 7-1). EQ is the most commonly used port symbol, so keep that one in mind.

Remember, you will encounter a lot of questions about cache configuration, logging, routing, and other configurations options that were introduced in this chapter. I explore all of those in detail in later chapters.

Key Point Summary

This chapter gave you a tour of the Proxy Server interface through the Internet Service Manager. By clicking each service's properties, you are presented with a number of configuration options.

- The Services tab is shared by all three services. From this tab, you can monitor current sessions, configure auto-dial, join an array, configure security, as well as backup and restore Proxy Server configuration.
- The Services tab also enables you to change the client configuration options and edit the LAT.
- The Permissions tab in the Web Proxy Services enables you to set permissions for users and groups to use various Web Proxy services, such as FTP Read and WWW.
- The Caching tab enables you to configure caching options.
- The Routing tab enables you to configure backup routes via another Proxy Server or an array.
- The Publishing tab enables you to configure your server for Internet Web traffic, or to redirect traffic to the Web server.
- The Logging tab, which is shared by all three services, enables you to configure logging options, such as saving logs to a file or to a SQL or ODBC database.
- In the Winsock Proxy Service, you can add or remove Winsock protocols in the Protocols tab.
- The Permissions tab in the Winsock Proxy Service functions like the Web Proxy Service, but it contains the Winsock Protocols, which can be assigned to users or groups. You also have an Unlimited Access feature, which enables assigned users or groups to access all available Winsock protocols.
- The Socks Service Permissions tab enables you to assign permissions to Socks clients by using a permit or deny function. Permit or Deny assignments can be given to all Socks clients, a particular domain, or on an individual basis.
- The Socks port options can be configured using EQ, NEQ, GT, LT, GE, or LE options.

Applying What You've Learned

The following review questions give you a chance to test your knowledge of the content in this chapter. Should you miss some, review the appropriate portions of the chapter. The answers to the Instant Assessment questions can be found in Appendix C.

Instant Assessment

1. What Properties tab is shared between all three Proxy Server services?

A. Protocol

B. Routing

C. Service

D. Logging

2. Where can you change the LAT configuration?

A. Local Address Table button on the Service tab

B. Local Address Table button on the Caching tab

C. Local Address Table button on the Publishing tab

D. Local Address Table button on the Routing tab

3. What is the name of the backup file Proxy Server creates?

A. `mspDD.mpc`

B. `mspMMDD.mpc`

C. `mspYYYYMMDD.mpc`

D. `mspback.mpc`

4. What happens if the Access Control check box is unchecked?

A. Clients cannot access the Internet.

B. Clients can access anything on the Internet.

C. Clients are restricted to only WWW.

D. Clients are restricted to only FTP.

5. Which is a logging option?

   A. Normal

   B. Complete

   C. Minimal

   D. Verbose

6. How can you give groups the right to use all Winsock protocols?

   A. Unlimited Access on the Permissions tab.

   B. Unlimited Access on the Protocols tab.

   C. Unlimited Access on the Logging tab.

   D. Unlimited Access on the Service tab

7. What are the two main permission functions of the Socks Permissions tab? (Choose two.)

   A. Permit

   B. Allow

   C. Grant

   D. Deny

8. If you wanted port information to be Equal To in the Socks Permissions, which code would you use?

   A. NEQ

   B. EQ

   C. GT

   D. LE

Critical Thinking Labs

These labs present you with analysis problems to test your critical thinking skills with the content in this chapter.

Lab 7.27 *Denying access in the Winsock Proxy Service*

A coworker would like to deny access to the Archie Protocol in the Winsock Proxy Service. What are the steps you would tell your coworker to follow?

Lab 7.28 *Assigning and managing Proxy Server permissions*

Your company is about to install and configure Proxy Server. What advice about users and groups would you offer to make permissions assignments easier and more manageable?

Lab 7.29 *Monitoring users*

You are afraid that Mary, a Proxy user, is abusing her privileges to use the Internet. You want to see how long she is staying connected to the Internet. How can you find this information?

Hands-on Labs

The Hands-on Labs give you an opportunity to practice skills you have learned in this chapter. Make sure you read the system requirements for each lab to be certain you have the correct configuration before beginning the lab.

Lab 7.30 *Giving WWW permissions to a selected group*

In this lab, you give WWW permissions to a selected group on your Proxy Server.

1. Click Start⇛Programs⇛Microsoft Proxy Server⇛Microsoft Management Console.
2. The MMC displays and you see the Internet Service Manager Console Root.
3. Expand the Internet Information Server directory and your server.
4. Right-click the Web Proxy Icon and select Properties.
5. Select the Permissions tab.
6. Access Control should be enabled in the check box. If it is not, click the box.
7. In the Protocol drop-down menu, select WWW.
8. Click Edit.
9. In the WWW Permissions dialog box that appears, click Add.
10. You see all the users and groups that are configured in your User Manager for Domains. Highlight the group you want to give WWW permissions to. You select Everyone if you want everyone on your network to have WWW access.
11. Once you have selected the desired group, click Add.
12. The group appears in the Add Names dialog box. You can now add additional groups if you wish.

13. Once you are finished adding groups, click OK at the bottom of the window.
14. In the WWW Permissions dialog box, click OK.
15. You can add rights to other protocols by selecting the protocol from the drop-down menu and completing these steps if you wish.
16. Once you are finished, click Apply, and then click OK.

Lab 7.31 *Backing up your Proxy Server configuration*

In this lab, you backup your current Proxy Server Configuration.

1. Click Start ⇒ Programs ⇒ Microsoft Proxy Server ⇒ Microsoft Management Console.
2. The MMC opens and you see the Internet Service Manager Console Root.
3. Expand the Internet Information Server directory and your server.
4. Right-click the Web Proxy icon and select Properties.
5. On the Services tab, click Server Backup.
6. The default directory is `C:\msp\config`. Accept the default and click OK.
7. The backup file is created.
8. Click OK on the Web Proxy Properties sheet.
9. Minimize the MMC.
10. Click Start ⇒ Programs ⇒ Windows NT Explorer.
11. The Explorer window appears.
12. Expand the MSP directory.
13. Double-click the Config directory.
14. You see the saved file of msp*YYYYMMDD*.mpc.
15. Double-click the file and select Notepad to open it.
16. Browse the backup file.

Lab 7.32 *Giving permissions for Winsock Proxy Service*

In this lab, you give permissions for the Winsock Proxy Service.

1. Click Start ⇒ Programs ⇒ Microsoft Proxy Server ⇒ Microsoft Management Console.
2. The MMC opens and you see the Internet Service Manager Console Root.
3. Expand the Internet Information Server directory and your server.

4. Right-click the Web Proxy icon and select Properties.
5. Right-click Winsock Proxy and select Properties.
6. Click the Protocols tab. Note the protocols now available.
7. Click the Permissions tab.
8. Enable Access Control should be selected. If it is not, click the check box.
9. In the Protocol drop-down box, select POP3, or another protocol if you do not want clients on your network to send Internet mail. You can also permit Unlimited Access by selecting this option.
10. Click Edit to open the POP3 Permissions page.
11. Click Add.
12. The users and groups currently available in User Manager for Domains appears. Select the group to whom you want to give permission and click Add.
13. The group appears in the Add Names dialog box. Click OK.
14. The POP3 Permissions dialog box reappears with your group added. Click OK.
15. This takes you back to the Winsock proxy Service Properties page. You may make additional entries by following the same steps. Once you are finished, click Apply, and then click OK.

Lab 7.33 *Denying permissions to a Socks client*

In this lab, you deny permissions to a Socks client.

1. Click Start ⇛ Programs ⇛ Microsoft Proxy Server ⇛ Microsoft Management Console.
2. The MMC opens and you see the Internet Service Manager Console Root.
3. Expand the Internet Information Server directory and your server.
4. Right-click the Socks Proxy icon and select Properties.
5. Click the Permissions tab, then click Add at the bottom of the tab.
6. In the action box, Deny should be selected. Choose a Socks client for whom you would like to deny a service. You need to know the client's IP address and subnet mask. If you do not have a Socks client, use an IP address of 10.0.0.7 and a subnet mask of 255.255.0.0.
7. Click the IP address radio button under the Source section and enter the IP address and subnet mask of the client.
8. Click to select the Port box at the bottom of the page.
9. You want this entry to be Equal To, so you accept the default of EQ.

10. In the Port number or service, enter **6667**. This denies chat access to this client. Click OK.

11. This returns you to the Permissions tab. You may perform further actions if you wish. Once you are finished, click Apply, and then click OK.

CHAPTER

8

Configuring the Proxy Client

About Chapter 8

This chapter shows you how to configure client computers to use the Proxy Server. I explore the processes, issues, and potential problems in configuring both Windows and non-Windows-based systems for the Web Proxy Service and the Socks Proxy Service. I also show you how to configure Windows clients to use the Winsock Proxy Service. There are two hands-on labs in this chapter for you to practice what you learn.

PROXY CLIENTS

If you have been working with Proxy Server and performing the labs in this book, you are probably discovering that Proxy Server is relatively easy to work with. The configuration options in the three Proxy services tend to be straightforward, and you have seen that the major configurations performed during the installation, such as the LAT and client configuration options, can be changed easily once installation is complete.

Proxy Server's client configuration follows this same formula — it's fast, easy, and generally problem free. I configure the Proxy client in this chapter for Web Proxy Services, and I also take a look at configuring the Winsock Proxy and Socks Proxy client.

Before you begin the client configuration, there are two actions to perform. I mentioned in Chapter 7 that the easiest way to assign Proxy services permissions is to establish groups of users to which permissions can be assigned. You may want to do this now in User Manager For Domains. To create a new group(s) in User Manager For Domains, follow these steps:

---

1. Click Start ⇒ Programs, Administrative Tools (common) ⇒ User Manager for Domains.
2. Click the User drop-down menu and select New Local Group. The New Local Group dialog box appears, as shown in Figure 8-1.

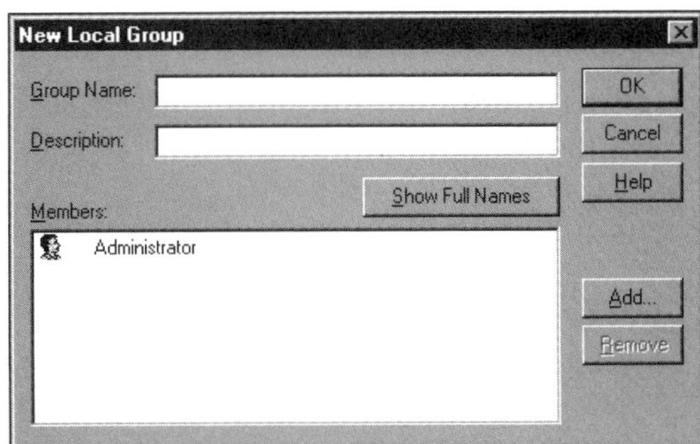

FIGURE 8-1 New Local Group selection

3. Assign a group name. You may want the group name to reflect the permissions of the group. Also, add a short description.

4. Next, click Add to add users or other global groups to the local group. When you finish, the dialog box should look similar to the one in Figure 8-2.

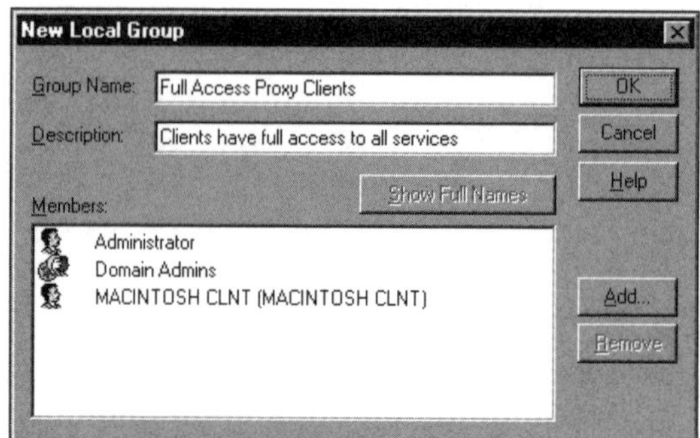

FIGURE 8-2 Completed New Local Group dialog box

5. Click OK to add the new local group. You can repeat these steps to add new groups.

A second action you should take before attempting client installation is to check client connectivity to the Proxy Server. This ensures that setup of the Proxy client is trouble free. You can do this with a ping test, such as `ping` *`server IP address`*. Once you have verified connectivity and you are happy with the group structure in User Manager for Domains, you're ready to begin.

Client Web Proxy

The Web Proxy Service functions with any CERN-compliant browser or application, regardless of platform. This means that it doesn't matter whether Internet Explorer or Netscape Navigator is running on a Windows 98 computer, a Macintosh, or even a UNIX computer. As long as the browser is CERN-compliant, it can use the Web Proxy Service. I focus on the Web Proxy configuration from both an Internet Explorer and a Netscape Navigator perspective, because these are the two most common Web browsers.

Internet Explorer

Each version of Internet Explorer is somewhat different in terms of configuration for Proxy Server. Because IE 4.01 is the most current version at the time of this writing, I focus on configuration of that version. The configuration options are accessed under the Internet Options selection in the View menu. This brings you to the Internet Options dialog box, as shown in Figure 8-3.

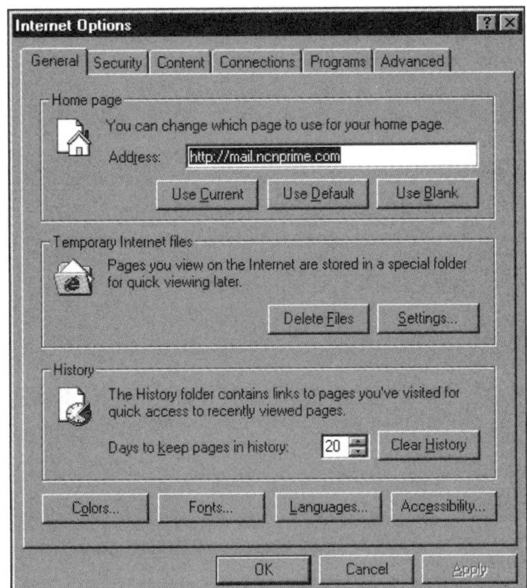

FIGURE 8-3 Internet Options Screen in IE 4.01

Click the Connection tab to access the option to connect via Proxy Server. By selecting the Access the Internet using a proxy server check box, the service is enabled. You need to supply the address of the Proxy Server, which can be the server's IP address, its DNS name, or NetBIOS computer name if the client is a Windows client.

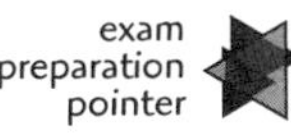

Although any CERN-compliant browser is supported on any platform, Web browsers do not support name resolution for Socks clients. So, if you are using Netscape on a UNIX computer, for example, you have to specify the Proxy Server by a DNS entry, then the DNS entry can be resolved to the Proxy Server.

You also need to specify the port, which is normally going be Port 80 for WWW services. Figure 8-4 shows a configured browser.

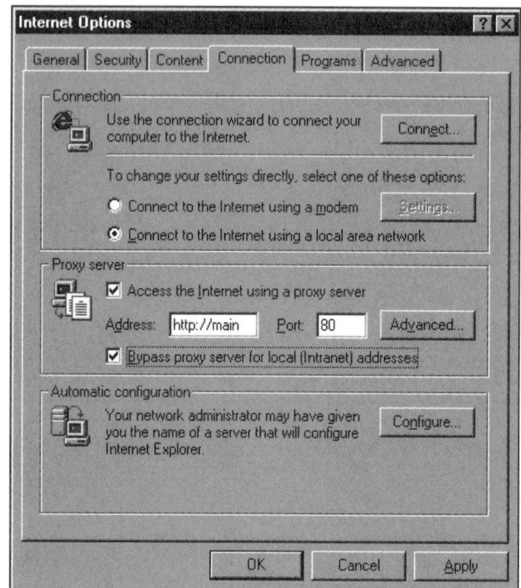

FIGURE 8-4 Connection tab

Click Advanced, and the Proxy Settings dialog box appears, as shown in Figure 8-5. This dialog box enables you to select multiple Proxy Servers for various functions, such as WWW, FTP, and so forth. Some environments use multiple Proxy Servers that are each dedicated for a particular service. For example, one server would be dedicated for WWW, while a different server is dedicated for FTP. The Proxy Settings dialog box enables you to configure these options.

If you want to use the same proxy server for all services, you would select the Use the same proxy server for all protocols check box.

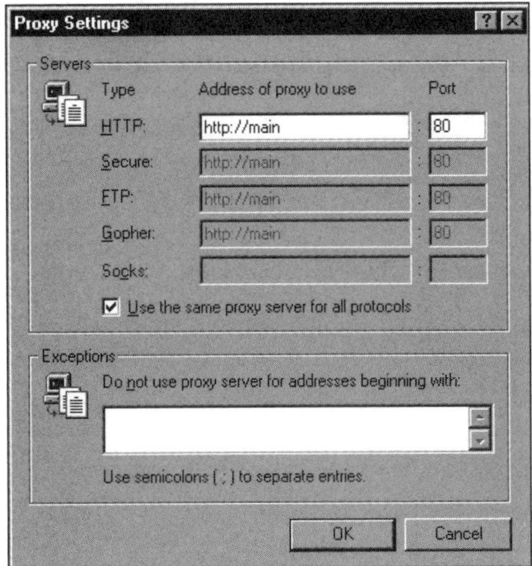

FIGURE 8-5 Proxy Settings dialog box

Netscape Navigator

To configure Netscape Navigator (or Communicator) 4.5, the latest version at the time of this writing, to use the Proxy Server, you perform a similar process as you would in Internet Explorer. From the Edit menu, choose Preferences. Netscape gives you a dialog box with a tree directory structure in the left pane and configuration options on the right. If you expand the Advanced directory and highlight the Proxies directory, you will see the options for configuration, as shown in Figure 8-6.

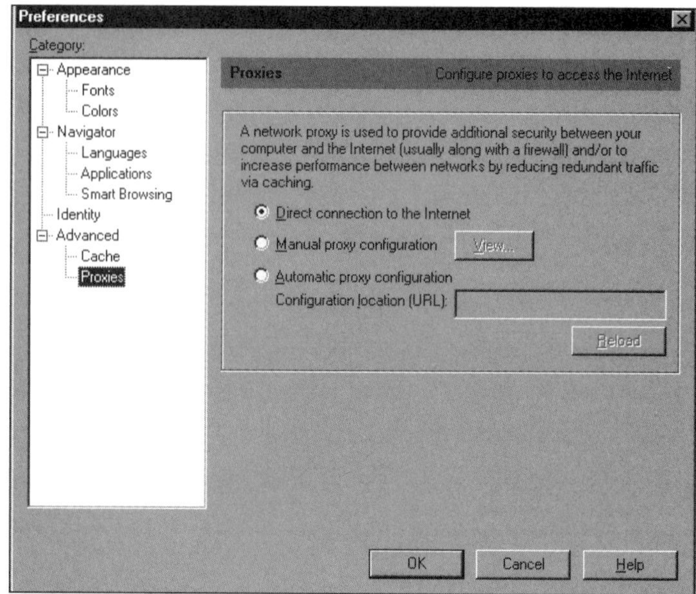

FIGURE 8-6 Netscape preferences

You need to manually configure Netscape Navigator for the Proxy Server by clicking the Manual proxy configuration button and clicking View. Once you do this, a dialog box that is similar to what you see in IE 4.01 (shown in Figure 8-7) appears. You have the option to assign different proxy servers to different protocols, but you there is no option to use the same proxy server for all, as there is in IE.

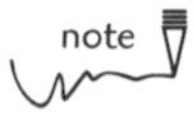

Notice the WAIS protocol in Figure 8-7. WAIS is an older Internet search protocol that was used to search for catalog resources, primarily used by education institutions. It is seldom used today.

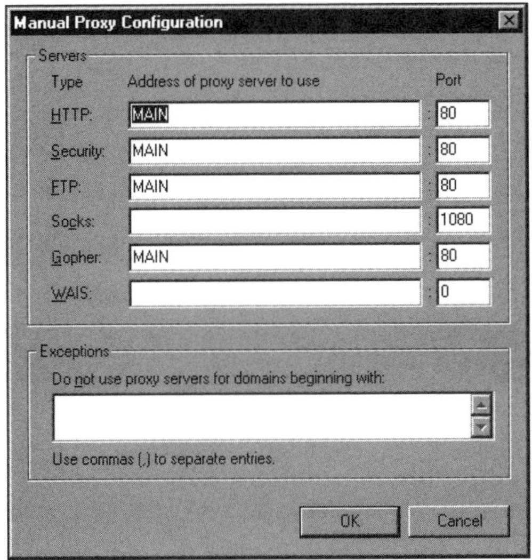

FIGURE 8-7 Netscape Manual Proxy Configuration dialog box

Winsock Proxy Client

Winsock is a shortened version of Windows Sockets. Only client computers running Microsoft Windows operating systems can be Winsock clients, and these clients must be configured with Winsock software.

When Proxy Server is installed, a share called `MSPCLNT`, contained in the `C:\MSP\Clients` directory, is created for Proxy client installations. This installation modifies the Winsock process on the client computer so that Winsock operations point to the Proxy Server. This enables the client to use Winsock applications, such as WS-FTP, transparently, as though the client is connected directly to the Internet. Because many Winsock applications do not have configuration options to use the Proxy Server, the client software modifies the Winsock access so these requests are forwarded to the Proxy Server service. As far as the Winsock application or user is concerned, the Proxy Server is invisible.

You have three major ways to install the Winsock Proxy client software. First, you can make a UNC connection at the run line by entering ***servername*\mspclnt\setup.exe**. This begins the installation of the client software, as shown in Figure 8-8.

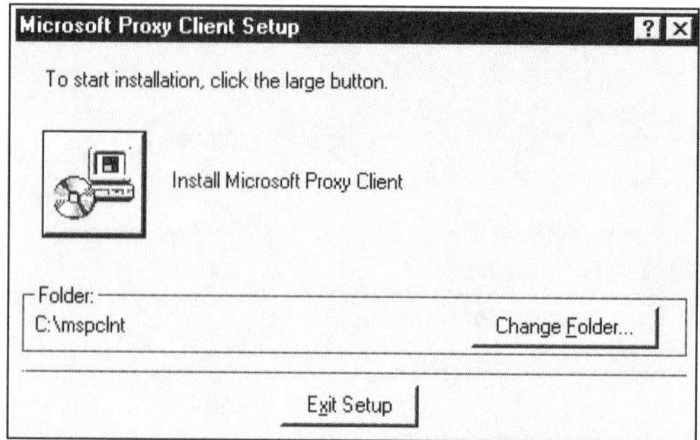

FIGURE 8-8 Proxy Client Software Setup

You can also run the installation from a Web browser by entering the URL `http://`*`servername`*`/msproxy`. You get a welcome page, as shown in Figure 8-9, with a link at the bottom to install the Winsock Proxy client software. This link takes you to the MSPCLNT directory and begins the installation. There is also a note on the welcome page about installing the Winsock Proxy client software using Netscape Navigator, which tells you to connect manually to the correct directory at the command prompt and run the `setup.bat` file.

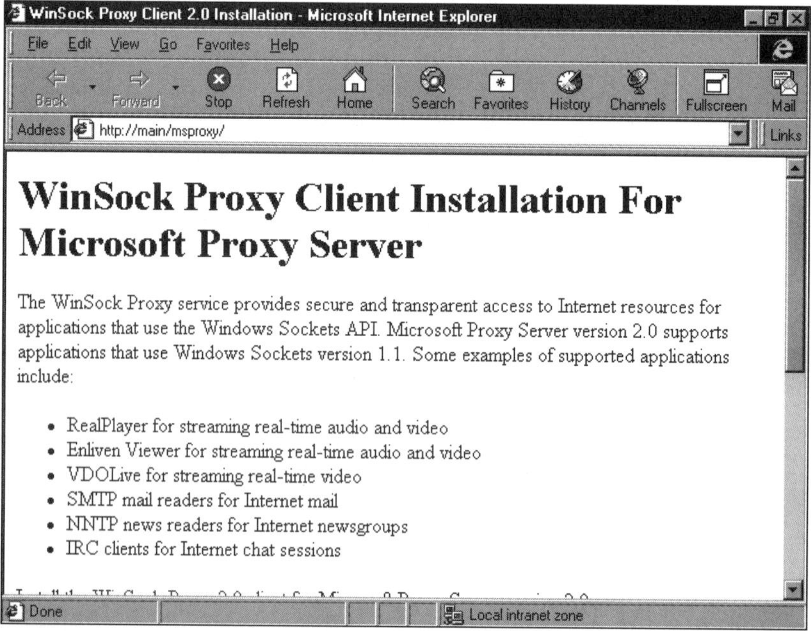

FIGURE 8-9 Browser Installation

Finally, you can install Proxy Server client software from a command prompt using the Setup command. You have a few switches you can use for the client setup. These are explained in Table 8-1.

TABLE 8-1 CLIENT SETUP SWITCHES

Switch	*Description*
`/r`	Reinstalls Proxy client software.
`/u`	Uninstalls the Winsock Proxy client application, but leaves the shared components.
`/q`	Runs client setup in quiet mode. The screen displays progress windows, but does not ask the user to approve or modify installation settings. There are some additional /q parameters available. Consult the Proxy Server documentation for additional information.

When using Winsock for Proxy, there are a few things to keep in mind. Some Winsock applications have options to configure them for use with a Proxy Server. Because you are using the Winsock Proxy DLLs and files, it is better not to configure the applications for Proxy. The applications will see the Internet as though they are directly connected. Additional configurations of the applications may cause you some problems. Also, you cannot use the Winsock Proxy client software on a computer running Microsoft Exchange Server. Client computers that use Exchange email programs, such as Outlook, can use the Winsock Proxy client software, but the actual server cannot.

When the Winsock Proxy client software is installed, `msplat.txt` and `mspclnt.ini` are copied to the client for use by the client software. The `msplat.txt` and the `mspclnt.ini` are overwritten and updated by the Proxy Server at regular intervals, so the clients always have a current copy of the LAT and the `.ini` file.

Once the software is installed, you have a few configuration options available on the Winsock Proxy client. You can access the WSP client icon in Control Panel, which calls the dialog box shown in Figure 8-10.

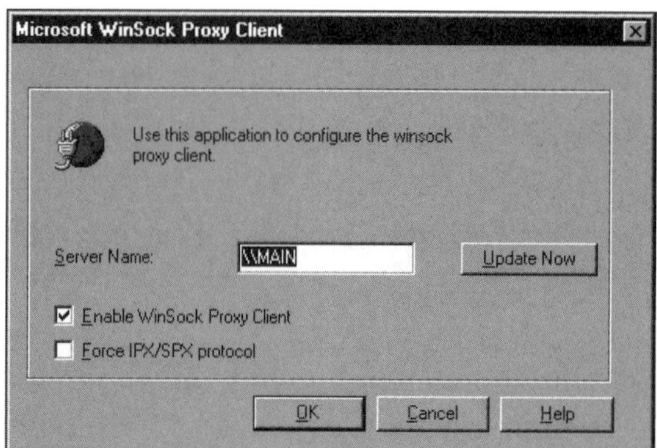

FIGURE 8-10 WSP Client dialog box

From this window, you can configure the server name, update the configuration by clicking Update Now, and you can select an option to force the IPX/SPX protocol for clients that have both TCP/IP and NWLink. This forces the computer to connect to the Proxy Server using NWLink instead of TCP/IP.

Anytime you make changes or updates to the Winsock Proxy client, you have to reboot for the changes to take effect.

Additional Configuration Options

The `mspclnt.ini` file can be used to configure Web browsers automatically. This action saves administrator time and ensures a uniform configuration across the organization. The `mspclnt.ini` modifies the browser as I did manually in the previous section. It identifies the Proxy Server and the port number, along with other configuration information. You can specify how the Proxy Server is to be contacted, either by NetBIOS name, DNS entry, or IP address. The `mspclnt.ini` file can be read and modified by using the Client Configuration dialog box on the Proxy Server or through a text editor as with any other `.ini` files. The `mspclnt.ini` file contains the configuration information, as you can see in the following section:

```
LocalBindTcpPorts=7070
[Net2fone]
ServerBindTcpPorts=0
[icq]
```

```
RemoteBindUdpPorts=0
ServerBindTcpPorts=0,1025-5000
NameResolutionForLocalHost=P
[Common]
WWW-Proxy=MAIN
Set Browsers to use Proxy=1
Set Browsers to use Auto Config=0
WebProxyPort=80
Configuration Url=http://MAIN:80/array.dll?Get.Routing.Script
Port=1745
Configuration Refresh Time (Hours)=6
Re-check Inaccessible Server Time (Minutes)=10
Refresh Give Up Time (Minutes)=15
Inaccessible Servers Give Up Time (Minutes)=2
Setup=Setup.exe
[Servers IP Addresses]
Name=MAIN
[Servers IPX Addresses]
[Master Config]
Path1=\\MAIN\mspclnt\
```

Note in the `.ini` file that the path1 will always point to the proxy server and that the refresh rate for the `.ini` file is every six hours or any time the computer is rebooted.

Browser Scripts

As I noted during installation, you can configure browsers by using an automated script. The default script is located at `http://`*`servername`*`:80/array.dll?Get.Routing.Script`, which you can see in the previous `mspclnt.ini` section. A custom script can also be used for this configuration. On the Client Installation/Configuration screen, you would click Configure to configure the use of a custom script. You can also configure the default script by clicking Properties at the bottom of the window.

The default script is created from the client configuration option selected during Setup. Using JavaScript, a custom script can be configured and used in place of the default script. Each time the browser is opened, the script is downloaded from the Proxy Server to configure the browser to gain Web access from the Proxy Server.

Scripts offer ease of administration. Because they are run when the browser is opened, configuration changes can be made easily and are automatic. Thus, any change made to the Proxy Server that impacts the client can be updated quickly in the script and automatically updated on the clients.

NWLink Clients

The Winsock Proxy client software supports clients using the IPX/SPX compatible protocol, NWLink. The same rules apply —the client has to be a Windows operating system, and a CERN-compliant browser has to be in use. Beyond that, the Winsock Proxy client software acts as an NWLink to TCP/IP gateway to the Proxy Server. You should note that the Winsock Proxy client software for NWLink does not support Windows 3.*x* clients.

Chapter 14 contains a troubleshooting section for NWLink Winsock Proxy clients.

Uninstalling the Winsock Client

If the need arises to uninstall the Winsock software from a client, the process is simple and straightforward. Follow these steps to perform the uninstallation:

1. Click Start ⇒ Run.
2. Enter **servername**\mspclnt\setup.exe.
3. The Setup Wizard begins and presents you with the option to add/remove client software, reinstall it, or uninstall it, as shown in Figure 8-11.

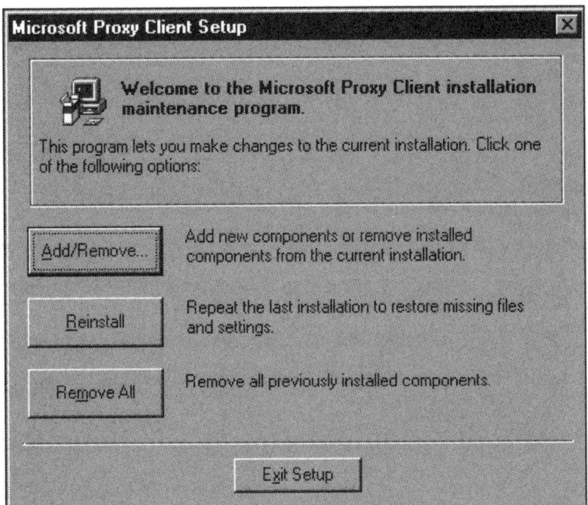

FIGURE 8-11 Uninstalling Winsock Client Software

4. Click uninstall. The Winsock client software is uninstalled.
5. Reboot the computer.

SOCKS CLIENT CONFIGURATION

Socks clients can access Proxy Server via the Web Proxy Service and the Socks Proxy Service. The Socks Proxy Service enables Socket applications to use the Proxy Server. By design, Sockets applications use a proxy server for access, whereas Winsock applications assume they have a direct Internet connection.

The Socket applications have to be configured manually to point to the proxy server. Depending on the permissions granted to the Socks clients, they are able to access the Internet via the Socket application.

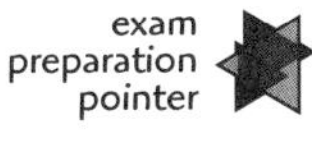

Socks clients, such as UNIX and Macintosh, must have TCP/IP configured. Winsock will translate NWLink to TCP/IP, but this is the only protocol it will translate. For example, Socks will not translate AppleTalk to TCP/IP. TCP/IP has to be installed on that machine with AppleTalk.

Exam Preparation Summary

Client configuration is usually straightforward, and you will not see a lot of exam questions concerning client configuration. Most questions you will see relate to Winsock configuration or Socks issues. Keep in mind that the client installation executable is stored in the MSPCLNT file on the Proxy Server. The installation of Winsock redirects Winsock requests to the Proxy Server, which is transparent to the application and the user. For UNIX and Macintosh Socks clients, you will need to specify the DNS entry for the Proxy Server and those clients must have TCP/IP installed in addition to any other protocol being used, such as AppleTalk. Keep in mind the location and name of the default browser configuration script, `http://servername:80/array.dll?Get.Routing.Script`.

Key Point Summary

This chapter showed you how to configure the Web Proxy, Winsock Proxy, and the Socks Proxy Services for use by Proxy Server clients:

- The Web Proxy Service can be used by any operating system that uses a CERN-compliant browser or application.
- Internet Explorer can be configured to use the Web Proxy Service by editing the Connection tab of the Internet Options page.
- Netscape Navigator can be configured via the Preferences page from the Edit menu.
- Winsock client software is located in the MSPCLNT directory on the Proxy Server or through the URL `http://servername/msproxy` if you are using a browser for Winsock client setup.
- Setup for Winsock can also be performed at the command line through the setup command.
- Winsock setup copies MSPLAT.TXT and MSPCLNT.INI to the client computer, which are modified and updated by the Proxy Server at regular intervals.
- Browsers can be configured automatically by using the default script created during Proxy Server installation, or from a custom Jscript. The default script is located at `http://servername:80/array.dll?Get.Routing.Script`.

- Winsock clients can use NWLink without TCP/IP, because Winsock performs the NWLink to TCP/IP translation. Socks clients must have TCP/IP installed in addition to any other protocol in use.

Applying What You've Learned

The following review questions give you a chance to test your knowledge of the content in this chapter. Should you miss some, review the appropriate portions of the chapter. The answers to the Instant Assessment questions can be found in Appendix C.

Instant Assessment

1. Which method can be used to install the Winsock software?

A. Browser

B. Execute `setup.exe` in the MSPCLNT directory

C. Command line

D. All of the above

2. What two files are copied to the client and updated on a regular basis? (Choose two)

A. `mspclnt.ini`

B. `locallat.txt`

C. `msplat.txt`

D. `locallat.ini`

3. Which kind of client can use Winsock? (Choose all that apply.)

A. Windows

B. Macintosh

C. UNIX

D. NetWare

4. What kind of browser can use the Web Proxy Service?

   A. IE 4.01

   B. IE 3.0

   C. Netscape Communicator

   D. Any CERN-compliant browser

5. What kind of platform can use the Web Proxy Service?

   A. Windows

   B. Macintosh

   C. UNIX

   D. All of the above

6. What is the default configuration script location?

   A. `C:\MSP\Proxy`

   B. `C:\MSP\Clients`

   C. `C:\MSP\Web`

   D. `C:\MSP\Winsock`

7. What is an older Internet search protocol used primarily in research and education institutions?

   A. TCP/IP

   B. SLIP

   C. FTP

   D. WAIS

Critical Thinking Labs

These labs present you with analysis problems to test your critical thinking skills with the content in this chapter.

Lab 8.34 *Configuring Proxy Server*

Your organization has just installed Proxy Server and needs to configure 400 client computer browsers to use the Proxy Server. You have been asked for suggestions to easily accomplish this task. What advice would you recommend?

Lab 8.35 *Avoiding Web Proxy Server problems*

Your company wants a small group of Macintosh clients to use the Web Proxy Service. These clients have only been communicating with each other in the past and not other Windows computers on the network. What should you check first to avoid potential problems?

Lab 8.36 *Proxy Server administration*

Your network has recently started using a Proxy Server. An administrator is worried that every change made to the Proxy Server will cause a big administrative load to configure the clients. What would you say regarding this concern?

Lab 8.37 *Netscape proxy configuration*

What actions should you take to configure Netscape Navigator to contact the Proxy Server for Internet access?

Lab 8.38 *UNIX clients*

What actions do you need to take to enable UNIX computers to use the Web Proxy Service and the SOCKS Proxy Service?

Lab 8.39 *NWLink clients*

An administrator is concerned that your network's NWLink clients will not be able to use the Winsock Service. What would you say to alleviate this concern?

Lab 8.40 *Using JavaScript*

How can JavaScript be used to create custom configuration solutions?

Lab 8.41 *Editing mspclnt.ini*

Your company needs to change the settings in the `mspclnt.ini` file so that users are directed to a new Proxy Server named ProxyCorpD. What line in the `mspclnt.ini` file should you change?

Hands-on Labs

The Hands-on Labs give you an opportunity to practice skills you have learned in this chapter. Make sure you read the system requirements for each lab to be certain you have the correct configuration before beginning the lab.

Lab 8.42 *Configuring Internet Explorer for Proxy Server*

In this lab, you manually configure Internet Explorer to use the Proxy Server.

1. Launch Internet Explorer.
2. Click the View menu and select Internet Options.
3. In the Internet Options dialog box, click the Connection tab.
4. Click the check box next to Access the Internet using a proxy server.
5. Once the check box is selected, the other areas are available. In the Address box, enter **`http://`servername** where ***servername*** is the NetBIOS name of your Proxy Server.
6. In the Port box, enter 80, which is the default selection for WWW services.
7. Click Advanced.
8. This takes you to the Proxy Setting dialog box.
9. In the middle of the dialog box, select the check box next to Use the same proxy server for all protocols.
10. Click OK.
11. You return to the Internet Options dialog box. Click Apply button and click OK.

Lab 8.43 *Installing Winsock client software*

In this lab, you will install the Winsock client software on your Windows computer.

1. On your Windows computer, click Start⇒Run.
2. In the Run box, enter **servername****MSPCLNT\setup.exe** where ***servername*** is the NetBIOS name of your Proxy Server. Click OK.
3. The client computer connects to the Proxy Server and begins the Winsock client software installation.
4. You see a dialog box to install the Winsock client software. Click the large button to install the software.
5. Setup checks for necessary disk space and installs the files.
6. When prompted, choose to reboot your computer.

CHAPTER

9

Creating a Secure Environment

About Chapter 9

One of the main functions of Proxy Sever is to provide ***firewall***, or security, services. Proxy Server's ability to manage both inbound and outbound Internet access provides a high level of security to the network. This chapter explores NT Server security and the server configuration Microsoft recommended to provide the highest level of protection. Secondly, this chapter explores Proxy Server security, including domain filters, packet filters, altering, and logging events. The critical thinking and hands-on labs give you a chance to practice implementing the security features you learn about in this chapter.

Proxy Server Security

One of the main functions of Proxy Server is to provide firewall services. In essence, this means that Proxy Server can protect your network against intruders from the Internet, but it can also restrict your internal clients from accessing certain kinds of information on the Internet. This entire function is designed to enable a network to utilize the Internet for business purposes while maintaining security.

Designing an effective security measure with Proxy Server is not difficult, but it tends to have a number of pitfalls along the way. One of the largest pitfalls is not Proxy Server itself, but rather Windows NT. Microsoft leaves many of the security features of Windows NT to the administrator to configure. It is not uncommon for someone who is new to Proxy Server to think the Proxy Server software will automatically fix any security holes — this is not the case. And with this thinking, the security issues concerning Windows NT and connectivity to the Internet can leave serious security breaches.

Windows NT Security

Windows NT is considered a highly secure, highly effective network operating system — and it is! Through its domain structure, authentication methods, NTFS, and a host of other features, Windows NT offers robust security. But we have to remember that security on the LAN or WAN is different than security connected to the Internet. If you take a multi-homed NT Server and connect it to the Internet, you can browse the Internet, but individuals on the Internet can also browse you and your network. Is it really that easy for Internet users to breach NT? Yes — if NT is not configured for Internet security, and in its default configuration, it is not. This is an area that is often overlooked, even when a proxy server is used.

IP Forwarding

One of the most critical aspects of Internet security with Windows NT is IP Forwarding. IP Forwarding is a part of the TCP/IP properties that enables the NT computer to pass IP packets to other segments of the network. Basically, if you are using a multi-homed computer connected to the Internet, and if IP Forwarding is permitted, Internet traffic can flow through the NT Server and to the LAN — not exactly what you want.

The IP Forwarding configuration is available on the Routing tab of the TCP/IP properties sheet, as shown in Figure 9-1.

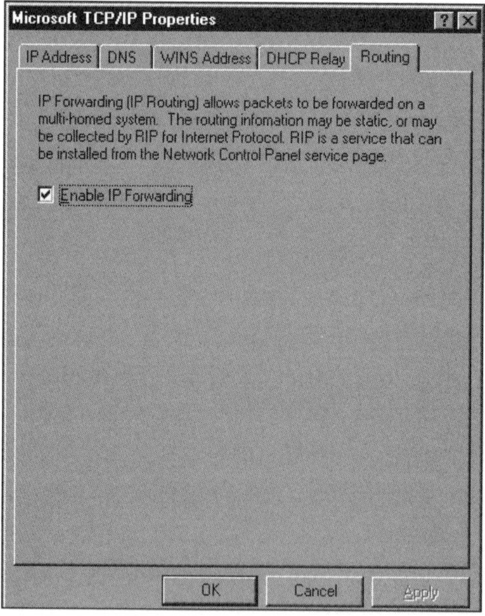

FIGURE 9-1 IP Forwarding configuration on the Routing tab of TCP/IP Properties

In Figure 9-1, the checkbox selects IP Forwarding. This means that IP packets from the Internet will be forwarded to other segments of the network. When connected to the Internet from a simple multi-homed computer or with Proxy Server installed, IP Forwarding must be unchecked.

This tab should be checked and rechecked to make certain IP Forwarding is not selected. Any time IP Forwarding is enabled, the network is open to intrusion from the Internet.

This seems simple enough, but you have to be careful. When you install TCP/IP, IP Forwarding is disabled by default. If it is enabled, a Proxy Server installation will disable it as well. However, if you make changes to some system configuration, such as installing RAS, it will be enabled again. The trick is to check this tab each time you make changes to the system to make certain IP Forwarding has not been enabled.

Why would you want to use IP Forwarding? There may be circumstances where you want to permit communication from the Internet to reach the network. In this case, you would want to enable IP Forwarding. But to create the most secure environment, IP Forwarding should be disabled. This cuts the direct link to the Internet, forcing all traffic to move through the Proxy Server.

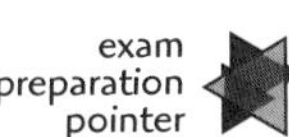

Expect a question or two about IP Forwarding on the exam. Make sure you know how to disable it and why you would want to do so.

TCP/IP Security

In addition to disabling IP Forwarding, there is an additional measure you can take to help reduce the likelihood of attacks against your Proxy Server. You can access the TCP/IP Security settings by clicking the Advanced button on the IP Address tab in TCP/IP properties. The Advanced IP Addressing dialog box is shown in Figure 9-2.

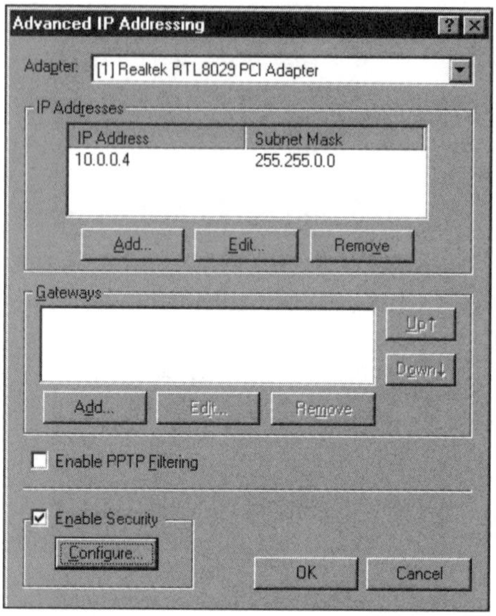

FIGURE 9-2 Advanced IP addressing dialog box

You can see configuration options for IP addresses and gateways, but notice the two checkboxes at the bottom of the window. One lets you enable filtering for Point to Point Tunneling Protocol (PPTP), and one lets you enable security. If you select the Enable Security checkbox and click the Configure button, you reach the TCP/IP Security dialog box, as shown in Figure 9-3.

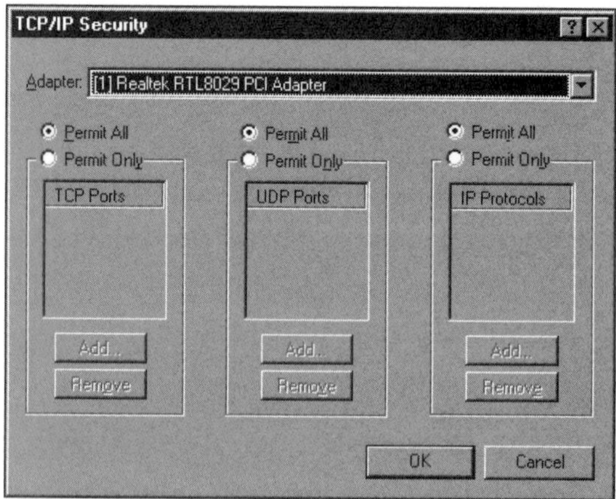

FIGURE 9-3 TCP/IP security dialog box

As you can see in Figure 9-3, the default is to permit all TCP, UDP, and IP protocols. You can further restrict this by defining what ports you want the Proxy Server to listen to. By selecting the adapter in the drop-down menu that is connected to the Internet, you can restrict access to ports by clicking the Permit Only radio button for either TCP, UDP, or IP protocols. If you click the Add button, you get the Security Add dialog box, as shown in Figure 9-4.

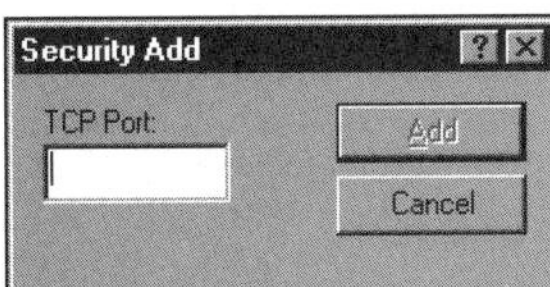

FIGURE 9-4 Security Add dialog box

You add the port by entering the port number that is to be permitted. For example, if you wanted to only permit access from TCP port 80, which is HTTP, you would enter 80 in the dialog box and click the Add button. Now, the only TCP port that is permitted is port 80, as shown in Figure 9-5.

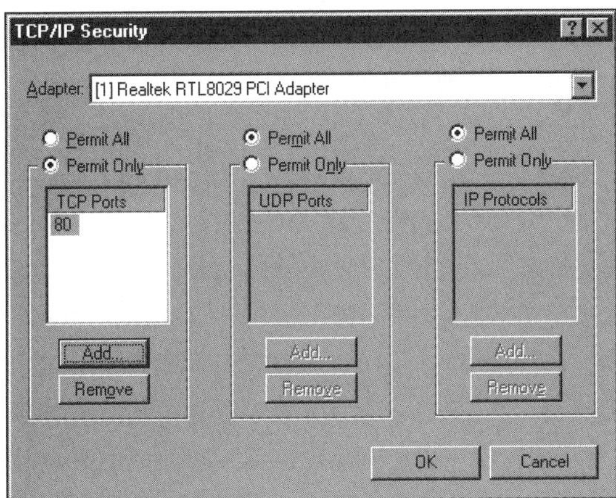

FIGURE 9-5 Restricted TCP port

Port restriction is not just available in Windows NT's TCP/IP Properties. Proxy Server can manage inbound port access as well, and I explain how that works in a later section.

General Security Issues

In addition to configuring IP Forwarding and TCP/IP Security, there are some additional measures you can take to reduce the possibly of attack from the Internet. Most of these are simply good server management techniques. It is important to remember that Proxy Server works with Windows NT Server, and good security strategies for NT Server will aid Proxy Server's firewall functionality.

- It is best to use Proxy Server on an NT Server that is dedicated for that purpose. Yes, the Proxy Server can also be a PDC or BDC, but this may cause security problems. The more services and functions you have running on the NT Server in conjunction with Proxy Server, the more likely you are to have security breaches. The best choice is to run Proxy Server on a dedicated NT Server that is configured specifically for communication with the Internet.
- Require usernames and passwords that conform to wise security configurations. Passwords should contain a mix of letters and numbers, with at least five characters. Note that passwords in NT are case sensitive.

  This approach makes password discovery difficult. Users should be strongly encouraged not to use their usernames as passwords, or the names of family members for passwords. This policy must be implemented at the network level since Proxy Server will use the domain login of a user. Although this point is preached extensively in all Microsoft documentation, many networks have very lax security when it comes to usernames and passwords. Also, strict account policies should be enforced from the administrator's end. For example, the administrator can specify how quickly the account password expires, which forces users to regularly change their passwords. Additionally, another useful feature is account lockout. This locks the account after a specified number of unsuccessful login attempts, with the default being three attempts. The account has to be unlocked by the administrator once it is locked. This helps prevent random password attacks since the Internet user only has three chances before the account is locked.
- The number of users who have administrative privileges or high-level access should be minimal and their names carefully guarded. The more users who have high-level access, the less secure your network becomes.

- Any server or client services that are not absolutely necessary should be disabled so they cannot run on the Proxy Server. For example, to reduce the possibility of Internet users gaining access to your NetBIOS to IP address name table, disable the WINS client on the external adapter.

Do not use Server Message Blocks (SMBs) over the Internet. Content and usernames can be easily gained from SMBs.

- No network drives should be mapped on the Proxy Server, especially if the Proxy Server is also the Web server. If they are, Internet users may be able to gain access to network resources through these mapped network drives.
- Remote procedure call (RPC) ports (1024 – 1029) should be disabled. This prevents remote users from using RPC commands on your network.
- Unbind any unnecessary service from the external adapter. DHCP settings should be removed from the server as well as DNS entries in the TCP/IP properties sheet. DNS and DHCP can be used, but they should be available only to the internal network. This action keeps Internet users from gaining this information and using it to penetrate your network
- Use only NTFS volumes. This enables you to implement security for your data and files.
- Do not allow your clients to configure DNS and gateway references. This prevents clients from bypassing the Proxy Server to gain access to the Internet.
- Microsoft recommends that Proxy Server be configured to be a stand-alone server in your domain. If you have multiple domains, you may consider setting up Proxy Server as the PDC in its own domain. A single one-way trust relationship can be established with another domain on your network, where the Proxy Server is the trusting domain and the internal domain is the trusted domain. This action also reduces the possibility of Internet users gaining access to the LAN or WAN.

Proxy Service Security

In addition to the security measures that are part of Windows NT, Proxy Server also plays a role in protecting your network. By configuring NT Server for optimal security on the Internet, you aid Proxy Server's ability to further refine and customize security options.

Web Proxy Permissions

As mentioned in Chapter 7, the administrator can define what permissions Web Proxy clients have concerning access to the Internet. This can be configured through the Permissions tab of the Web Proxy Service, as shown in Figure 9-6.

Notice that access control has to be enabled to restrict protocol usage. The protocol can be selected, and by using the Edit button users and groups can be given access to particular protocols. With access control enabled, no users or groups have default permissions. Every user or group must be explicitly granted the right to use the various Web protocols.

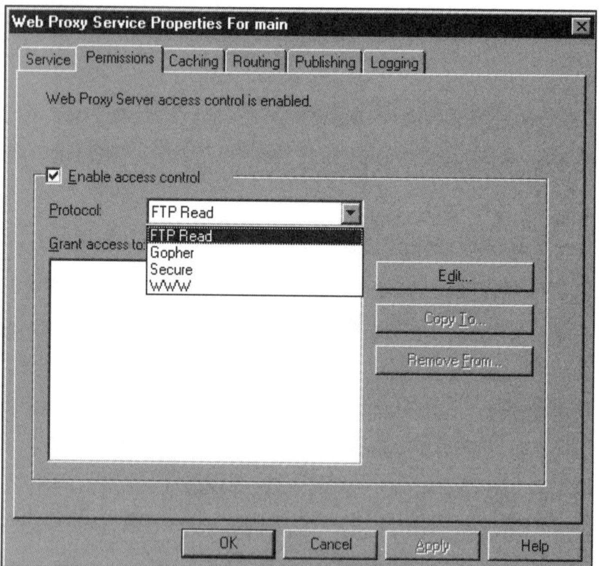

FIGURE 9-6 Permissions tab of Web Proxy Service Properties

As a general rule of thumb, only grant access to protocols that are needed for company-related business. This creates a more secure environment and discourages users from playing on the Internet.

Winsock Security

Security for Winsock applications is set in the same manner as the Web Proxy Service. Access can be granted via protocol in the Permissions tab of the Winsock Proxy Service Properties page, as shown in Figure 9-7.

As with the Web Proxy Service, once access control is enabled, you must explicitly grant permissions to users and groups — no users or groups are given default permissions. You have a number of Winsock protocols that can be granted to users, and you have the option to grant Unlimited Access to users or groups for the Winsock Service.

For security purposes, it is usually best to grant unlimited access only to administrator or high-level groups. This action creates a tighter security model and keeps more ports closed. Also, this action reduces certain unwanted protocol usage, such as IRC (chat).

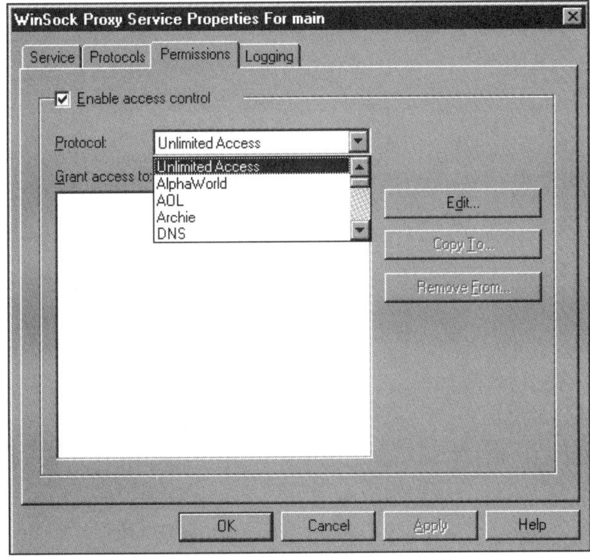

FIGURE 9-7 Permissions tab of Winsock Proxy Service Properties

Socks Security

The Socks security model functions somewhat differently. The permissions for Socks can be set on the Permissions tab of the Socks Proxy Properties sheet, as shown in Figure 9-8.

Protocols can be added to give Socks clients rights to use explicit ports. Socks does not use Windows NT Challenge/Response security login, but rather it uses the IP address and the Identification protocol (IdentD) to authenticate Socks clients.

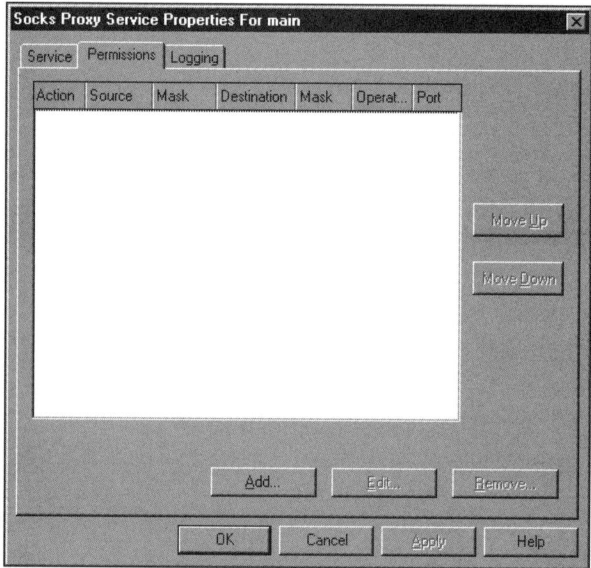

FIGURE 9-8 Permissions tab of Socks Proxy Properties

The Socks Proxy Service is dependent on the Web Proxy Service and will not function if the Web Proxy Service is not running.

By clicking the Add button, the Permissions tab of the Socks Proxy Service Properties page becomes available, as shown in Figure 9-9.

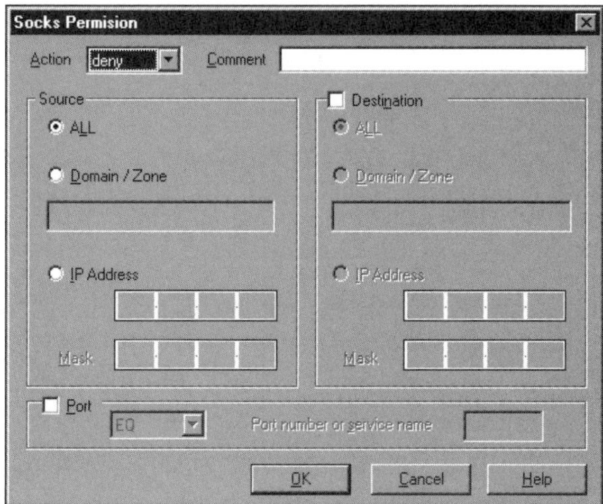

FIGURE 9-9 Socks Permission dialog box

All access is denied by default, so the administrator must grant explicit rights to Socks services. Port options can also be configured for the permit action that is performed.

Refer to Chapter 7 for a detailed discussion of the port options available.

Anonymous Access

An additional issue concerning security is anonymous access. As I mentioned in Chapter 4, IIS installs a default anonymous account named IUSR_*computername*. The anonymous account is a guest account that permits a guest user to access certain services and resources. The user can typically access Web and FTP sites by using the Anonymous user name and his or her e-mail address as the password. I should note that some FTP sites require an e-mail user name as the password for anonymous FTP client access. In this case, the e-mail name sent by Proxy Server is `proxyuser@domain`, where *domain* is the current Internet DNS domain setting in use.

By default, the Anonymous account has permission to access the Web Proxy service, and the user does not need to have further permissions. Proxy Server can be used to extend this functionality by granting anonymous access to both the Winsock and Web Proxy services by disabling access control in each service.

However, this is usually not a wise security plan. If anonymous access is permitted, all client applications can use the account. The only way to prevent this is to disable anonymous logon.

When using a Proxy Server array, the IUSER_*computername* account is not replicated correctly across the array because of issues with the SAM database on each server. In this case, you can use the Everyone account in place of the anonymous account if you want to permit anonymous access.

As a further security measure, you may want to disable this access if your organization has no need for an anonymous account. This action forces all users to log on with a valid account and password.

TO DISABLE (OR LATER RE-ENABLE) THE ANONYMOUS ACCOUNT, FOLLOW THESE STEPS:

1. In the Internet Service Manager, double-click the computer name beneath the WWW Service.
2. In the WWW Service Properties dialog box, select the Allow Anonymous checkbox. You can clear the check box to disable anonymous access or check it to re-enable anonymous access.
3. IApply the changes you made and click OK.

When the Allow Anonymous is the only checkbox enabled in the WWW Service, Access Control is automatically disabled for the Web Proxy Service.

IdentD

As previously mentioned, the IdentD Simulation Service is used by Socks clients as a part of the logon process. The IdentD Simulation Service assigns a temporary security identifier to each Socks user. This service creates a random username and assigns it to requesting servers in order to provide Socks clients with the ability to log on. If you have Socks clients on your network, the IdentD Simulation Service can be installed through the Proxy Server CD-ROM.

TO INSTALL THE IDENTD SIMULATION SERVICE, FOLLOW THESE STEPS:

1. Create a directory named IdentD on the Proxy Server computer.
2. Copy `Identd.exe`, located in the IdentD directory of the Proxy Server CD-ROM, to the new directory on the Proxy Server.
3. From the command prompt, change to the IdentD directory on the server, and then type identd -install.
4. From the command prompt, type net start identd.
5. Create a bidirectional packet filter for this service that uses TCP port 113.

Creating packet filters is discussed later in this chapter.

Domain Filters

Domain filters are additional security measures designed to control access by internal clients. A domain filter can limit access to certain Internet sites, or the filter can deny access to all sites except certain ones that are specified. Domain filters apply to every user and group on the network — it is not possible to deny access to sites based on individual users and groups.

Domain filters are configured under the Security section of the shared Web, Winsock, and Socks Proxy Services. To access section, simply click on Service tab of either the Web, Winsock, or Socks Proxy Properties sheet, and then click the Security button. The Security dialog box is shown in Figure 9-10.

Notice that with the Enable filtering checkbox selected, domain filters can be added. Also, the Enable filtering checkbox also tells us that a direct Internet connection is required. This notice applies to Proxy Servers used in a chain. If there is not direct Internet access for the upstream Proxy Server computer in the chain, name resolution cannot take place and domain filtering does not work.

Using multiple Proxy Servers is discussed in Chapter 12.

Notice that you have the option to grant access or deny access. If you want the users on your network to have access to all Internet sites with the exception of a few, use the Granted radio button. Consider this example. Suppose your company's fiercest competitor is XYZ Company. You want your users to have full access to all Internet domains, but you don't want them accessing XYZ Company. You can use the Granted radio button and add the exception to the list. If you click the Add button, you are given a Deny Access To dialog box, as shown in Figure 9-11.

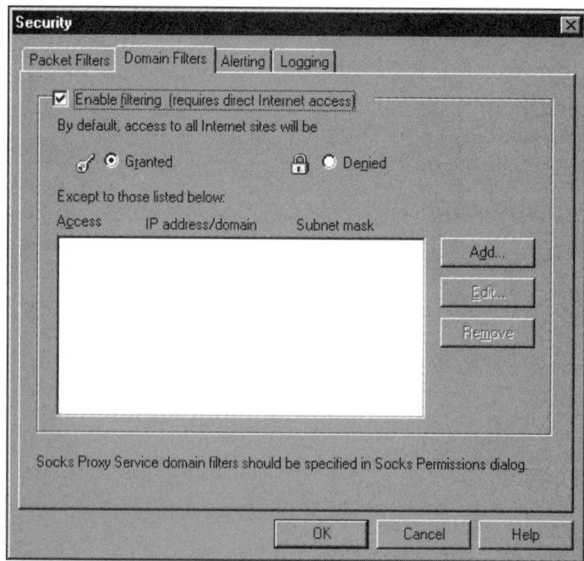

FIGURE 9-10 Security dialog box

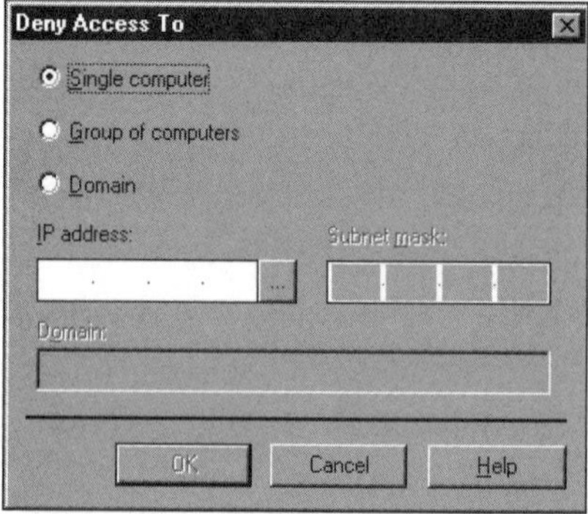

FIGURE 9-11 Deny Access To dialog box

If you want to deny access to XYZ Company to everyone in the domain, select the Domain radio button and type the URL in the Domain space, as shown in Figure 9-12.

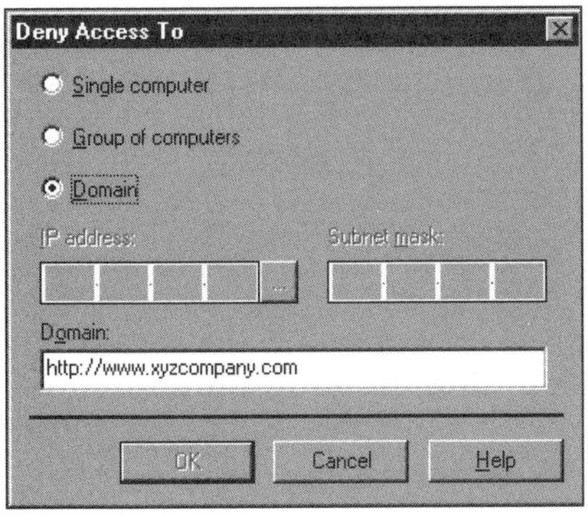

FIGURE 9-12 Denying access to XYZ Company

When you click OK, the domain filter is added to the list. Now, the domain can access all Internet sites except `xyzcompany.com`, as shown in Figure 9-13.

You can also deny access to a single computer by IP address, or a group of computers by IP address and subnet mask.

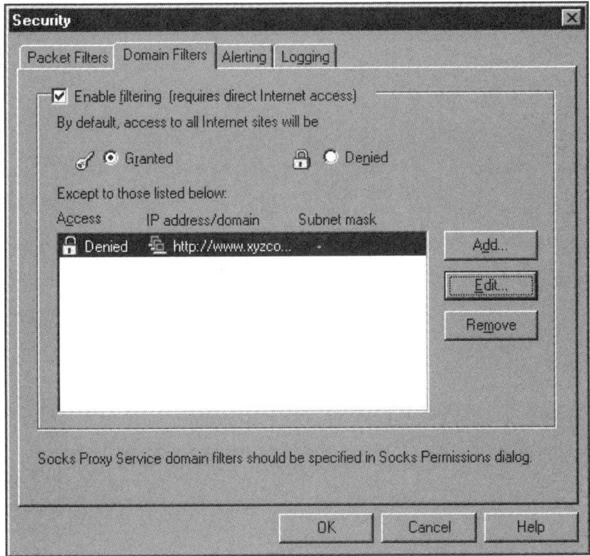

FIGURE 9-13 Enabled domain filter

You can also turn this situation around. Suppose you have a highly restrictive environment and you only want your clients to be able to access `xyzcompany.com`, but no other domains. Click the Denied radio button on the Security tab, as shown in Figure 9-14.

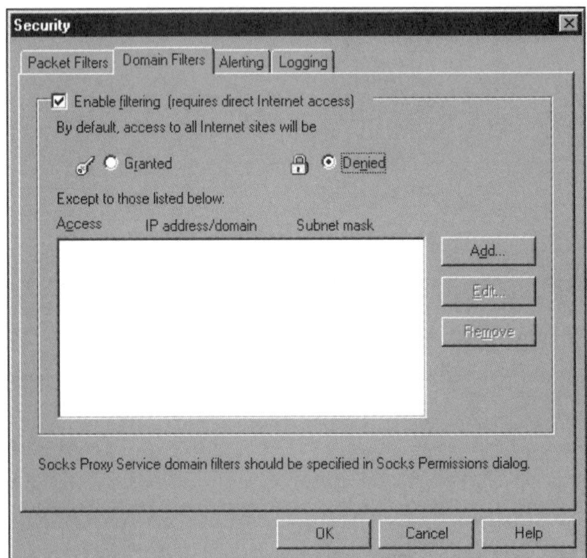

FIGURE 9-14 Denied domain filter

Now, anything you add to the exception list will be granted to users, but only the domains or computers listed in the exception list will be accessible. Once a domain is added, access is granted to the site, as shown in Figure 9-15.

Once domain filtering is implemented, the filter restricts all clients. If a client attempts to connect to an Internet domain that is not allowed, the Proxy Server will issue a *proxy report* to the client informing the client that access is denied.

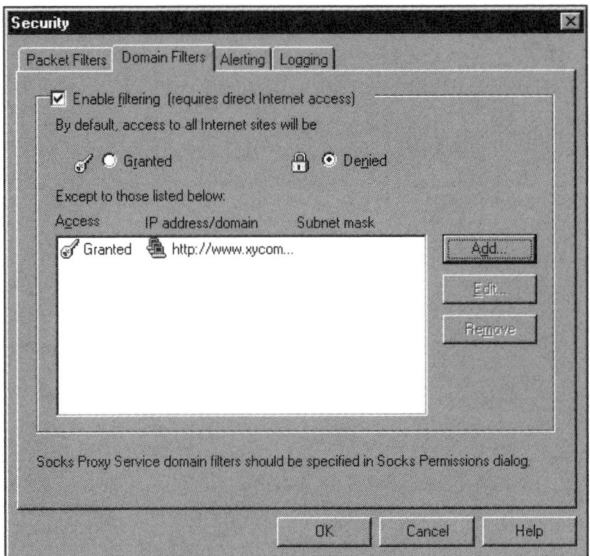

FIGURE 9-15 Granted domain filter

Packet Filtering

Domain filtering is used to control outbound access; packet filtering is used to control outbound access as well as inbound access. By definition, packet filtering does just that — it filters IP packets specified by the administrator. This controls what kind of information is allowed in or out of the network. Packet filtering intercepts and examines every packet that attempts to pass through the Proxy Server to determine if it is allowed or not. Packet filtering even contains options to reject address spoofing and FRAG attacks, and can block packets that come from specific Internet sites.

As with domain filtering, packet filtering is configured by accessing Security in the shared Proxy Services and clicking on the Packet Filters tab, as shown in Figure 9-16.

An external adapter must be present to configure packet filtering. If you are using a dial-up adapter, such as a modem, you must configure auto-dial before configuring packet filters. Configuring auto-dial is addressed in Chapter 13.

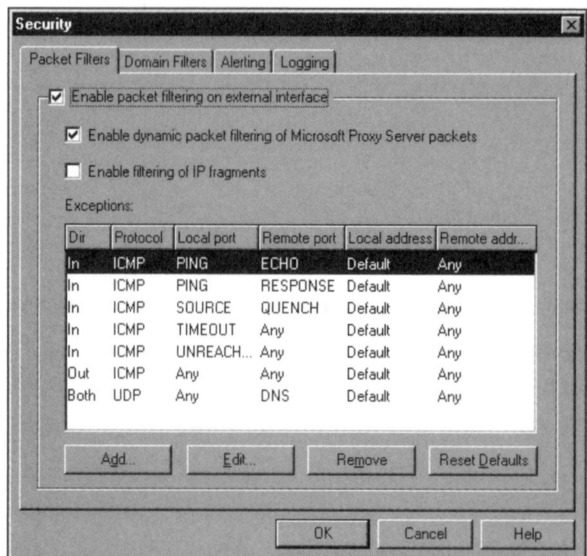

FIGURE 9-16 Packet Filters tab

As with domain filters, you have to enable packet filtering by clicking the first checkbox. Once this is done, you have a number of options for configuring packet filters.

By default, all packets are filtered except those listed in the exception list. The second checkbox in the window allows the administrator to enable dynamic packet filtering of Microsoft Proxy packets, which is enabled by default. Dynamic filtering enables Proxy Server to automatically block specified packets and to open and close ports as needed. When a port needs to be opened for a certain communication, Proxy opens the port, then closes the port when it is no longer needed. This is a security feature to keep minimal ports open on the Internet. If the dynamic filtering checkbox is unchecked, the packet filtering becomes static; in other words, all ports in the exception list remain open at all times. The third checkbox can be used to provide even more security by filtering IP fragments.

Packet filters apply to the external adapter. The internal adapter can still function on the network as it normally would. As you can see in Figure 9-16, a number of filters are added to the exception list by default. Remember that all packets are filtered except what appears in the exception list. You can add additional exceptions by clicking the Add button, which takes you to the Packet Filter Properties dialog box, as shown in Figure 9-17.

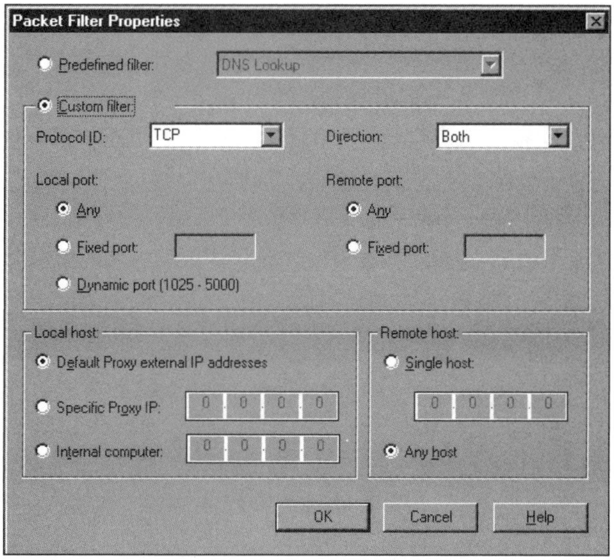

FIGURE 9-17 Packet Filter Properties dialog box

You can add a custom filter by specifying the Protocol ID and configuring port information. Suppose you want to permit bidirectional TCP traffic. In the Direction drop-down menu, choose Both, the protocol ID is TCP, and you can configure the Local and Remote ports as well as the Local and Remote hosts. You can also accept the defaults. When you click OK, the filter is added to the exception list, as shown in Figure 9-18.

You can also add additional predefined filters. By clicking the Add button, selecting the Predefined filter, and selecting the Protocol ID in the drop-down menu, you can easily add new filters, such as SMTP, PPTP, and POP3, as shown in Figure 9-19.

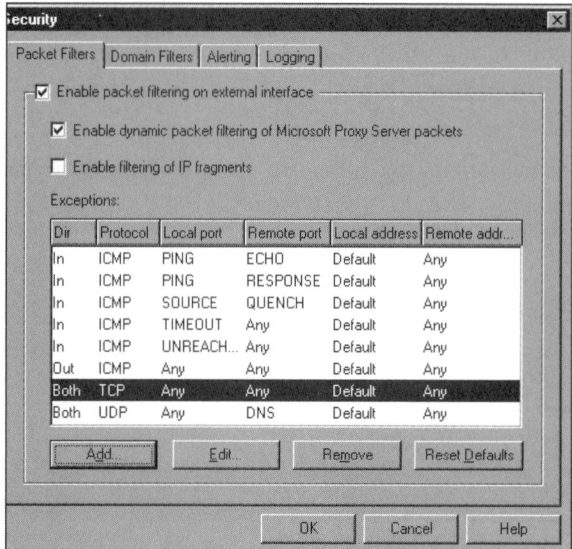

FIGURE 9-18 Configured TCP custom filter

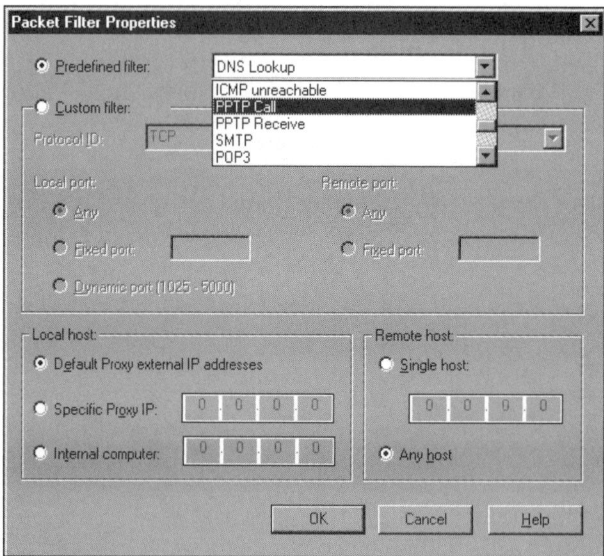

FIGURE 9-19 Predefined packet filters

You have probably noticed that domain and packet filter configuration is rather quick and easy. This is by design, and it is a huge plus for busy and stressed network administrators. With only a small amount of administrative overhead, Proxy Server is able to provide tight security automatically.

The following is a list of all the Predefined filters available in the drop-down menu.

DNS Lookup	PPTP Receive
ICMP All Outbound	SMTP
ICMP Ping Response	POP3
ICMP Ping Query	IdentD
ICMP SRC Quench	HTTP Server (port 80)
ICMP Timeout	HTTPS Server (port 443)
ICMP Unreachable	NetBIOS (WINS clients only)
PPTP Call	NetBIOS (all)

Note that some protocols require multiple filters to function properly. For example, to use PPTP, you have to use a PPTP Call and PPTP Receive filter.

Security Alerts and Reporting

The final aspect of Proxy Server's security features is its ability to log events and send event alerts to administrators. Proxy Server offers full alert and logging features that can be configured to fit virtually any need.

Proxy Alerts

Proxy Server enables administrators to configure proxy security alerts so they will be notified of potentially dangerous or damaging attacks or events. The Proxy alerts can be configured on the Alerting tab of the Security screen, as shown in Figure 9-20.

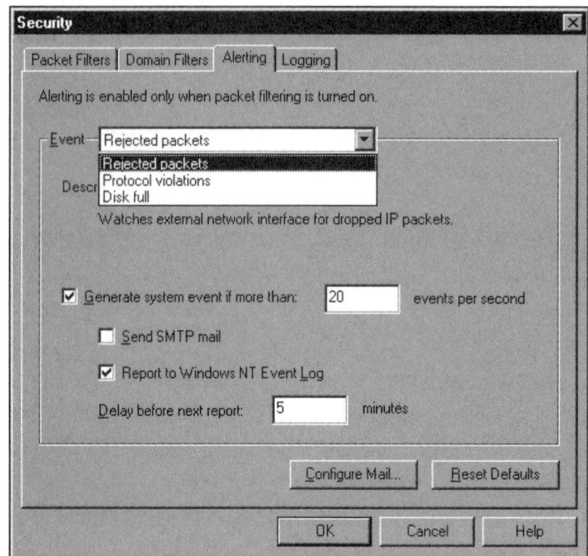

FIGURE 9-20 Security Alerting tab

Proxy Server can send an administrative alert for three events: Rejected packets, Protocol violations, and Disk full. Rejected packets are dropped; in other words, because packet filtering, they are not permitted to pass through the Proxy Server. A high rate of rejected packets may indicate an attack on the network. Notice in Figure 9-20 that the default alert is 20 events per second. So, if 20 or more packets are dropped per second, Proxy Server generates an alert. The same is true for a protocol violation, which is attempted communication using illegal IP packets. The default alert for protocol violations is one event per second. The last alert event is disk full, which can be used to alert the administrator that disk storage is running low.

To generate rejected packet and protocol violation alerts, packet filtering must be enabled.

You can receive an alert by reporting it to the Windows NT Event Log, and you can also receive an SMTP mail alert if desired. By clicking the checkbox next to Send SMTP mail and then clicking the Configure Mail button, you are given a Configure Mail Alerting screen, as shown in Figure 9-21.

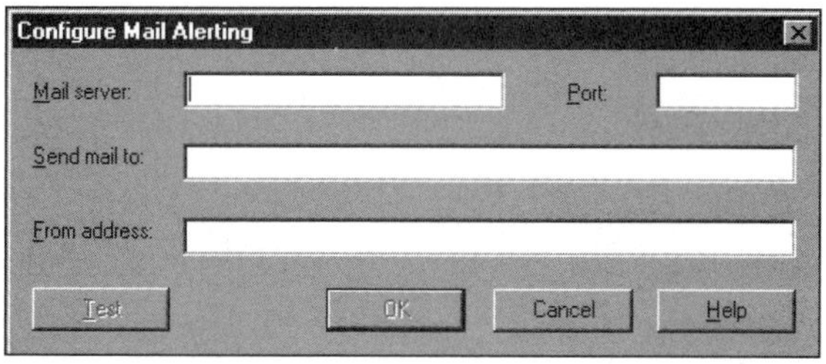

FIGURE 9-21 **Configure Mail Alerting dialog box**

Once you configure the mail alert, you can send a test e-mail to make certain it is working properly.

Proxy Logging

As mentioned, you can log Proxy alerts, but Proxy logging also logs additional events for the Web Proxy Service, the Winsock Proxy Service, and the Socks Proxy Service. A Logging tab is available on the properties sheet of each service, as well as the Security tab for packet logging, and all of the log configuration tabs are virtually the same. The security logging makes it possible to log dropped or rejected packets.

Proxy Server logs are stored in `C:\winnt\system32\msplogs`. Each log has a different name, although they all follow the *yymmdd*`.log` format with some variations, depending on whether the log is a daily, weekly, or monthly log. The log filenames for the services are as follows:

- The Web Proxy log: `W3`*yymmdd*`.log`
- The Winsock Proxy log: `Ws`*yymmdd*`.log`
- The Socks Proxy log: `Sp`*yymmdd*`.log`
- The Packet Filter log: `Fp`*yymmdd*`.log`

Logging for packet filtering can be configured by accessing the Logging tab of the Security properties sheet, as shown in Figure 9-22.

As you can see in Figure 9-22, logging can be enabled using Regular or Verbose format. Regular format records basic information with limited data fields while verbose logging records all information.

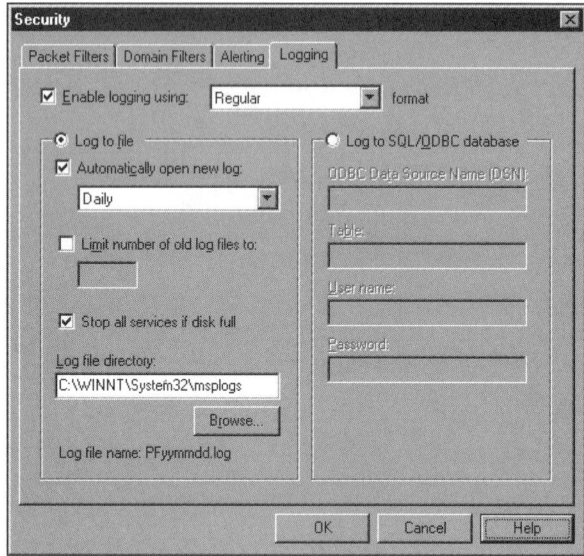

FIGURE 9-22 Logging tab

Verbose logging creates extensive logs and consumes much more disk space than regular logging. Make sure you have a specific reason before implementing verbose logging.

Regular logging contains the entries shown in Table 9-1.

TABLE 9-1 REGULAR LOG ENTRIES

Entry	*Description*
Date	The day the packet was received
Time	The time the packet was received
SRC IP	The IP address of the originating remote host
SRC Port	The remote service port used to open the connection
Protocol	The protocol used to make the connection
Dest IP	The destination IP address of the internal local host
Dest Port	The destination port number
Action	Statement of whether the packet was dropped or accepted
Interface	The interface on which the packet was received

Verbose mode stores this information as well, but also adds information such as Raw IP Header and Raw IP Packet.

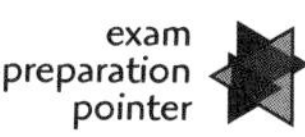

You should be aware of how logging works for the exam, but you will not be expected to distinguish the data storage differences between regular and verbose logging.

You have two logging choices: logging to a file or logging to a database. If you log to a file, you can log daily, weekly, or monthly, and you can also specify a limit to the number of old logs. By default, all services will stop if the disk becomes full.

You can choose a directory. `C:\winnt\system32\msplogs` is the default, but you can browse to store the log in another location. The log files can be stored on a different server, although for security and performance purposes, it is usually best if you store them on the Proxy Server.

If you choose to log to a database, select the radio button. Proxy can log to Open Database Connectivity (ODBC) databases, which is a standard API to construct open platform databases. Examples of ODBC databases are Microsoft Access and SQL. As with log files, you can store the log in a local database or another database on the network by specifying the database, the table, and the username and password.

Exam Preparation Summary

Because security is one of the major functions of Proxy Server, you can expect to have several related questions on the exam. For NT security, you should pay careful attention to the points in the "General Security Issues" section of this chapter. You may see a question that says, "How can you stop Internet users from gaining access to your NetBIOS to IP address name table?" or related questions from that section. You should also expect a question or two about IP Forwarding.

You should know the ins and outs of configuring domain filters and packet filters. The best way to get ready for these questions is to study the sections in this chapter and experiment with setting up filters on your computer. The exam question may ask, "You want users on your network to have unlimited Internet access, with the exception of `www.xyzcompany.com`. How can you configure this?" Often, domain and packet filter questions will be in a scenario situation asking you for the correct configuration action. The scenario questions begin with a problem or situation, then provide you with desired results, optional results, and a solution to the problem. You will have to determine the outcome of the proposed solution, such as the "meets the required result and optional results, meets the required result and one optional result," and so forth. You may also see an interface question or two concerning security. In these questions, you will be presented with a portion of the Proxy Server interface and asked to configure the interface to produce a requested outcome.

You will not see extensive questions about configuring alerts and logging. You should know what options are available, such as sending an SMTP alert and logging to ODBC-compliant databases, but the alert and logging questions are usually straightforward.

Key Point Summary

This chapter explored the configuration of a secure Proxy Server environment.

- IP Forwarding must be disabled to create a secure environment. This forces all traffic to flow through the Proxy Server.
- Additional port configuration can be performed on the TCP/IP Security screen.
- The Proxy Server should be reserved for that purpose. For security reasons, it is best to have the fewest number of services possible running on the Proxy Server.
- Additional services, such as WINS, should be disabled from the external adapter to tighten security.
- RPC ports should be disabled on the Proxy Server.
- Use only NTFS volumes on the Proxy Server.
- Permissions to clients for various protocols can each be configured on the Permissions tab of the Web, Winsock, and Socks Proxy Service tabs.
- IdentD is used by Socks clients to gain a random, temporary logon ID.
- Domain filters are used to restrict access to outbound traffic. Filters can be configured by domain, group of computers, or single computer. Domain filters apply to all users — you cannot assign filters to certain users or groups.

- Packet filters are used to control what kind of IP packets are allowed both in and out of the network. The Proxy Server inspects each packet and drops packets that are not allowed.
- Proxy filter alerts can be configured for rejected packets, protocol violations, and disk full.
- Proxy filter alerts can be logged in a file or sent via SMTP mail.
- Proxy logging is available in regular or verbose formats. Logs can be text files or they can be configured for storage in ODBC-compliant databases such as Microsoft Access and SQL.

Applying What You Have Learned

The following review questions give you a chance to test your knowledge of the content in this chapter. Should you miss some, review the appropriate portions of the chapter. The answers to the Instant Assessment questions can be found in Appendix C.

Instant Assessment

1. Which logging format logs all information?
   A. Regular
   B. Standard
   C. Verbose
   D. Full
2. Where are Proxy logs stored by default?
   A. `C:\MSProxy`
   B. `C:\MSP\Logs`
   C. `C:\winnt\system32\msplogs`
   D. `C:\winnt\system32\winntlogs`

3. What is the default name for a packet filter log?

A. `dd.log`

B. `mmdd.log`

C. `Fpyymmdd.log`

D. `MSPdd.log`

4. Which of the following is a standard database API?

A. SQL

B. Access

C. ODBC

D. ASPLOG

5. How can IP Forwarding be disabled?

A. In Proxy Server Web Proxy Service Properties

B. In Proxy Server Winsock Proxy Service Properties

C. In ISM Connectivity Properties

D. In TCP/IP Properties

6. Why should SMBs not be used on the Internet?

A. They are incompatible with TCP/IP.

B. They can be read and intercepted.

C. They slow WAN traffic.

D. They should be used on the Internet.

7. Why should services such as WINS be disabled from the external adapter?

A. To create tighter security

B. To avoid TCP interference

C. To avoid client access problems

D. To avoid external adapter failure

8. Which policies for passwords are good tactics to keep security high? (Choose all that apply.)

A. Minimum lengths

B. Combination of letters and numbers

C. Account lockout options for failed password attempts

D. Password expirations

9. How could you restrict access to IRC?

   A. Through Web Proxy Protocol options

   B. Through Winsock Proxy Protocol options

   C. Through Socks Proxy Protocol options

   D. This cannot be done.

10. Which groups should have unlimited Winsock access?

   A. All users

   B. Administrators

11. Which client would use IdentD?

   A. UNIX

   B. Windows NT Workstation

   C. Windows 95

   D. Windows 98

12. How can you create a domain filter for a particular user?

   A. In Web Proxy Properties

   B. In Winsock Proxy Properties

   C. In Socks Proxy Properties

   D. This cannot be done.

Critical Thinking Labs

These labs present you with analysis problems to test your critical thinking skills with the content in this chapter.

Lab 9.44 *Password parameters*

Two of your coworkers are having a disagreement. They want to roll out a new password policy to the network, but can't determine the parameters the users should use for their passwords. What would you recommend?

Lab 9.45 *Configuring filters*

Your company wants to use PPTP and has established a PPTP Call filter. However, PPTP still does not work. What mistake was made?

Lab 9.46 *Restricting protocol access*

Your company does not want any users to have access to IRC, RealAudio, and a number of other Winsock protocols. The administrators, however, should have access to all Winsock protocols. How would you configure this?

Lab 9.47 *Restricting anonymous access*

Your company does not want anyone to be able to use the Web Proxy Service via an anonymous account. What steps can you take to disable this account?

Lab 9.48 *Windows NT Security parameters*

Your company has asked you to recommend a set of Windows NT Security parameters. What are some of issues you should discuss to implement an effective security policy?

Hands-on Labs

The Hands-on Labs give you an opportunity to practice skills you have learned in this chapter. Make sure you read the system requirements for each lab to be certain you have the correct configuration before beginning the lab.

Lab 9.49 *Configuring a domain filter*

In this lab, you will configure a domain filter.

1. On the Proxy Server computer, click Start ⇛ Programs ⇛ Proxy Server ⇛ Microsoft Management Console.
2. The Console opens. Expand the Internet Information Server folder and the Proxy Server computer. Right-click Web Proxy and select Properties.
3. The Properties sheet appears. Click the Security button on the Service tab.
4. The Security properties window appears. Click the Domain Filters tab.
5. Click the Enable filtering checkbox at the top of the tab.
6. The Granted radio button is selected by default. This means users have access to all Internet sites.
7. To create an exception, click the Add button.
8. The Deny Access To dialog box appears. Click the Domain radio button. The domain box becomes active.

9. In the domain box, type **`http://www.infoseek.com`** and click OK. Now `infoseek.com` is denied access.
10. From a client computer, use a browser to try to connect to `www.infoseek.com` through the Proxy Server. What happens?
11. Once you have tested the filter, you can remove it by selecting the filter in the exception list and clicking the Remove button. Now users can once again access `infoseek.com`.

Lab 9.50 *Configuring a predefined packet filter*

In this lab, you will configure a predefined packet filter.

1. On the Proxy Server computer, click Start ⇒ Programs ⇒ Proxy Server ⇒ Microsoft Management Console.
2. The Console opens. Expand the Internet Information Server folder and the Proxy Server computer. Right-click Web Proxy and select Properties.
3. The Properties sheet appears. Click the Security button on the Service tab.
4. The Security properties window appears. Click the Packet Filters tab.
5. Click the Enable packet filtering on external interface checkbox. The rest of the screen becomes active.
6. To add a predefined filter, click the Add button.
7. The Packet Filter Properties sheet appears. At the top of the screen, click the Predefined filter radio button. The drop-down menu becomes active.
8. Click the drop-down menu and select SMTP, then click OK.
9. The TCP SMTP filter is added to the exception list.

Lab 9.51 *Configuring packet filter alerting and logging*

In this lab, you will configure packet filter alerts and logs.

1. Open the Internet Service Manager and click the Security button found on the Service tab.
2. The Security sheet appears. Click the Alerting tab.
3. In the Event dialog box, you have the option to generate alerts for rejected packets, protocol violations, or a disk full warning. Select Rejected Packets.
4. Alerts are generated by default is if there are at least 20 events per second. Accept the default.

5. You can choose to write the alerts to the Windows NT Event Log, which is selected by default, but you can also have the system send you SMTP mail. If you select this option, click the Configure Mail button and enter the name of the mail server and your mail address.
6. Click the logging tab. Generally, you want to accept the defaults of enable "regular" logging, but you can change this to verbose if you choose. Also, you may choose to log to a SQL/ODBC-compliant database as well.

CHAPTER

10

Caching with Proxy Server

About Chapter 10

This chapter explores the caching features of Microsoft Proxy Server 2.0. In this chapter, you learn how to configure passive and active caching, how to manipulate and change cache drives, and how to configure cache filters to customize your caching needs. This chapter contains five labs to practice the skills you learn.

How Caching Works

I introduced caching in previous chapters. Aside from Proxy Server's firewall capabilities, Proxy Server also provides complex caching features. The combination of Proxy Server 2.0's firewall and caching capabilities is why Proxy Server is a hybrid product. Firewalls and proxy servers were originally available as separate products until Microsoft meshed the two together. The result is a product that provides both a high level of security against attacks from the Internet and effective caching features.

The purpose of caching is performance. The Proxy Server can *cache*, or temporarily store, Internet objects so the objects are served to the clients from the cache instead of being retrieved from the Internet. This process is transparent to the client who requests objects through a browser as though directly connected. The result is the objects are quickly returned to the client.

When a client first requests an Internet object, Proxy Server will check its cache. If the object is current and resides in the cache, the object is returned to the client from the cache, as shown in Figure 10-1.

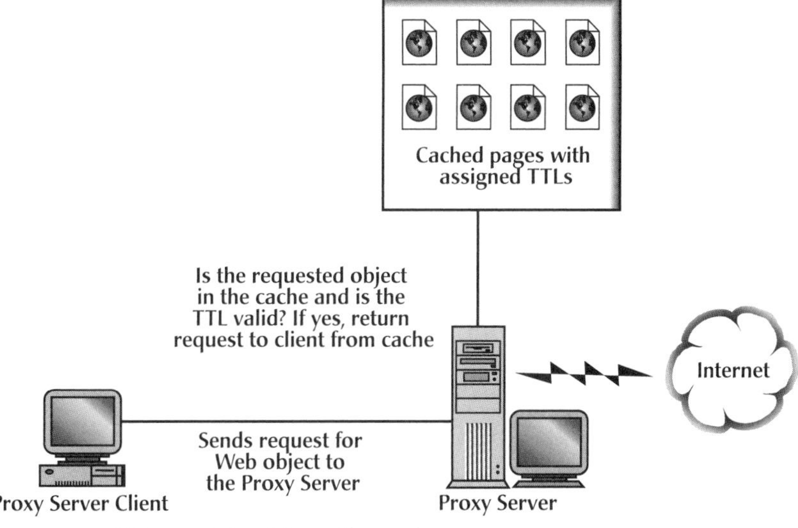

FIGURE 10-1 Object retrieval from the cache

If the object is not in the cache, Proxy Server retrieves the object from the Internet, places it in the cache, then serves the object to the client, as shown in Figure 10-2.

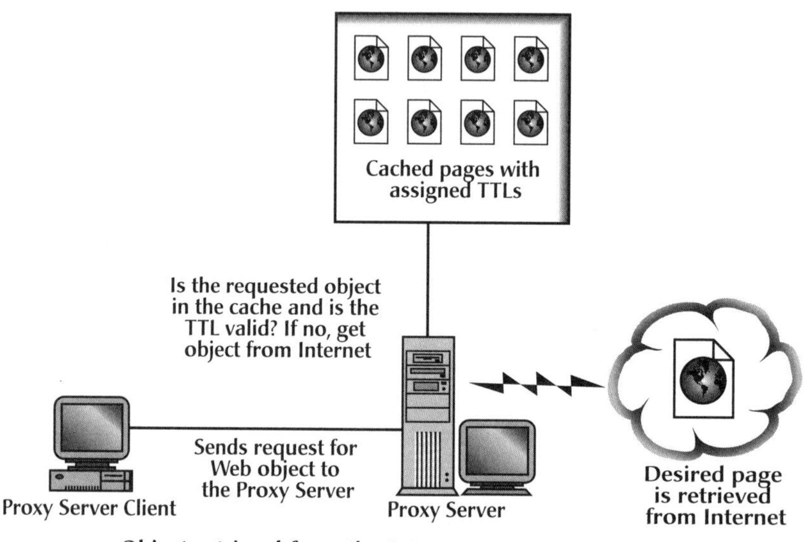

FIGURE 10-2 Object retrieval from the Internet

Through this caching model, LAN and WAN environments can provide fast and effective Internet service for clients.

What Can Be Cached?

Any HTTP or FTP objects, as well as any Uniform Resource Locator (URL), can be cached. Any object associated with a URL can be cached as well. However, some Internet objects, due to their nature, simply cannot be stored in the cache properly. Objects that are dynamically generated using input from the user do not function in the cache. These objects require processing by the server that hosts the object and cannot be provided from the Proxy Server while the object is stored in the cache. URLs or other HTTP objects that require user authentication or SSL also will not function in the cache.

Proxy Server uses a set of criteria to determine if an object can be cached. The Internet object must meet the following criteria:

- The request must be a `GET` command.
- There must be no basic keyword logons.
- The HTTP response header must not include the following commands:
  - WWW-Authenticate
  - Pragma: No-cache
  - Cache-control: Private
  - Cache-control: No-cache
  - Set-cookie
- The date in the Expires header field must be later than the date in the Date header field.
- The HTTP result code must be `success`.
- The object must be encrypted or sent via SSL.
- There can be no Authorization header in the HTTP request header.

If the object meets these criteria, the object can be stored in the Proxy Server cache. If not, the object is retrieved from the Internet directly each time a client request is made.

Passive and Active Caching

I introduced the concept of passive and active caching earlier in this book. With passive caching, each cached object is assigned a TTL. When a request for an object is made, the cache is checked for the object using the `Urlcache.dll`. If the TTL has expired, Proxy Server uses the RetrieveUrlFile API to get the object from the cache.

If the object's TTL has expired, Proxy Server checks the object on the Internet. If the object has changed, Proxy Server recaches the object using the CreateUrlFile API and returns the object to the client. If it has not changed, Proxy Server updates the TTL and returns the object to the client from the cache.

If the object is not in the cache, Proxy Server checks the Internet to see if the object is available and if it can be cached. If it is available and can be cached, Proxy Server caches the object and returns it to the client. If it cannot be cached, it returns the object directly to the client.

Active caching works with passive caching and can be thought of as an additional set of rules for passive caching. The main difference between active and passive caching is Proxy Server's role. In passive caching, Proxy Server's caching functions are dependant on requests made by the client — Proxy Server is reactive in passive caching. In active caching, Proxy Server does not have to wait for client requests to manipulate and update the cache — Proxy Server is proactive in active caching.

In active caching, Proxy Server takes on a managerial role concerning the cache. Without prompting from clients, the Proxy Server can examine TTLs, update changed objects, extend TTLs, and remove old items from the cache. The Proxy Server makes decisions for the cached objects based on three qualities:

- **Popularity:** Based on the number of client requests for the particular object, Proxy Server determines the "popularity" of an object. Proxy Server keeps the most popular objects regularly updated and constantly available to clients from the cache.
- **TTL:** Proxy Server automatically checks TTLs that are close to expiration and determines whether to update the TTL or remove the object.
- **Server load:** During low-traffic times, Proxy Server performs more active caching processes than when Proxy traffic is high.

You can learn more about caching architecture in Chapter 6.

Passive and Active Caching Configuration

Configuration options for passive and active caching are available on the Caching tab of the Web Proxy Properties screen, as shown in Figure 10-3.

As you can see in Figure 10-3, you have the option to enable caching, which is passive, and the option to enable active caching by using the two checkboxes. Beneath each checkbox, you have three radio buttons to configure how you want Proxy Server to handle passive and active caching. This seems simple enough, but the radio button selections are often a point of confusion.

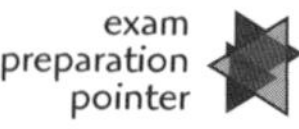

You will see several questions on the exam concerning these radio buttons. Study the following section carefully!

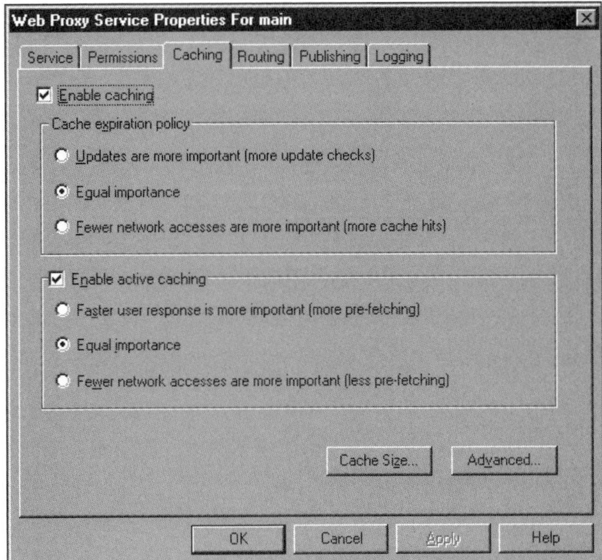

FIGURE 10-3 Caching tab of Web Proxy Properties

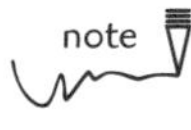

No controls on the Caching tab are available unless at least one drive on the Proxy Server is formatted with NTFS for caching, which you configured during setup. Also, see the next section, "Configuring Cache Drives" for additional information.

In the cache expiration policy section, which applies to passive caching, you have three configuration options:

- **Updates are more important (more update checks)**: This option causes the Proxy Server to perform more update checks to make certain the most current object is available in the cache. You would use this option if the most current data from the Internet is required; however, this option generates more Internet traffic. The Proxy Server checks the cache objects for freshness more often with this option selected.
- **Equal importance:** This option strikes a balance between freshness and best cache performance. Objects are not updated as frequently as the first option, but Internet traffic is reduced and clients experience better cache return. If Internet objects do not need to be the most current to service the needs of your organization, the Equal importance option should be selected. This option is enabled by default.

- **Fewer network accesses are more important (more cache hits):** This option provides the best user response since objects are served from the cache more frequently; however, objects are updated the least using this option. If your network tends to use static URLs and Web objects that seldom change, this would be your best option. The objects are served from the cache and updated the least using this option.

Active caching builds on these three configuration options and adds the following three additional options for active caching:

- **Faster user response is more important (more pre-fetching):** This option provides the best cache performance because Proxy Server will extensively seek to update and refresh the cache. This provides the freshest cache objects, but generates the most Internet traffic as Proxy Server constantly updates the cache.
- **Equal importance:** Once again, equal importance is the default in the active caching section as well. This option strikes a balance between the freshest cache data and the best cache performance.
- **Fewer network accesses are more important (less pre-fetching):** This option causes Proxy Server to use the least amount of pre-fetching to update cache objects. This option causes the least amount of Internet traffic, but provides older cache data instead of the most current copy from the Internet.

Configuring Cache Drives

Cache drives are configured and established during Proxy Server setup. However, with changing network needs, it is not uncommon to have to reconfigure cache parameters from time to time. Proxy Server provides an easy method of reconfiguring cache drives through the Internet Service Manager.

By accessing the Cache tab in the Web Proxy Service, you will see the main caching screen. If you click the Cache Size button, you will see the cache configuration screen that you saw during Proxy Server installation, as shown in Figure 10-4.

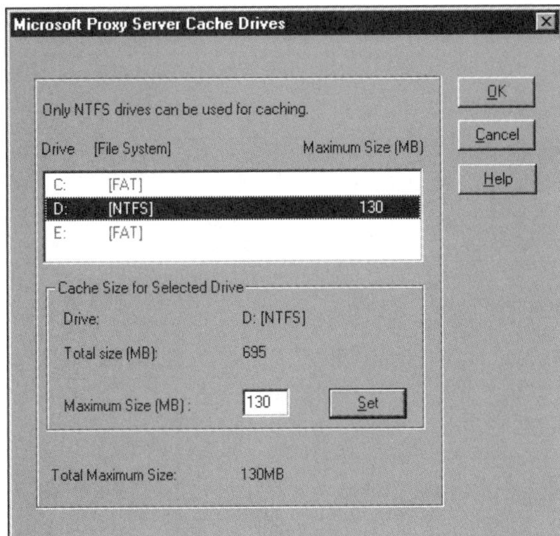

FIGURE 10-4 Proxy Server Cache Drives dialog box

At any time during Proxy Server operation, you can add new cache drives or adjust the size of the cache drive as needed.

Remember, any drive used for caching must formatted with NTFS. Proxy Server 2.0 does not use FAT drives for caching.

Use caution before lowering the size of the cache drive. Some of the cache data may be lost. If you increase the size of a current cache drive, there is no effect on the cache data.

The screen gives the size (in megabytes) of the drive itself, and you are able to configure the size of the cache by entering the amount, in megabytes, in the dialog box and clicking the Set button.

Advanced Cache Configuration

The Advanced Cache Policy options makes it possible for you to define what Internet objects and URLs are added to the cache. To configure the advanced cache policy, click the Advanced button on the Caching tab of the Web Proxy Service properties page, which brings up the Advanced Cache Policy dialog box shown in Figure 10-5.

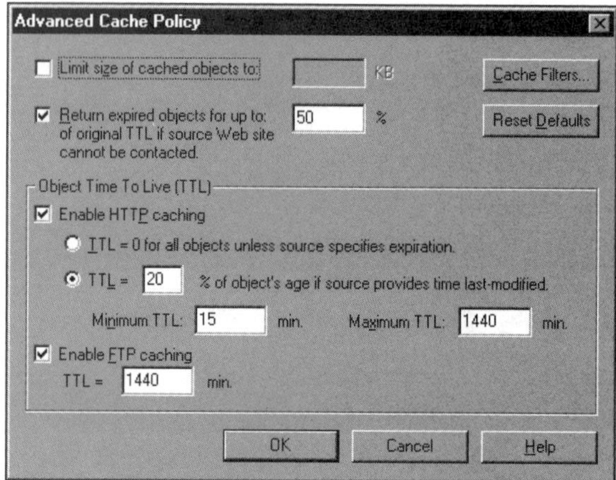

FIGURE 10-5 Advanced Cache Policy dialog box

Cache Size and TTL Policies

You have a number of configuration options in the Advanced Cache Policy screen. First, as you can see at the top of the screen in Figure10-5, you can choose a limit for the size of cached objects. By default, this option is not enabled, which means there is no size limit for cache objects. If you choose to limit the size of cache objects, click the checkbox and enter an amount (in kilobytes) to limit the size.

It is usually better to leave the default open so there are no size restrictions on cached objects. Configuring a cached object restriction to 2MB or less may limit your caching performance, depending on the kind of objects your environment normally caches.

With the next option, you determine whether Proxy Server returns an expired object to the clients if the Web server that hosts those objects becomes unavailable. This option is useful if an Internet site should go down. Even though the object has expired in the cache, it can still be served to the client while waiting for the Internet site to come back online. The default percentage is 50 percent. This amount makes it possible for Proxy Server to use half of the object's original TTL once it has expired in order to continue serving the object to the client. If you would rather Proxy Server to not provide expired objects, uncheck this option.

The client will receive no data until the Internet site comes back online. You can also change the percentage of the TTL that Proxy Server can use to serve expired objects.

The second half of the Advanced Cache Policy screen is where you configure Object Time To Live (TTL). This configuration determines how long an Internet object lives in the cache before it is updated. As you can imagine, the configuration options here affect passive and active caching greatly. The shorter a TTL, the more work Proxy Server has to do to keep the object current and available from the cache.

As you can see in Figure 10-5, HTTP caching and FTP caching are enabled by default and have default values. You should keep both HTTP and FTP caching available. By unchecking the Enable HTTP caching checkbox, you basically cripple the caching functions of Proxy Server, since most cached objects are HTTP-based.

To configure HTTP caching, you have two options. You can select a TTL that equals zero for all objects unless the object's source specifies an expiration time. This option is not selected by default and is not an option you would normally want to use. It causes objects to have a TTL of zero, with the exception of objects that are configured by the source for a TTL. Basically, with this option, objects that do not have a preconfigured TTL are not cached.

With the second option, you specify the TTL by a percentage of the object's age if the source provides the time it was last modified. In essence, you set a time span between object updates. The lower the percentage, the more frequently the object is updated. The default for this option is 20 percent.

You can also configure a minimum TTL and a maximum TTL in minutes, as shown in Figure 10-5. The default minimum time is 15 minutes and the default maximum time is 1,440 minutes (24 hours). Again, the way you choose to configure this determines how long an object can live in the cache before it is updated. The default settings provide optimal performance, so make sure you have a specific reason before altering the TTL.

Finally, you can specify the TTL for FTP objects by entering an amount in minutes in the dialog box. The default is 1,440 minutes.

Cache Filters

Cache filters give you the ability to specify particular sites and pages within a site that you want Proxy Server to cache or not cache. This feature is useful if a company uses a handful of Internet sites everyday. The cache filter can be created to make certain caching for those sites is performed in a manner that speeds service to the clients.

To access the Cache Filters page, click the Cache Filters button on the Advanced Cache Policy Page, as shown in Figure 10-6.

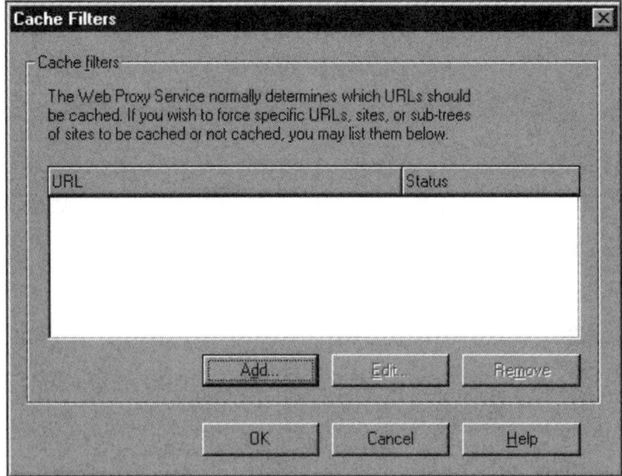

FIGURE 10-6 Cache Filters dialog box

Using the Cache Filters page, you can force which URLs are cached and how they are cached. This page overrides Proxy Server's normal caching configuration in the Web Proxy Service. You can add filters by clicking the Add button, which takes you to the Cache Filter Properties screen, as shown in Figure 10-7.

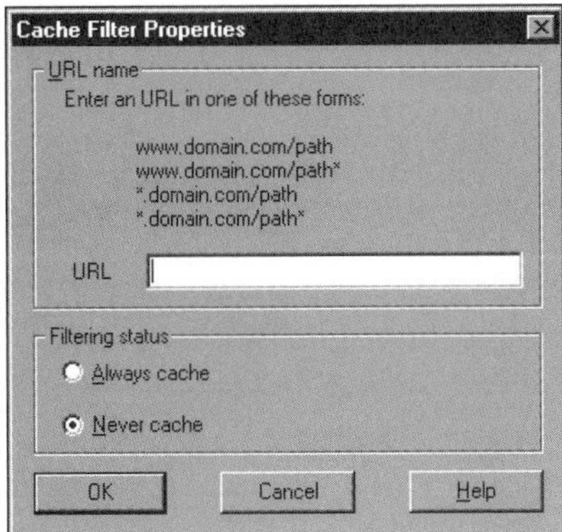

FIGURE 10-7 Cache Filter Properties dialog box

Notice in Figure 10-7 that you are asked to enter a URL in a particular form. The cache filters use an asterisk (*) to signify a wildcard. The following sections explain each of the wildcard functions.

You will see several questions asking you how to use the wildcard feature to configure a cache filter. You should memorize the following sections for the exam.

www.domain.com/path

This option allows you to specify a certain location in a particular domain. For example, if you always wanted to cache `www.idgbooks.com/mismt`, you would enter the URL and path in the URL dialog box and click the Always cache button, as shown in Figure 10-8.

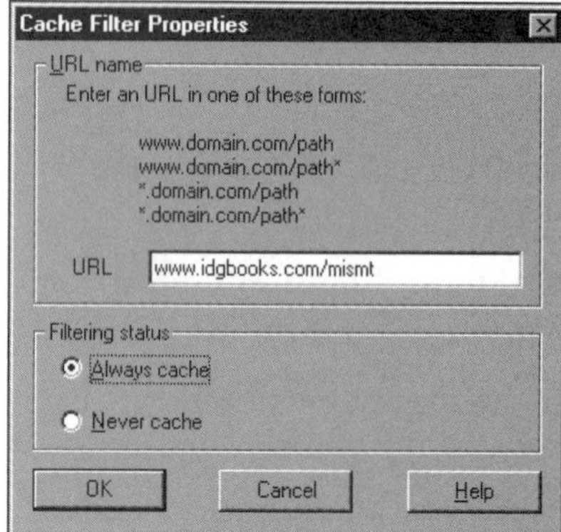

FIGURE 10-8 Specific domain and path caching

This specific domain and path option enables you to always cache a particularly favorite page on a Web site, or you can choose to never cache that particular page, by clicking the Never cache button. This is useful if a certain page changes constantly and you want the most current page returned to the clients from the Internet.

*www.domain.com/path**

The next option you have is a domain and a path with a wildcard option. This function allows you to select a certain domain and path as well as every page that is a subset of that path. For example, if you wanted to cache `www.idgbooks.com/mismt` and every page following the `/mismt` path, you would use the `/mismt*` wildcard, as shown in Figure 10-9.

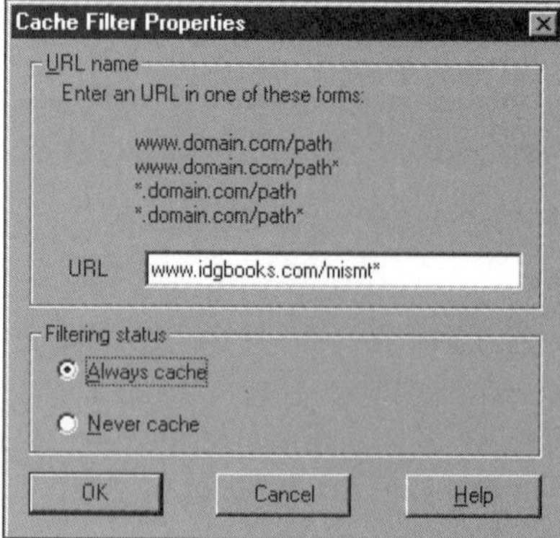

FIGURE 10-9 Domain and path wildcard caching

Once you use the wildcard, any page following /mismt is cached as well. Figure 10-10 shows you the actual page. Once a user requests this page, the page is forced into the cache because of the cache filter that has been created.

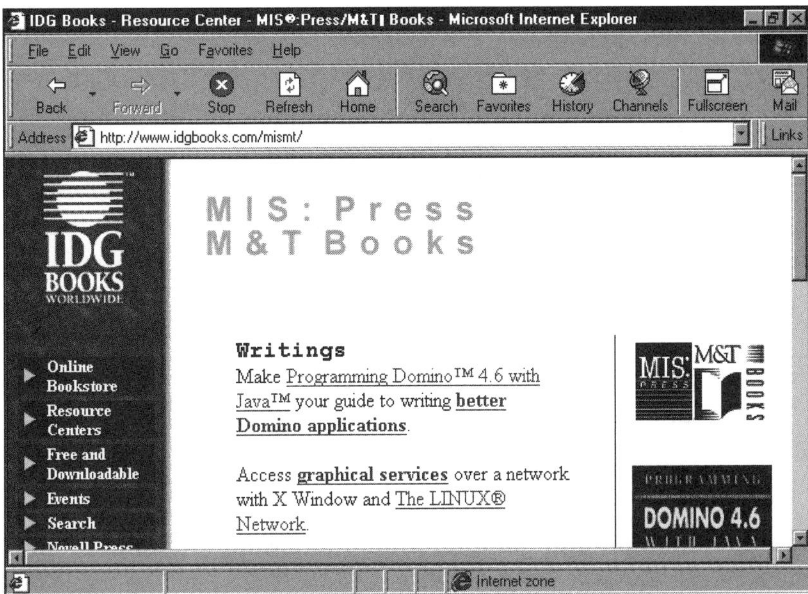

FIGURE 10-10 www.idgbooks.com/mismt

If a user clicks on one of the links within the /mismt path, that page will be forced into the cache because of the wildcard character.

*domain.com/path

With this option, you can wildcard the beginning extension of the domain and path. By using this option, you can cache or never cache any beginning extension of that particular domain and path. By using this option, you are able to specify www, ftp, mail, and other options, as shown in Figure10-11.

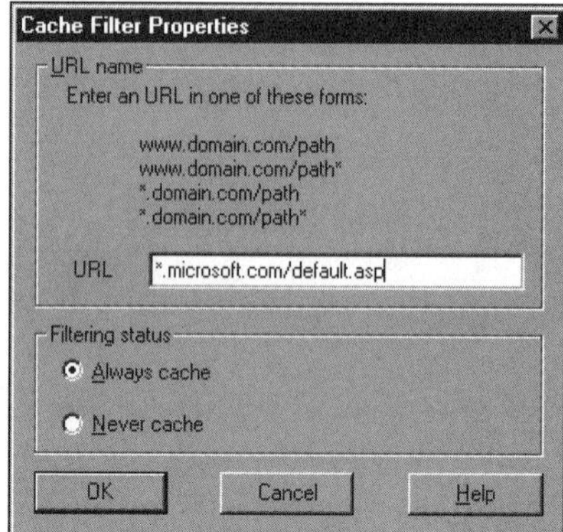

FIGURE 10-11 Wildcard domain and path extension

With this wildcard, any site at `microsoft.com/default.asp`, whether it be www of ftp, will be cached. As with the other options, you can choose the Never cache option.

.domain.com/path

This option provides the same functionality as the previous wildcard, but an additional wildcard is added to path. This way, anything under the path is affected by the additional wildcard as well as the extension wildcard, as shown in Figure 10-12.

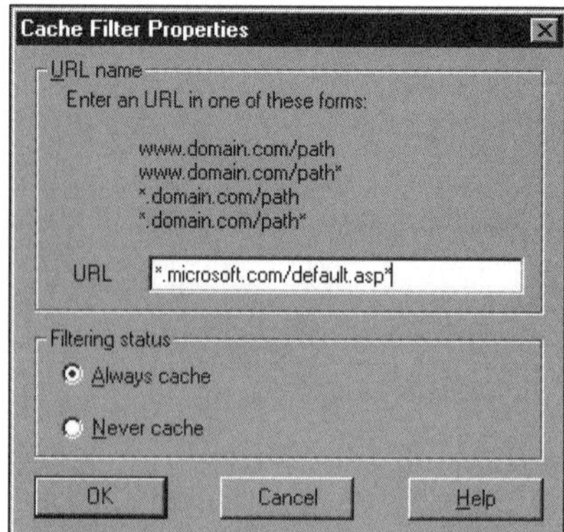

FIGURE 10-12 Domain and path wildcards

Once you create the cache filters you desire, each filter is added to the list in the Cache Filters dialog box, as shown in Figure 10-13. Note that you can create filters for other domains, such as .edu, .gov, .mil, and so forth. For each filter created, you have the option of always caching the filter or never caching the filter.

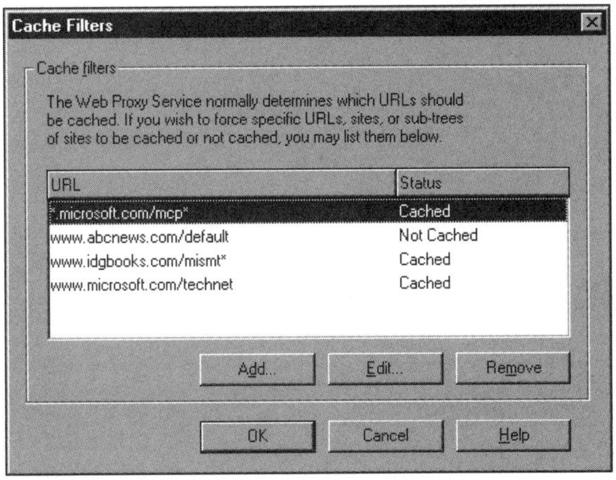

FIGURE 10-13 Cache Filters list

Once you have created the cache filters, you can modify or remove them at any time using the Edit or Remove buttons.

Cache Filter Exceptions

Cache filters can also be used to create exception policies. This approach is useful if you do not want to cache a site in general, but do want to cache a certain page or pages under a certain path, or vice versa.

To create an exception, you perform the same steps used to create the filters. For example, if you never wanted to cache information from `www.microsoft.com/mcp`, you would create a wildcard filter as `www.microsoft.com/mcp*`. This action would not cache `/mcp` or any pages under the `/mcp` tree. However, you can create an exception to this. If you wanted to cache `www.microsoft.com/mcp/certsteps/steps.htm`, you could create a filter to always cache it. This creates an exception to the earlier wildcard.

You can also use a wildcard in an exception. If you wanted to cache any pages under `/steps.htm`, you would add the wildcard character `/steps.htm*`. This action will cache `/steps.htm` and pages under that path. When you create an exception, the exceptions will appear as normal cache filters in the Cache Filters page, as shown in Figure 10-14.

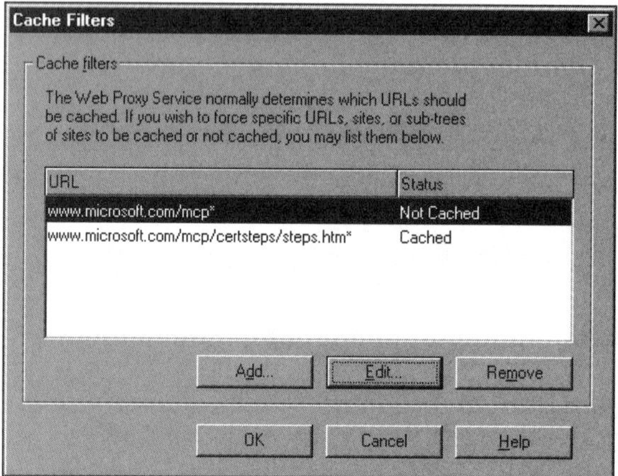

FIGURE 10-14 Cache Filter exception

Exam Preparation Summary

Because caching is one Proxy Server's main functions, you can expect a number of exam questions to focus on this issue. The exam questions will focus on two major areas of caching: passive and active caching configuration and the configuration of cache filters.

You need to know the difference between the more cache hits, more prefetching, and the other options that you can configure. You have six radio buttons to select from; three for passive caching and three for active caching. You should expect the exam to mix questions about these options together in a confusing manner, so it's important you have a clear understanding of the configuration options in order to answer those questions correctly.

You will have a number of questions concerning cache filtering. These questions will often give you a scenario with a desired outcome and ask you how to configure a cache filter to meet those results. These questions are generally easy, but you do have to know how to use the wildcard character to configure the cache filters.

Key Point Summary

This chapter explored the caching configuration options available in Proxy Server.

- Passive caching responds to client requests and caches Internet objects by assigning a TTL.
- Active caching enables Proxy Server to update TTLs based on an object's popularity, TTL, and the server load.
- Most Internet objects can be cached. The exceptions are generally dynamic objects and objects that require authentication.
- Cache drives can be altered at any time, or additional cache drives can be added as necessary through the Caching tab of the Internet Service Manager.

Applying What You've Learned

The following review questions give you a chance to test your knowledge of the content in this chapter. Should you miss some, review the appropriate portions of the chapter. The answers to the Instant Assessment questions can be found in Appendix C.

Instant Assessment

1. What kind of caching enables Proxy Server to automatically update cache items?

A. Passive

B. Active

C. Reactive

D. Proxy Server cannot do this.

2. What does the Cache Size button on the Caching Tab enable you to do?
   - **A.** Reconfigure cache filters
   - **B.** Reconfigure cache policies
   - **C.** Reconfigure cache drives
   - **D.** Set the URL TTL
3. What is one of the main factors Proxy Server uses to determine updating of TTLs in active caching?
   - **A.** Object size
   - **B.** Object popularity
   - **C.** Object location
   - **D.** Object protocol type
4. What is default maximum TTL (in minutes)?
   - **A.** 15
   - **B.** 60
   - **C.** 870
   - **D.** 1,440
5. Which passive caching option would you use to enable Proxy Server to perform the most update checks?
   - **A.** Updates are more important
   - **B.** Equal
   - **C.** Fewer network accesses are more important
   - **D.** This cannot be done.
6. What does the more pre-fetching option in active caching mean?
   - **A.** Objects are pre-fetched and updated often.
   - **B.** Objects are not updated until requests are made by clients.
   - **C.** Objects are updated at equal intervals.
   - **D.** This is not an active caching option.

7. What would happen if you use the cache filter `www.microsoft.com/mcp` set to always cache?

   A. Everything at microsoft.com would be cached.

   B. Nothing at `microsoft.com` would be cached.

   C. Only the domain and path would be cached.

   D. The domain, path and all subtrees would be cached.

8. What would happen if you use the cache filter `www.microsoft.com/mcp*` set to always cache?

   A. Everything at `microsoft.com` would be cached.

   B. Nothing at `microsoft.com` would be cached.

   C. Only the domain and path would be cached.

   D. The domain, path and all subtrees would be cached.

9. What would happen if you use the cache filter `*.microsoft.com/mcp`?

   A. Everything at `microsoft.com` would be cached.

   B. Nothing at `microsoft.com` would be cached.

   C. Only the domain and path would be cached if www was used.

   D. Any domain and path would be cached, including www, ftp, and so forth.

10. What is meant by the concept of cache filter exception?

   A. An exception is made to another cache filter.

   B. An exception is made to all cache filters.

   C. An exception is made to particular user.

   D. An exception is made to a particular group.

Critical Thinking Labs

These labs present you with analysis problems to test your critical thinking skills with the content in this chapter.

Lab 10.52 *Active caching*

You have been asked to explain how Proxy Server uses active caching. How would you explain active caching and the configuration options?

Lab 10.53 *Cache filters*

You have been asked to configure Proxy Server so that it never caches `www.infoseek.com` or any of its subtrees. How would you configure the filter?

Lab 10.54 *Cache filter exceptions*

Your company has the cache filter `www.microsoft.com/default.asp*` set to Always cache. However, you company would like to never cache `www.microsoft.com/technet`. Is it possible to configure this exception, and if so, how?

Hands-on Labs

The Hands-on Labs give you an opportunity to practice skills you have learned in this chapter. Make sure you read the system requirements for each lab to be certain you have the correct configuration before beginning the lab.

Lab 10.55 *Creating a cache filter*

In this lab you will create an Always cache filter for `www.microsoft.com/mcp` and all of the path's subtrees.

1. To create a cache filter, click Start ⇛ Programs ⇛ Proxy Server ⇛ Microsoft Management Console.
2. The Internet Service Manager appears. Expand the Internet Information Server folder and expand the name of the Proxy Server.
3. Right-click the Web Proxy icon and click Properties. The properties sheet appears.
4. Click the Caching tab. Make certain that both the Enable caching and Enable active caching checkboxes are selected.
5. Click the Advanced button. The Advanced Cache Policy screen appears.
6. Click the Cache Filters button. The Cache Filters screen appears.
7. Click the Add button. The Cache Filter Properties screen appears.
8. Since you want to create a cache filter for a domain, path, and all subtrees under that path, type **www.microsoft.com/mcp*** in the URL box.

9. Click the Always cache radio button and click OK.
10. The new filter appears in the filter list.

Lab 10.56 *Creating a cache filter exception*

In this lab, you will create an exception policy to the cache filter `www.idgbooks.com/default*`.

1. To create a cache filter, click Start ⇒ Programs ⇒ Proxy Server ⇒ Microsoft Management Console.
2. The Internet Service Manager appears. Expand the Internet Information Server folder and expand the name of the Proxy Server.
3. Right-click the Web Proxy icon and click Properties. The properties sheet appears.
4. Click the Caching tab. Make certain that both the Enable caching and Enable active caching checkboxes are selected.
5. Click the Advanced button. The Advanced Cache Policy screen appears.
6. Click the Cache Filters button. The Cache Filters screen appears.
7. Click the Add button. The Cache Filter Properties screen appears.
8. Since you want to create a cache filter for a domain, path, and all subtrees under that path, type **www.idgbooks.com/default*** in the URL box.
9. Click the Never cache radio button and click OK. Since you have used a wildcard character for the default page, no pages under `idgbooks.com` will be cached.
10. The new filter appears in the filter list.
11. To create an exception to the filter, click the Add button. This returns you tot he Cache Filter Properties page.
12. To create an exception that caches `www.idgbooks.com/mismt`, type **www.idgbooks.com/mismt** in the URL box and click the Always cache button. Click OK.
13. The exception appears in the filter list. This causes the `/mismt` page to always be cached.

CHAPTER

11

Proxy Server in the Enterprise

About Chapter 11

Previous chapters focus on the configuration of a single proxy server. Yet, many large environments use multiple proxy servers to achieve effective Internet connectivity and caching for all of their clients. This chapter explores the methods and configuration issues for using multiple Proxy Servers in a single LAN or WAN. This chapter covers Proxy arrays, Proxy chains, the Cache Array Routing Protocol, how to configure multiple proxy servers, and how to use reverse proxying and reverse hosting. There are several labs at the end of this chapter for you to practice the skills you learn.

THE MULTISERVER ENVIRONMENT

Like most Microsoft products, Proxy Server is scalable. It can work its magic in a small LAN, or on a WAN with thousands of users and with various configurations. Multiple Proxy Servers can work together, and Proxy Servers can work with other servers such as Web servers and Exchange Servers.

As a general rule of thumb, a single Proxy Server can handle about two thousand client computers, if there is not an overabundance of Internet traffic. However, for many large and complex environments, a single Proxy Server sitting between the LAN and the Internet just isn't enough.

Microsoft addresses this issue by enabling a LAN or WAN to use multiple Proxy Servers in the same environment. The multiple servers work together to achieve the common goals of Internet object service, protection, and high-speed caching.

Proxy Server Arrays

A Proxy Server *array* is method to connect multiple Proxy Server computers together to create distributed caching among the array members. This model enables the Proxy Servers in the array to create a logical cache among all servers, as shown in Figure 11-1.

Each server's cache is logically combined to create one large cache. To the user, this process is transparent, but Proxy Server arrays are able to provide superior performance in the following ways:

- **Caching Performance:** All array members keep their own array membership table and communicate with each other in a peer-to-peer fashion.
- **Load Balancing:** Each array member carries its share of the load. This keeps one array member from becoming overwhelmed with client requests.
- **Fault Tolerance:** If one of the array members should fail, the array can continue to function without that array member.
- **Administration:** Proxy Server computers in an array can be administered as one machine.

Because the array forms one distributed cache, client requests are routed within the array to the appropriate array member. This is done using the Cache Array Routing Protocol (CARP), which is explained further later in this chapter.

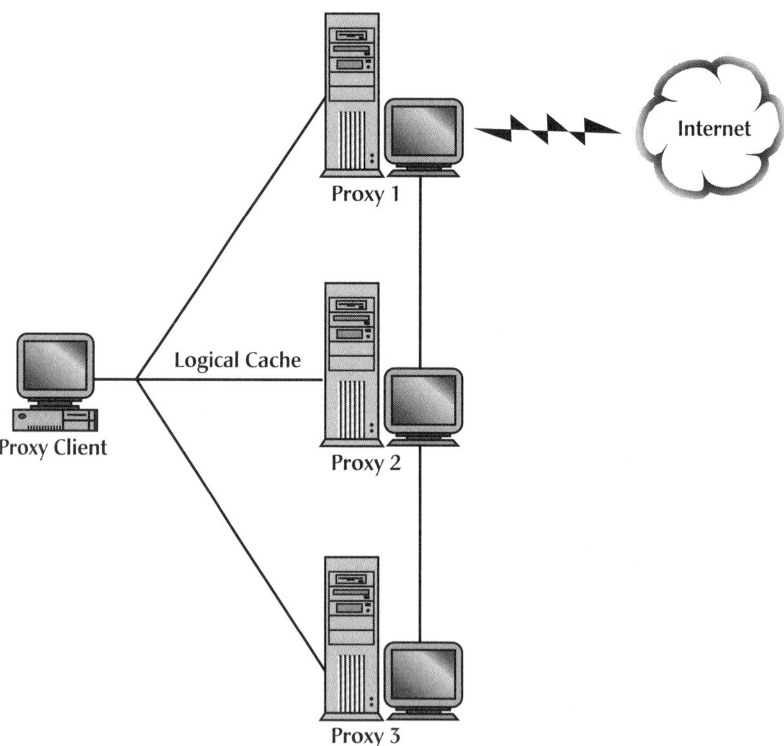

FIGURE 11-1 Proxy Server array

Proxy Server Chain

A *Proxy Server chain* is generally a WAN solution that links single Proxy Server computers or Proxy Server arrays in a chained method. This configuration provides a single Internet access point for a larger environment, as shown in Figure 11-2.

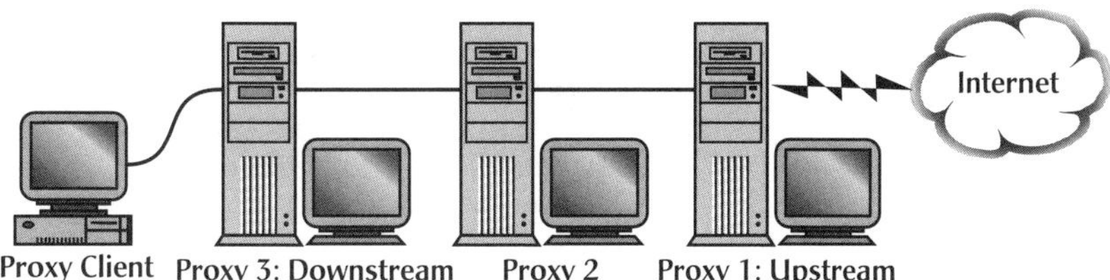

FIGURE 11-2 Proxy Server chain

This configuration is known as *hierarchical caching* because the computers communicate in an upstream method. The Proxy Server computer or Proxy Server array that connects to the Internet is known as the *upstream* computer, and the computer or array that is most far from the Internet, or closest to the clients, is known as the *downstream* server or array. Proxy chains enable you to chain LANs within a WAN environment together to provide better caching and load balancing. This way, traffic is balanced with all servers and arrays within a network, as shown in Figure 11-3.

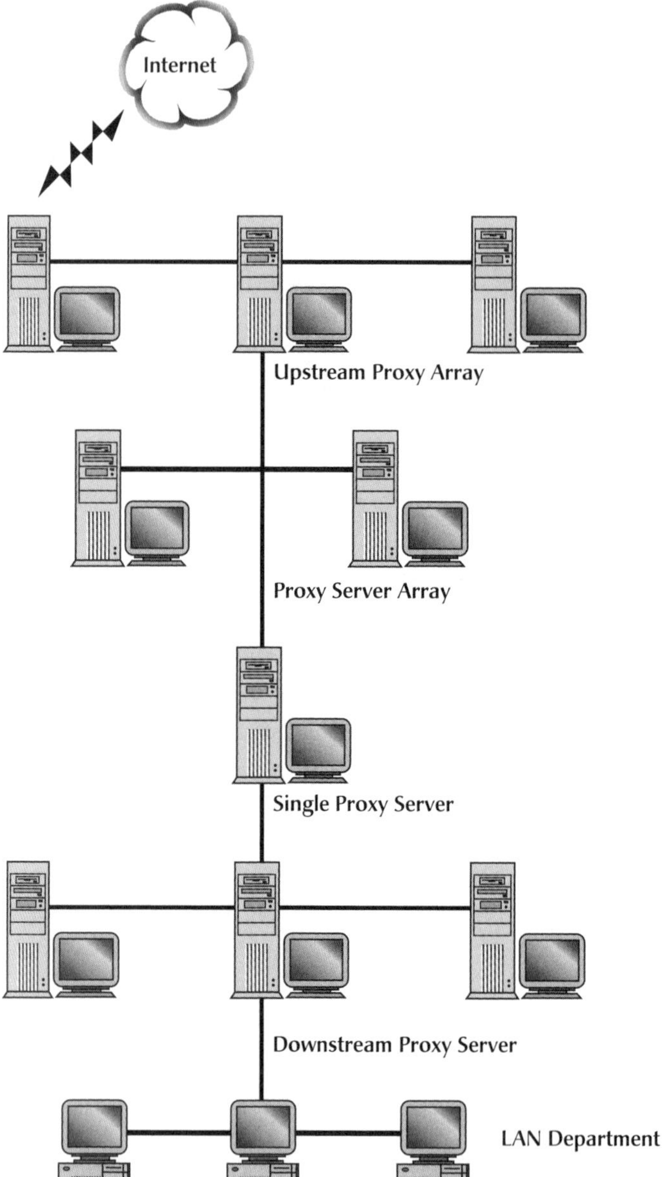

FIGURE 11-3 Single Proxy Servers and arrays in a chain

As within an array, the chain is transparent to the user. If the downstream computer or array cannot satisfy a request from its cache, the request is forwarded to the next chain member, and so on until the unsatisfied request is serviced by the upstream computer or array, or retrieved from the Internet.

Arrays can only be formed among computers running Proxy Server 2.0. However, chains can be formed with Proxy Server 2.0, Proxy Server 1.0, as well as third-party firewalls and proxy servers.

Cache Array Routing Protocol

Proxy servers in a chain are able to know where particular URLs are stored in arrays or single members within a chain through the Cache Array Routing Protocol (CARP). CARP was introduced as an answer to problems associated with Internet Cache Protocol (ICP) introduced in the mid-1990s.

ICP used a query method to find which server held a particular URL in its cache. This method created high amounts of query traffic in large environments, and wasn't particularly effective. In essence, each server was blind to what URLs the other servers held and could only find this information through a query.

CARP uses a mathematical formula called a *hash algorithm* to avoid this query process. This hash formula enables the Proxy Servers to calculate which server will store a particular URL and know exactly where each URL is stored. A hash uses two inputs to calculate the formula: the list of available servers, and the URL of the client request. The hash formula enables each Proxy Server computer that is a member of an array to know the location of the stored cache information within the logical array cache drive. Because of the hash, the Proxy servers within the array do not have to query each other for the location of a particular Internet object.

Each Proxy Server in the array has a hash number, and each URL has a hash number. The two numbers are combined to create a final hash. The server with the highest hash number stores that particular URL. This hash routine is repeated for each URL, so that URLs are stored evenly across the array members' cache drives. This creates a logical cache, because the array members know what is in the other array members' caches as well as what is in their own. Here's an example of how this works.

First, the array membership table is examined and a hash number for each array member is computed, as shown in Table 11-1.

TABLE 11-1 ARRAY MEMBER HASH CALCULATION.

ARRAY MEMBER	HASH CALCULATION
CorpProxy1	14
CorpProxy2	7
CorpProxy3	4

Second, a request URL is given a hash calculation by the routing algorithm. For example, suppose say `www.idgbooks.com` is given a hash of 24. The URL hash and the array member hashes are combined, as shown in Table 11-2.

TABLE 11-2 HASH COMPUTATION

ARRAY MEMBER	HASH	URL HASH	TOTAL
CorpProxy1	14	24	38
CorpProxy2	7	24	31
CorpProxy3	4	24	28

For the URL `www.idgbooks.com`, CorpProxy1 has the highest hash number, so CorpProxy1 will store this URL in its cache. The next URL to be cached will repeat this same process, but the routing algorithm will take into account each server's load factor when determining the hash. This way, the cache is load-balanced across each server. This process provides superior performance, is transparent to the client, and has the following features:

- **Logical single cache:** This feature enables the cache drives of the Proxy Server computers within the array to behave as one logical cache. Because CARP uses a hash to calculate URL location within the cache, there is no data repeated among the servers. This way, two servers don't have the same Internet data cached.
- **Dynamic configuration:** ICP was a manual protocol; it could not adapt to a changing environment. CARP, however, can adapt to changes within the

array. For example, if one array member should fail, CARP enables the redirection of requests and caching hash to account for the failed server.

- **Support for current browsers:** Today's browsers are a lot smarter than they were a few years ago. Most current browsers today are CARP aware. This means that the browser uses a Proxy AutoConfig File (PAC) to anticipate where cached data is stored and to attempt to retrieve data directly from that server in the array through one hop. If the browser is not capable of this, the Proxy Server will forward the request, which will be fulfilled with two hops.

You are expected to understand the concept of the hash algorithm on the exam, although you will not see complex questions about hashing.

You can view the membership table of any array member using a browser and typing the address `http://`*`servername`*`/array.dll?Get.Info.v1`. The information you will receive will look similar to the following:

```
Proxy Array Information / 1.0
ArrayEnabled: 1
ConfigID: 796254318
ArrayName: CorpArray
ListTTL: 2000
MAIN 10.0.0.4 80 http://MAIN:80/array.dll MSProxy /2.0 72456
 Up 100 150
CORPPROXY 10.0.0.8 80 http://CORPPROXY:80/array.dll MSProxy
 /2.0 72456 Up 100 200
```

The opening lines give you the array name and the array configuration IP. The lines explaining the server are described as follows:

- The Proxy array member's computer name.
- The Proxy array member's IP address.
- The TCP port number used for communication within the array. The default port is 80.
- The URL for `array.dll`.
- The version of Proxy Server the member is running.

- The amount of time in seconds the array member has been operational.
- The array member's state, displayed as either "up" or "down."
- The load factor of the member. The default is 100, and this number is used by the hashing algorithm to determine where Internet objects should be cached.
- The cache size of the array member, in megabytes.

You can also use the command line to view array information using the RemotMSP utility. You can execute the RemotMSP utility from the C:\MSP directory to access the switches available for the utility. If you want to view the status of a particular array member, the command line syntax is `RemotMSP status -member:proxyservername -V`. This will give you a command line version similar to using `http://servername/array.dll?Get.Info.v1`. RemotMSP provides a number of additional functions such as starting and stopping, status, synchronization, and backup and restore functions for remote management of Proxy Server arrays.

Configuring Arrays

An array can be configured by accessing the shared Service tab of either the Web, Winsock, or Socks Proxy Service properties sheets, as shown in Figure 11-4. When you click the Array button, the Array window opens, as shown in Figure 11-5.

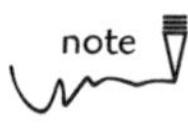

You should administer only one member of an array at a time so synchronization will perform correctly.

When joining an array, you can link two Proxy Server computers in an array, or you can simply join an array that currently exists. The controls in the Array window are rather easy and straightforward.

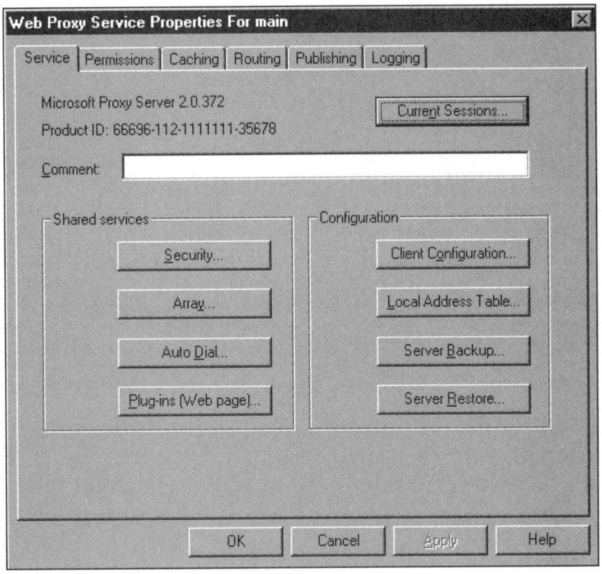

FIGURE 11-4 Shared Service tab

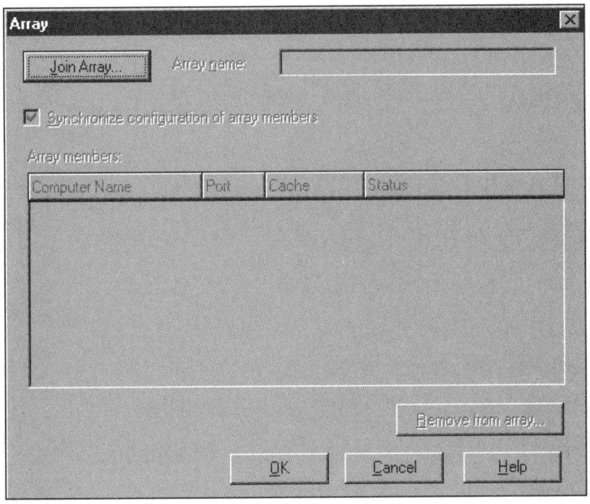

FIGURE 11-5 Array window

To join an array, click the Join Array button. A dialog box appears asking for the computer name to form an array with, as shown in Figure 11-6.

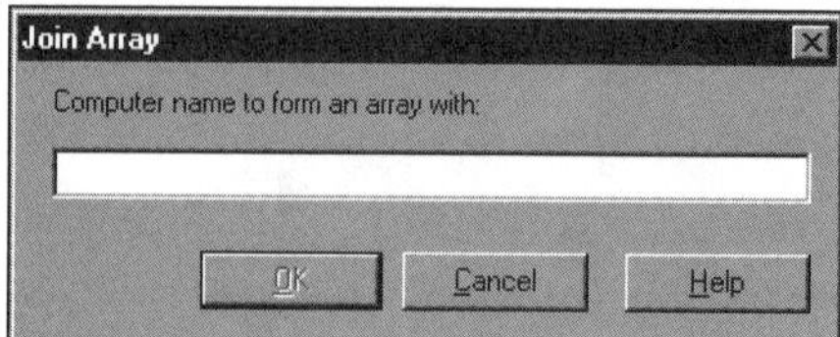

FIGURE 11-6 Join Array dialog box

If no current array exits, you see a New Array dialog box to name the new array. The new server(s) now appear in the Array dialog box. The Join Array button changes to Leave Array. If you choose to remove the local machine from the array, you can click this button to remove it. You will see a dialog box telling you the Proxy Server will become a stand-alone server.

As a security measure, you should use Windows NT Challenge/Response authentication when creating or modifying arrays. This action gives you additional protection from an unauthorized user creating or modifying a Proxy Server.

Load Balancing the Proxy Array

Once you have configured computers for array membership, there are a few other things you should do so the clients can properly use the Proxy array.

First, if your network uses DNS, you need to create an array CNAME in DNS that can resolve the names of the array members. This CNAME resource should include both the name of the array and each array member's unique IP address. This creates a *one point* of contact, as though the array were one machine. Downstream arrays, proxy servers, and clients can be configured to contact the array by the new DNS entry.

Because the DNS entry is be an alias that services an array of multiple computers, DNS resolves the requests in a round-robin fashion so each Proxy Server gets equal service and an equal workload.

You are likely to see a question about arrays and DNS. Remember that an array should have one alias name, but the unique IP address of each array member. This enables DNS to load balance by using a round-robin approach.

Second, if you are using Winsock clients for the Proxy server array, you need to add sections to the `Mspclnt.ini` file on the Proxy Server computer manually to tell the Winsock client which array member to use. This can be done using a text editor and inputting the correct Proxy Server information. This `Mspclnt.ini` file is copied to the clients so the changes will take effect.

Third, in a multisegment LAN or WAN environment that uses WINS, it's best to add a static multi-homed entry for each Proxy Server computer that you want to load balance. This helps avoid one server being inundated with requests while another is mostly idle. With the static WINS entry, the WINS server will attempt to provide the IP address of a Proxy Server that is on the same segment as the client. If this cannot be done, it will provide the IP address of a Proxy Server on the same network. If this fails as well, WINS will provide the IP address of any Proxy Server available. This method helps keep Proxy traffic local and evenly distributes the load of requests among the network.

Array Synchronization

When an array is configured, all members in the array share information with each other if synchronization is enabled. The array shares the following parameters:

- Domain Filters
- Web Proxy service protocol access control information
- Web Proxy service caching options
- Web Proxy service upstream routing options
- Reverse proxying information
- Winsock Proxy service protocol definition
- Winsock proxy service access control information
- Socks Proxy service permissions
- Logging configuration
- Packet filter alerting information
- LAT information
- Client configuration information

The following parameters are not replicated or shared in the array:

- Web Proxy service enable cache flag
- Web Proxy cache size

- Web Proxy cache disk location
- Web Proxy directory information
- Logging directories for each service
- Packet filters
- IIS WWW service password authentication settings

Any time additional changes are made to an array member, those changes are synchronized with the other array members. Any time an array member goes down, a message will appear in the Event Viewers of the other array members noting that a particular array member is down.

If you are making changes to an array member while another administrator is also making changes to an additional array member, and that administrator saves his or her changes before you, you will receive a message telling you your changes have not been applied. You have two options: refresh or overwrite. If you use the refresh option, all changes you made will be discarded. Microsoft recommends this option because it keeps your server synchronized with the rest of the array. If you choose overwrite, your changes will stay in place and be replicated across the array, which means that changes made by another administrator to another array member are overwritten. This creates a synchronization conflict.

Another possibility is your server detects the changes from another array member after your changes have been saved. This creates an Array Configuration Conflict message. If this happens, you can choose the synchronize now option, and choose an array member to synchronize with. This is the best option to restore a synchronized array. You can also click the Cancel button, which will keep the changes to your server, but not synchronize them with the array members.

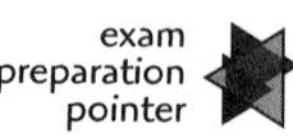

You are likely to see a question on the refresh or overwrite functions. Remember that to keep your changes intact, you have to choose the overwrite function, but this will overwrite the changes made by another administrator on another server.

The issue with multiple Proxy Servers in an array being administered at one time is a scheduling issue. In a network environment, you can avoid problems such as this by having a detailed maintenance schedule. This way, multiple administrators are not performing tasks that overlap or conflict with each other.

Routing

Routing within Proxy Server enables you to configure how your server communicates with other Proxy Servers or arrays within a chain. Essentially, routing tells the Proxy Server how to find its way to upstream connections or arrays. The routing algorithm automatically detects whether the Proxy Server computer in the upstream chain is online or not.

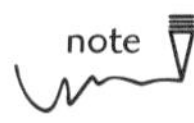

Upstream routing applies only to Web Proxy Service requests. Winsock and Socks requests do not support chained configurations.

Routing within multiserver environments can be configured from the Web Proxy Service by clicking the Routing tab, as shown in Figure 11-7.

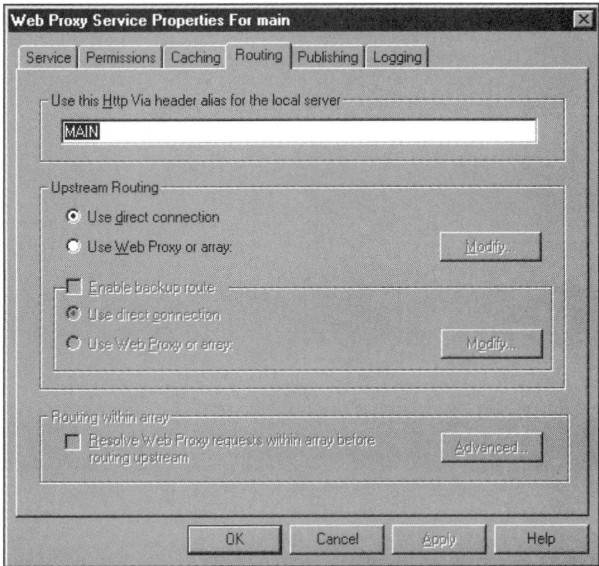

FIGURE 11-7 **Routing tab of the Web Proxy Service properties page**

The middle section of this tab enables you to configure either a direct connection to the Internet for the Web Proxy request, or to an array. The direct connection is selected by default, but if you want to use an array for upstream routing, click the second radio button and click the Modify button. This takes you to the Advanced Routing Options screen, as shown in Figure 11-8.

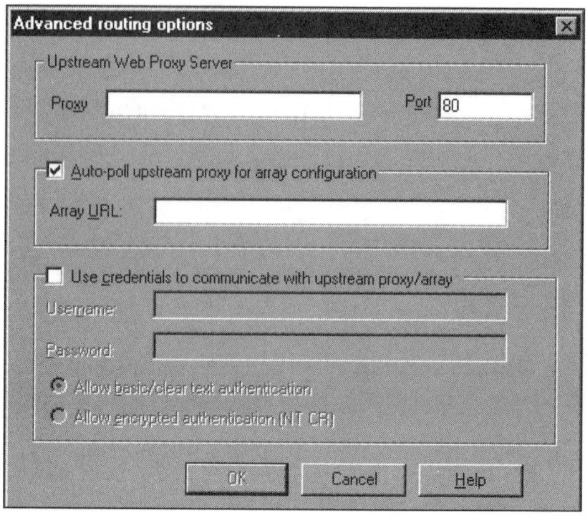

FIGURE 11-8 Advanced routing options

To use an array for upstream routing, type the name of the array in the Proxy dialog box and change the port if necessary (80 is the default). When you type the proxy array name, the Array URL in the Auto-poll upstream proxy for array configuration field is automatically entered as `http://`*`servername`*`:80/array.dll`, as shown in Figure 11-9.

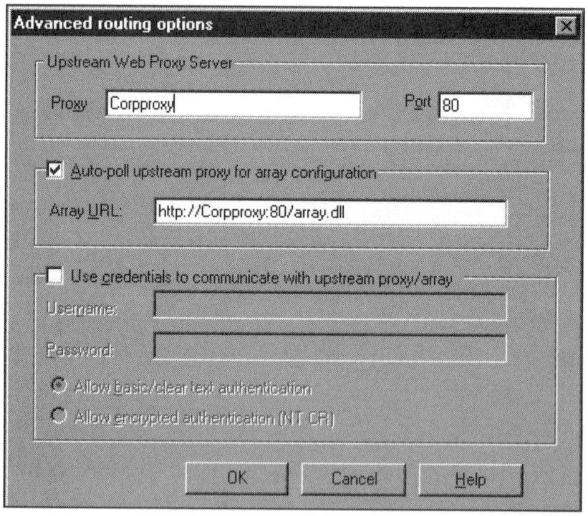

FIGURE 11-9 Configured Upstream Web Proxy Server

The auto-poll feature enables the server to automatically poll the upstream array to get the array configuration information. If you are using an array, you should keep this option selected so your server can get the appropriate configuration information for routing.

You also have the option to use logon credentials to communicate with the upstream server or array. This is an additional security measure for your network. To use this feature, click the Use credentials to communicate with upstream proxy/array checkbox. Then, enter a valid username and password. You can also select either basic/clear text authentication or NTCR, depending on the security parameters of your network. Figure 11-10 shows a configured credentials section.

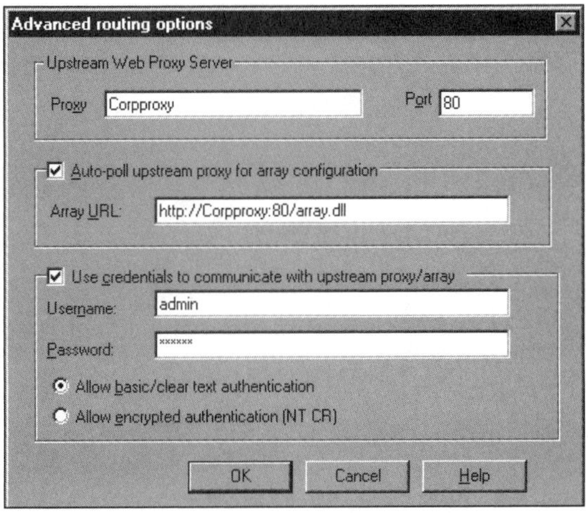

FIGURE 11-10 Configured routing credentials

Once you have made your entries in the Advanced Routing Options window, click OK to return to the Routing tab. You also have the option to configure a backup route should your main upstream route fail. If you check the Enable backup route checkbox, you can use a direct connection to the Internet to service the client request or configure an additional Proxy Server or array. This is useful in environments that have multiple routes and access points. Consider the diagram in Figure 11-11.

In this example, the WAN has two Internet access points, or two "upstream" arrays in two locations, Dallas and New York. A small office in Houston has been opened, and rather than provide a direct connection, the office is linked to Dallas as the primary route, because this is the closest city. However, the backup route can be to New York in case the Dallas site goes down. This helps provide continuous service to Houston.

You can configure the closest array for upstream service and use the other array as a backup route should the main array fail or be taken offline. The backup route operates exactly like the primary route and is fully functional. If the primary route fails, Proxy Server uses the backup route while continuing to query the primary route until it comes back online.

The last configuration option is for routing within an array. This checkbox is available on the Routing tab at the bottom of the screen. This configuration tells Proxy Server to attempt to service all Web Proxy requests from the array before routing the request upstream. As discussed in earlier sections, this is accomplished through CARP. Service from the array is limited to one hop before the request is passed upstream.

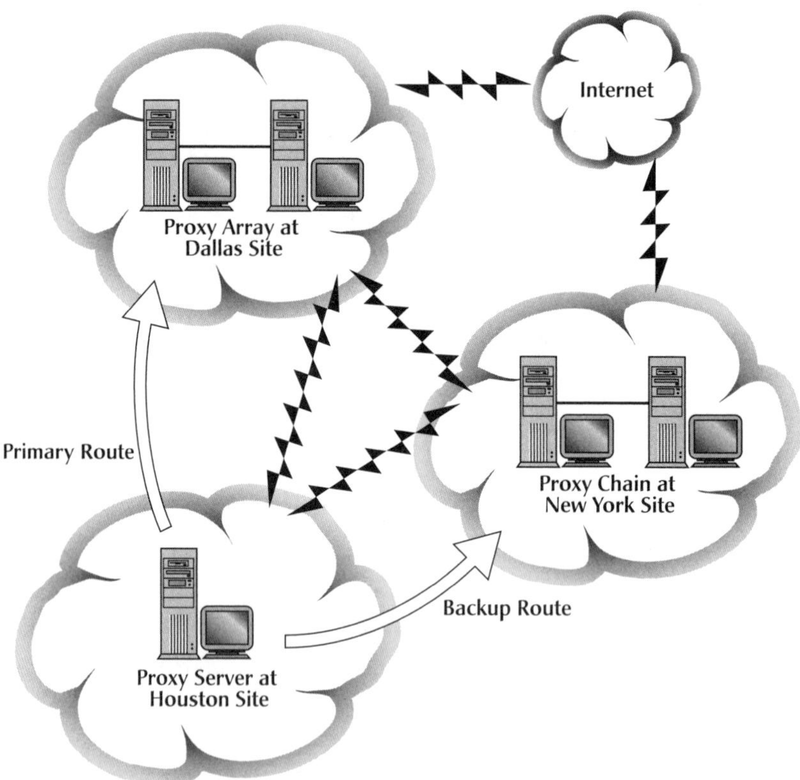

FIGURE 11-11 Multiple access point WAN

Server Proxying

Just as multiple Proxy Servers can work together, a single Proxy Server or a Proxy Server chain can function with other servers. Server proxying is the process of locating different servers behind the Proxy Server(s) so they are protected from the Internet, but are still provided with Internet communications. Common examples are a Web server or an Exchange Server. By using Server proxying, all inbound and outbound traffic to these servers is passed through the Proxy Server, as shown in Figure 11-12.

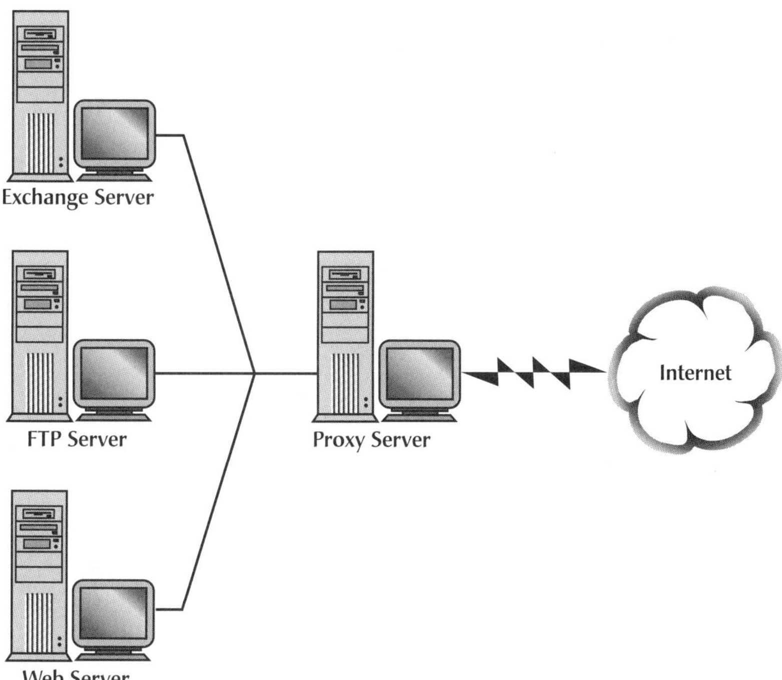

FIGURE 11-12 Server proxying

With this configuration, Proxy Server examines inbound packets and determines which server should get those packets. It then forwards the packets to the appropriate server for service. To Internet users, the Proxy Server is transparent and it appears they are directly sending requests to the Web server, Exchange Server, FTP Server, and so forth. This process is accomplished by binding the desired service to the external adapter.

For example, if you wanted to permit Internet mail to come to your internal Exchange Server, you must bind DNS entries to your external NIC. For mail, you would configure an MX record, which stands for Mail eXchanger, so the Proxy Server will accept Internet mail and forward that mail to the Exchange Server. You also need to configure an Address DNS (A DNS) record to identify the Fully Qualified Domain Name (FQDN) such as `www.`*`yourcompany`*`.com`.

note **Using Proxy Server with Exchange Server is covered later in this chapter.**

Reverse Proxying and Reverse Hosting

Reverse proxying provides Web publishing while maintaining a secure network. Reverse proxying listens to incoming requests and forwards HTTP requests to the internal Web server for service. This process is transparent to the Internet client and makes the Proxy Server appear to be the Web server. The process can be thought of as reverse proxy because the Proxy Server is providing the same service to Internet users as it does to the internal clients, as shown in Figure 11-13.

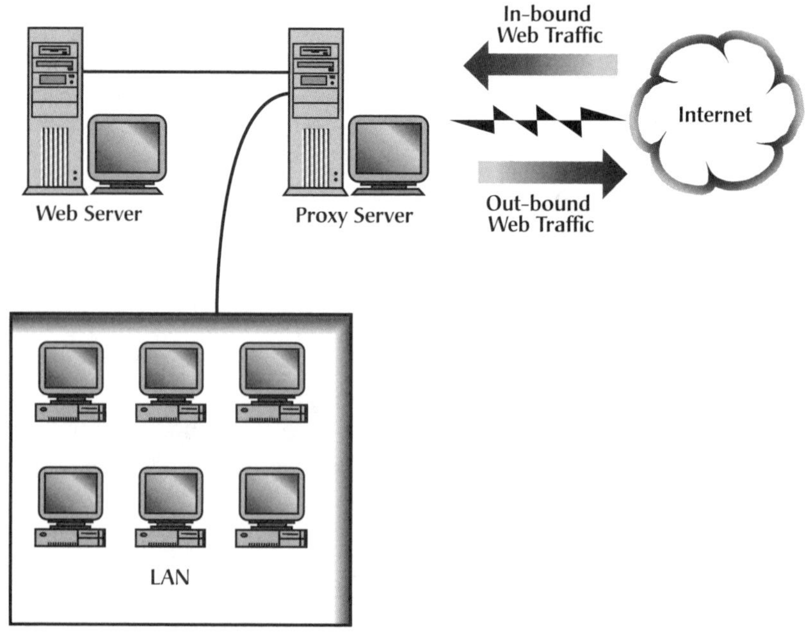

FIGURE 11-13 Reverse Proxying

Reverse hosting is one step above reverse proxying in that it enables multiple internal servers to publish to the Internet. Proxy Server maintains a list of internal servers that publish to the Internet, and routes traffic to the appropriate server. Again, this process is transparent to Internet users. Proxy Server simply redirects the incoming URL to the appropriate internal server.

For example, suppose your company has two Web servers to host its Web site, which sells products. One server contains a database to record all sales information, and the other simply returns HTTP pages to clients for information. So, one server takes orders while another sells products. The order server is called `www.xyzcompany.com/order`, and the other server is simply `www.xyzcompany.com`. Any requests received from the Internet with the URL `www.xzycompany.com/order` are be sent to the order server, and others are sent to the main server, as shown in Figure 11-14.

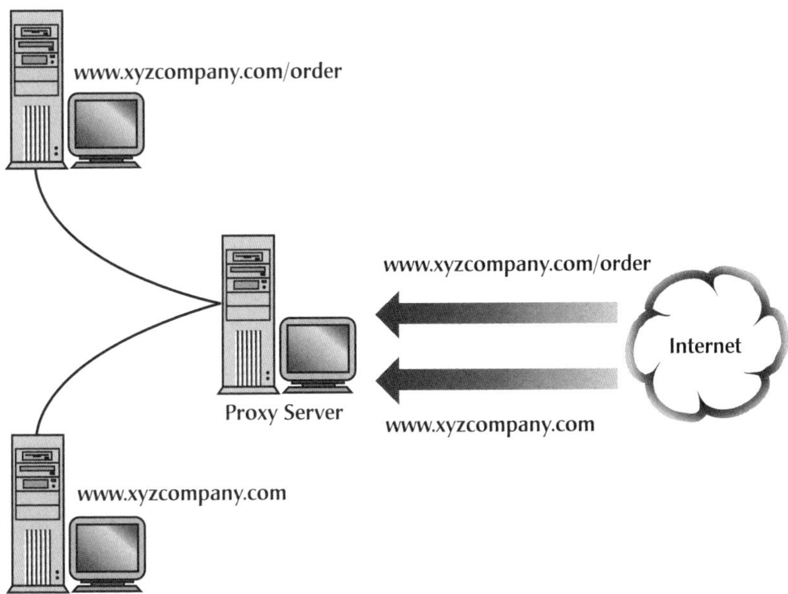

FIGURE 11-14 Reverse hosting

Reverse proxying and reverse hosting maintain security by providing one point of contact for all in-bound and out-bound traffic. This way, there is only one way in and one way out, which is a much safer configuration than each Web server having its own link to the Internet. Also, because reverse proxying and reverse hosting cache content from the internal Web servers, response to Internet requests is faster.

You should test all publishing content and links for compatibility with Proxy Server. Although most will work fine, there may be problems with redirect messages.

Reverse proxying and reverse hosting can be configured on the Publishing tab of the Web Proxy Server Properties page, as shown in Figure 11-15.

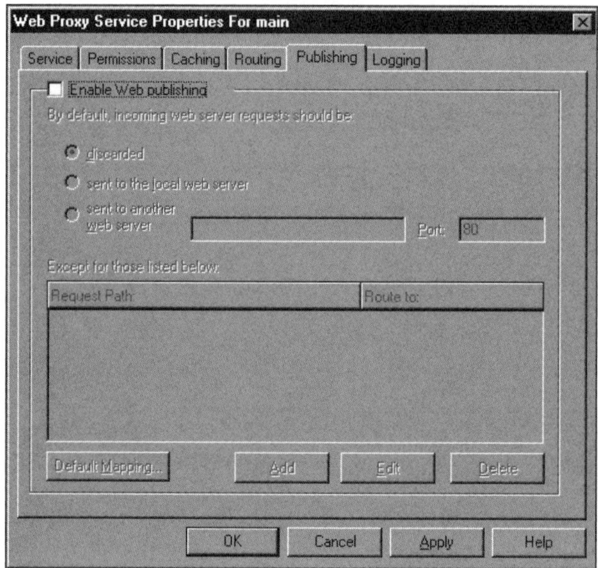

FIGURE 11-15 Publishing tab

By clicking the Enable Web publishing check box, you can select what to do with incoming Web server requests. The radio button options are to discard the request, send it to the local Web server, or send it to another Web server by specifying the location and port. Next is an exception list. This enables you to exclude certain requests from the rule you have created. For example, if incoming requests should be sent to the local Web server, except for `www.xyzcompany.com/sales`, you can create an exception and provide the route. You can do this by clicking the Add button, as shown in Figure 11-16.

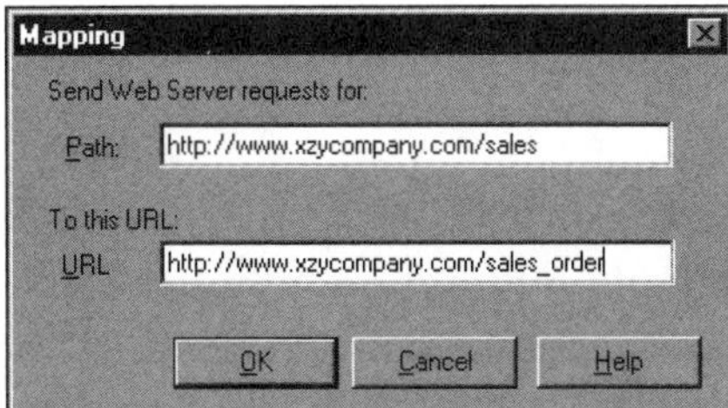

FIGURE 11-16 Mapping dialog box

The mapping dialog box enables you to configure where a certain URL should be sent. You will also be asked to enter the default local host name to support legacy Internet applications, as shown in Figure 11-17.

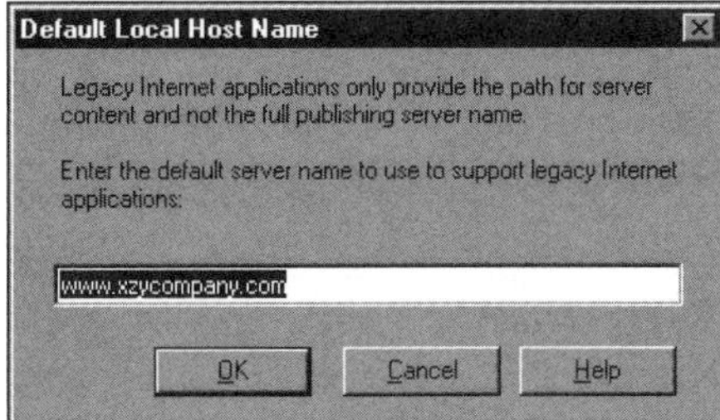

FIGURE 11-17 Default local Host Name dialog box

Once you have completed the configuration, the exception appears in the exception list as shown in Figure 11-18.

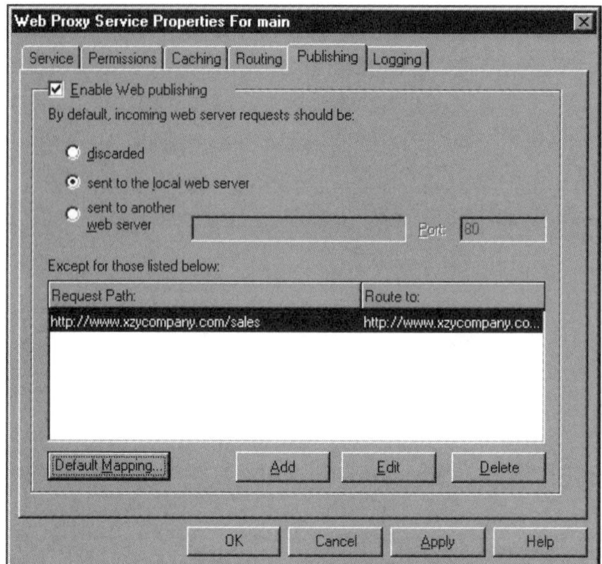

FIGURE 11-18 Exception list

Proxy Server and Exchange Server

As noted previously, Proxy Server can be used to forward incoming Exchange Server requests. This configuration enables your company to exchange mail with other companies or Internet users while maintaining the security you desire for the environment.

Microsoft Exchange Server is mostly commonly thought of as messaging software, but it is actually a group of related services that provide complex functions. Proxy Server and Exchange Server can be installed on the same computer if desired, but appropriate packet filters must be enabled to allow the Exchange Server to communicate using the external NIC. Because Exchange Server is a complicated product, most environments choose to use a server dedicated to Exchange Server, and have Proxy Server forward Internet requests via server proxying.

As I noted earlier, to enable Proxy Server to forward Exchange service requests, you need to configure an MX DNS and an A DNS record for the external interface to identify the server that should receive these requests.

For the exam, keep the MX and A DNS records in mind when configuring a Proxy Server to send Internet requests to an Exchange Server.

You also need to add `Wspcfg.ini` files to the Exchange directory where the server stores its executable files. You need a `Wspcfg.ini` file that contains entries for the Exchange SMTP service. You need to add the following entries to the file and place the file in the directory where the `Msexcimc.exe` file is located. This binds the SMTP port to the Proxy Server computer's port 25.

```
[Msexcimc]
ServerBindTcpPorts=25
Persistent=1
KillOldSessions=1
```

You also need to a second `Wspcfg.ini` file that contains entries for the Exchange Store. You can add additional ports as needed, depending on the communication needs of your environment. The listed ports are POP on port 110 and NNTP on port 119.

```
[Store]
ServerBindTcpPorts=110,119
Persistent=1
KillOldSessions=1
```

Once the Exchange services are stopped and restarted using the configuration above, you should be able to connect to the Exchange Server from the Proxy Server's external NIC by using SMTP, POP, or NNTP.

You can learn more about Proxy Server and Exchange Server by referring to the Proxy Server documentation and the Exchange Server documentation.

Proxy Server and the Intranet

It wasn't too many years ago that companies communicated with their employees by stuffing memos in employee mailboxes. That method has widely been replaced by e-mail and by intranets. An intranet is simply an internal Internet — it is designed to communicate important information to employees or provide employee services. An intranet is a regular HTTP site — it can provide any function or service of a regular Internet site.

Proxy Server can provide services to internal clients for your intranet. Two of the main services it can provide are caching and IPX-to-IP gateway services for IPX/SPX networks. This way, IPX/SPX networks can enjoy an intranet without worrying about TCP/IP connectivity.

For Proxy Server, an intranet works the same as the Internet. A browser is used to contact a URL, which is actually an internal URL. Proxy Server fulfills the request from the internal intranet server and can provide the same caching features as if the intranet site were an Internet site. Of course, for this to occur, the clients must be configured to contact the Proxy Server to reach the intranet server.

Multiple Server and Mixed Environments

Configuring multiple Proxy Servers in arrays and chains is easy if your network is a Windows NT network using Proxy Server 2.0 on all the Proxy Servers. However, in large environments, this is seldom the case. Many large environments use a mix of protocols, operating systems, and even proxy servers. This section takes a look at a few of the major scenarios you are likely to encounter on the job.

Mixed Proxy Servers

If an environment uses Proxy Server 2.0, Proxy Server 1.0, and perhaps even third-party products such as Netscape, a couple of issues arise.

The first concerns caching. Array members must use Proxy Server 2.0. Proxy Server cannot contain arrays with Proxy Server 1.0 and/or third-party products. You can still chain a mix of products together, but caching will be affected because these products are not CARP-aware. However, requests can still be routed to an upstream Proxy Server or array for service.

The second issue concerns load balancing. As mentioned earlier, DNS is the key. The Proxy Server array should have one CNAME entry, such as `corp.proxy.com`. Each array member will have this entry, but with the entry will be the IP address of each of the array members. The IP addresses are be treated in a round-robin fashion so all of the servers get equal service requests.

DNS is normally your best approach for load balancing in a mixed Proxy environment. Of course, a HOST file can be used to statically assign a particular

Proxy Server to particular clients. This method is not as desirable because of the overhead, however.

IPX Environments

Making certain the Proxy Server load is evenly distributed becomes a little more interesting in IPX environments. Remember that Proxy Server can function as an IPX/SPX-to-TCP/IP gateway. This way, your network can use IPX while still having the functionality of the Internet, which only uses TCP/IP.

However, load balancing requires a little more work. In order to communicate with the array, the IPX addresses of the member servers in the array must be used. This information is found in the `LOCAL-ADDR.DUMP` file located in the `C\MSP\Clients` directory on each Proxy Server in the array. This data from each server will have to be merged together and placed in the Servers IPX Addresses sections of the `mspclnt.ini` file. This creates a merged file, which can then be copied to the other members of the array so load balancing can be performed.

Issues with DNS, WINS, and DHCP

In complex networks, you normally need full name resolution provided by DNS and WINS, as well as the automatic assignment of IP addresses by DHCP. Proxy Server, because of its scalability, is designed to function in complex environments where DNS, WINS and DCHP Servers are used. There are two major issues that should be addressed when using DNS, WINS, and DCHP with Proxy Server:

- Load Balancing
- Security

Both of these issues are addressed in earlier chapters. With DNS in environments that use multiple Proxy Severs, Address name DNS records should include all the Proxy Servers and their IP addresses so round-robin requests are fulfilled. This way, all the Proxy Servers get equal traffic.

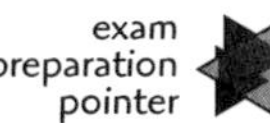

It is important to keep the round-robin method with DNS in mind for the exam. You are likely to see a question concerning this issue.

WINS load balancing is somewhat different. The WINS Manager should be used to create a static mapping for the Proxy Servers. This ensures that proper load balancing occurs among Proxy Server for WINS by providing a search order so a Proxy request is sent to a Proxy Server on the local subnet first, before using a Proxy Server on another subnet.

Also, any service that absolutely does not have to be installed on the external adapter should be disabled. WINS is a good example. Disabling WINS from the external adapter protects your NetBIOS names from Internet intruders.

Exam Preparation Summary

The exam is not overly focused on multiple Proxy Server environments. You are, however, expected to have an understanding of the major concepts discussed in this chapter. You should understand the difference between Proxy arrays and Proxy chains. Keep in mind that only servers running Proxy Server 2.0 can be array members, though Proxy Server 2.0, Proxy Server 1.0, and third-party firewalls and Proxy Servers can function within a chain.

You should keep in mind the major advantages of CARP, especially the hashing algorithm and the functionality it provides to Proxy arrays so they no longer have to use a query method to learn the location of a particular URL.

Also, remember that if a network uses DNS and Proxy Server arrays, you need to create a CNAME alias that represents all array members. For example, the CNAME could be `proxy.corproxy.com`. This CNAME record points to all IP addresses, instead of pointing to one server. DNS sends requests round-robin style so there is equal load balancing.

Remember that you can view the membership table of any array member using a browser and the URL `http://`*`servername`*`/array.dll?Get.Info.v1`.

Finally, keep in mind that if you change the configuration of an array member while another administrator is changing the configuration of another array member, you will get a message asking you to refresh or overwrite. If you refresh, you will lose the changes you made, but your server will remain synchronized with the rest of the array. Overwrite accepts your changes, but overwrites the changes the other administrator made, which creates a synchronization conflict.

You are not likely to see complex questions concerning reverse proxying or reverse hosting, but you are expected to have a conceptual understanding of these issues.

Key Point Summary

This chapter explored the use of multiple Proxy Servers in large LAN or WAN environments.

- Proxy Servers can be configured in an array format. This enables the Proxy Server to create one logical cache that provides superior performance.
- Chains can be used to create an upstream path to the Proxy Server or array that connects to the Internet.
- CARP is used to configure and keep track of the URLs stored in the arrays and chains. This protocol enables the Proxy Servers to know the location of cached URLs without having to query the servers for the location. This is performed using a hash algorithm.
- Arrays are configured using the Array button on the Service tab of the shared Web, Winsock, and Socks Proxy properties sheet.
- In networks that use DNS, a CNAME alias should be used for the array members so proper load balancing can take place.
- Care should be taken when making configuration changes to an array member. Another administrator should be making changes at the same time. This can create a synchronization conflict.
- Primary and backup upstream routes can be configured on the Routing tab of the Web Proxy Service properties page.
- Server proxying is the process of sending packets to internal servers for request fulfillment, such as an Exchange Server.
- Reverse proxying and reverse hosting redirect Internet traffic to the appropriate Web servers for service.

Applying What You've Learned

The following review questions give you a chance to test your knowledge of the content in this chapter. Should you miss some, review the appropriate portions of the chapter. The answers to the Instant Assessment questions can be found in Appendix C.

Instant Assessment

1. Which of the following is a benefit of Proxy Server arrays?
   - **A.** Caching performance
   - **B.** Fault tolerance
   - **C.** Ease of administration
   - **D.** All of the above
2. Which statement is true about array membership?
   - **A.** Only Proxy Server 2.0 servers can be array members.
   - **B.** Only Proxy Server 2.0 and Proxy Server 1.0 servers can be array members.
   - **C.** Proxy Server 2.0 and some third-party Proxy Servers can be array members.
   - **D.** CARP permits any proxy server from any vendor to function as an array member.
3. An algorithm used by CARP to determine the location of a URL is:
   - **A.** ProxySPC
   - **B.** Hash
   - **C.** `Array.dll`
   - **D.** Chain
4. If another administrator makes changes to an array member at the same time you make your changes, what should you do to preserve array synchronization?
   - **A.** Choose the Overwrite option.
   - **B.** Choose the Refresh option.
   - **C.** Resynchronize the array.
   - **D.** Do nothing. Proxy Server will correct the problem.
5. Which protocol did CARP replace?
   - **A.** TCP/IP
   - **B.** IPX
   - **C.** ICMP
   - **D.** ICP

6. What is the correct URL to view an array member's membership table?

   A. `http://`*`servername`*`/array.dll?Get.Info.v1`

   B. `http://`*`servername: 80`*`/array.dll?Get.Info.v1`

   C. `http://`*`servername`*`/array.dll?Get.List.v1`

   D. `http://`*`servername`*`/array.dll?`

7. Which default TCP port is used for communication within an array?

   A. 23

   B. 38

   C. 65

   D. 80

8. Which command line utility can be used to get array membership tables?

   A. Ping

   B. Ipconfig /all

   C. RemotMSP

   D. arp -a

9. Your company uses DNS and multiple Proxy Servers in an array. What should be done so load balancing for client requests will be performed correctly?

   A. Create a static entry in DHCP.

   B. Create a CNAME alias in DNS for all array members.

   C. Create a static WINS entry for all array members.

   D. CARP will enable load balancing to function automatically.

10. When configuring routing, what logon option(s) are available?

    A. Basic Text only

    B. Clear Text only

    C. NTCR

    D. Basic Text and NTCR

11. What is the process of sending Web server requests to multiple Web servers within the network?

    A. Reverse proxying

    B. Reverse hosting

    C. Reserve storage

    D. Reverse service

Critical Thinking Labs

These labs present you with analysis problems to test your critical thinking skills with the content in this chapter.

Lab 11.57 *Primary and backup routes*

You company has two large networks — one in Denver and one in San Diego. Each network uses a Proxy Server array and has a direct connection. Your company opens a small office in Atlanta, and you want to chain the Proxy Server there to the other networks. Draw a diagram showing which network should be the primary route and which network should be the backup route. Explain your answer.

Lab 11.58 *CARP*

You have been asked to present an overview of CARP at an upcoming meeting, highlighting its advantages to multiple Proxy Server environments. What are some of the things you will say?

Lab 11.59 *Using DNS*

A coworker does not understand why DNS is important in environments that use multiple Proxy Servers. How can you explain the importance of DNS and the DNS records that may be needed?

Lab 11.60 *Multiple Proxy administrators*

You have multiple Proxy Server administrators on your network with several Proxy Server arrays. You insist on creating a maintenance schedule so that no administrators are making changes to an array at the same time. Your administrators question you on this. How would you explain your actions?

Lab 11.61 *Proxy Server and an intranet*

An executive at your company heard there are certain advantages to using Proxy Server for the company intranet, even when Internet access is not permitted. You have been asked to outline the possible advantages at an upcoming meeting. What will you say?

Lab 11.62 *IPX environments*

A coworker is concerned about configuring Proxy Server to act as an IPX gateway for IPX clients. What actions do you need to take to accomplish this?

Lab 11.63 *WINS Servers*

You are having problems with one of your WINS Servers. The server does not seem to be providing client access to the Proxy Server. What are some actions you can take?

Hands-on Labs

The Hands-on Labs give you an opportunity to practice skills you have learned in this chapter. These labs assume you have at least two functioning Proxy Servers on a network.

Lab 11.64 *Configuring a Proxy Server array*

In this lab, you will configure a Proxy Server array.

1. To join an array, click Start ⇒ Programs ⇒ Proxy Server ⇒ Microsoft Management Console.
2. The Internet Service Manager appears. Expand the Internet Information Server folder and expand the name of the Proxy Server.
3. Right-click the Web Proxy icon and click Properties. The properties sheet appears.
4. On the Service tab, click the Array button. The Array dialog box appears.
5. Click the Join Array button. The Join Array dialog box appears.
6. Enter the computer name of the Proxy Server you want to form an array with. You need only enter the name, such as CorpProxy. Click OK.
7. If you are not joining an existing array, a dialog box appears asking you to name the array. Type in the appropriate name for the array and click OK.
8. The array members now appear in the Array Members list.

9. The Join Array button has changed to read Leave Array. If you want to remove a member from the array, highlight the appropriate computer and click the Leave Array button. You see a dialog box telling you the server leaving the array will become a stand-alone server.

Lab 11.65 *Configuring routing options*

In this lab, you will configure routing options to other arrays. If you are not working in an environment that has multiple arrays or if you are not permitted to make changes to the current configuration, you can still practice this lab. Just don't apply the changes you make.

1. To configure routing options, click Start ⇒ Programs ⇒ Proxy Server ⇒ Microsoft Management Console.
2. The Internet Service Manager appears. Expand the Internet Information Server folder and expand the name of the Proxy Server.
3. Right-click the Web Proxy icon and click Properties. The properties sheet appears.
4. Click the Routing tab. In the Upstream Routing section, click the Use Web Proxy or array radio button, and then click Modify.
5. The Advanced Routing Options window appears. In the Proxy dialog box, type the name of the upstream server or array. If you do not have an upstream server or array, type CorpProxy. Note that the Auto-poll Array URL dialog box is automatically configured with `http://`***servername***`:80/array.dll`.
6. If you want to use credentials to communicate with the upstream server or array, click the check box, and then type in an appropriate username and password. If you want to use NTCR, click the radio button. Click OK.
7. If you want to enable a backup route, click the check box and repeat steps 5 and 6.
8. If you want to use this configuration, click the Apply button and click OK. If you do not, click the Cancel button.

Lab 11.66 *Reverse Proxying*

In this lab, you will configure reverse proxying. If you do not have a Web server on your network, you can use `www.xyzcompany.com` for experimental purposes.

1. Click Start ⇒ Programs ⇒ Microsoft Proxy Server ⇒ Microsoft Management Console.

2. The Internet Service Manager appears. Expand the Internet Information Server directory and expand the computer name.
3. Right click the Web Proxy Service and select Properties. The Properties sheet appears.
4. Click the Publishing tab and click the Enable Web Publishing check box.
5. Select the radio button that tells Proxy Server what to do with incoming Web server requests. You can select the send to local Web server button if you do not actually have a Web server to point to.
6. Click the Add button to create exceptions to this rule. If you do not have actual exceptions to configure, you can simply make up a URL and a path for experimental purposes. Once you have entered the information, click OK.
7. You may see the Default Mapping dialog box. If this appears, enter the name of your Web server or `www.xyzcompany.com` for experimental purposes, and then click OK.
8. The new entry appears in the exception list. Click Apply to apply the changes, then click OK, or click cancel if you do not want to save the changes.

CHAPTER

Proxy Server and RAS

12

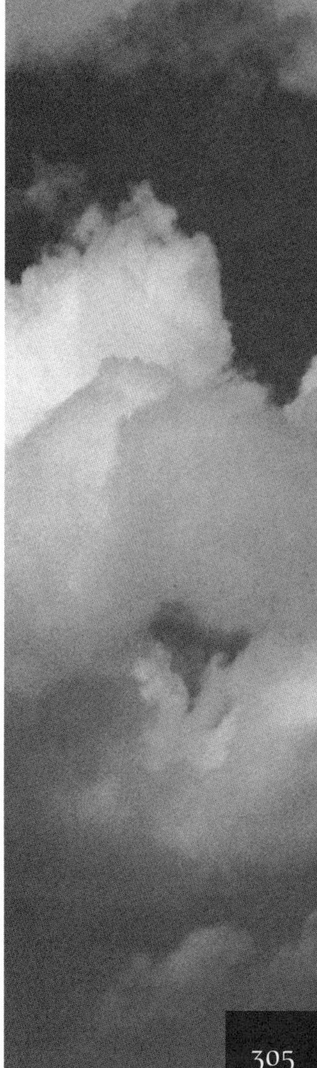

About Chapter 12

Proxy Server can use Windows NT's Remote Access Service (RAS) to connect to an ISP using a modem or an ISDN line. In this chapter, you learn how to configure NT's RAS for use with Proxy Server, and how to configure Proxy Server to provide dial-out service to clients and the situation where a modem connection is appropriate for use with Proxy Server. There are five labs in this chapter to practice the skills you learn.

Dial-Up for Proxy Server

Proxy Server has the ability to use dial-up networking to connect with an ISP for Internet connectivity. You may ask, why? After all, dial-up accounts using a modem have a maximum baud rate of 56 Kbps, and are often unreliable. Why would a network use a Proxy Server to connect to the Internet with a modem?

There are two major reasons for this configuration. First, for a small workgroup or a LAN, a dial-up account with a modem or ISDN line is the most cost-effective solution. The network can use Proxy Server for caching and security while still providing Internet access to the users. The link may be slow, but in a small workgroup or LAN, a dial-up account is often enough to meet the needs of the group and is least expensive.

Second, dial-up accounts are often used as a backup measure if the main link goes down. This is an effective fault tolerance solution to provide continuous Internet access in case of a primary link failure.

Proxy Server contains a number of options for configuring dial-up networking and functions seamlessly with Window NT RAS or Windows NT Routing and Remote Access Service (RRAS). Before Proxy Server's services for dial-up connectivity can be configured, RAS or RRAS must be configured on the server.

RAS

Windows NT RAS is designed to permit a remote client to function and act and though it was connected to the network. RAS is more than simple dial-up software; it enables clients to log into a LAN and participate on the LAN as a member. In other words, RAS is not simply logging into another server and asking that server to do all the work. The RAS client has an actual place on the network and can function as though it were directly connected.

RAS is normally used in a Point to Point Protocol (PPP) configuration, although some networks still use the older Serial Line Internet Protocol (SLIP) configuration. RAS supports clients running MS-DOS, Windows 3.1, Windows 95/98, and Windows NT.

Before installing and configuring RAS, you need to install a modem or ISDN adapter. Remember that Windows NT is not plug-and-play compliant, so it's best to check the Windows NT Hardware Compatibility List (HCL) to find a modem that is compatible with NT. You can check out the hardware compatibility list at `www.microsoft.com/hwtest/hcl`.

Installing a Modem

After you have selected an appropriate modem for Windows NT, you can install the modem by physically adding the hardware to the computer (follow the manufacturer's directions), rebooting the computer, and accessing the Modems icon in Control Panel, as shown in Figure 12-1.

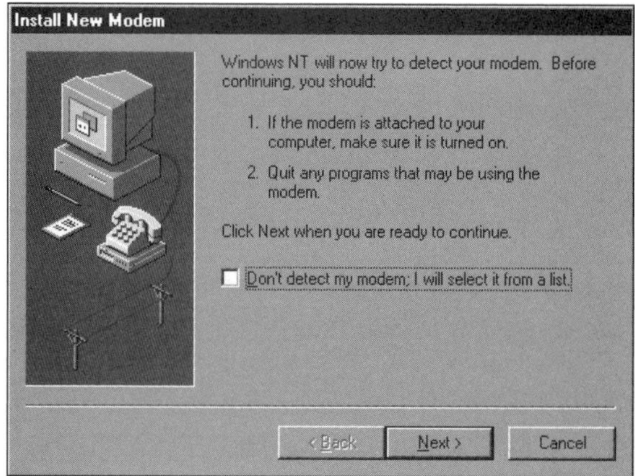

FIGURE 12-1 Install New Modem Wizard

The Install New Modem Wizard begins. You can let Windows NT try to detect your modem, or you may want to select the check box that tells NT to let you select your modem from a list. If you select this option, the Wizard provides you with a list of manufacturers and the model models to choose from, as shown in Figure 12-2.

From this point, you can select the modem you want to install, or you click the Have Disk button to manually install the modem from a diskette.

Once you complete the Wizard, the modem is installed. From this point on, if you double-click the Modems Icon in control panel, you are given a modem properties sheet, as shown in Figure 12-3.

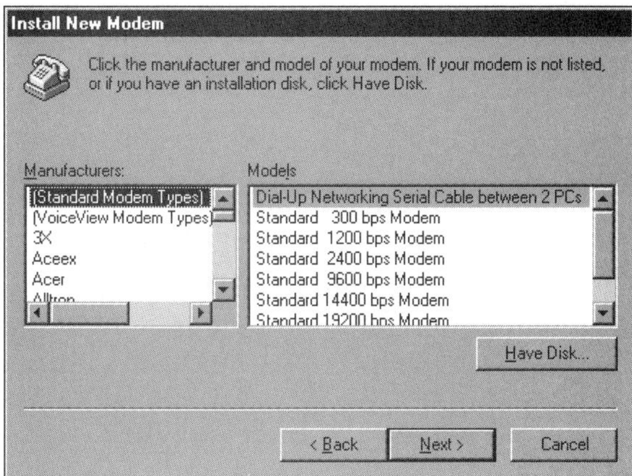

FIGURE 12-2 Install New Modem selection list

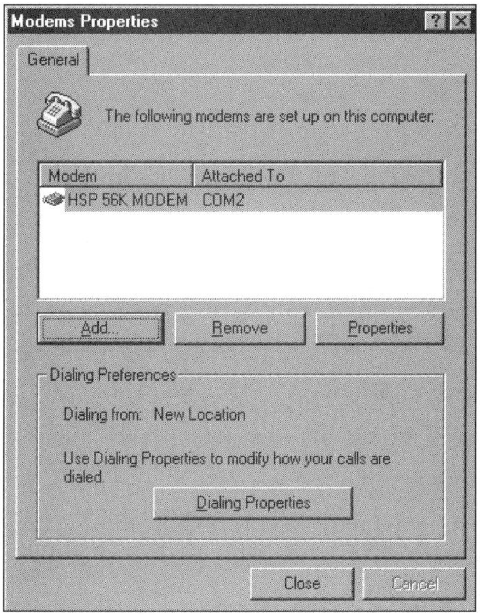

FIGURE 12-3 Modem Properties sheet

From the Properties sheet, you can add new modems by clicking the Add button. This starts the Installation Wizard. You can also remove a modem by using the Remove button. If you click the Properties button, you are be taken to an additional Properties sheet with two tabs: General and Connection, as shown in Figure 12-4.

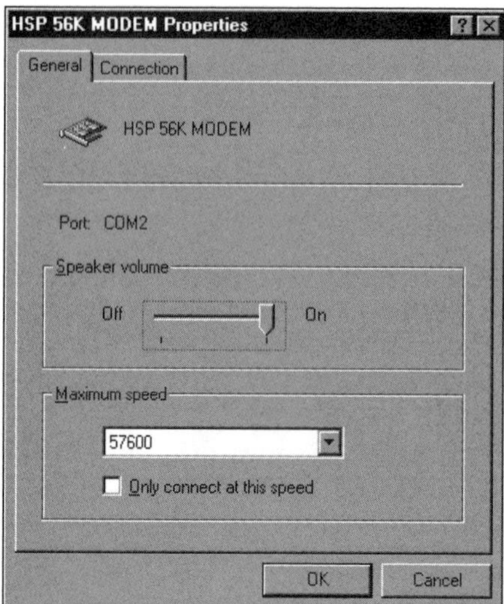

FIGURE 12-4 General tab of the Modem Properties sheet

You can configure the speaker volume of the modem and the maximum speed you want the modem to connect at. You can also check the Only connect at this speed option. This tells Windows NT to try to establish a certain speed connection that you select, although this speed is not guaranteed.

The Connection tab gives you a list of Connection preferences, such as data bits, parity, and stop bits. You can also configure Call preferences. These tell the modem how to handle the call connection. You can specify a time to disconnect the modem if the system becomes idle for a certain period of time (the default is 30 minutes). Figure 12-5 shows the Connection tab.

Clicking the Advanced button takes you to the Advanced Connection Settings where you can make changes to the error control and flow control selections. You can also change the modem type and add additional modem initialization strings. Refer to the manufacturer's documentation before making changes to these settings or adding new settings. Figure 12-6 shows the Advanced Connection Settings dialog box.

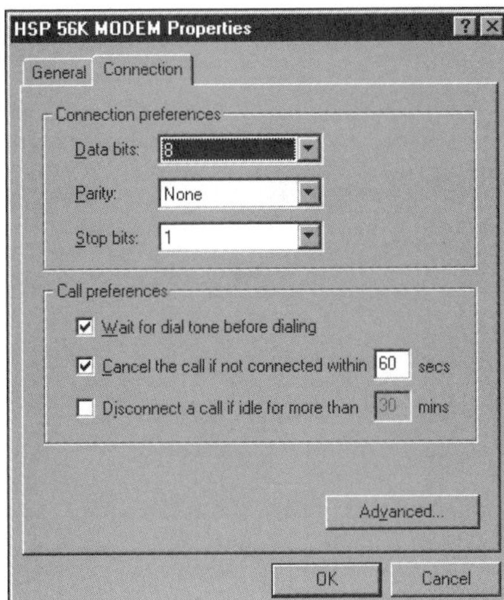

FIGURE 12-5 Connection tab of the Modem Properties sheet

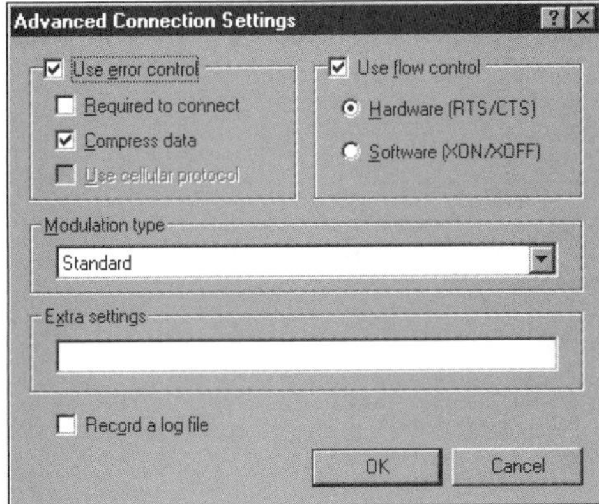

FIGURE 12-6 Advanced Connection Settings dialog box

RAS Settings

If RAS is already installed on your server, installing a new modem or ISDN adapter automatically configures RAS to use the hardware. RAS can be accessed from the Network icon in Control Panel. Click the Services tab, highlight the Remote Access Service, and click the Properties button. Your modem appears in the Remote Access Setup dialog box, as shown in Figure 12-7.

note **If RAS was not installed on your NT Server during setup, Lab 12.70 shows you how to install RAS.**

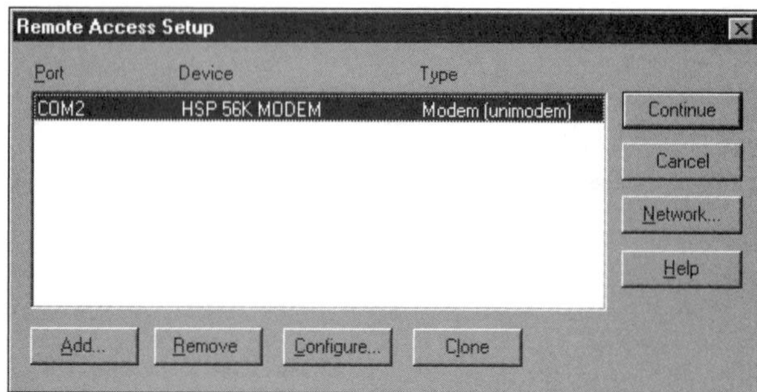

FIGURE 12-7 Remote Access Setup dialog box

As in the Modem Properties dialog box, you can add or remove a modem from the list. If you click the Configure button, you see the Configure Port Usage dialog box, as shown in Figure 12-8.

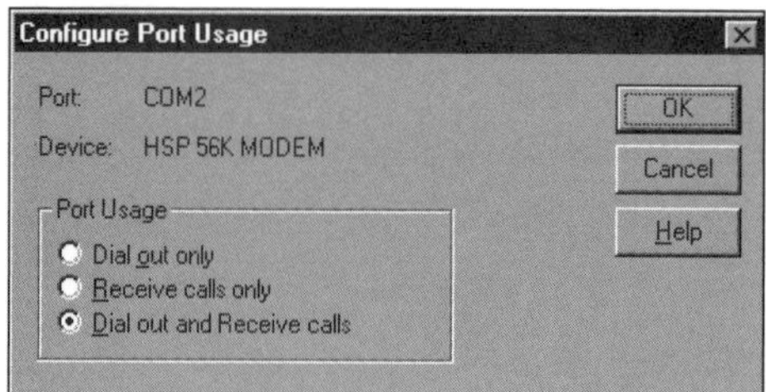

FIGURE 12-8 Configure Port Usage dialog box

You should take special note of the configuration options. You have three radio buttons: Dial out only, Receive calls only, and Dial out and Receive calls. You need to make the modem selection appropriate for your network. Will your Proxy Server only dial out to get Internet objects for clients? Or, will the server both dial out and receive calls? You need to make the appropriate selection here to give your server the functionality desired; however, you should be aware that Microsoft does not recommend using the Proxy Server to dial out and receive calls. Your clients' Internet connectivity may be limited if you select this. when the same lines are used for both Proxy Server and RAS, and it also opens a potential security threat.

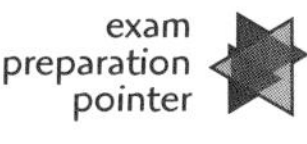

You are likely to see a question about these selections. The best option is to permit Proxy Server to dial out to fulfill Internet requests, but not permit external clients to dial in to the Proxy Server.

If you click the Network button in the Remote Access Setup dialog box, you have the option to configure Network settings, such as dial out protocols, server settings, and encryption settings. Also, if you want to use a Multilink configuration, you can enable it from this screen. The Network Configuration dialog box is shown in Figure 12-9.

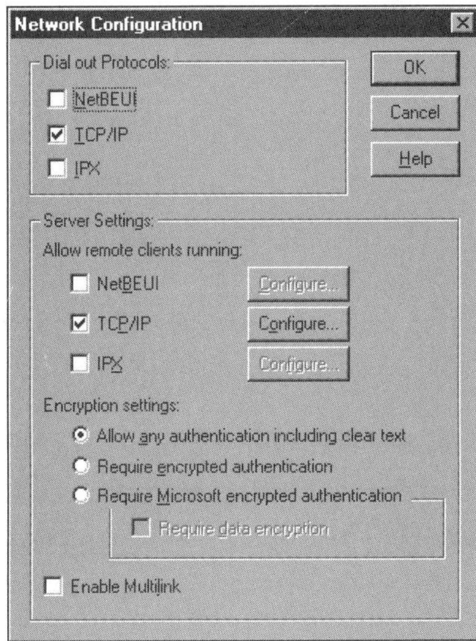

FIGURE 12-9 Network Configuration dialog box

Of course, the dial-out protocol you want to select is TCP/IP. However, you can permit remote clients running NetBEUI or even IPX to use NT's RAS services for dial-up connectivity. If clients are permitted to dial in to access the Proxy Server (which is not recommended), you need to click the Configure button next to the protocol the remote clients are running. For example, if your clients use only TCP/IP, click the Configure button next to TCP/IP to see the dialog box shown in Figure 12-10.

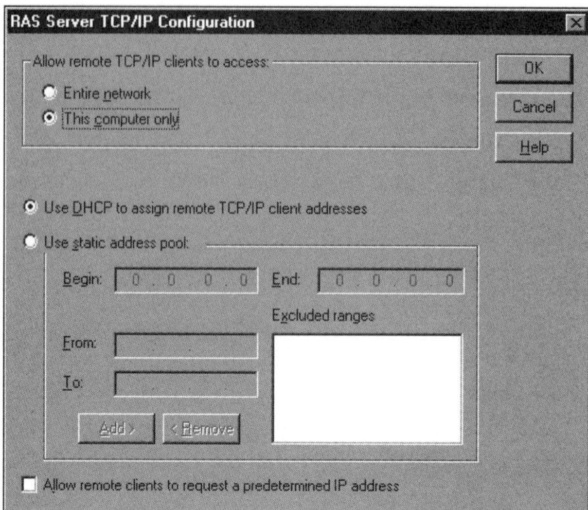

FIGURE 12-10 RAS Server TCP/IP Configuration

At the top of the window, in the Allow remote TCP/IP clients to access: section, you should select the This computer only radio button. This limits the dial-in clients to the Proxy Server. If you select the Entire network setting, IP forwarding is enabled, which creates a security hole in your network.

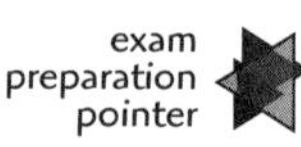

Permitting dial-in clients is not recommended, but if you choose to permit this, they should not under any circumstances be granted access to the entire network. This enables IP forwarding and is a serious security breach.

Configuring a Phone Book Entry

Before you can use the dial-up functionality of Proxy Server, you need to configure a phone book entry to dial-out to your ISP. This must be done from NT's Dial-Up Networking directory and cannot be configured from the Proxy Server interface.

TO CONFIGURE A PHONE BOOK ENTRY, FOLLOW THESE STEPS:

1. Click Start ⇒ Programs ⇒ Accessories ⇒ Dial-Up Networking.
2. If other Phonebook Entries have not been configured previously, the New Phonebook Entry Wizard begins, as shown in Figure 12-11. Type in the

desired name of the entry and click Next. If you have other PhoneBook entries configured and want to add a new one, click the New button on the Dial-Up Networking screen that appears.

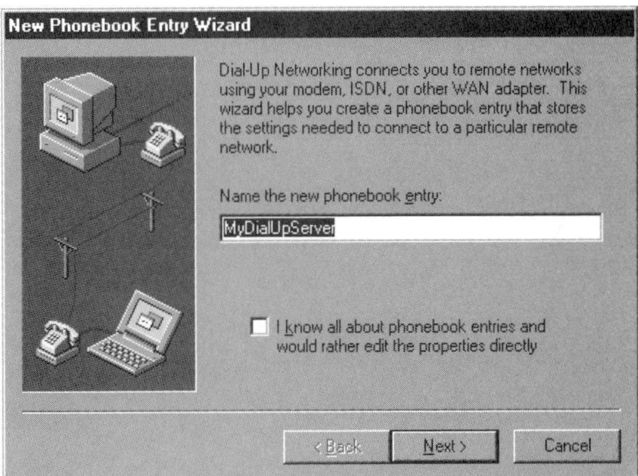

FIGURE 12-11 New Phonebook Entry Wizard

3. The Server dialog box tab appears. Click the check boxes that are appropriate for your ISP, as shown in Figure 12-12, and click Next.

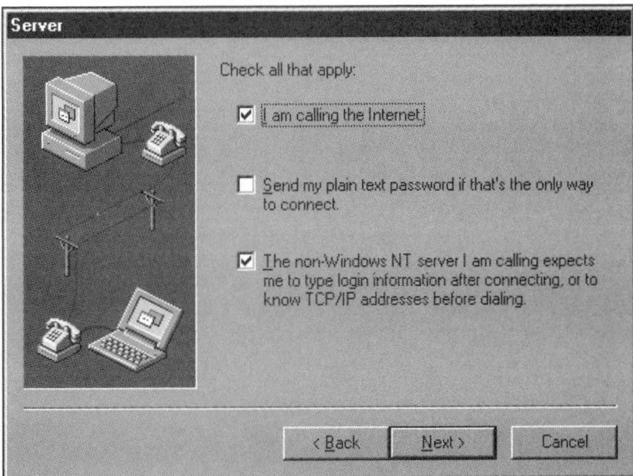

FIGURE 12-12 Server dialog box

4. The Phone Number dialog box appears. Enter the Country code and the area code and phone number of the ISP you are calling, as shown in Figure 12-13. You can also click the Alternates button to enter additional numbers. Click Next.

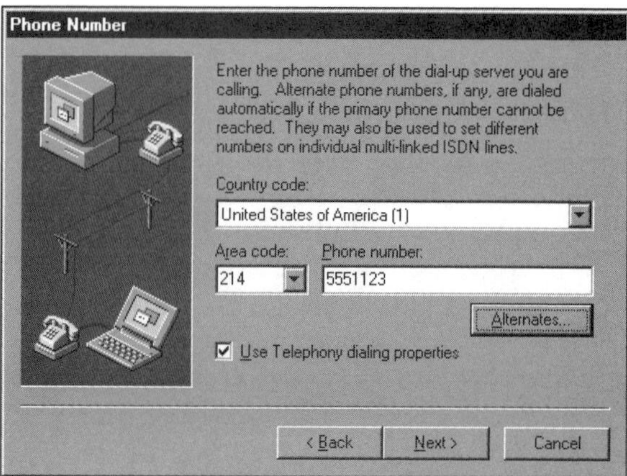

FIGURE 12-13 Phone Number dialog box

5. The Serial Line Protocol dialog box appears, as shown in Figure 12-14. Choose the serial line protocol you want. PPP is selected by default, and this is normally what you would use. Accept the default or change to SLIP if necessary and click Next.

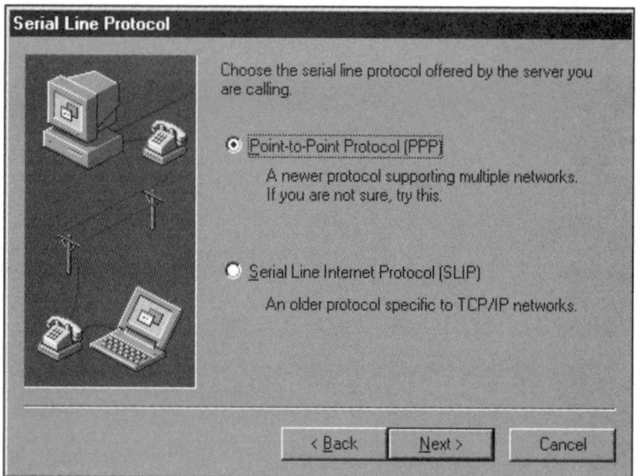

FIGURE 12-14 Serial Line Protocol dialog box

6. The Login Script dialog box appears, as shown in Figure 12-15. This window enables you to configure additional scripting options to log on to the server. These scripts are not used by most ISPs. None is selected by default. If you need to make changes, click the appropriate radio button or click Edit script. If not, accept the default of None by clicking Next.

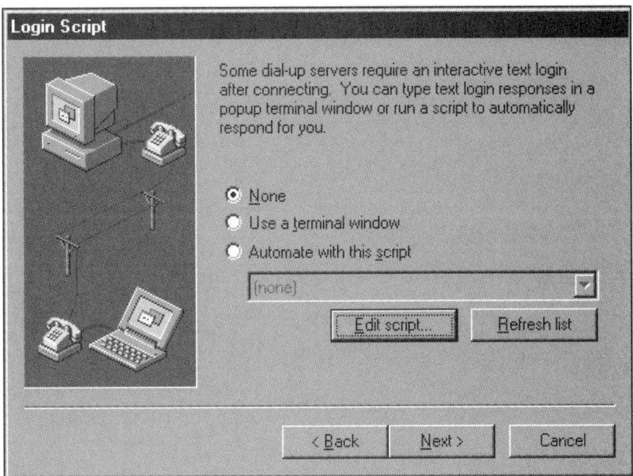

FIGURE 12-15 Login Script dialog box

7. The IP address dialog box appears, as shown in Figure 12-16. This window enables you to enter an IP address for use on the remote server, or you can accept the default of 0.0.0.0 if the ISP provides the IP address, which is usually the case. Make certain you do not enter an IP address that is the same as your internal NIC — this is a security breach. Click Next.

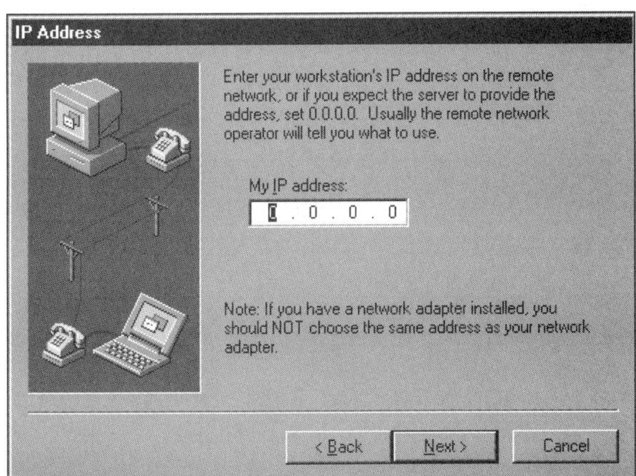

FIGURE 12-16 IP Address dialog box

8. The Name Server Address dialog box appears, as shown in Figure 12-17. Again, enter the remote WINS and DNS IP addresses, or leave them as 0.0.0.0 if they are provided by the ISP, which is normally the case. Click Next.

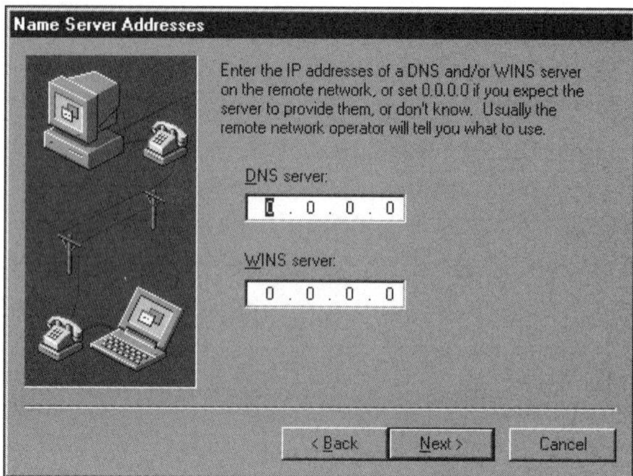

FIGURE 12-17 Name Server Addresses

9. The New Phonebook Entry window appears, telling you that the phonebook has been configured. Click the Finish button to complete the setup.

Configuring RAS for Autodial

Once you have your phonebook entry configured, you need to tell RAS to use Auto-Dial for Proxy Server Autodial to work. This enables Proxy Server to dial on demand when a client requests an Internet object or needs to perform a Winsock or Socks function.

TO CONFIGURE RAS FOR AUTODIAL, PERFORM THE FOLLOWING STEPS:

1. In Control Panel, double-click Services.
2. The Services dialog box appears. Select the Remote Access Autodial Manager and click Startup, as shown in Figure 12-18.

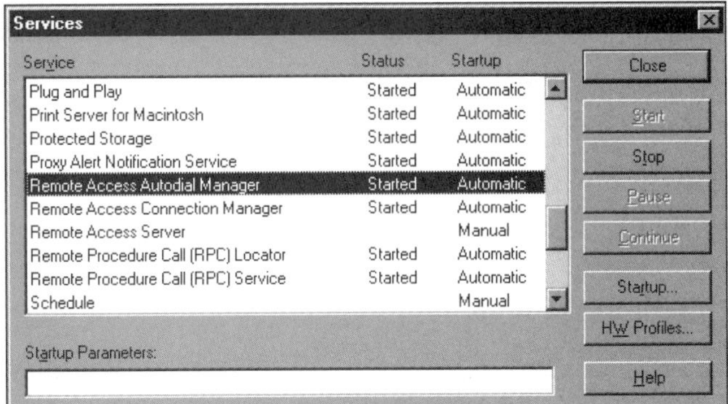

FIGURE 12-18 Remote Access Autodial Manager

3. The Service dialog box appears, as shown in Figure 12-19. Under Startup Type, click Disabled and then click OK.

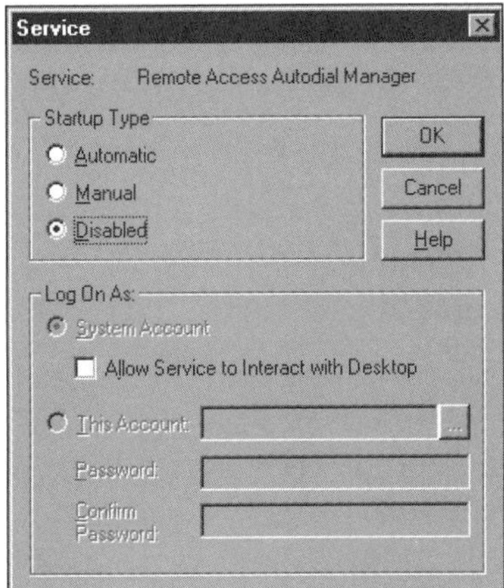

FIGURE 12-19 Service dialog box

4. This returns you to the Services dialog box. Select Remote Access Connection Manager, and click Startup.
5. This returns you to same dialog box as in Figure 12-19. Under Startup Type, click Automatic and click OK. Then click close on the Services dialog box.

Unbinding the WINS Client

Finally, the last portion of RAS configuration for Proxy Server is to unbind the WINS client from the external adapter. This provides additional security for your environment and prevents Internet users from compromising your NetBIOS names.

TO UNBIND THE WINS CLIENT FROM THE EXTERNAL ADAPTER, FOLLOW THESE STEPS:

1. In Control Panel, double-click the Network icon.
2. Click the Bindings tab. In the Show Bindings for field, click the drop-down menu and select all adapters, as shown in Figure 12-20.

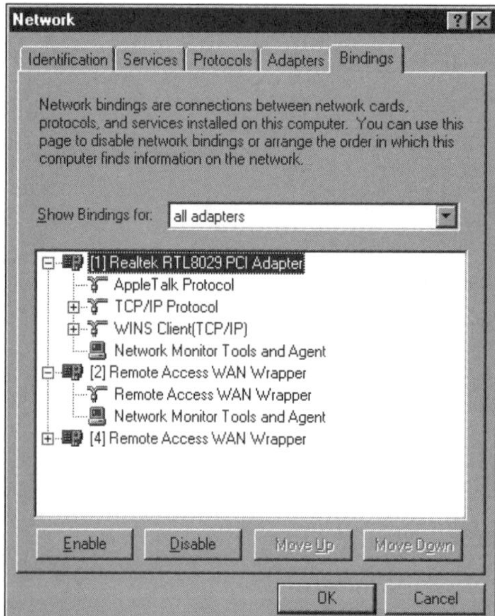

FIGURE 12-20 Bindings tab

3. In the bindings list, click the plus sign next to Remote Access Server Service to expand the view.
4. Select the WINS Client (TCP/IP) and click the Disable button, as shown in Figure 12-21.

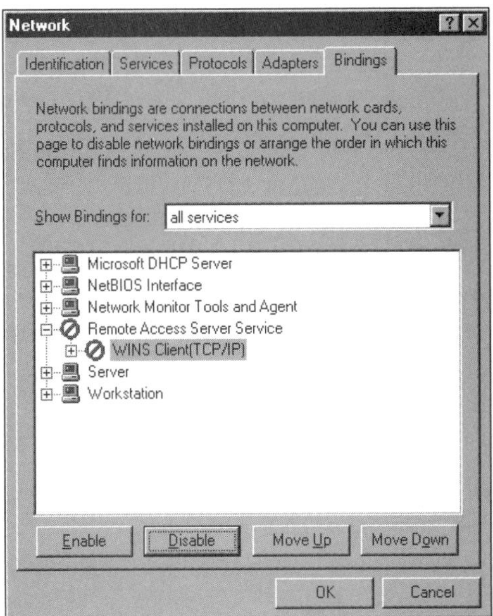

FIGURE 12-21 Disable WINS Client

5. Click the OK button.

For additional information on RAS configuration or troubleshooting RAS, refer to the Windows NT documentation or visit `www.microsoft.com/technet`.

RRAS

Routing and Remote Access Service is an add-on product designed to enable dial-up routing between two networks. RRAS's primary function is to create Virtual Private Networks (VPNs) for use with Point to Point Tunneling Protocol (PPTP). A VPN and PPTP enable two networks to use the Internet as a virtual LAN link. This method avoids the expense of an actual T1 line between two sites.

PPTP functions by *encapsulating*, or hiding, the local LAN protocol inside of what appears to be a PPP packet. This way, the packet can travel over the Internet, even though it is actually an Internet incompatible protocol, such as NetBEUI.

The result is the secure transmission of data over the Internet without a huge expense.

The RRAS PPTP server service can be used on a Proxy Server computer, but you have to establish a PPTP call and PPTP receive filter when using packet filtering for PPTP to function on the Proxy Server. The PPTP call and PPTP receive filters permit both inbound and outbound PPTP traffic.

You should always check `www.microsoft.com` **for any late hot fixes for add-on products, such as RRAS. This can save you a lot of time and problems if there is a fix that needs to be applied.**

This functionality does has the potential to cause a number of problems. Though PPTP is permitted for use with Proxy Sever, Microsoft does not recommended it. Because PPTP is designed to be a call-and-receive protocol, it enables IP forwarding and opens a number of potential security holes in your network. So, it's important to consider other options carefully before using PPTP with Proxy Server.

Proxy Server Dial-Up

Proxy Server provides dial-on-demand service for the Web, Winsock, and Socks Proxy Services. When a client makes a request that must be retrieved from the Internet, Proxy Server dials the ISP and services the request in this manner.

Dial-up parameters for Proxy Server can be configured on the shared Service tab of the Web, Winsock, and Socks Proxy Service Properties page, as shown in Figure 12-22.

In the Shared Services section, there is a button for Auto Dial. This is where you configure Proxy Server's dial-out functions. Click the Auto Dial button to access the Auto Dial Properties page, as shown in Figure 12-23.

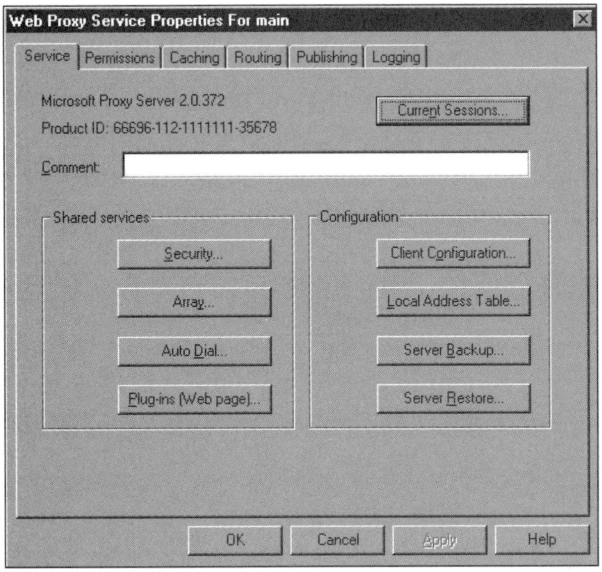

FIGURE 12-22 Service tab

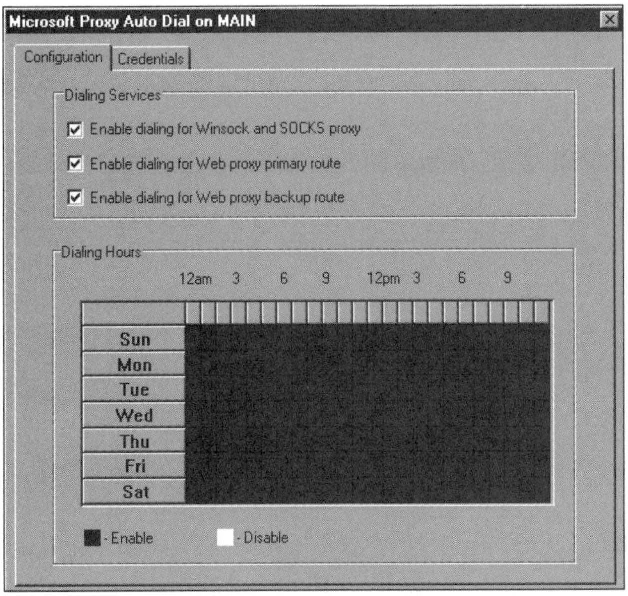

FIGURE 12-23 Auto Dial Properties page

In the Dialing Services section, there are three check boxes: Enable dialing for Winsock and SOCKS proxy, Enable dialing for Web proxy primary route, and Enable dialing for Web proxy backup route. Auto Dial can service Winsock and Socks requests by dialing out to the Internet. For the Web Proxy Service, the cache is checked first, and then Auto Dial can be used to retrieve the Internet objects that are not in the cache. If the dial-up account is your primary link, such as in a small workgroup or LAN, you should check the Enable dialing for Web proxy primary route check box. If dial-up is only a backup in case the main link fails, you should select the Enable dialing for Web proxy backup route option.

Next you can configure the dialing hours that Proxy Server is available. This is useful if you want to restrict the hours that users can access the Proxy Server for services, as you might if there are hourly usage charges from your ISP, or for further security.

To change the hours the Proxy Server is available for dial-out service, simply click the blue grid squares so they become white. You can adjust the dialing hours according to both hours of the day and the day itself. In Figure 12-24, the dialing hours have been adjusted so that dial-out is only available from Monday through Friday, from 8:00 A.M. to 5:00 P.M. If you need to change the dialing hours, they can be easily adjusted by enabling or disabling the appropriate time grids.

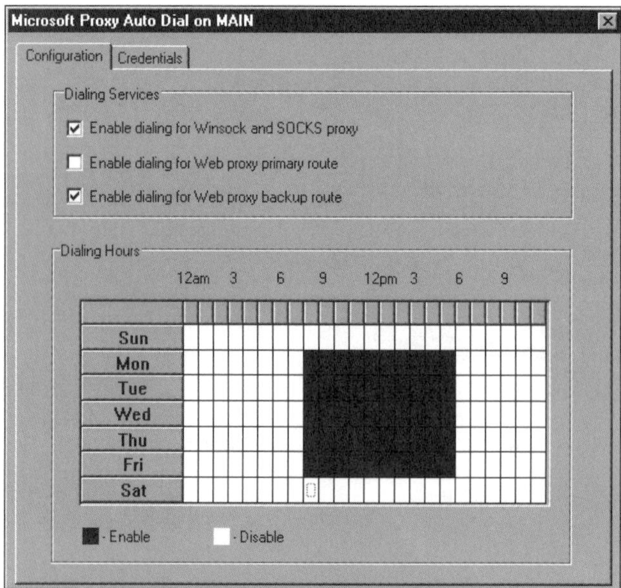

FIGURE 12-24 Adjusted dialing hours

If you click the Credentials tab, you can select the RAS phonebook entry you previously configured to launch the Internet connection. If there are multiple phone book entries on your server, click the drop-down menu next to Entry Name to select the appropriate ISP. You can also input your user name and password on this tab, as shown in Figure 12-25.

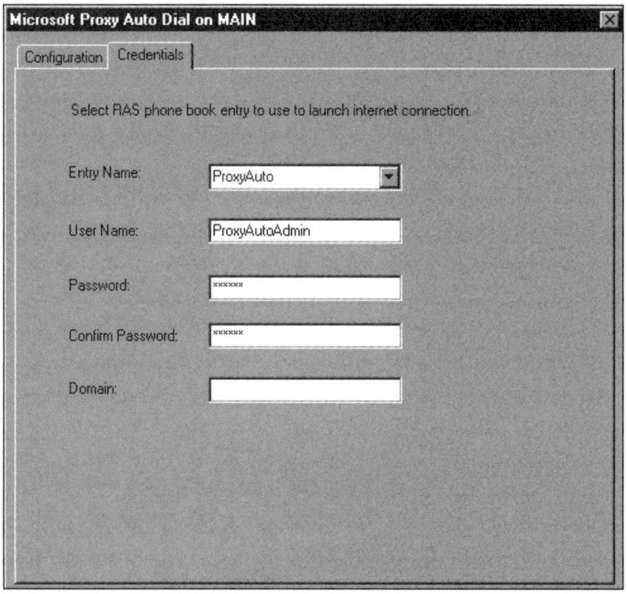

FIGURE 12-25 Credentials tab

After you configure Auto Dial for the first time, or if you clear the configuration, you need to stop and restart the Web, Winsock, and Socks Proxy Services to initialize the changes. After you have initialized the configuration, you can make further changes without stopping and restarting the services. You can stop and start the services from the Internet Service Manager or using the command prompt. The syntax for stopping and starting services at the command prompt is provided in Table 12-1.

TABLE 12-1 COMMAND LINE SYNTAX TO STOP AND START SERVICES

Service	*Syntax*
Web Proxy	`Net stop	start w3svc`
Winsock Proxy	`Net stop	start wspsvc`
Socks Proxy	`Net stop	start spsvc`

Exam Preparation Summary

You will not see many exam questions on Auto Dial. You are likely to see planning questions that ask you how to use a modem installed on your Proxy Server when there is a T1 link available as well. Remember that using a modem and dial-up for Proxy Server is a good backup measure if the main link fails. This enables your network to continue using Proxy services until the main link is repaired. You will also see a few questions about configuring RAS for use with Proxy Server. Remember that you have to configure RAS for Auto Dial for the Proxy Server to be able to use it, and you should unbind the WINS client from the external adapter. Also, if you permit users to dial-in to the Proxy Server, you should not permit them to have access to the entire network, but rather to the Proxy Server only. Otherwise, IP forwarding is enabled, which is a security breach. Proxy Server can be used with RRAS to establish PPTP connections, but remember that it does so at a performance loss and creates potential security holes.

Key Point Summary

In this chapter, you learned about using RAS and RRAS to perform Auto-dial functions with Proxy Server.

- Proxy Server can provide dial-on-demand services in conjunction with Windows NT RAS.
- RAS configuration provides dial in, dial out, or both functions. As a general rule to preserve security, Proxy Server should be used as dial out only.
- If RAS is installed on your server, you can install new modems using the Install New Modem Wizard. RAS configures itself to use the new modem.

- If client dial in is permitted on the Proxy Server, you should limit the clients to the Proxy Server computer and not the entire network. If you permit clients to access the entire network, IP forwarding is enabled on the routing tab of TCP/IP properties, which is a serious security breach.
- A phonebook entry for your ISP must be configured before configuring Proxy Server's Auto Dial properties.
- RAS must be configured to permit Auto-Dial before you configure Proxy Server's Auto-dial properties.
- The WINS client should be disabled from the external adapter.
- RRAS is an add-on product to RAS that permits the creation of VPNs using PPTP. This configuration is not recommended to use in conjunction with Proxy Server.
- Proxy Server dial-up can be configured for use as the primary or backup route, and the dialing hours can be adjusted at the administrator's discretion.
- The Proxy Server services must be stopped and restarted when the Auto Dial tabs are configured or cleared.

Applying What You've Learned

The following review questions give you a chance to test your knowledge of the content in this chapter. Should you miss some, review the appropriate portions of the chapter. The answers to the Instant Assessment questions can be found in Appendix C.

Instant Assessment

1. What resource should be checked before installing a modem on NT Server?

A. NT's documentation

B. HCL

C. *TechNet*

D. *Winnt* Magazine

2. Which modem configuration is recommended for use with Proxy Server?

   A. Dial in

   B. Dial out

   C. Dial in and Dial out

   D. None of the above

3. For client dial-in, which TCP/IP configuration setting should be selected to preserve security?

   A. Entire network

   B. This computer only

   C. This subnet only

   D. This network only

4. What should you do to prevent your NetBIOS names from being compromised by Internet users?

   A. Unbind DHCP from the external adapter.

   B. Unbind DNS from the external adapter.

   C. Unbind WINS from the external adapter.

   D. Unbind TCP/IP from the external adapter.

5. What protocol is used by RRAS when creating a VPN?

   A. TCP

   B. SLIP

   C. PPP

   D. PPTP

6. What is the correct command line syntax to start the Socks Proxy Service?

   A. `Net start spsvc`

   B. `Net start w3spc`

   C. `Net start wspsvc`

   D. `Net start socks`

Critical Thinking Labs

These labs present you with analysis problems to test your critical thinking skills with the content in this chapter.

Lab 12.67 *Unbinding WINS*

Why should WINS be unbound from the external adapter of any Proxy Server?

Lab 12.68 *Auto Dial setup*

A coworker is setting up Auto Dial on the company's Proxy Server. When he clicks the credentials tab, the entries are all blank. What is causing this and what should your coworker do?

Lab 12.69 *Using RRAS*

You company wants to use RRAS to establish PPTP connections on the Proxy Server computer. What advice would you give?

Hands-on Labs

The Hands-on Labs give you an opportunity to practice skills you have learned in this chapter. These labs assume you have at least a functioning Proxy Server on a network.

Lab 12.70 *Installing RAS*

In this lab, you will install RAS on your server if it is not already installed.

1. Open Control Panel and double-click the Network icon.
2. Click the Services tab and click the Add button.
3. A selection service list appears. Highlight Remote Access Service and click OK.
4. NT prompts you for the location of the files needed for the installation, which you normally install from the NT Server CD-ROM I386 directory. Select the appropriate directory and click Continue.
5. The files are copied. If a modem is installed, it appears in the RAS Capable Devices list. Click OK, and then click Continue.
6. The RAS Server TCP/IP configuration will appear. Under the Allow remote TCP/IP clients to access section, click This computer only. This will prevent IP forwarding.

7. RAS is configured and installed. Click the OK button and click Close to save the binding information.
8. You are prompted to reboot the computer.

Lab 12.71 *Configuring Auto Dial*

In this lab, you configure Proxy Server for Auto Dial. This lab assumes you have a modem installed in your server and RAS configured. You must also set up a phonebook entry, configure RAS for Auto Dial, and unbind the WINS client from the external adapter. Refer to the step-by-step instructions for each of these actions within this chapter and complete them before performing this lab.

1. Click Start ⇒ Programs ⇒ Microsoft Proxy Server ⇒ Microsoft Management Console.
2. The Internet Service Manager appears. Expand the Internet Information Server directory and expand the computer name.
3. Right-click the Web Proxy Service and select Properties. The Properties sheet appears.
4. Click the Auto Dial button. On the configuration tab, click Enable dialing for Winsock and SOCKS proxy. If you are using dial-up for your primary route, click the Enable dialing for Web proxy primary route option. If you are using dial-up for the backup route, click the Enable dialing for Web proxy backup route option.
5. Configure the Dialing hours by clicking the blue grids. All are selected by default. Blue grids are enabled and white grids are disabled.
6. Click the Credentials tab. Select the Entry Name of the phonebook entry you configured to use for Proxy Dial out. If you have more than one phonebook on your computer, use the drop-down menu to select the correct ISP.
7. Enter your ISP username and password.
8. When finished, click OK.

PART

Optimizing Proxy Server

IV

In Part IV, you learn how to manage and optimize Proxy Server's performance. In Chapter 13, you learn how to use Windows NT tools, such as Performance Monitor, to track and examine Proxy Server performance, and how to identify potential problems. You also learn about the counters Proxy Server adds to Windows NT Performance Monitor.

In Chapter 14, you explore troubleshooting the Proxy Server and the Proxy Client. A number of common problems and event messages are examined, and you learn valuable troubleshooting strategies.

CHAPTER

13

Proxy Server Performance

About Chapter 13

As with all server products, the process of monitoring and tuning the performance of the product is an ongoing and often challenging task. Proxy Server, however, makes performance management easier by adding Proxy counters to Performance Monitor. The extensive counters available enable the administrator to see how well Proxy Server is the handling the requests of the Web, Winsock, and Socks Proxy Server services as well as the caching functions. This chapter shows you how to use Proxy Server's counters in Performance Monitor, and the labs at the end of the chapter give you a chance to practice the skills you learn.

Performance Monitoring

The concept of *performance monitoring* often does not get the attention it deserves in networking environments. Because of time constraints and often overworked network administrators, many environments tend to be reactive in terms of performance problems or issues — in other words, fix it when it's broken, but don't worry about it until then.

This approach is ineffective and often leads to network downtime, which costs companies a lot of money and often leaves users waiting on the network. The best approach is a preventative measure — monitor the network and resolve potential problems before they ever become problems. This preventative approach saves both time and money in the end.

Windows NT provides a wide scope of performance monitoring counters in both Network Monitor and Performance Monitor that you can easily view and configure. These tools enable administrators to watch what is happening and identify potential problems on both the server and the network.

In conjunction with NT's Performance Monitor, Proxy Server adds its own set of counters during setup, so the performance of the Proxy Server, the services, and the cache can be monitored. These counters enable network administrators to gain a clear view of the Proxy Server's performance.

Performance Bottlenecks

Before you examine the Proxy Server Performance Monitor and its configuration, you should note some common server problems, or typical performance issues that tend to arise in all servers on all networks. The common term to identify these problems is either a server or network bottleneck.

Bottlenecks are common performance problems in network environments. A bottleneck is a device, whether it be a router or a CPU, that cannot handle the load that is placed on it by the network. It's a lot like an entry ramp to a freeway. Often, the entry ramp is too small to handle the amount of traffic placed on it at 5:00 in the afternoon. The traffic backs up and each car has to wait to be serviced, or wait until it can get on the freeway. If a server's CPU is too slow to handle the amount of network requests, it becomes a bottleneck — there are too many packets needing service, so the packets have to wait. This slows performance down and can become a serious performance problem.

There are a number of common devices that can become bottlenecks:

- **CPU:** If the CPU is not fast enough to handle the amount of network and system requests placed on it, it becomes a bottleneck. The system runs slowly and requests have to wait to be serviced. As networks grow, server CPUs often have to be upgraded to handle the work load. The main CPU counter you should watch is listed under the Processor object as %Processor Time. This counter gives you the percentage of processor time that is busy. Typically, the lower the %Processor Time counter, the better. If the %Processor Time goes over 80 percent, you probably need to upgrade to a faster processor.
- **Memory:** The common wisdom is often true—the more RAM a system has, the better it will perform. A server must have enough RAM to meet the system's services and demands. It is common today for network servers to have over 100MB of RAM. For the Memory object, you should watch the Page Fault/sec counter to determine how the system is using the swap file. If the system is constantly having to use the swap file to store files, and then return them to physical memory, you probably need more RAM.
- **Disk:** The physical disks of the server must be large enough to handle general storage and caching needs. The disk counter to watch is Disk Queue Length, as this gives you information about the queue length waiting to transfer information to the disk. If there is too much queue data, this usually means the disk is too slow and there may even be a problem with the disk I/O subsystem.
- **NIC:** Network Interface Cards are often sources of bottlenecks. Regardless of the speed or memory of the server, the NIC must be able to handle the amount of network traffic placed on it. You can accomplish this by making certain you use network interface cards that can match the bandwidth offered by your network.

Performance Monitor

The Windows NT Performance Monitor is available in the Administrative Tools (Common) menu. Use Performance Monitor to evaluate the performance of the server. Basically, Performance Monitor enables you to create charts that track the performance of a variety of system components. This enables you to see each resource and its performance, so you can identify potential bottlenecks.

To create a new chart, select File ⇛ New Chart. Then, select Edit ⇛ Add to Chart. This gives you an Add to Chart dialog box, as shown in Figure 13-1, where you can add counters such as %Processor Time, Interrupts/sec, and a variety of other counters.

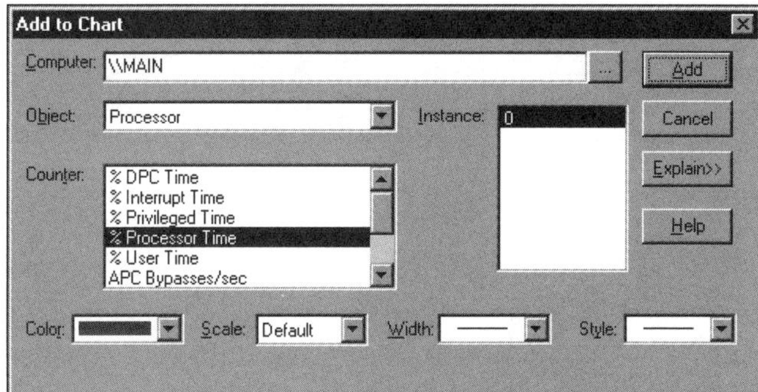

FIGURE 13-1 Add to Chart dialog box in Performance Monitor

Each counter is displayed in a different color, which enables you to view a variety of counters in one chart, as shown in Figure 13-2.

You can also use Performance Monitor to create log files, which you can use to help determine problems and identify configuration changes that you need to make. To add a log, simply click the Log button on the toolbar, and then click the + button on the toolbar to add components to the log file.

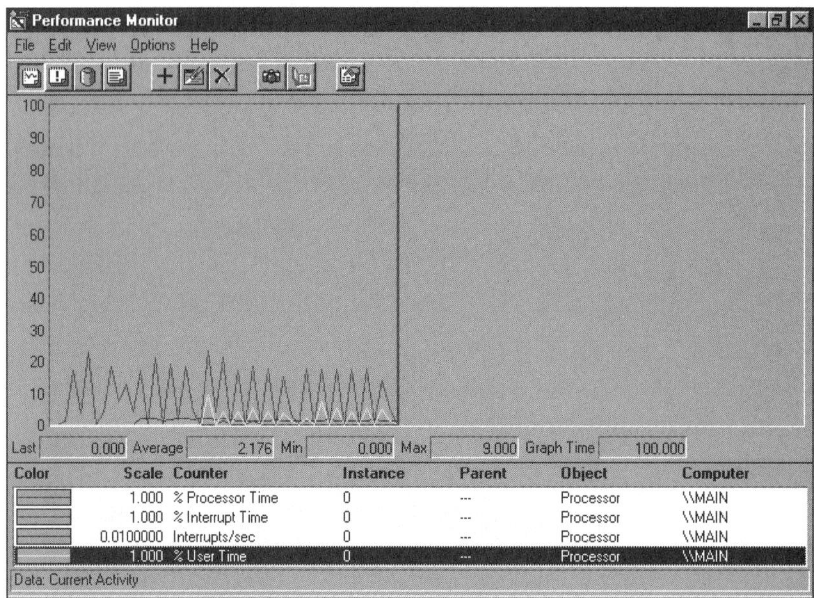

FIGURE 13-2 Performance Monitor

If you want to view disk performance, which you will need to do for some Proxy Server counters, you must turn on disk monitoring by using the Diskperf utility at the command line, as shown in Figure 13-3.

```
C:\WINNT\System32\cmd.exe
Microsoft(R) Windows NT(TM)
(C) Copyright 1985-1996 Microsoft Corp.

C:\>diskperf

Disk Performance counters on this system are currently set to never start.

DISKPERF [-Y[E] | -N] [\\computername]

  -Y[E] Sets the system to start disk performance counters
        when the system is restarted.

     E  Enables the disk performance counters used for measuring
        performance of the physical drives in striped disk set
        when the system is restarted.
        Specify -Y without the E to restore the normal disk
        performance counters.

  -N    Sets the system disable disk performance counters
        when the system is restarted.

  \\computername       Is the name of the computer you want to
                       see or set disk performance counter use.

C:\>
```

FIGURE 13-3 DiskPerf utility options

There are a couple of options, but you will mainly want to use the -y switch to turn on disk monitoring. Keep in mind that you need to reboot the system to start monitoring. You should to monitor the system over a few days to get an accurate look at the disk performance, and you should turn off DiskPerf once you have finished because of the drain it places on the system.

Network Monitor

Where Performance Monitor enables you to gather information about the performance of the server, Network Monitor enables you to gather information about the performance of the network. Network Monitor is also accessible in Administrative Tools (Common) and enables you to capture network data, as shown in Figure 13-4.

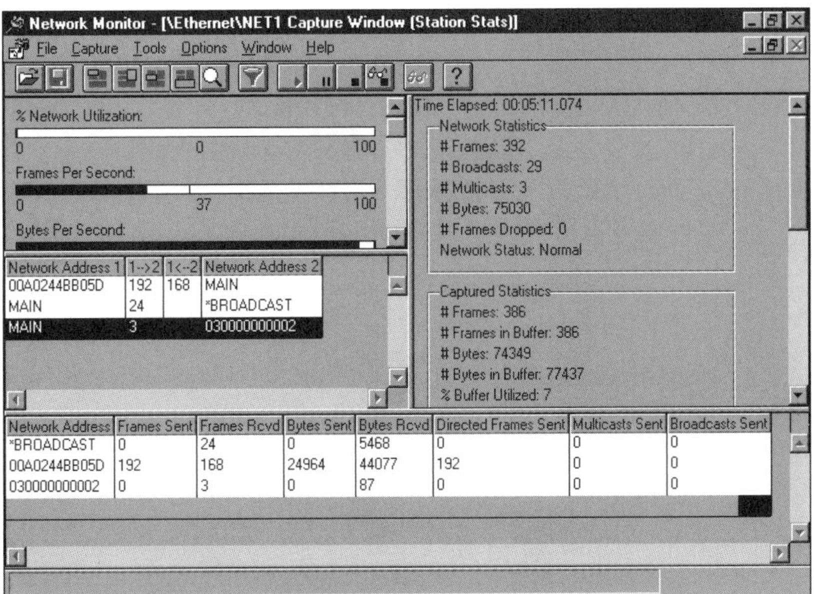

FIGURE 13-4 Network Monitor

Network Monitor gathers information with counters such as % Network Utilization, Frames Per Second, Bytes Per Second, and statistical information on the network and the captured data.

Network Monitor is an effective tool to capture data during slow network periods. For example, if the network seems to become sluggish every day at 3:00 P.M., you can use Network Monitor to capture data during that slow period. The data gathered can help identify potential problems or network bottlenecks.

You can start a network capture by clicking Capture ⇒ Start. Once a capture is complete, you can use the Capture menu can be used to stop the capture and Display Captured data. This gives you a series of columns that provide data about the network activity, as shown in Figure 13-5.

Network Monitor - [Capture:1 (Summary)]

File Edit Display Tools Options Window Help

Frame	Time	Src MAC Addr	Dst MAC Addr	Protocol	Description
1	10.432	MAIN	030000000002	BONE	Station Query Request C (0x00)
2	10.968	MAIN	*BROADCAST	BROWSER	Workgroup Announcement [0x0c] PROXY
3	11.527	MAIN	030000000002	BONE	Station Query Request C (0x00)
4	12.527	MAIN	030000000002	BONE	Station Query Request C (0x00)
5	22.866	MAIN	*BROADCAST	DHCP	Discover (xid=5AF141BB)
6	32.479	MAIN	*BROADCAST	DHCP	Discover (xid=5AF141BB)
7	34.715	MAIN	*BROADCAST	NBT	NS: Query req. for JSPNRMPTGSBSSDIR
8	35.463	MAIN	*BROADCAST	NBT	NS: Query req. for JSPNRMPTGSBSSDIR
9	36.214	MAIN	*BROADCAST	NBT	NS: Query req. for JSPNRMPTGSBSSDIR
10	43.681	MAIN	*BROADCAST	ARP_RARP	ARP: Request, Target IP: 10.0.0.5
11	43.681	WIN98 CLNT	MAIN	ARP_RARP	ARP: Reply, Target IP: 10.0.0.4 Target
12	43.681	MAIN	WIN98 CLNT	NBT	NS: Query (Node Status) resp. for MAIN,
13	43.682	WIN98 CLNT	MAIN	TCP	....S., len: 8, seq: 9153298-915330
14	43.682	MAIN	WIN98 CLNT	TCP	.A..S., len: 4, seq: 584540-584543
15	43.682	WIN98 CLNT	MAIN	TCP	.A...., len: 0, seq: 9153299-915329
16	43.682	WIN98 CLNT	MAIN	NBT	SS: Session Request, Dest: MAIN
17	43.683	MAIN	WIN98 CLNT	NBT	SS: Positive Session Response, Len: 0
18	43.683	WIN98 CLNT	MAIN	SMB	C negotiate, Dialect = NT LM 0.12
19	43.685	MAIN	WIN98 CLNT	SMB	R negotiate, Dialect # = 5
20	43.690	WIN98 CLNT	MAIN	SMB	C session setup & X, Username = WIN98 CL
21	43.866	MAIN	WIN98 CLNT	TCP	.A...., len: 0, seq: 584638-584638
22	45.305	MAIN	WIN98 CLNT	SMB	R session setup & X, and R tree connect
23	45.306	WIN98 CLNT	MAIN	SMB	C transact2 Query file system info

F#: 1/417 Off: 17 (x11) L: 12 (xC)

FIGURE 13-5 Network Monitor captured data

Proxy Server Performance Counters

As I mentioned previously, installing Proxy Server adds Proxy Server counters to Performance Monitor. You can access the counters through the standard Performance Monitor, or by clicking Start ⇒ Programs ⇒ Microsoft Proxy Server ⇒ Monitor Microsoft Proxy Server Performance. If you create a new chart, you will see under the Object drop-down list that Proxy Server adds counters for the Web

Proxy Server Service, the Winsock Proxy Service, the Socks Proxy Service, the Web Proxy Server Cache, and Packet Filtering, as shown in Figure 13-6.

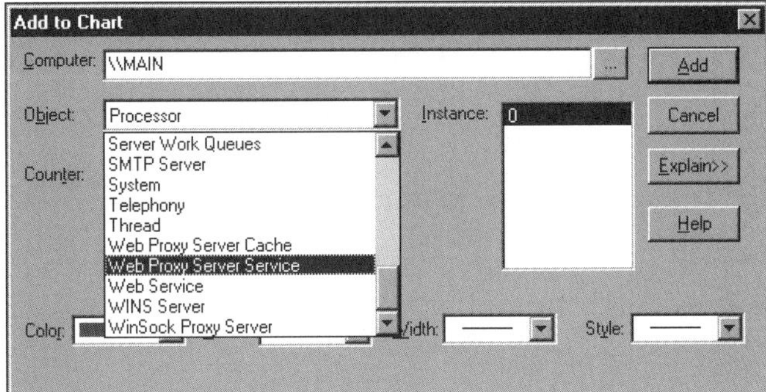

FIGURE 13-6 Proxy Server objects

By selecting the appropriate object, you can choose from a variety of counters that enable you to monitor Proxy Server's performance. The following sections examine each of the objects and counters.

Web Proxy Server Service

The Web Proxy Server Service object provides with many counters to monitor the performance of all aspects of the Web Proxy Service. Table 13-1 gives you a complete list of the counters available for the Web Proxy Service and an explanation of the information each counter provides.

TABLE 13-1 WEB PROXY SERVER SERVICE COUNTERS

Web Proxy counter	*Explanation*
Array Bytes Received/sec	The rate at which bytes of data are received from other Proxy Servers in the same array
Array Bytes Sent/sec	The rate at which bytes of data are sent to other Proxy Servers in the same array
Array Bytes Total/sec	The sum of Array Bytes Received/sec and Array Bytes Sent/sec

continued

TABLE 13-1 *(continued)*

Web Proxy counter	Explanation
Cache Hit Ratio (%)	The percentage of Web Proxy client requests that have been served by using cache data out of the total number of client requests
Client Bytes Received/sec	The rate at which data bytes are received from clients
Client Bytes Sent/sec	The rate at which data bytes are sent to clients
Client Bytes Total/sec	The sum of Client Bytes Received/sec and Client Bytes Sent/sec
Current Average Milliseconds/request	The mean number of milliseconds required to service a client request
Current Users	The current number of users connected to the service
DNS Cache Entries	The current number of DNS domain name entries cached
DNS Cache Flushes	The total number of times that the DNS cache has been flushed
DNS Cache Hits	The total number of times a DNS domain name was found in the DNS cache
DNS Cache Hits (%)	The percentage of DNS names serviced by the DNS cache out of the total of all DNS entries that have been retrieved
DNS Retrievals	The total number of DNS domain names that have been retrieved
Failing Requests/sec	The rater per second that client requests have been completed with some type of error
FTP Requests	The number of FTP requests that have been made
Gopher Requests	The number of Gopher requests that have been made
HTTP Requests	The number of HTTP requests that have been made
HTTPS Sessions	The total number of secure HTTP sessions that have been serviced by the SSL Tunnel
Maximum Users	The maximum number of users that have connected to the service at the same time
Requests/sec	The number of incoming requests that have been made, per second

Web Proxy counter	Explanation
Reverse Bytes Received/sec	The rate at which bytes of data are received from Web publishing servers in response to reverse proxy requests
Reverse Bytes Sent/sec	The rate at which bytes of data are sent to Web publishing servers in response to reverse proxy requests
Reverse Bytes Total/sec	The sum of Reverse Bytes Received/sec and Reverse Bytes Sent/sec
Sites Denied	The total number of Internet sites that the service has denied access
Sites Granted	The total number of Internet sites that the service has granted access
SNEWS Session	The total number of SNEWS sessions serviced by the SSL Tunnel
SSL Client Bytes Received/sec	The rate at which secure SSL data bytes are received from secure clients
SSL Client Bytes Sent/sec	The rate at which secure SSL data bytes are sent to secure clients
SSL Client Bytes Total/sec	The sum of SSL Client Bytes Received/sec and SSL Client Bytes Sent/sec
SSL Sessions Scavenged	The number of SSL sessions closed because of idle time-out and excessive SSL demand
Thread Pool Active Sessions	The number of Web Proxy client sessions being actively served by thread pool threads
Thread Pool Failures	The number of client requests rejected because the thread pool was overcommitted
Thread Pool Size	The number of threads in the thread pool
Total Array Fetches	The total number of client requests that have been serviced by requesting data from other array members
Total Cache Fetches	The total number of client requests that have been serviced by using cached data
Total Failing Requests	The total number of client requests that have failed because of errors
Total Requests	The total number of requests that have ever been made to the Proxy Server

continued

TABLE 13-1 *(continued)*

Web Proxy counter	Explanation
Total Reverse Fetches	The total number of reverse Proxy requests that have been serviced from Web publishing servers
Total Upstream Fetches	The total number of requests that have been serviced using data from remote servers on the Internet or from an upstream chained proxy servers
Total SSL Sessions	The total number of SSL sessions received by the SSL Tunnel
Total Successful Requests	The total number of requests that have been successfully processed.
Total Users	The total number of users ever connected to the service
Upstream Bytes Received/sec	The rate at which bytes are received from servers on the Internet or upstream chained proxy servers
Upstream Bytes Sent/sec	The rate at which bytes are sent to servers on the Internet or upstream chained proxy servers
Upstream Bytes Total/sec	The sum of Upstream Bytes Sent/sec and Upstream Bytes Received/sec
Unknown SSL Sessions	The total number of unknown SSL sessions serviced by the SSL Tunnel

Obviously, although there are many counters to choose from, however, there are some major counters that you will normally focus on:

- **Cache Hit Ratio %:** This counter tells you what percentage of the Web Proxy Server requests were serviced from the cache. This percentage gives you a good idea of how well your cache is being utilized. If the percentage is low, this means that most requests are being filled directly from the Internet. You may have too many restrictions on what objects are cached, or your cache drive may be too small to adequately store objects that can be cached.
- **Client Bytes Total/sec:** This counter tells you the transfer speed of data from the Proxy Server to the client, and from the client to the Proxy Server. This counter can help you determine if the network is adequately handling the traffic from the Proxy Server to the clients and vice versa.

- **Current Average Milliseconds/Request:** This counter tells you how long it takes for Proxy Server to service a client request. This information tells you if the server is adequately handling the client request load.
- **HTTP Requests:** This counter gives you an idea of how much HTTP request traffic the Proxy Server is receiving from the clients. This can give you an indication of how often users are using the Internet and if Proxy Server is able to handle the volume of requests.

It is not important to know all the counters for the exam, but you should understand these major counters and when you would want to use them.

Web Proxy Server Cache

The Web Proxy Server Cache object provides you with counters to monitor the performance of your cache drives. These counters help you determine how the cache is being utilized, and if the cache drives are able to accommodate the caching needs of the Server. Table 13-2 is the complete counter list for the Web Proxy Server Cache object.

TABLE 13-2 WEB PROXY SERVER CACHE COUNTERS

Cache Counter	*Explanation*
Active Refresh Bytes Rate	The number of bytes of data per second retrieved from the Internet to actively refresh popular URLs in the cache
Active URL Refresh Rate	The number of popular URLs per second that are actively refreshed from the Internet in the cache
Bytes Committed Rate	The number of bytes per second committed to disk storage in the cache
Bytes in Cache	The total number of bytes of data currently contained in the cache
Bytes Retrieved Rate	The number of bytes of data per second retrieved from disk storage in the cache
Max Bytes Cached	The maximum number of bytes of data that have been stored in the cache

continued

TABLE 13-2 *(continued)*

CACHE COUNTER	EXPLANATION
Max URLs Cached	The maximum number of URLs that have been stored in the cache
Total Actively Refreshed URLs	The total number of popular URLs in the cache that have been actively refreshed from the Internet
Total Bytes Actively Refreshed	The total number of bytes that have been actively refreshed from the Internet
Total Bytes Cached	The total number of bytes that have been stored in the cache
Total Bytes Retrieved	The total number of bytes that have been retrieved from the cache
Total URLs Cached	The total number of URLs that have been stored in the cache
Total URLs Retrieved	The total number of URLs that have been retrieved from the cache
URL Commit Rate	The number of URLs per second committed to the cache
URL Retrieve Rate	The number of URLs per second retrieved from the cache
URLs in Cache	The current number of URLs in the cache

There are a few counters you would use to determine it your cache drives are performing adequately:

- **Active Refresh Bytes/sec:** For active caching, this counter tells you how active the refresh rate is — in other words, how much active caching and pre-fetching Proxy Server is performing. If the value is too high, you may need to take a look at your active caching policy and make some adjustments so the Proxy Server is not doing a lot of pre-fetching.
- **Max Bytes Cached:** This counter tells you the maximum size the cache has reached. If the value is consistently high, most of the cache storage space is constantly being used. You may need to increase the size of the cache to accommodate cache growth.

- **Total Actively Refreshed URLs:** This counter measures the total number of URLs that have been actively refreshed. This gives you an idea of how many URLs in the cache are being pre-fetched. As with the Active Refresh Bytes/sec counter, this tells you how much active caching Proxy Server is performing.
- **URLs in Cache:** This counter is a quick way to determine how many URLs the cache is currently storing.

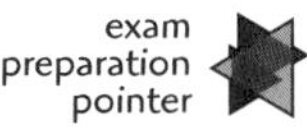

You do not need to memorize all the cache counters, but you should be familiar with these.

Winsock Proxy Service

The Winsock Proxy Service object counters give you performance data about Winsock utilization and performance. These counters help you determine how the Proxy Server is servicing Winsock requests. Table 13-3 lists counters available for the Winsock Proxy Service object.

TABLE 13-3 Winsock Proxy Service Counters

Winsock Proxy Service counter	*Explanation*
Accepting TCP Connections	The number of connection objects that are waiting for a TCP connection from the Winsock Proxy client after a successful remote connection
Active Sessions	The number of active Winsock Proxy client sessions
Active TCP Connections	The number of active TCP connections
Active UDP Connections	The number of active UDP connections
Available Worker Threads	The number of control channel threads that are available or waiting in the completion port queue
Back-Connecting TCP Connections	The total number of connections that are waiting for an inbound connect API call to finish
Bytes Read/sec	The number of bytes of data read per second by the data pump

continued

TABLE 13-3 *(continued)*

Winsock Proxy Service counter	Explanation
Bytes Written/sec	The number of bytes of data written per second by the data pump
Connecting TCP Connections	The total number of connections that are waiting for a remote connect API call to finish
DNS Cache Entries	The current number of DNS domain name entries cached as a result of Winsock service activity
DNS Cache Flushes	The total number of times the DNS domain name cache has been flushed or cleared by the Winsock service
DNS Cache Hits	The total number of times a DNS domain name was found in the DNS cache by the Winsock service
DNS Cache Hits (%)	The percentage of DNS domain names received by the DNS cache out of the total of all DNS entries that have been retrieved by the Winsock service
DNS Retrievals	The total number of DNS domain names that have been retrieved by the Winsock service
Failed DNS Resolutions	The number of API calls to `gethostname/gethostaddr` that have failed.
Listening TCP Connections	The number of connection objects that are waiting for TCP connections from the Internet after a successful listen
Non-connected UDP Mappings	The number of mappings for UDP connections
Pending DNS Resolutions	The number of API calls to `gethostname/gethostaddr` that have not yet returned
Successful DNS Resolutions	The number of API calls to `gethostname/gethostaddr` that have returned successfully
Worker Threads	The number of control channel worker threads and data pumps worker threads that are active

The following are the main counters you would use to give you information about the Winsock Service:

- **Active Sessions:** This counter tells you how many active Winsock sessions are currently in progress. This gives you information on how clients are using the Winsock Proxy Service and the number of clients that are using the service.
- **Active TCP Connections** and **Active UDP Connections:** These two counters give you data about the number of active TCP and UDP connections. These counters are useful to gain utilization information concerning the Winsock Service.

It is not necessary to memorize all the Winsock Service counters for the exam, but you should be familiar with these.

Socks Proxy Service

The Socks Proxy Service object gives you counters to monitor Socks connections and activity. Table 13-4 is a list of the counters available for the Socks Proxy Service object

TABLE 13-4 Socks Proxy Service Counters

Socks Proxy Service counter	*Explanation*
Socks Client Bytes Received/sec	The rate at which bytes of data are received from Socks clients
Socks Client Bytes Sent/sec	The rate at which bytes of data are sent to Socks clients
Socks Clients Bytes Total/sec	The sum of Socks Client Bytes Received/sec and Socks Client Bytes Sent/sec
Socks Sessions	The total number of Socks client sessions serviced by the Socks Proxy service
Total Failed Socks Sessions	The total number of Socks client requests that were not serviced because the client did not have access rights to satisfy the request or because of an initial protocol error
Total Socks Sessions	The total number of Socks client sessions
Total Successful Socks Sessions	The total number of Socks client requests that were successfully serviced

You would primarily use the following two counters to monitor the Socks Service:

- **Total Failed Socks Sessions:** This counter gives you information about the total number of Socks sessions that have failed because of access rights or protocol error. If this number is unusually high, you should take a look at the permissions you have assigned Socks clients and see if the permissions are too restrictive.
- **Total Socks Sessions:** This counter enables you to see the total number of Socks client sessions. This is useful to determine if clients are utilizing the Socks Proxy Service.

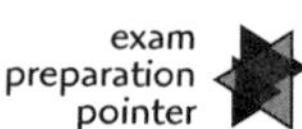

You are not likely to see any exam questions on Socks Proxy Service counters on the exam.

Packet Filter

The Packet Filter object provides you with counters to view packet filter performance. These counters can be helpful in determining the number of rejected packets, which could indicate attacks from the Internet. Table 13-5 gives you the counters for the Packet Filtering object.

TABLE 13-5 PACKET FILTERING COUNTERS

Packet Filter counter	*Explanation*
Frames Dropped Due to Filter Denial	The total number of frames dropped because of data rejection by dynamic packet filters
Frames Dropped Due to Protocol Violations	The total number of frames dropped because of a protocol anomaly
Total Dropped Frames	The total number of dropped or filtered frames
Total Incoming Connections	The total number of incoming connections established through filtered interfaces
Total Lost Logging Frames	The total number of dropped frames that cannot be logged

You would primarily use the following packet filter counters:

- **Frames Dropped Due to Filter Denial:** This counter gives you a good idea of the number of frames that have been dropped because the filter denied access.
- **Frames Dropped Due to Protocol Violations:** This counter enables you to see the number of frames that have been dropped because of protocol violations or errors.

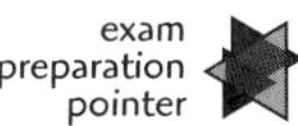

You do not need to memorize all the packet filter counters for the exam, but you should be familiar with these.

Performance Tips

Performance Monitor and Network Monitor help you identify problems or performance issues with Proxy Server, but it is up to you to keep Proxy Server's performance at an acceptable level. The best way to do this is through some simple preventative tips. These tips will help you avoid performance problems, or at least solve them before they have an adverse effect on network users.

- Make sure your cache drives are large enough to permit network growth. Keep a sharp eye on network growth and remember to adjust the cache size using the cache formula so the cache is large enough to service the needs of all the clients.
- If additional demands are placed on the Proxy Server computer, such as Web hosting or other network functions, make sure your CPU can handle the load and that your system has enough RAM to handle the tasks the server will be required to perform.
- If there are changes in the network or additional loads are placed on the Proxy Server, establish a new baseline of performance so you will know what is abnormal and what is normal.
- Make sure that your domain and cache filters protect your network and block any activity by users you want to restrict, but don't make the services more restrictive than necessary. This leads to poor performance and a lot of complaints from the users.

- Use Performance Monitor to check the services from time to time to see how the server is running — even if no problems are evident.
- Create logs you can review. This helps identify potential problems and issues that need to be addressed.

Simple Network Management Protocol

Simple Network Management Protocol (SNMP) is a protocol in the TCP/IP suite that enables administrators to monitor performance information on server products as well as network devices such as routers and hubs. Proxy Server supports the use of SNMP.

SNMP is not a protocol that is available by default. Any device that is monitored with SNMP must use an SNMP software package to gather information about the device. Information that is gathered is stored in a Management Information Base (MIB) file.

Proxy Server allows the use of SNMP to manage and evaluate its performance of the Web and Winsock Proxy Server Services. The software for SNMP, however, is not installed by default. The SNMP files, `w3p.mib` and `wsp.mib` are available on the installation CD-ROM in the PERFCTRS directory. The administrator has to copy these two files manually and compile them with the SNMP package.

To learn more about SNMP and SNMP packages offered by Microsoft, visit `www.microsoft.com`.

Exam Preparation Summary

You will most likely see several questions on the exam about Performance Monitor as it relates to Proxy Server, as well as some general Performance Monitor and Network Monitor questions. You may be asked to determine which Monitor would be best for which situation. You should remember that Network Monitor is used to watch the activity of the network, whereas Performance Monitor is used to watch the performance of the local machine. So, if a question asks you about the CPU of the Proxy Server, you would use Performance Monitor to monitor the %Processor Time counter.

You will also be asked about various Proxy Server counters. You should review the counters pointed out in this chapter, as those are the ones you will most likely see as answer choices on the exam.

Key Point Summary

In this chapter, you learned how to configure various Proxy Server Performance Monitor counters.

- Windows NT Performance Monitor is used to watch the performance of the server's system and can be used to monitor the processor, the memory, and many other system components.
- Network Monitor is used to view performance and statistical information concerning network traffic. Traffic can be monitored and captured, then the captured information can be reviewed.
- During installation, Proxy Server adds a number of counters for the Web, Winsock, and Socks Proxy Server services, as well as caching and filter counters.
- Any server or network device that is not able to handle the traffic or demands placed on it is considered a bottleneck.
- For the Web Proxy Server service counters, the most important counters to use are Cache Hit Ratio %, Client Bytes Total/sec, Current Average Milliseconds/Request, and HTTP Requests.
- For the Web Proxy Server cache counters, the most important counters to use are Active Refresh Bytes/sec, Max Bytes Cached, Total Actively Refreshed URLs, and URLs in Cache.
- For the Winsock Proxy Service, the most important counters to use are Active Sessions, Active TCP Connections, and Active UDP Connections.
- For the Socks Proxy Service, the most important counters to use Total Failed Socks Sessions and Total Socks Sessions.
- For the Packet Filter counters, the most important counters to use are Frames Dropped Due to Filter Denial and Frames Dropped Due to Protocol Violation.

Applying What You've Learned

The following review questions give you a chance to test your knowledge of the content in this chapter. Should you miss some, review the appropriate portions of the chapter. The answers to the Instant Assessment questions can be found in Appendix B.

Instant Assessment

1. Which counter should you use to view information about protocol violations?
   - **A.** Frames Dropped Due to Filter Denial
   - **B.** Frames Dropped Due to Protocol Violations
   - **C.** Total Failed Socks Sessions
   - **D.** Total Socks Sessions
2. If you want to know how many URLs are in the cache, which counter should you use?
   - **A.** Total Actively Refreshed URLs
   - **B.** DNS Cache Entries
   - **C.** Connecting TCP Connections
   - **D.** URLs in Cache
3. In a Proxy Server with active caching, which counter should you use to gather performance information to see how much pre-fetching the server is performing?
   - **A.** Max Bytes Cached
   - **B.** Active Refresh Bytes/sec
   - **C.** Total URLs cached
   - **D.** URL Commit Rate
4. You want to view how fast Proxy Server is transmitting bytes to the client and vice versa. Which counter should you use?
   - **A.** Cache Hit Ratio %
   - **B.** Current Average Milliseconds/Requests

C. Current Bytes Total/sec

D. Unknown SSL Sessions

5. Which counter should you use to determine if you should add more RAM to your Proxy Server?

A. Upstream Bytes/sec

B. Disk Queue Length

C. %Processor Time

D. Page Faults/sec

Critical Thinking Labs

These labs present you with analysis problems to test your critical thinking skills with the content in this chapter.

Lab 13.72 *Performance Monitor and active caching*

Your company wants to use Performance Monitor to gain information about the performance of active caching. Which counters would you recommend?

Lab 13.73 *Performance Monitor and processor speed*

You want to see if your system processor is able to handle the demands placed on the system by Proxy clients. Which counters should you use?

Lab 13.74 *Performance Monitor and client utilization*

You want to see how the Winsock and Socks clients are utilizing the related Proxy Server services. Which counters should you use?

Lab 13.75 *Performance Monitor logs*

How can you configure Performance Monitor to create a log file?

Lab 13.76 *Internet traffic*

You want to analyze the Internet traffic coming in and out of your environment. How can you do this?

Hands-on Labs

The Hands-on Labs give you an opportunity to practice skills you have learned in this chapter. These labs assume you have at least a functioning Proxy Server on a network.

Lab 13.77 *Configuring Performance Monitor*

In this lab, you will configure Performance Monitor to allow physical disk counters.

1. Click Start⇒Run. Type **CMD** and click OK.
2. At the command prompt, type `Diskperf`.
3. You are given a switch list. Since you want to allow the system to run disk performance counters, type **diskperf -y** and press the Enter key.
4. You will be prompted to reboot the computer. Close the command prompt and reboot to activate the disk performance counters.

Lab 13.78 *Configuring Web Proxy Service counters*

In this lab you will configure Web Proxy Service counter.

1. Click Start⇒Programs⇒Microsoft Proxy Server⇒Monitor Microsoft Proxy Server Performance.
2. Click the File menu and click New Chart.
3. Click the Edit menu and click Add to Chart.
4. The Add to Chart window appears. In the object drop-down menu, select Web Proxy Server Service.
5. In the Counter menu, select Cache Hit Ratio % and click the Add button.
6. Click Bytes Total/sec and click the Add button.
7. Click Average Milliseconds/Request and click the Add button.
8. Click HTTP Requests and click the Add button, then click Done.
9. View the performance counters and take note of any high percentages. This could denote performance issues or problems.
10. Click the File⇒New Chart.
11. Click the Edit⇒Add to Chart.
12. Select another one of the Proxy Server objects and add counters that you wish to view. Continue to experiment with Performance Monitor until you are comfortable using it.

CHAPTER

14

Troubleshooting Proxy Server

About Chapter 14

This chapter examines troubleshooting Proxy Server and the Proxy client. You learn about Windows NT tools and Proxy Server tools that help the system administrator find and even prevent problems. I also discuss some of the most common error messages concerning Proxy Server and the Proxy client. This chapter has four labs that give you a chance to practice the skills you learn.

Troubleshooting

Troubleshooting is one of those skills you need to have as a network administrator, but you hope you seldom use. Any time you work with complex operating systems and server software, the potential problems can be equally complex. In terms of Proxy Server, you have to not only troubleshoot Proxy Server services, but you also have to troubleshoot IIS and Windows NT.

Each system administrator has his or her own method of troubleshooting, and you no doubt have your own system if you have experience troubleshooting networks or systems. There are no hard rules, but you should ask yourself some questions when troubleshooting. The following questions can help you examine a problem logically and find the solution to that problem.

- **Where is the problem?** Is the problem most likely a server problem or is it an actual Proxy Server service problem?
- **What has changed in the environment?** Often, changes may trigger error messages or some other problem within the environment. Note any changes that have been made.
- **What resources are available for research?** Unfortunately, some administrators use a trial-and-error approach to troubleshooting. This method is ineffective and may actually create more problems. The best approach is to research the problem using the Windows NT documentation, the Proxy Server documentation, Microsoft TechNet, the Microsoft Knowledge Base, or even the white papers available at the Proxy Server home page at `www.microsoft.com/proxy`.
- **What is the course of action?** Determine a course of action to resolve the problem, then try that course of action.
- **Has the course of action resolved the problem?** If so, congratulations. If not, you should try some alternative courses of action or perform some further research.

Troubleshooting Tools

Fortunately, Windows NT provides you with some tools to assist in troubleshooting. These tools can assist you in determining the likely cause of the problem and even solving the problem. Of course, there are not specific troubleshooting tools for all situations, but you can use a number of resources to help you more quickly identify and resolve problems.

Event Viewer

Your first step to understanding a problem is to examine the error message in Event Viewer. Event Viewer is available in Windows NT's Administrative Tools and gives you a list of system events, as shown in Figure 14-1.

Event Viewer - System Log on \\MAIN

Log View Options Help

Date	Time	Source	Category	Event
11/11/98	8:34:36 AM	DCOM	None	1000
11/11/98	8:34:34 AM	Wins	None	4097
11/11/98	8:32:35 AM	SMTPSVC	None	525
11/11/98	8:32:29 AM	SMTPSVC	None	554
11/11/98	8:32:29 AM	SMTPSVC	None	423
11/11/98	8:32:13 AM	SMTPSVC	None	531
11/11/98	8:31:16 AM	DhcpServer	None	1024
11/11/98	8:30:57 AM	BROWSER	None	8015
11/11/98	8:30:02 AM	AppleTalk	None	3
11/11/98	8:30:02 AM	Serial	None	11
11/11/98	8:30:02 AM	Serial	None	22
11/11/98	8:30:02 AM	Serial	None	22
11/11/98	8:29:43 AM	EventLog	None	6005
11/11/98	8:30:02 AM	Serial	None	36
11/10/98	5:48:52 PM	BROWSER	None	8033
11/10/98	8:42:47 AM	DCOM	None	1000

FIGURE 14-1 Event Viewer

Event Messages are displayed according to the event that occurred. Blue buttons indicate that a service or process has started and do not signify errors. Red buttons indicate a Stop event, and yellow errors indicate warning events. If you double-click an event, you are taken to a detail page that gives you more information about that event, as shown in Figure 14-2.

As you can see in Figure 14-2, this Stop error concerns the Service Control Manager and tells you there is a problem with RAS configuration. This information can give you clues about how to begin the troubleshooting process and what areas of the system to focus on.

By using the Log menu in Event Viewer, you can choose view system, security, or application events, which all follow the same display pattern just discussed.

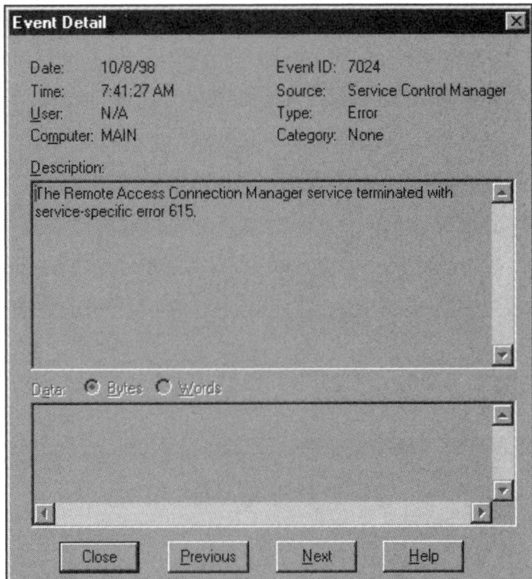

FIGURE 14-2 Event Viewer detail

Proxy Server Logs

Another resource to explore is the Proxy Server log files. Depending on the kind of problem you are having, there are various log files you may want to consult. For example, if you are having client setup problems, a log file is generated and stored in `C:\Mpcsetup.log` on the client computer. Server problems can be explored through the Proxy logs located on the server in `C:\winnt\system32\msplogs`, or you can explore additional NT log files located in `C:\winnt\system32\logfiles`.

The Registry

The Registry is one of those tools that can save the day or strike fear into the heart of even the most adept administrator. Essentially, the Registry is nothing more than one giant database of system settings. It replaces the older `.ini` files and organizes data so it can be easily found and manipulated. However, the Registry is not a place where you want to make mistakes. Incorrect changes, or accidental changes, can render the system non-bootable, so you should take great care before using the Registry as a primary troubleshooting tool. It is always best to tackle problems through the user interface and Control Panel if at all possible.

The Registry can be viewed and edited by using the Registry Editor, which comes in two forms — Regedit and Regedt32. Regedit is the standard Registry Editor for use with Windows 95, and Regedt32 is the 32-bit editor that comes with Windows NT. Regedt32 is a powerful tool that provides more functionality than Regedit. Regedt32 works with the entire Registry, but it enables you to manage and edit individual subtrees as well. In addition, Regedt32 shows additional values not available in Regedit, and it can be used for auditing purposes. To access Regedt32, type **regedt32** at the command line. This opens the Registry Editor, as shown in Figure 14-3.

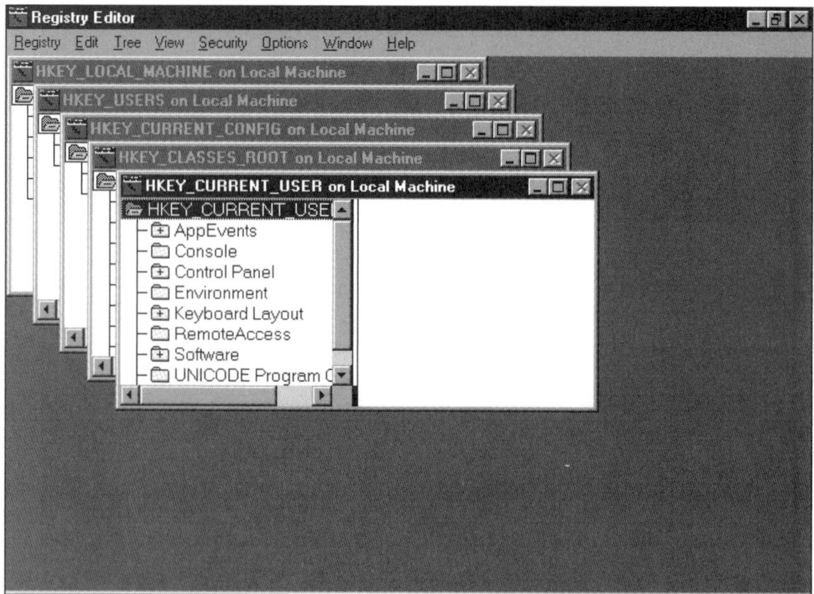

FIGURE 14-3 Regedt32

The Registry is organized in a tree structure with five subtrees, as you can see in Figure 14-3. The following is a short description of each subtree:

- **HKEY_LOCAL_MACHINE:** This subtree contains the system settings and hardware configurations. Any configuration for the server is stored in this subtree. Figure 14-4 shows the expanded subtree.

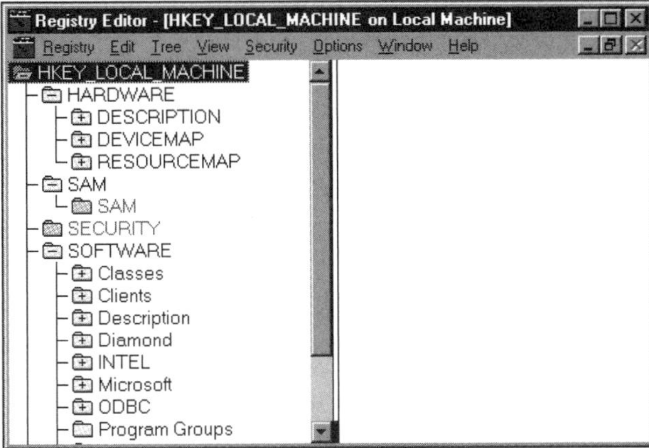

FIGURE 14-4 HKEY_LOCAL_MACHINE

- **HKEY_USERS:** This subtree contains information about users and the profile for each user on the local machine. Figure 14-5 shows the expanded subtree.

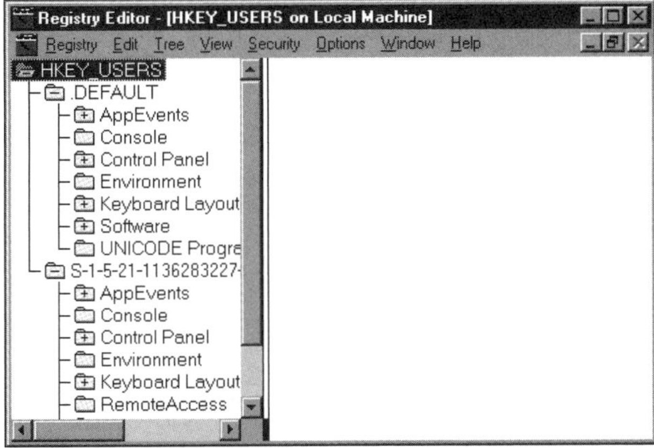

FIGURE 14-5 HKEY_USERS

- **HKEY_CURRENT_USER:** This subtree contains information about the current user's settings and profile information. Figure 14-6 shows the expanded subtree.

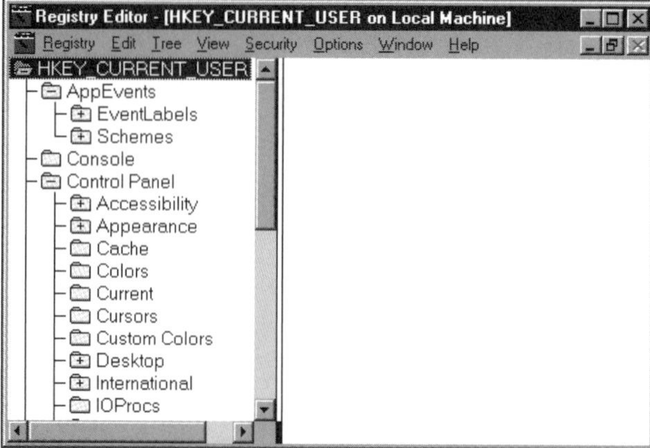

FIGURE 14-6 HKEY_CURRENT_USER

- **HKEY_CURRENT_CONFIG:** This subtree contains information about the current system configuration. Figure 14-7 shows the expanded subtree.

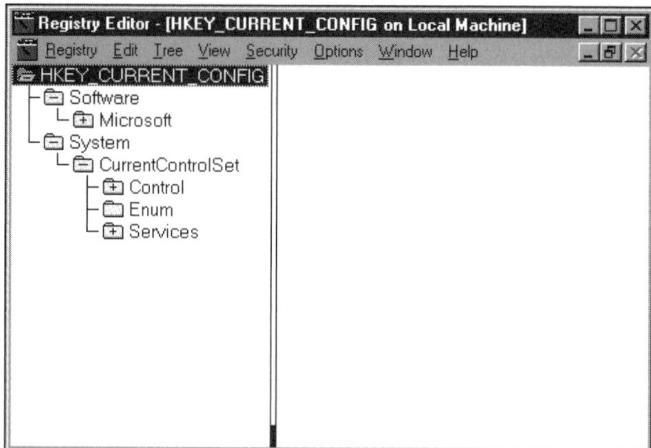

FIGURE 14-7 HKEY_CURRENT_CONFIG

- **HKEY_CLASSES_ROOT:** This subtree contains software configuration data. Figure 14-8 shows the expanded subtree.

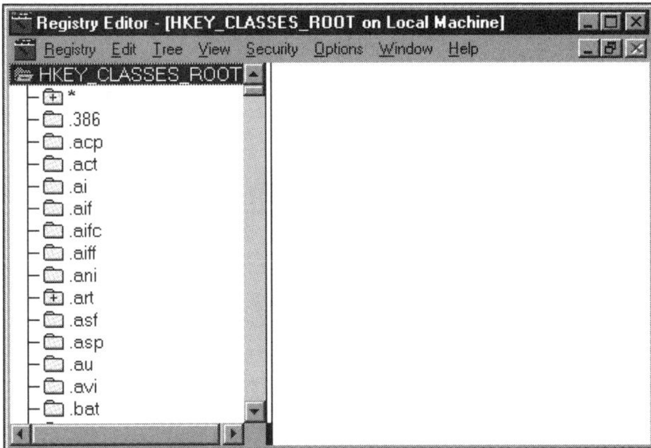

FIGURE 14-8 HKEY_CLASSES_ROOT

Each subtree is made up of keys and subkeys. Also, a group of keys is sometimes called a *hive*. By expanding the subtree, the appropriate key and subkeys as necessary, you are able to make changes to system configurations. For example, the Proxy Server registry entries are stored within five key locations, all within `HKEY_LOCAL_MACHINE\SYSTEM\CurrentControlSet\Services`, as shown in Figure 14-9.

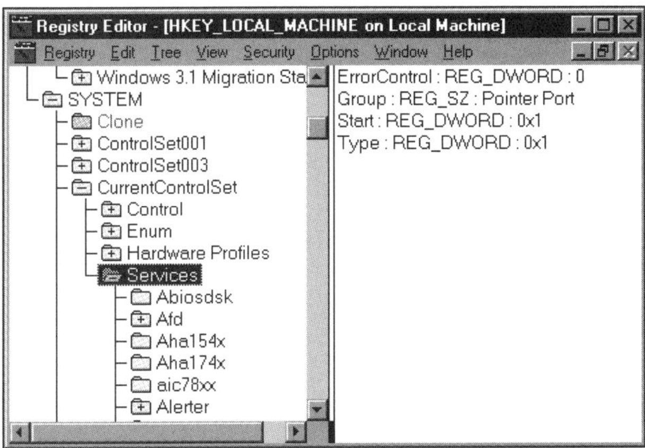

FIGURE 14-9 Proxy Server Registry entry location

From this point, you can view the registry entries and edit entries based on the service or Proxy Server function. For example, Figure 14-10 shows the W3PCache key and the Parameters subkey.

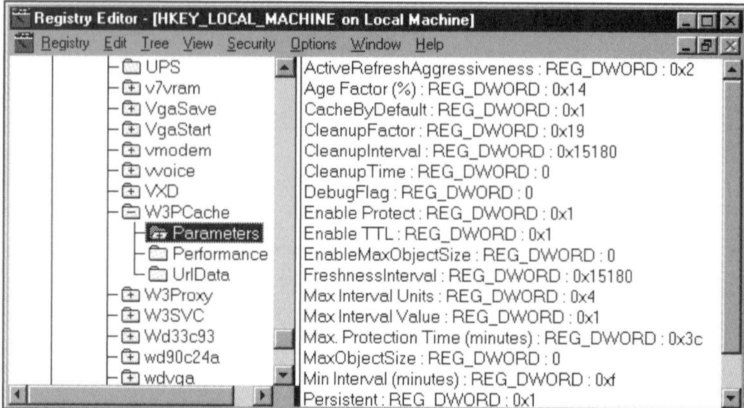

FIGURE 14-10 Parameters subkey

Table 14-1 gives the Proxy Server services and functions and the key locations for those services and functions.

TABLE 14-1 PROXY SERVER SERVICE REGISTRY KEY LOCATIONS

Service or function	*Key location*
Web Proxy Service	`W3Proxy\Parameters`
Web Proxy Cache	`W3PCache\Parameters`
Winsock Proxy Service	`WSPSRV\Parameters`
Socks Proxy Service	`W3Proxy\Parameters\Socks`
Reverse Proxy	`W3Proxy\Parameters\ReverseProxy`
Packet Filtering	`MSPAdmin\Filters`
Domain Filtering	`W3Proxy\Parameters\Dofilter`
Array Membership	`W3Proxy\Parameters\MemberArray`
Chain Membership	`W3Proxy\Parameters\ChainedArray`
Logging	`MSPAdmin\Parameters`

Remember that the Registry is simply a database that houses all the system settings, configurations, and user information. The Registry Editor can be a great troubleshooting tool, but again, you should use extreme caution when editing the Registry directly. You should back up the Registry before making any changes, make only a few changes at a time, and keep detailed notes about what you have changed.

You can learn more about the Registry and editing the Registry by consulting the Windows NT documentation.

Performance Monitor and Network Monitor

Often, server or network problems are actually performance issues. In other words, you have not received specific error messages, but the system is simply not functioning as it should. You can use Performance Monitor to examine the performance of the local machine, and you can use Proxy Server counters to search for problems that could be degrading performance. Network Monitor enables you to examine network traffic and look for problems that may be associated with actual network performance.

You can learn more about Performance Monitor and Network Monitor in Chapter 13.

CHKWSP

Because of the nature of the Winsock Proxy service and the potential for problems, Proxy Server includes a utility called Chkwsp to display Winsock information. The utility comes in both a 16-bit and a 32-bit form and is available in the MSPCLNT subdirectory, as shown in Figure 14-11.

You can run this utility from the command line and use the `-F` switch to display full information. The utility provides you with protocol information, Winsock file information, and the current status.

FIGURE 14-11 Chkwsp32

Proxy Client Event Messages and Problems

Except for performance-related problems, most of your troubleshooting work concerning Proxy Server will focus on event messages. By using Event Viewer, you can see the event message and an explanation of the message. The following sections highlight some of the most common event messages and general problems related to various Proxy Server client services and functions.

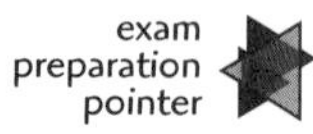

The following event messages and problems are some of the most common. You should be aware of them and their solutions for the exam. Many troubleshooting exam questions give you situations or problems where event messages are presented. You should pay careful attention to any error messages regarding the LAT.

Client Setup Event Messages

The following event messages are some of the most common ones encountered during Proxy client setup.

- **Please set a description of the internal network.** This error message occurs if the `Msplat.txt` file is not present on the computer. You should make certain that your logon credentials are accurate, and that you have enough disk space available.
- **Setup could not find `Wsock32.dll` on your system.** Make sure the `Wsock32.dll` is present in `C:\winnt\system32` on the NT client.

Web Proxy Client Event Messages

The following event messages are some of the most common ones encountered for the Web Proxy client.

- **A connection with the server could not be established.** This event message is for all IIS services, and tells you that a connection could not be established. Verify that the server is operational and available, and that the server name was entered correctly.
- **Access is Denied / HTTP Error 5.** The client does not have permission to access the requested URL.
- **The connection with the server was reset.** This error occurs if the server cleared the connection, or if the server is taken offline. Try to reconnect again to complete the request.
- **The URL is invalid.** This error occurs if the URL was not typed correctly.

Winsock Proxy Client Event Messages

The following event messages are some of the most common ones encountered for the Winsock Proxy client.

- **The Winsock Proxy service has denied client authentication.** This error occurs if the user account or password is entered incorrectly or has expired.
- **Message too long.** This error occurs if the message length is longer than the current limit for the application. This may mean there is an incorrect protocol setting or mismatched port type between the server and client.

IPX Client Problems

The following problems are some of the most common ones encountered for the IPX Proxy client.

- **Failure to refresh configuration files or failure to connect to server.** This problem occurs when an IPX client cannot connect to the Mspclnt share on the Proxy Server computer. This message may also indicate that TCP/IP is installed on the IPX client, but is not available on the internal NIC of the Proxy Server. The best solution is to remove TCP/IP from the IPX client and force the clients to use only IPX for all Winsock Proxy connections.
- **Windows for Workgroups clients that use IPX are not able to access the Winsock Proxy service for Proxy Server.** IPX is only supported for Windows 95, 98, and NT clients.

General Client Performance Problems

The following general problems are some of the most common ones encountered by the Proxy client.

- **Connection is slow from a client that uses Windows Sockets connected application on a local network.** When certain local addresses are slow, the Winsock Proxy Server may be attempting to redirect a local connection. Make sure the local connection is contained in the LAT.
- **Internal network performance is slow for all clients accessing the same server.** If a connection is slow for all client requests to a particular server on the internal network, check to make sure the IP address of the server is included in the LAT.

Proxy Server Event Messages and Problems

Except for performance-related problems, most of your troubleshooting work concerning Proxy Server will focus on event messages. By using Event Viewer, you can see the event message and an explanation of the message. The following sections highlight some of the most common event messages and general problems related to various Proxy Server services and functions.

Server Setup Event Messages

The following are common event messages during a Proxy Server installation:

- **Proxy Server Setup requires administrator privileges.** If you receive this message, you have attempted to install Proxy Server from an account that does not have administrator privileges, which are required to install the software.
- **Setup could not find the IIS virtual root Scripts directory.** Make sure you have not removed or renamed the default scripts directory set up by IIS. The default directory location is `C:\InetPub\scripts`.
- **This software can only be installed on Windows NT Server version 4.0 build *buildnumber* or later.** This error message occurs if you attempt to install Proxy Server on a preliminary release of NT Server 4.0. You need to upgrade Windows NT 4.0 to the current build number.

Web Proxy Service Event Messages

The following are common Web Proxy Service event messages:

- **HTTP/1.0 server error (*-number*).** This error occurs when Windows NTCR authentication is used to validate Web Proxy clients.
- **HTTP/1.0 server error.** This error occurs when Proxy Server binaries are not installed in the correct directory for Proxy Server scripts. Check the location of your IIS scripts directory.

Web Proxy Cache Event Messages

The following are common Web Proxy Cache Event Messages:

- **113 – Web Proxy cache failed to initialize the URL cache on disk.** You need to reset the default settings. Stop the Web Proxy Service. On the Caching tab, click the Advanced button and click Reset Defaults. Restart the Web Proxy Service.

- **114 – The hard disk used by the Web Proxy server to cache popular URLs is full.** You need to free up space, or reconfigure the Web Proxy cache to resume normal operation.

Web Proxy Array and Chain Event Messages

The following are common array and chain event messages:

- **130 and 131 – The Web Proxy Service detected that the upstream proxy *servername* is (down or back up).** This message is generated when an upstream Proxy Server is down or when it comes back online.
- **132 and 133 – The Web Proxy service detected that the array member *servername* is (down or back up).** This message is generated when an array member is down or when it comes back online.

Winsock Proxy Service Event Messages

The following are common Winsock Proxy Service event messages:

- **2 – The Winsock Proxy service failed to initialize the network. The data is the error.** This message is generated if the service was not able to process a client request, usually because of missing or corrupt files. Stop and restart the services.
- **4 – The Winsock Proxy service cannot initialize due to a shortage of available memory. The data is the error.** The server needs more memory.
- **17 – Incorrect network configuration. None of the server's addresses are internal.** The LAT needs to be modified to include the internal adapter's IP address.

Exam Preparation Summary

For troubleshooting questions on the exam, you should have a firm understanding of how to use Event Viewer, Performance Monitor, and Network Monitor, and when those tools would help you in troubleshooting situations. You will not see detailed questions about editing the Registry. Most of the troubleshooting questions you will encounter give you a situation and ask what the problem is or ask for a solution. You will see questions concerning the LAT and issues with IPX clients. Remember that Proxy Server 2.0 only supports Windows 95, 98, or NT IPX clients — not Windows 3.*x* or Windows For Workgroups. You should be familiar with the major error messages discussed in this chapter and you should review the complete list of error messages found in Appendix F.

Key Point Summary

This chapter explored troubleshooting the Proxy client and the Proxy Server.

- Administrators should take an orderly approach to troubleshooting a problem, which includes identifying the problem, researching it, and making orderly solution attempts.
- Troubleshooting resources can be found in the Windows NT documentation, the Proxy Server documentation, Microsoft TechNet, the Microsoft Knowledge Base, and through white papers at `www.microsoft.com/proxy`.
- Event Viewer can be used to find information on system events and problems.
- Performance Monitor and Network Monitor are excellent tools for troubleshooting performance problems.
- The Registry can be used as a troubleshooting tool, although you should take great care using the Registry.
- Chkwsp is a Proxy Server utility that gives you data on the Winsock Proxy Service.
- A number of error messages that you should know are presented in this chapter.

Applying What You've Learned

The following review questions give you a chance to test your knowledge of the content in this chapter. Should you miss some, review the appropriate portions of the chapter. The answers to the Instant Assessment questions can be found in Appendix C.

Instant Assessment

1. What kind of system event is displayed in red in Event Viewer?
   A. Stop
   B. Warning
   C. Wait
   D. Pause
2. Which Registry subtree would contain information about modem configurations?
   A. HKEY_CURRENT_USER
   B. HKEY_CLASSES_ROOT
   C. HKEY_CURRENT CONFIG
   D. HEKY_LOCAL_MACHINE
3. Which Registry subtree would contain information about software configurations?
   A. HKEY_CURRENT_USER
   B. HKEY_CLASSES_ROOT
   C. HKEY_CURRENT CONFIG
   D. HEKY_LOCAL_MACHINE
4. Which Registry subtree would contain information about the policies for the current user?
   A. HKEY_CURRENT_USER
   B. HKEY_CLASSES_ROOT
   C. HKEY_CURRENT CONFIG
   D. HEKY_LOCAL_MACHINE
5. Which Proxy Server utility can be used to view information about Winsock?
   A. `Ping`
   B. `Chkwsp`
   C. `Ipconfig /all`
   D. `Chkpserver`

Critical Thinking Labs

These labs present you with analysis problems to test your critical thinking skills with the content in this chapter.

Lab 14.79 *Client setup troubleshooting*

During client setup, you receive the message **Please set a description of the internal network.** What is most likely causing this error?

Lab 14.80 *Troubleshooting the cache*

You receive the following message about the Web Proxy cache: **113 – Web proxy cache failed to initialize the URL cache on disk.** What is most likely causing this error?

Lab 14.81 *Troubleshooting the Winsock Proxy Service*

You receive the following message: **17 – Incorrect network configuration. None of the server's addresses are internal.** What is most likely causing this error?

Hands-on Labs

The Hands-on Labs give you an opportunity to practice skills you have learned in this chapter. These labs assume you have at least a functioning Proxy Server on a network.

Lab 14.82 *Troubleshooting the Registry*

In this lab, you will explore the Registry. You will not modify any of the Registry settings. Warning! Great care should be taken when you perform this lab! If you modify Registry settings, you may not be able to boot the system.

1. Click Start ⇒ Run, and enter **regedt32**.
2. The Registry Editor opens. Expand HKEY_LOCAL_MACHINE.
3. Select the System key, and then click Tree ⇒ Expand.
4. Select CurrentControlSet subkey, and then click Tree ⇒ Expand.
5. Select the Services subkey, and then click Tree ⇒ Expand.
6. Scroll through the list and you will see the Proxy Server subkeys, such as the W3Pcache, W3Proxy, and so forth.
7. Select the W3Proxy subkey, and then click Tree ⇒ Expand.

8. Select the Parameters subkey. A listing of settings appears in the right column. Click Tree ⇒ Expand.
9. Select the ReverseProxy subkey. Information appears in the right pane concerning default local hosts, Reverse Proxy name, and so forth.
10. Click through the other keys and explore the registry settings, as you desire. Make certain that you do not alter any of the settings.
11. Once you are finished exploring, click Close.

Resources

APPENDIX A

Proxy Server 2.0 Exam Objectives

The Proxy Server 2.0 exam, number 70-88, counts as an elective certification toward the Microsoft Certified Systems Engineer certification, and earns the Microsoft Certified Product Specialist certification if you have previously passed the Networking Essentials exam. Also, exam 70-88 counts toward the MCSE + Internet certification as one of the possible core requirements. Exam 70-88 measures your skills to implement and support Proxy Server 2.0 in the following areas:

Planning

- Choose a secure access strategy for various situations. Access includes outbound access by users to the Internet and inbound access to your Web site. Considerations include:
  - Translating addresses from the internal network to the Local Address Table (LAT)
  - Controlling anonymous access
  - Controlling access by known users and groups
  - Setting protocol permissions
  - Auditing protocol access
  - Setting Microsoft Windows NT security parameters

- Plan an Internet site or an intranet site for stand-alone servers, single-domain environments, and multiple-domain environments. Tasks include:
  - Choosing appropriate connectivity methods
  - Choosing services
  - Using Microsoft Proxy Server in an intranet that has no access to the Internet
  - Choosing hardware
- Choose a strategy to balance Internet access across multiple Proxy Server computers. Strategies include:
  - Using DNS
  - Using arrays
  - Using Cache Array Routing Protocol (CARP)
- Choose a rollout plan for integrating a Proxy Server with an existing corporate environment.
- Choose a fault tolerance strategy. Strategies include:
  - Using arrays
  - Using routing

Installation and Configuration

- Create a LAT.
- Configure server authentication. Authentication options include:
  - Anonymous logon
  - Basic authentication
  - Microsoft Windows NT Challenge/Response authentication
- Configure Windows NT to support Microsoft Proxy Server.
- Configure the various Proxy Server services.
- Configure Microsoft Proxy Server for Internet access. Situations include:
  - Configuring Proxy Server to provide Internet access through a dial-up connection to an ISP.
  - Configuring Proxy Server to act as an IPX gateway.
  - Configuring multiple Microsoft Proxy Servers for Internet access.

  - Configuring multiple Proxy Servers spread across several different geographic locations.
- Select and use software configuration management tools (for example, Control Panel, Windows NT Setup, Regedt32).
- Configure auditing.
- Given a scenario, decide which user interface to use to perform administrative tasks.
- Identify the licensing requirements for a given Proxy Server site.
- Configure Proxy Server arrays.
- Configure arrays to provide fault-tolerance for Web Proxy client requests.
- Use packet filtering to prevent unauthorized access. Tasks include:
  - Using packet filtering to enable a specific protocol.
  - Configuring packet filter alerting and logging.
- Configure hierarchical caching.

Setting Up and Managing Resource Access

- Grant or restrict access to the Internet for selected outbound users and groups who use the various Proxy Server services to access the Internet.
- Grant or restrict access to specific Internet sites for outbound users.
- Choose the location, size, and type of caching for the Web Proxy service.
- Configure active caching and passive caching.
- Implement Web publishing to enable reverse proxying.
- Back up and restore Proxy Server configurations.
- Implement reverse hosting.

Integration and Interoperability

- Use the Proxy Server client Setup program to configure client computers.
- Configure Proxy Server and Proxy Server client computers to use the Proxy Server services. Configurations include:
  - Microsoft Internet Explorer client computers

    - Netscape Navigator client computers
    - Macintosh client computers
    - UNIX client computers
    - Client computers on an IPX-only network
- Configure a RAS server to route Internet requests.
- Write JavaScript to configure a Web browser.
- Change settings in Mspclnt.ini.

Monitoring and Optimization

- Configure Proxy Server to log errors when they occur.
- Monitor performance of various functions by using Microsoft Windows NT Performance Monitor. Functions include HTTP and FTP sessions.
- Analyze performance issues. Performance issues include:
    - Identifying bottlenecks
    - Identifying network-related performance issues
    - Identifying disk-related performance issues
    - Identifying CPU-related performance issues
    - Identifying memory-related performance issues
- Optimize performance for various purposes. Purposes include:
    - Increasing throughput
    - Optimizing routing
- Use Performance Monitor logs to identify the appropriate configuration.
- Perform Internet traffic analysis by using Windows NT Server tools.
- Monitor current sessions.

Troubleshooting

- Resolve Proxy Server and Proxy Server client installation problems.
- Resolve Proxy Server and Proxy Server client access problems.
- Resolve Proxy Server client computer problems.

- Resolve security problems
- Resolve caching problems.
- Troubleshoot a WINS server to provide client access to Proxy Servers.
- Troubleshoot hardware-related problems such as network interfaces and disk drives.
- Troubleshoot Internet/intranet routing hardware and software. Software includes Microsoft Routing and Remote Access Service (RRAS).

Important Exam Note

In the fall of 1998, Microsoft began implementing adaptive testing technologies in many of its exams. The Proxy Server 2.0 exam may contain adaptive testing technologies. To learn more about adaptive testing, visit the MCP page at `www.microsoft.com/mcp`.

Exam Objective Cross-Reference to Chapter Content and Labs

The following table gives you a cross reference to the exam objectives and where those objectives are covered in the book, as well as the labs that cover the objectives. You can use this table to check your knowledge and skills before you take the exam and to review areas in which you feel weak.

TABLE A-1 Proxy Server 2.0 Objectives Cross-Reference Chart

Exam Objective	Chapter(s)	Section(s)	Lab(s)
Planning			
Choose a secure access strategy for various situations. Access includes outbound access by users to the Internet and inbound access to your Web site.	Chapter 7	The Proxy Server Interface	Lab 7.27, Lab 7.28, Lab 7.29, Lab 7.30, Lab 7.32, Lab 7.33
	Chapter 9	Creating a Secure Environment	Lab 9.46, Lab 9.49

continued

TABLE A-1 *(continued)*

Exam Objective	Chapter(s)	Section(s)	Lab(s)
Considerations include:			
• Translating addresses from the internal network to the Local Address Table (LAT)	Chapter 3	Examining Your Network	
	Chapter 5	Installing Proxy Server 2.0	Lab 5.19
	Chapter 9	Proxy Service Security	
• Controlling anonymous access	Chapter 9	Proxy Service Security	Lab 9.47
• Controlling access by known users and groups	Chapter 7	Permissions	Lab 7.27, Lab 7.28, Lab 7.30, Lab 7.32, Lab 7.33
	Chapter 9	General Security Issues Proxy Service Security Domain Filters	Lab 9.46, Lab 9.49
• Setting protocol permissions	Chapter 7	Permissions	Lab 7.27, Lab 7.28, Lab 7.30, Lab 7.32, Lab 7.33
	Chapter 9	Proxy Service Security	Lab 9.46, Lab 9.49, Lab 9.50
• Auditing protocol access	Chapter 7	Permissions	Lab 7.27, Lab 7.29
• Setting Microsoft Windows NT security parameters	Chapter 9	Windows NT Security	Lab 9.48
Plan an Internet site or an intranet site for stand-alone servers, single-domain environments, and multiple-domain environments.	Chapter 3	Before You Install Proxy Server	Lab 3.5, Lab 3.6, Lab 3.7, Lab 3.9
	Chapter 11	Multiple Proxy Environments	
Tasks include:			
• Choosing appropriate connectivity methods	Chapter 3	Examining Your Network	Lab 3.5, Lab 3.6

EXAM OBJECTIVE	CHAPTER(S)	SECTION(S)	LAB(S)
◦ Choosing services	Chapter 3	Examining Your Network	
	Chapter 7	The Web Proxy Service The Winsock Proxy Service The Socks Proxy Service	Lab 7.27, Lab 7.29, Lab 7.30
◦ Using Microsoft Proxy Server in an intranet that has no access to the Internet	Chapter 11	Proxy Server and the Intranet	Lab 11.61
◦ Choosing hardware	Chapter 3	Local Machine Requirements	Lab 3.5
Choose a strategy to balance Internet access across multiple Proxy Server computers. Strategies include:	Chapter 11	Multiple Proxy Environments	Lab 11.57, Lab 11.58, Lab 11.60, Lab 11.64 Lab 11.65, Lab 11.66
◦ Using DNS	Chapter 11	Issues with DNS, WINS, and DHCP	Lab 11.59
◦ Using arrays	Chapter 11	Proxy Server Arrays	Lab 11.65
◦ Using Cache Array Routing Protocol (CARP)	Chapter 11	Cache Array Routing Protocol	Lab 11.58
Choose a rollout plan for integrating a Proxy Server with an existing corporate environment.	Chapter 3	Before You Install Proxy Server	Lab 3.5, Lab 3.9
Choose a fault tolerant strategy. Strategies include:	Chapter 11	Multiple Proxy Environments	Lab 11.57
◦ Using arrays	Chapter 11	Proxy Server Arrays Configuring Arrays	Lab 11.65
◦ Using routing	Chapter 11	Routing	Lab 11.66
Installation and Configuration			
Create a LAT	Chapter 5	Installing Proxy Server 2.0	Lab 5.19, Lab 5.22

continued

TABLE A-1 *(continued)*

Exam Objective	Chapter(s)	Section(s)	Lab(s)
Configure server authentication. Authentication options include:	Chapter 11	Routing	Lab 9.48, Lab 11.65
• Anonymous logon	Chapter 9	Proxy Service Security	Lab 9.47
• Basic authentication	Chapter 11	Routing	Lab 11.65
• Microsoft Windows NT Challenge/Response authentication	Chapter 11	Routing	Lab 11.65
Configure Windows NT to support Proxy Server	Chapter 3	Before You Install Proxy Server	Lab 3.9, Lab 3.10
	Chapter 4	Internet Information Server Overview	Lab 4.16
Configure various Proxy Server Services.	Chapter 7	The Proxy Server Interface	Lab 7.27, Lab 7.28, Lab 7.29, Lab 7.30, Lab 7.31, Lab 7.32
Configure Microsoft Proxy Server for Internet access. Situations include:	Chapter 9	Creating a Secure Environment	
	Chapter 11	Multiple Proxy Environments	Lab 11.57, Lab 11.64
	Chapter 12	Proxy Server and RAS	Lab 12.70, Lab 12.71
• Configuring Proxy Server to provide Internet access through a dial-up connection to an ISP.	Chapter 12	Proxy Server and RAS	Lab 12.67, Lab 12.68, Lab 12.69, Lab 12.70, Lab 12.71
• Configuring Proxy Server to act as an IPX gateway.	Chapter 11	IPX Environments	Lab 11.62
• Configuring multiple Microsoft Proxy Servers for Internet access	Chapter 11	Multiple Proxy Environments	Lab 11.64, Lab 11.65
• Configuring multiple Proxy Servers spread across several different geographic locations.	Chapter 11	Multiple Proxy Environments	Lab 11.52, Lab 11.53

EXAM OBJECTIVE	CHAPTER(S)	SECTION(S)	LAB(S)
Select and use software configuration management tools (for example, Control Panel, Windows NT Setup, Regedt32)	Chapter 14	Troubleshooting Tools	Lab 14.82
Configuring auditing	Chapter 7	The Web Proxy Service	Lab 7.29
Given a scenario, decide which user interface to use to perform administrative tasks.	Chapter 7	The Proxy Server Interface	Lab 7.27, Lab 7.30, Lab 7.31, Lab 7.32, Lab 7.33
Identify the licensing requirements for a given Proxy Server site	Chapter 5	Installation Requirements	Lab 5.19
Configure Proxy Server arrays	Chapter 11	Configuring Arrays	Lab 11.64
Configure arrays to provide fault-tolerance for Web Proxy client requests	Chapter 11	Configuring Arrays	Lab 11.57, Lab 11.64, Lab 11.65
Use packet filtering to prevent unauthorized access. Tasks include:	Chapter 9	Packet Filtering	Lab 9.50
• Using packet filtering to enable a specific protocol	Chapter 9	Packet Filtering	Lab 9.50
• Configuring packet filter alerting and logging.	Chapter 9	Security Alerts and Reporting	Lab 9.51
Configure hierarchical caching	Chapter 11	The Multiserver Environment	Lab 11.64
Setting Up and Managing Resource Access			
Grant or restrict access to the Internet for selected outbound users and groups who use the various Proxy Server services to access the Internet.	Chapter 9	Creating a Secure Environment	Lab 9.49
Grant or restrict access to specific Internet sites for outbound users	Chapter 9	Creating a Secure Environment	Lab 9.49

continued

TABLE A-1 *(continued)*

Exam Objective	*Chapter(s)*	*Section(s)*	*Lab(s)*
Choose the location, size, and type of caching for the Web Proxy service	Chapter 10	Caching with Proxy Server	Lab 10.52, Lab 10.53, Lab 10.54, Lab 10.55, Lab 10.56
Configure active caching and passive caching	Chapter 10	Passive and Active Caching Configuration	Lab 10.52
Implement Web publishing to enable reverse proxying	Chapter 11	Reverse Proxying and Reverse Hosting	Lab 11.65
Back up and restore Proxy Server configurations	Chapter 7	Service Tab	Lab 7.31
Implement reverse hosting	Chapter 11	Reverse Proxying and Reverse Hosting	Lab 11.66
Integration and Interoperability			
Use the Proxy Server client Setup program to configure client computers.	Chapter 8	Browser Scripts	Lab 8.34, Lab 8.38
Configure Proxy Server and Proxy Server client computers to use the Proxy Server services. Configurations include:	Chapter 8	Configuring the Client	Lab 8.34, Lab 8.35, Lab 8.36, Lab 8.37, Lab 8.38, Lab 8.39, Lab 8.42, Lab 8.43
• Microsoft Internet Explorer client computers	Chapter 8	Internet Explorer	Lab 8.36
• Netscape Navigator client computers	Chapter 8	Netscape Navigator	Lab 8.37
• Macintosh client computers	Chapter 8	Socks Client Configuration	Lab 8.35
• UNIX client computers	Chapter 8	Socks Client Configuration	Lab 8.38
• Client computers on an IPX only network	Chapter 8	NWLink Clients	Lab 8.39
Configure a RAS server to route Internet requests	Chapter 12	RAS	Lab 12.70
Write JavaScript to configure a Web browser	Chapter 8	Browser Scripts	Lab 8.40

Exam Objective	Chapter(s)	Section(s)	Lab(s)
Change settings in Mspclnt.ini	Chapter 8	Additional Configuration Options	Lab 8.41
Monitoring and Optimization			
Configure Proxy Server to log errors when they occur	Chapter 9	Proxy Logging	Lab 9.51
Monitor performance of various functions by using Microsoft Windows NT Performance Monitor. Functions include HTTP and FTP sessions.	Chapter 13	Performance Monitor	Lab 13.72, Lab 13.73, Lab 13.74, Lab 13.77, Lab 13.78
Analyze performance issues. Performance issues include:	Chapter 13	Performance Monitor	Lab 13.72, Lab 13.73, Lab 13.74, Lab 13.77, Lab 13.78
• Identifying bottlenecks	Chapter 13	Performance Bottlenecks	Lab 13.73
• Identifying network-related performance issues	Chapter 13	Network Monitor	Lab 13.78
• Identifying disk-related performance issues	Chapter 13	Performance Bottlenecks	Lab 13.77, Lab 13.78
• Identifying CPU-related performance issues	Chapter 13	Performance Bottlenecks	Lab 13.73
• Identifying memory-related performance issues	Chapter 13	Performance Bottlenecks	Lab 13.78
Optimize performance for various purposes. Purposes include:	Chapter 13	Proxy Server Performance	Lab 13.72, Lab 13.73, Lab 13.74, lab 13.77, Lab 13.78
• Increasing throughput	Chapter 11	Routing	Lab 11.65
• Optimizing routing	Chapter 11	Routing	Lab 11.65
Use Performance Monitor logs to identify the appropriate configuration	Chapter 13	Performance Monitor	Lab 13.75
Perform Internet traffic analysis by using Windows NT Server tools.	Chapter 13	Network Monitor	Lab 13.76

continued

TABLE A-1 *(continued)*

Exam Objective	Chapter(s)	Section(s)	Lab(s)
Monitor current sessions	Chapter 7	Service Tab	Lab 7.29
Troubleshooting			
Resolve Proxy Server and Proxy client installation problems	Chapter 14	Client Setup Event Messages Server Setup Event Messages	Lab 14.79
Resolve Proxy Server and Proxy client access problems	Chapter 14	General Client Performance Problems Proxy Server Event Messages and Problems	Lab 14.81
Resolve Proxy Server client computer problems	Chapter 14	Proxy Client Event Messages and Problems	Lab 14.79
Resolve security problems	Chapter 9	Creating a Secure Environment	Lab 9.44, Lab 9.45, Lab 9.46, Lab 9.47, Lab 9.48, Lab 9.49, Lab 9.50, Lab 9.51
Resolve caching problems	Chapter 14	Web Proxy Cache Event Messages	Lab 14.80
Troubleshoot a WINS server to provide client access to Proxy Servers	Chapter 11	Issues with DNS, WINS, and DHCP	Lab 11.63
Troubleshoot hardware-related problems such as network interfaces and disk drives.	Chapter 14	Performance Monitor and Network Monitor	Lab 13.73
Troubleshoot Internet/ Intranet routing hardware and software. Software includes Microsoft Routing and Remote Access Service (RRAS)	Chapter 11 Chapter 12	Routing RRAS	Lab 11.57 Lab 12.68, Lab 12.69, Lab 12.71

APPENDIX

Mini-Lab Manual

B

This appendix serves as your own mini-lab manual. These are all the critical thinking and hand-on labs from each chapter put together in one section for easy reference and practice. There is no substitute for actually using the Proxy Server software and practicing the administrative and configuration skills you learn in the labs. Before you take the exam, it is a good idea to use this mini-lab manual for review and further practice. Each hands-on lab includes the system requirements you need to complete the lab. Table B-1 is a list of all the labs in this book.

TABLE B-1

LAB NUMBER	TYPE OF LAB	LAB TITLE	CHAPTER
2.1	Critical thinking	Connectivity tests	2
2.2	Critical thinking	IP address classes	2
2.3	Critical thinking	Subnet masks	2
2.4	Hands-on	Installing TCP/IP	2
3.5	Critical thinking	Configuring the network	3
3.6	Critical thinking	Internet connectivity	3
3.7	Critical thinking	Establishing a baseline	3
3.8	Critical thinking	Needs Assessment	3
3.9	Hands-on	Local IP addresses using DHCP	3
3.10	Hands-on	Local IP addresses without DHCP	3
4.11	Critical thinking	IIS features	4
4.12	Critical thinking	Securing transactions	4
4.13	Critical thinking	Multiple administrators	4
4.14	Critical thinking	Checking FrontPage Extensions	4
4.15	Hands-on	Installing the NT 4.0 Option Pack	4
4.16	Hands-on	The IIS interface	4
4.17	Hands-on	Viewing properties	4
5.18	Critical thinking	NWLink and Proxy	5
5.19	Critical thinking	Building the LAT	5
5.20	Critical thinking	Troubleshooting Setup	5
5.21	Critical thinking	Proxy licensing	5
5.22	Hands-on	Installing Proxy Server	5
6.23	Critical thinking	Proxy Server clients	6
6.24	Critical thinking	Wsock32.dll file	6
6.25	Critical thinking	Active and passive caching	6
6.26	Critical thinking	Proxy Server services	6
7.27	Critical thinking	Denying access in the Winsock Proxy Service	7
7.28	Critical thinking	Assigning and managing Proxy Server permissions	7

LAB NUMBER	TYPE OF LAB	LAB TITLE	CHAPTER
7.29	Critical thinking	Monitoring users	7
7.30	Hands-on	Giving WWW permissions to a selected group	7
7.31	Hands-on	Backing up your Proxy Server configuration	7
7.32	Hands-on	Giving permissions for Winsock Proxy Service	7
7.33	Hands-on	Denying permissions to a Socks client	7
8.34	Critical thinking	Configuring Proxy Server	8
8.35	Critical thinking	Avoiding Web Proxy Server problems	8
8.36	Critical thinking	Proxy Server administration	8
8.37	Critical thinking	Netscape Proxy configuration	8
8.38	Critical thinking	UNIX clients	8
8.39	Critical thinking	NWLink clients	8
8.40	Critical thinking	Using JavaScript	8
8.41	Critical thinking	Editing mspclnt.ini	8
8.42	Hands-on	Configuring Internet Explorer for Proxy Server	8
8.43	Hands-on	Installing Winsock client software	8
9.44	Critical thinking	Password parameters	9
9.45	Critical thinking	Configuring filters	9
9.46	Critical thinking	Restricting protocol access	9
9.47	Critical thinking	Restricting anonymous access	9
9.48	Critical thinking	Windows NT Security parameters	9
9.49	Hands-on	Configuring a domain filter	9
9.50	Hands-on	Configuring a predefined packet filter	9
9.51	Hands-on	Configuring packet filter alerting and logging	9
10.52	Critical thinking	Active caching	10
10.53	Critical thinking	Cache filters	10
10.54	Critical thinking	Cache filter exceptions	10
10.55	Hands-on	Creating a cache filter	10

Continued

TABLE B-1 *(continued)*

LAB NUMBER	TYPE OF LAB	LAB TITLE	CHAPTER
10.56	Hands-on	Creating a cache filter exception	10
11.57	Critical thinking	Primary and backup routes	11
11.58	Critical thinking	CARP	11
11.59	Critical thinking	Using DNS	11
11.60	Critical thinking	Multiple Proxy administrators	11
11.61	Critical thinking	Proxy Server and an intranet	11
11.62	Critical thinking	IPX environments	11
11.63	Critical thinking	WINS Servers	11
11.64	Hands-on	Configuring a Proxy Server array	11
11.65	Hands-on	Configuring routing options	11
11.66	Hands-on	Reverse proxying	11
12.67	Critical thinking	Unbinding WINS	12
12.68	Critical thinking	Auto Dial setup	12
12.69	Critical thinking	Using RRAS	12
12.70	Hands-on	Installing RAS	12
12.71	Hands-on	Configuring Auto Dial	12
13.72	Critical thinking	Performance Monitor and Active Caching	13
13.73	Critical thinking	Performance Monitor and processor speed	13
13.74	Critical thinking	Performance Monitor and client utilization	13
13.75	Critical thinking	Performance Monitor logs	13
13.76	Critical thinking	Internet traffic	13
13.77	Hands-on	Configuring Performance Monitor	13
13.78	Hands-on	Configuring Web Proxy Service counters	13
14.79	Critical thinking	Client setup troubleshooting	14
14.80	Critical thinking	Troubleshooting the cache	14
14.81	Critical thinking	Troubleshooting the Winsock Proxy Service	14

LAB NUMBER	TYPE OF LAB	LAB TITLE	CHAPTER
14.82	Hands-on	Troubleshooting the Registry	14

Lab 2.1 *Connectivity tests*

You are having problems connecting to a server on your TCP/IP network. The server's name is `CorpServerD`, and you have WINS enabled on your network. What are two quick tests you can perform at your client computer to test connectivity?

Lab 2.2 *IP address classes*

A friend asks you to explain the differences between IP Classes A, B, and C, and the default subnet mask for each. How would you explain this?

Lab 2.3 *Subnet masks*

Some networks choose to use a subnet mask that differs from the IP class. For example, some Class B networks use a Class C subnet mask. What are the benefits of this?

Lab 2.4 *Installing TCP/IP*

For this lab, you need a computer running either Windows NT Workstation 4.0 or Windows NT Server 4.0 on which TCP/IP is *not* installed. It is not necessary that this computer reside on a network. In this lab, you will install and configure TCP/IP on your computer. Follow each step completely:

1. Right click Network Neighborhood and choose Properties from the menu that appears.
2. The Network properties sheet appears. Click the Protocols tab.
3. Click the Add button.
4. NT builds a protocol list. Select TCP/IP from the list. You computer gives you a message asking if you would like NT to use a DHCP server. Click No. Your computer may ask you for the location of the setup files; you should either specify a directory or your CD-ROM drive.
5. The computer installs the protocol. Click the Close button on the Network properties sheet. The binding configuration is stored, and the TCP/IP properties sheet appears.

6. Because you do not want to use a DHCP server for this lab, you must input an IP address and a subnet mask manually. Assign this computer an IP address of 10.0.0.4 by entering the address in the IP Address section of the dialog box. You can accept the default subnet mask of 255.255.0.0, and you do not need to enter a default gateway. Click Apply, and then click OK.
7. You are asked to reboot the computer. Do so.
8. Once your computer has rebooted, you can verify the install by right-clicking Network Neighborhood, and selecting Properties from the list. When the Network property sheet appears, click the Protocols tab again, and you will see the TCP/IP protocol installed. That's all there is to it!

Lab 3.5 *Configuring the network*

Lewis Manufacturing Company has 1000 users on an NT network. They would like to provide Internet access to all of the users with Proxy Server. How much disk space should be allocated for the cache, and what type of ISP connection would be best for this amount of traffic?

Lab 3.6 *Internet connectivity*

As a consultant, you have been asked to outline the advantages and disadvantages of ISDN connectivity and T1 connectivity for a LAN of 600 users so management can make a decision about which one to purchase. What would you say?

Lab 3.7 *Establishing a baseline*

A friend has heard of establishing a baseline of performance, but doesn't understand the concept. How would you explain this to your friend, and what tools would you suggest to establish a network performance baseline?

Lab 3.8 *Needs assessment*

You have been hired by a small company that is considering adding Internet access to their LAN to perform a needs assessment. What are two major questions you should ask and why are those questions important?

Lab 3.9 *Local IP addresses using DHCP*

This lab assumes you are using NT Server 4.0 with TCP/IP installed on a TCP/IP network. In preparation for Proxy Server installation, it is a good idea to gather information about the TCP/IP address range of your network for the LAT construction during setup. This lab will guide you through a two-part process, depending on your network configuration.

To gather the IP address range for a network using DHCP Server, follow these steps:

1. In NT Server, click Start ⇛ Administrative Tools ⇛ DHCP Manager.
2. The DHCP Manager interface appears, as shown in Figure B-1.
3. Click the Scope menu. You can view the scope properties and IP address range of your network. Note this address range should be noted and include it in the LAT. Make sure you include any reserved IP addresses as a part of the LAT.

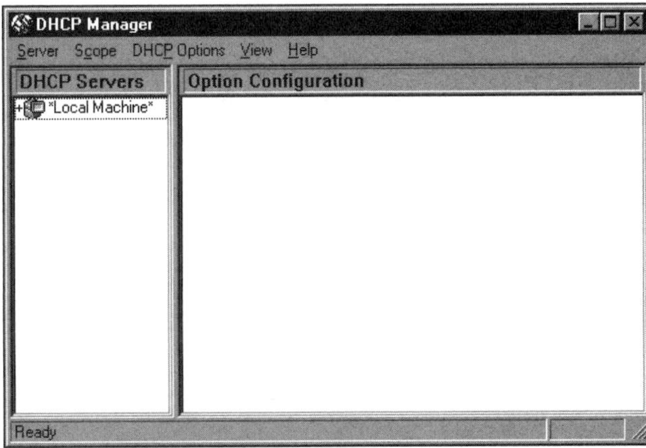

FIGURE B-1 DHCP Manager

4. If you are using a multi-homed computer, as recommended, make certain that the IP address of the NIC that is bound to the local network is included in the LAT. If the Server's IP address is assigned statically, view its IP address by right-clicking Network Neighborhood, choosing the Protocols tab, selecting TCP/IP Protocol, and clicking the "Properties" button. This page shows you the NIC and the IP address assigned to it.

Lab 3.10 *Local IP addresses without DHCP*

This lab assumes you use a network that does not have a DCHP Server, such as in a small workgroup or LAN.

1. If your workgroup or LAN does not use DHCP Server, you must note the IP address of each machine and network node manually.

2. First, find any documentation about the network. Hopefully, records have been kept for the network addresses that have been assigned to each node.
3. Whether a document exists or not, it is a good idea to go to each machine and check each IP address manually so you have an accurate range when you install Proxy Server.
4. To check the IP address of each NT machine, right-click Network Neighborhood, choose Properties, select the Protocol tab, select TCP/IP, and then click the Properties button. This gives you the IP address of the computer.
5. For Windows 95/98 computers, right-click Network Neighborhood, choose Properties, select TCP/IP Adapter, and then click the Properties button. This gives you the IP address of the computer.
6. If you are using Macintosh computers in your NT network, you can view the TCP/IP address of a Mac by opening control panel and double-clicking TCP/IP. This gives you the IP address of the computer.

Lab 4.11 *IIS features*

Your company is considering implementing IIS to host the company's new Web site and its forthcoming intranet site. You have been asked to give an overview of IIS's features and functions at a meeting. What are some of the things you will say?

Lab 4.12 *Securing transactions*

Your company uses IIS and needs to perform secure transfers of financial records over the Internet. As the administrator, you are asked how the company can do this so that no data is corrupted during transit. What IIS component should you use and why?

Lab 4.13 *Multiple administrators*

Your company is hosting a number of Web sites and the administrative load has become too much for you to handle. You would like for some other people within your company to have administrative privileges over these sites. How can you do this?

Lab 4.14 *Checking FrontPage Extensions*

There seems to be a problem with the FrontPage Server Extensions on your IIS server. What easy way can you check and repair errors to the Extensions?

Lab 4.15 *Installing the NT 4.0 Option Pack*

This lab assumes you are using an NT 4.0 operating system and have the NT 4.0 Option Pack. The Option Pack is available on CD through a TechNet subscription or it is downloadable from Microsoft at `http://www.microsoft.com/ntserver/nts/downloads/recommended/NT4OptPk/default.asp`

1. Open the option pack CD or launch Setup from the downloaded version. Internet Explorer opens and you are shown a Welcome Screen.
2. In left pane, click the Install link. This takes you to the installation page.
3. Follow the steps given on the installation screen. Begin by reading the licensing agreement.
4. Next, if you have beta releases of IIS 4.0 prior to beta 3 installed, you need to uninstall them. Go to Control Panel, select Add/Remove Programs, and select IIS from the list. Then click the Add/Remove button. The beta version of IIS is uninstalled and you may be required to reboot your system.
5. If you do not have Service Pack 3 installed on your NT 4.0 Server, choose the option to install the service pack. The Service Pack is installed, and you will have to reboot your computer.
6. If you are not using at least Internet Explorer 4.0, choose to upgrade to IE 4.01.
7. Once these steps are complete, you are ready to install the Option Pack. Click the Install Option Pack link. You are taken to a welcome screen. Click Next.
8. The next screen presents you with the End User License Agreement. You must accept the agreement for the installation to continue. Click Accept, and then click Next.
9. Next, you are asked to select either Update or Update Plus. Update Plus will install the core components and enable you to install additional components if you wish to do so. Choose the Update Plus option and click Next.
10. You are taken to a selection screen that enables you to choose the components you wish to install. Spend a few moments looking at the options and the subcomponents for each. Highlight the main component and click the Show Subcomponents button to view the subcomponents.

11. Select the components to install by clicking the check box beside each component. If you are unsure of what you need, simply accept the defaults and add components at a later time if you need them.
12. If you selected additional components, you may be presented with various screens asking for a local directory or additional information about administrative rights. Accept the defaults on these unless you know that you need to make specific changes.
13. Setup begins at this point by copying the files to your computer and beginning the installation process. A status bar is provided. This process usually takes from 10 to 15 minutes.
14. When the installation phase is complete, you are given a screen asking you to click Finish to finish the installation. Click Finish.
15. You are prompted to reboot your computer.

Lab 4.16 *The IIS interface*

This lab assumes you have installed IIS successfully in Lab 4-15. In this lab, you will explore the IIS interface.

1. Click Start ⇛ Programs ⇛ Windows NT Option Pack ⇛ Microsoft Internet Information Server, and then select Internet Service Manager.
2. The MMC launches and opens ISM. In the left pane, a Console Root with IIS is listed and perhaps other directories, depending on what you have installed.
3. Expand the IIS directory. You see the name of your computer with a computer icon, and perhaps others depending on your network configuration. Expand your computer.
4. You see a default Web site and default FTP site. Click the default Web site.
5. In the right pane, you see a listing of all of the files within the default Web site. Notice that new icons that have appeared on the toolbar. Click each one to see what they do, and then close the windows after you have seen them.
6. As you clicked on each icon, you are presented with NT's User Manager for Domains, NT's Server Manager, Event Viewer, Performance Monitor, and IIS's Key Manager.
7. Notice the computer icon on the toolbar. Click it. You see a dialog box, which enables you to connect to another server. Close the dialog box.

8. Also on the toolbar, you see an icon to Show/Hide Scope. If you click this button, it removes the left pane of MMC.
9. Notice the Action and View tabs. Click the Action tab. This enables you to explore, browse, start, stop, and pause various services, as well as to further configure the interface.
10. Click the View tab. In this tab, you can change the icon size, and also select list or detail.
11. At the top of the MMC screen, click the Console drop-down menu. Notice that you have several options here specific to the MMC. Click Add/Remove Snap-in.
12. You are presented with a screen to add new snap-ins to the Console root or to the other directories available. You would use this if you had additional snap-ins you wanted to use.
13. Close the snap-ins dialog box and close the MMC.

Lab 4.17 *Viewing properties*

This lab assumes you have successfully installed IIS in Lab 4.5. In this lab, you will view properties sheets within IIS.

1. Click Start ⇛ Programs ⇛ Windows NT Option Pack ⇛ Microsoft Internet Information Server, and then select Internet Service Manager.
2. MMC launches, and opens ISM. In the left pane, a Console Root with IIS is listed and perhaps other directories, depending on what you have installed.
3. Expand the IIS directory. You see the name of your computer with a computer icon, and perhaps others depending on your network configuration. Expand your computer.
4. You see a default Web site and a default FTP site. Click the default Web site.
5. On the toolbar, click the Properties icon. You are given a sheet of default Web site properties.
6. Take a moment to browse the various tabs.
7. Click the Operators tab. Notice that from this tab, you can give operator permissions to other users on the network.
8. Click the HTTP Headers tab. Notice that you can enable content expiration and configure expiration time. Notice also that there is a content rating section. Click the edit rating button. Notice that you can enable various ratings for the Web sites as needed. Close this tab.

9. Click Directory Security tab. Notice that there are three areas: Anonymous Access and Authentication Control, Secure Communications, and IP Address and Domain Name Restrictions. Click the Edit button for Anonymous Access and Authentication Control.
10. You see the authentication methods discussed in this chapter.
11. Click the Performance tab. Notice that there are several options to fine-tune the performance of your Web site, including bandwidth throttling.
12. Close the Properties window. Take a moment to look at the properties of the default FTP site and continue to look around the interface until you are comfortable with its content.

Lab 5.18 *NWLink and Proxy*

Your company uses NWLink only, but wants to gain Internet access with a Proxy Server. Many people think they will have to change the network protocol to TCP/IP. What would you tell them?

Lab 5.19 *Building the LAT*

A friend is about to perform a Proxy Server installation, but doesn't understand the LAT and how to build one. How would you explain the LAT, its construction, and what warnings would you give?

Lab 5.20 *Troubleshooting Setup*

During Setup, a coworker receives the Proxy error message "None of the Proxy Server's computer's addresses are internal." What is most likely the cause of the problem?

Lab 5.21 *Proxy licensing*

Your company is considering using Proxy Server, but is concerned about the administration and expense of licensing. You have been asked to give an overview of Proxy Server licensing at an upcoming meeting. How would you explain?

Lab 5.22 *Installing Proxy Server*

This lab assumes you have a computer running Windows NT Server 4.0, Service Pack 3, and IIS 3.0 or greater, and that you have an NTFS drive to use for the cache. To install Proxy Server, follow these steps:

1. Insert the Proxy Server CD-ROM. `Autorun.inf` will initialize, or you can double-click Setup in the root directory of the CD-ROM to begin setup.
2. The Welcome Screen and End User License Agreement appears. Read the agreement and click Continue.
3. The CD key screen Enter the CD Key found on the CD-ROM case and click OK.
4. The Product Identification screen appears. Note the ID for future use. Click OK.
5. Setup searches the system for previously installed components, and then present an Installation Options screen. You can accept the default directory or change it if you wish. Start the installation by clicking the large button with a computer icon on it.
6. The Installation Options screen appears with the default options of installing Proxy Server, the Administrative Tool, and the documentation selected. If you click the Change Option button, you see additional client share options. Accept the defaults and click OK to return to the main screen.
7. Accept the defaults and click Continue.
8. Setup stops the WWW Services.
9. The Cache Drives dialog box appears. Select the drive you want to use for caching. Notice that any FAT drives are grayed out.
10. Next, you need to enter the cache size in the Maximum Size field. Use the cache size formula to calculate this. Enter the number and click the Set button. Click OK.
11. The LAT Configuration box appears. If you click the Construct Table button, you will be given some additional options that are selected by default. Click OK. You get a message telling you to make sure you edit out any external NIC addresses. Click OK.
12. Once you have configured the addresses you want to include in the LAT and made any editorial changes, click OK.
13. Next, you see the Client Installation/Configuration dialog box. Notice that if you enable the Configure Web browsers to use Automatic Configuration, you see the default Configuration URL. You can configure this by clicking the Configure button. Accept the default.
14. If you click the Properties button of the Browser automatic configuration script, you will see additional options for Client configuration. Click Cancel.
15. Click OK in the Client Installation/Configuration dialog box.

16. The Access Control dialog box appears. Access control for Winsock and Web Proxy Services are selected by default. Click OK to accept the default settings.
17. Proxy Server performs the installation.
18. You see a dialog box telling you that Packet Filtering can be set via the administration tool. Click OK. Setup updates the system and restarts the WWW services.
19. Once the WWW services are started, you see a dialog box telling you that Proxy Server setup was completed successfully. Click OK.

Lab 6.23 *Proxy Server clients*

Your company is migrating from Macintosh to Windows platforms. Currently about half of the client computers are Macintosh. You use an NT Server on the network. Your company is considering adding a proxy server, but is concerned about the connectivity options for Macintosh clients with Microsoft Proxy Server. What would you say to alleviate their concerns?

Lab 6.24 *Wsock32.dll file*

One of your coworkers doesn't understand why the `wsock32.dll` file is necessary for his Windows 98 computer. How would you explain this?

Lab 6.25 *Active and passive caching*

A friend asks you to explain the difference between active and passive caching. How would you explain this?

Lab 6.26 *Proxy Server services*

You have been asked to present an overview of the services provided by the three Proxy Server services and what functionality is provided by each service. How will you explain this?

Lab 7.27 *Denying access in the Winsock Proxy Service*

A coworker would like to deny access to the Archie Protocol in the Winsock Proxy Service. What are the steps you would tell your coworker to follow?

Lab 7.28 *Assigning and managing Proxy Server permissions*

Your company is about to install and configure Proxy Server. What advice about users and groups would you offer to make permissions assignments easier and more manageable?

Lab 7.29 *Monitoring users*

You are afraid that Mary, a Proxy user, is abusing her privileges to use the Internet. You want to see how long she is staying connected to the Internet. How can you find this information?

Lab 7.30 *Giving WWW permissions to a selected group*

In this lab, you give WWW permissions to a selected group on your Proxy Server.

1. Click Start ⇒ Programs ⇒ Microsoft Proxy Server ⇒ Microsoft Management Console.
2. The MMC displays and you see the Internet Service Manager Console Root.
3. Expand the Internet Information Server directory and your server.
4. Right-click the Web Proxy Icon and select Properties.
5. Select the Permissions tab.
6. Access Control should be enabled in the check box. If it is not, click the box.
7. In the Protocol drop-down menu, select WWW.
8. Click Edit.
9. In the WWW Permissions dialog box that appears, click Add.
10. You see all the users and groups that are configured in your User Manager for Domains. Highlight the group you want to give WWW permissions to. You select Everyone if you want everyone on your network to have WWW access.
11. Once you have selected the desired group, click Add.
12. The group appears in the Add Names dialog box. You can now add additional groups if you wish.
13. Once you are finished adding groups, click OK at the bottom of the window.
14. In the WWW Permissions dialog box, click OK.
15. You can add rights to other protocols by selecting the protocol from the drop-down menu and completing these steps if you wish.
16. Once you are finished, click Apply, and then click OK.

Lab 7.31 *Backing up your Proxy Server configuration*

In this lab, you back up your current Proxy Server Configuration.

1. Click Start⇛Programs⇛Microsoft Proxy Server⇛Microsoft Management Console.
2. The MMC opens and you see the Internet Service Manager Console Root.
3. Expand the Internet Information Server directory and your server.
4. Right-click the Web Proxy icon and select Properties.
5. On the Services tab, click Server Backup.
6. The default directory is `C:\msp\config`. Accept the default and click OK.
7. The backup file is created.
8. Click OK on the Web Proxy Properties sheet.
9. Minimize the MMC.
10. Click Start⇛Programs⇛Windows NT Explorer.
11. The Explorer window appears.
12. Expand the MSP directory.
13. Double-click the Config directory.
14. You see the saved file of `msp`*`YYYYMMDD`*`.mpc`.
15. Double-click the file and select Notepad to open it.
16. Browse the backup file.

Lab 7.32 *Giving permissions for Winsock Proxy Service*

In this lab, you give permissions for the Winsock Proxy Service.

1. Click Start⇛Programs⇛Microsoft Proxy Server⇛Microsoft Management Console.
2. The MMC opens and you see the Internet Service Manager Console Root.
3. Expand the Internet Information Server directory and your server.
4. Right-click the Web Proxy icon and select Properties.
5. Right-click Winsock Proxy and select Properties.
6. Click the Protocols tab. Note the protocols now available.
7. Click the Permissions tab.
8. Enable Access Control should be selected. If it is not, click the check box.

9. In the Protocol drop-down box, select POP3, or another protocol if you do not want clients on your network to send Internet mail. You can also permit Unlimited Access by selecting this option.
10. Click Edit to open the POP3 Permissions page.
11. Click Add.
12. The users and groups currently available in User Manager for Domains appears. Select the group to whom you want to give permission and click Add.
13. The group appears in the Add Names dialog box. Click OK.
14. The POP3 Permissions dialog box reappears with your group added. Click OK.
15. This takes you back to the Winsock proxy Service Properties page. You may make additional entries by following the same steps. Once you are finished, click Apply, and then click OK.

Lab 7.33 *Denying permissions to a Socks client*

In this lab, you deny permissions to a Socks client.

1. Click Start ⇒ Programs ⇒ Microsoft Proxy Server ⇒ Microsoft Management Console.
2. The MMC opens and you see the Internet Service Manager Console Root.
3. Expand the Internet Information Server directory and your server.
4. Right-click the Socks Proxy icon and select Properties.
5. Click the Permissions tab, then click Add at the bottom of the tab.
6. In the action box, Deny should be selected. Choose a Socks client for whom you would like to deny a service. You need to know the client's IP address and subnet mask. If you do not have a Socks client, use an IP address of 10.0.0.7 and a subnet mask of 255.255.0.0.
7. Click the IP address radio button under the Source section and enter the IP address and subnet mask of the client.
8. Click to select the Port box at the bottom of the page.
9. You want this entry to be Equal To, so you accept the default of EQ.
10. In the Port number or service, enter **6667**. This denies chat access to this client. Click OK.
11. This returns you to the Permissions tab. You may perform further actions if you wish. Once you are finished, click Apply, and then click OK.

Lab 8.34 *Configuring Proxy Server*

Your organization has just installed Proxy Server and needs to configure 400 client computer browsers to use the Proxy Server. You have been asked for suggestions to easily accomplish this task. What advice would you recommend?

Lab 8.35 *Avoiding Web Proxy Server problems*

Your company wants a small group of Macintosh clients to use the Web Proxy Service. These clients have only been communicating with each other in the past and not other Windows computers on the network. What should you check first to avoid potential problems?

Lab 8.36 *Proxy Server administration*

Your network has recently started using a Proxy Server. An administrator is worried that every change made to the Proxy Server will cause a big administrative load to configure the clients. What would you say regarding this concern?

Lab 8.37 *Netscape Proxy configuration*

What actions should you take to configure Netscape Navigator to contact the Proxy Server for Internet access?

Lab 8.38 *UNIX clients*

What actions do you need to take to enable UNIX computers to use the Web Proxy Service and the SOCKS Proxy Service?

Lab 8.39 *NWLink clients*

An administrator is concerned that your network's NWLink clients will not be able to use the Winsock Service. What would you say to alleviate this concern?

Lab 8.40 *Using JavaScript*

How can JavaScript be used to create custom configuration solutions?

Lab 8.41 *Editing mspclnt.ini*

Your company needs to change the settings in the `mspclnt.ini` file so that users are directed to a new Proxy Server named ProxyCorpD. What line in the `mspclnt.ini` file should you change?

Lab 8.42 *Configuring Internet Explorer for Proxy Server*

In this lab, you manually configure Internet Explorer to use the Proxy Server.

1. Launch Internet Explorer.
2. Click the View menu and select Internet Options.
3. In the Internet Options dialog box, click the Connection tab.
4. Click the check box next to Access the Internet using a proxy server. Once the check box is selected, the other areas are available. In the Address box, enter **http://servername** where ***servername*** is the NetBIOS name of your Proxy Server.
5. In the Port box, enter **80**, which is the default selection for WWW services.
6. Click Advanced.
7. This takes you to the Proxy Setting dialog box.
8. In the middle of the dialog box, select the check box next to Use the same proxy server for all protocols.
9. Click OK.
10. You return to the Internet Options dialog box. Click Apply button and click OK.

Lab 8.43 *Installing Winsock client software*

In this lab, you will install the Winsock client software on your Windows computer.

1. On your Windows computer, click Start⇒Run.
2. In the Run box, enter **\\servername\MSPCLNT\setup.exe** where ***servername*** is the NetBIOS name of your Proxy Server. Click OK.
3. The client computer connects to the Proxy Server and begins the Winsock client software installation.
4. You see a dialog box to install the Winsock client software. Click the large button to install the software.
5. Setup checks for necessary disk space and installs the files.
6. When prompted, choose to reboot your computer.

Lab 9.44 *Password parameters*

Two of your coworkers are having a disagreement. They want to roll out a new password policy to the network, but can't determine the parameters the users should use for their passwords. What would you recommend?

Lab 9.45 *Configuring filters*

Your company wants to use PPTP and has established a PPTP Call filter. However, PPTP still does not work. What mistake was made?

Lab 9.46 *Restricting protocol access*

Your company does not want any users to have access to IRC, RealAudio, and a number of other Winsock protocols. The administrators, however, should have access to all Winsock protocols. How would you configure this?

Lab 9.47 *Restricting anonymous access*

Your company does not want anyone to be able to use the Web Proxy Service via an anonymous account. What steps can you take to disable this account?

Lab 9.48 *Windows NT Security parameters*

Your company has asked you to recommend a set of Windows NT Security parameters. What are some of issues you should discuss to implement an effective security policy?

Lab 9.49 *Configuring a domain filter*

In this lab, you will configure a domain filter.

1. On the Proxy Server computer, click Start ⇛ Programs ⇛ Proxy Server ⇛ Microsoft Management Console.
2. The Console opens. Expand the Internet Information Server folder and the Proxy Server computer. Right-click Web Proxy and select Properties.
3. The Properties sheet appears. Click the Security button on the Service tab.
4. The Security properties window appears. Click the Domain Filters tab.
5. Click the Enable filtering checkbox at the top of the tab.
6. The Granted radio button is selected by default. This means users have access to all Internet sites.
7. To create an exception, click the Add button.
8. The Deny Access To dialog box appears. Click the Domain radio button. The domain box becomes active.
9. In the domain box, type **http://www.infoseek.com** and click OK. Now `infoseek.com` is denied access.

10. From a client computer, use a browser to try to connect to `www.infoseek.com` through the Proxy Server. What happens?
11. Once you have tested the filter, you can remove it by selecting the filter in the exception list and clicking the Remove button. Now users can once again access `infoseek.com`.

Lab 9.50 *Configuring a predefined packet filter*

In this lab, you will configure a predefined packet filter.

1. On the Proxy Server computer, click Start ⇛ Programs ⇛ Proxy Server ⇛ Microsoft Management Console.
2. The Console opens. Expand the Internet Information Server folder and the Proxy Server computer. Right-click Web Proxy and select Properties.
3. The Properties sheet appears. Click the Security button on the Service tab.
4. The Security properties window appears. Click the Packet Filters tab.
5. Click the Enable packet filtering on external interface checkbox. The rest of the screen becomes active.
6. To add a predefined filter, click the Add button.
7. The Packet Filter Properties sheet appears. At the top of the screen, click the Predefined filter radio button. The drop-down menu becomes active.
8. Click on the drop-down menu and select SMTP, then click OK.
9. The TCP SMTP filter is added to the exception list.

Lab 9.51 *Configuring packet filter alerting and logging*

In this lab, you will configure packet filter alerts and logs.

1. Open the Internet Service Manager and click the Security button found on the Service tab.
2. The Security sheet appears. Click the Alerting tab.
3. In the Event dialog box, you have the option to generate alerts for rejected packets, protocol violations, or a disk full warning. Select Rejected Packets.
4. Alerts are generated by default is if there are at least 20 events per second. Accept the default.
5. You can choose to write the alerts to the Windows NT Event Log, which is selected by default, but you can also have the system send you SMTP mail. If you select this option, click the Configure Mail button and enter the name of the mail server and your mail address.

6. Click the logging tab. Generally, you want to accept the defaults of enable "regular" logging, but you can change this to verbose if you choose. Also, you may choose to log to a SQL/ODBC-compliant database as well.

Lab 10.52 *Active caching*

You have been asked to explain how Proxy Server uses active caching. How would you explain active caching and the configuration options?

Lab 10.53 *Cache filters*

You have been asked to configure Proxy Server so that it never caches `www.infoseek.com` or any of its subtrees. How would you configure the filter?

Lab 10.54 *Cache filter exceptions*

Your company has the cache filter `www.microsoft.com/default.asp*` set to Always cache. However, you company would like to never cache `www .microsoft. com/technet`. Is it possible to configure this exception, and if so, how?

Lab 10.55 *Creating a cache filter*

In this lab you will create an Always cache filter for `www.microsoft.com/mcp` and all of the path's subtrees.

1. To create a cache filter, click Start ⇛ Programs ⇛ Proxy Server ⇛ Microsoft Management Console.
2. The Internet Service Manager appears. Expand the Internet Information Server folder and expand the name of the Proxy Server.
3. Right-click the Web Proxy icon and click Properties. The properties sheet appears.
4. Click the Caching tab. Make certain that both the Enable caching and Enable active caching checkboxes are selected.
5. Click the Advanced button. The Advanced Cache Policy screen appears.
6. Click the Cache Filters button. The Cache Filters screen appears.
7. Click the Add button. The Cache Filter Properties screen appears.
8. Since you want to create a cache filter for a domain, path, and all subtrees under that path, type **www.microsoft.com/mcp*** in the URL box.
9. Click the Always cache radio button and click OK.
10. The new filter appears in the filter list.

Lab 10.56 *Creating a cache filter exception*

In this lab, you will create an exception policy to the cache filter `www.idgbooks.com/default*`.

1. To create a cache filter, click Start ⇒ Programs ⇒ Proxy Server ⇒ Microsoft Management Console.
2. The Internet Service Manager appears. Expand the Internet Information Server folder and expand the name of the Proxy Server.
3. Right-click the Web Proxy icon and click Properties. The properties sheet appears.
4. Click the Caching tab. Make certain that both the Enable caching and Enable active caching checkboxes are selected.
5. Click the Advanced button. The Advanced Cache Policy screen appears.
6. Click the Cache Filters button. The Cache Filters screen appears.
7. Click the Add button. The Cache Filter Properties screen appears.
8. Since you want to create a cache filter for a domain, path, and all subtrees under that path, type **www.idgbooks.com/default*** in the URL box.
9. Click the Never cache radio button and click OK. Since you have used a wildcard character for the default page, no pages under `idgbooks.com` will be cached.
10. The new filter appears in the filter list.
11. To create an exception to the filter, click the Add button. This returns you to the Cache Filter Properties page.
12. To create an exception that caches `www.idgbooks.com/mismt`, type **www.idgbooks.com/mismt** in the URL box and click the Always cache button. Click OK.
13. The exception appears in the filter list. This causes the `/mismt` page to always be cached.

Lab 11.57 *Primary and backup routes*

You company has two large networks — one in Denver and one in San Diego. Each network uses a Proxy Server array and has a direct connection. Your company opens a small office in Atlanta, and you want to chain the Proxy Server there to the other networks. Draw a diagram showing which network should be the primary route and which network should be the backup route. Explain your answer.

Lab 11.58 *CARP*

You have been asked to present an overview of CARP at an upcoming meeting, highlighting its advantages to multiple Proxy Server environments. What are some of the things you will say?

Lab 11.59 *Using DNS*

A coworker does not understand why DNS is important in environments that use multiple Proxy Servers. How can you explain the importance of DNS and the DNS records that may be needed?

Lab 11.60 *Multiple Proxy administrators*

You have multiple Proxy Server administrators on your network with several Proxy Server arrays. You insist on creating a maintenance schedule so that no administrators are making changes to an array at the same time. Your administrators question you on this. How would you explain your actions.

Lab 11.61 *Proxy Server and an intranet*

An executive at your company heard there are certain advantages to using Proxy Server for the company intranet, even when Internet access is not permitted. You have been asked to outline the possible advantages at an upcoming meeting. What will you say?

Lab 11.62 *IPX environments*

A coworker is concerned about configuring Proxy Server to act as an IPX gateway for IPX clients. What actions do you need to take to accomplish this?

Lab 11.63 *WINS Servers*

You are having problems with one of your WINS Servers. The server does not seem to be providing client access to the Proxy Server. What are some actions you can take?

Lab 11.64 *Configuring a Proxy Server array*

In this lab, you will configure a Proxy Server array.

1. To join an array, click Start ⇛ Programs ⇛ Proxy Server ⇛ Microsoft Management Console.

2. The Internet Service Manager appears. Expand the Internet Information Server folder and expand the name of the Proxy Server.
3. Right-click the Web Proxy icon and click Properties. The properties sheet appears.
4. On the Service tab, click the Array button. The Array dialog box appears.
5. Click the Join Array button. The Join Array dialog box appears.
6. Enter the computer name of the Proxy Server you want to form an array with. You need only enter the name, such as **CorpProxy**. Click OK.
7. If you are not joining an existing array, a dialog box appears asking you to name the array. Type in the appropriate name for the array and click OK.
8. The array members now appear in the Array Members list.
9. The Join Array button has changed to read Leave Array. If you want to remove a member from the array, highlight the appropriate computer and click the Leave Array button. You see a dialog box telling you the server leaving the array will become a stand-alone server.

Lab 11.65 *Configuring routing options*

In this lab, you will configure routing options to other arrays. If you are not working in an environment that has multiple arrays or if you are not permitted to make changes to the current configuration, you can still practice this lab. Just don't apply the changes you make.

1. To configure routing options, click Start ⇒ Programs ⇒ Proxy Server ⇒ Microsoft Management Console.
2. The Internet Service Manager appears. Expand the Internet Information Server folder and expand the name of the Proxy Server.
3. Right-click the Web Proxy icon and click Properties. The properties sheet appears.
4. Click the Routing tab. In the Upstream Routing section, click the Use Web Proxy or array radio button, and then click Modify.
5. The Advanced Routing Options window appears. In the Proxy dialog box, type the name of the upstream server or array. If you do not have an upstream server or array, type, **CorpProxy**. Note that the Auto-poll Array URL dialog box is automatically configured with `http://`*`servername`*`:80/array.dll`.
6. If you want to use credentials to communicate with the upstream server or array, click the check box, and then type in an appropriate username and password. If you want to use NTCR, click the radio button. Click OK.

7. If you want to enable a backup route, click the check box and repeat steps 5 and 6.
8. If you want to use this configuration, click the Apply button and click OK. If you do not, click the Cancel button.

Lab 11.66 *Reverse proxying*

In this lab, you will configure reverse proxying. If you do not have a Web server on your network, you can use `www.xyzcompany.com` for experimental purposes.

1. Click Start ⇛ Programs ⇛ Microsoft Proxy Server ⇛ Microsoft Management Console.
2. The Internet Service Manager appears. Expand the Internet Information Server directory and expand the computer name.
3. Right click the Web Proxy Service and select Properties. The Properties sheet appears.
4. Click the Publishing tab and click the Enable Web Publishing check box.
5. Select the radio button that tells Proxy Server what to do with incoming Web server requests. You can select the send to local Web server button if you do not actually have a Web server to point to.
6. Click the Add button to create exceptions to this rule. If you do not have actual exceptions to configure, you can simply make up a URL and a path for experimental purposes. Once you have entered the information, click OK.
7. You may see the Default Mapping dialog box. If this appears, enter the name of your Web server or `www.xyzcompany.com` for experimental purposes, and then click OK.
8. The new entry appears in the exception list. Click Apply to apply the changes, then click OK, or click cancel if you do not want to save the changes.

Lab 12.67 *Unbinding WINS*

Why should WINS be unbound from the external adapter of any Proxy Server?

Lab 12.68 *Auto Dial setup*

A coworker is setting up Auto Dial on the company's Proxy Server. When he clicks the credentials tab, the entries are all blank. What is causing this and what should your coworker do?

Lab 12.69 *Using RRAS*

You company wants to use RRAS to establish PPTP connections on the Proxy Server computer. What advice would you give?

Lab 12.70 *Installing RAS*

In this lab, you will install RAS on your server if it is not already installed.

1. Open Control Panel and double-click the Network icon.
2. Click the Services tab and click the Add button.
3. A selection service list appears. Highlight Remote Access Service and click OK.
4. NT prompts you for the location of the files needed for the installation, which you normally install from the NT Server CD-ROM I386 directory. Select the appropriate directory and click Continue.
5. The files are copied. If a modem is installed, it appears in the RAS Capable Devices list. Click OK, and then click Continue.
6. The RAS Server TCP/IP configuration will appear. Under the Allow remote TCP/IP clients to access section, click This computer only. This will prevent IP forwarding.
7. RAS is configured and installed. Click the OK button and click Close to save the binding information.
8. You are prompted to reboot the computer.

Lab 12.71 *Configuring Auto Dial*

In this lab, you configure Proxy Server for Auto Dial. This lab assumes you have a modem installed in your server and RAS configured. You must also set up a phonebook entry, configure RAS for Auto Dial, and unbind the WINS client from the external adapter. Refer to the step-by-step instructions for each of these actions within this chapter and complete them before performing this lab.

1. Click Start ⇛ Programs ⇛ Microsoft Proxy Server ⇛ Microsoft Management Console.
2. The Internet Service Manager appears. Expand the Internet Information Server directory and expand the computer name.
3. Right-click the Web Proxy Service and select Properties. The Properties sheet appears.
4. Click the Auto Dial button. On the configuration tab, click Enable dialing for Winsock and SOCKS proxy. If you are using dial-up for your primary

route, click the Enable dialing for Web proxy primary route option. If you are using dial-up for the backup route, click the Enable dialing for Web proxy backup route option.

5. Configure the Dialing hours by clicking the blue grids. All are selected by default. Blue grids are enabled and white grids are disabled.
6. Click the Credentials tab. Select the Entry Name of the phonebook entry you configured to use for Proxy Dial out. If you have more than one phonebook on your computer, use the drop-down menu to select the correct ISP.
7. Enter your ISP username and password.
8. When finished, click OK.

Lab 13.72 *Performance Monitor and Active Caching*

Your company wants to use Performance Monitor to gain information about the performance of active caching. Which counters would you recommend?

Lab 13.73 *Performance Monitor and processor speed*

You want to see if your system processor is able to handle the demands placed on the system by Proxy clients. Which counters should you use?

Lab 13.74 *Performance Monitor and client utilization*

You want to see how the Winsock and Socks clients are utilizing the related Proxy Server services. Which counters should you use?

Lab 13.75 *Performance Monitor logs*

How can you configure Performance Monitor to create a log file?

Lab 13.76 *Internet traffic*

You want to analyze the Internet traffic coming in and out of your environment. How can you do this?

Lab 13.77 *Configuring Performance Monitor*

In this lab, you will configure Performance Monitor to allow physical disk counters.

1. Click Start ⇒ Run. Type **CMD** and click OK.

2. At the command prompt, type `Diskperf`.
3. You are given a switch list. Since you want to allow the system run disk performance counters, type **diskperf -y** and press the Enter key.
4. You will be prompted to reboot the computer. Close the command prompt and reboot to activate the disk performance counters.

Lab 13.78 *Configuring Web Proxy Service counters*

In this lab you will configure Web Proxy Service counter.

1. Click Start ⇒ Programs ⇒ Microsoft Proxy Server ⇒ Monitor Microsoft Proxy Server Performance.
2. Click the File menu and click New Chart.
3. Click the Edit menu and click Add to Chart.
4. The Add to Chart window appears. In the object drop-down menu, select Web Proxy Server Service.
5. In the Counter menu, select Cache Hit Ratio % and click the Add button.
6. Click Bytes Total/sec and click the Add button.
7. Click Average Milliseconds/Request and click the Add button.
8. Click HTTP Requests and click the Add button, then click Done.
9. View the performance counters and take note of any high percentages. This could denote performance issues or problems.
10. Click the File ⇒ New Chart.
11. Click the Edit ⇒ Add to Chart.
12. Select another one of the Proxy Server objects and add counters that you wish to view. Continue to experiment with the Performance Monitor until you are comfortable using it.

Lab 14.79 *Client setup troubleshooting*

During client setup, you receive the message **Please set a description of the internal network.** What is most likely causing this error?

Lab 14.80 *Troubleshooting the cache*

You receive the following message about the Web Proxy cache: **113 – Web proxy cache failed to initialize the URL cache on disk.** What is most likely causing this error?

Lab 14.81 *Troubleshooting the Winsock Proxy Service*

You receive the following message: **17 – Incorrect network configuration. None of the server's addresses are internal.** What is most likely causing this error?

Lab 14.82 *Troubleshooting the Registry*

In this lab, you will explore the Registry. You will not modify any of the Registry settings. Warning! Great care should be taken when you perform this lab! If you modify Registry settings, you may not be able to boot the system.

1. Click Start ⇛ Run, and enter **regedt32**.
2. The Registry Editor opens. Expand HKEY_LOCAL_MACHINE.
3. Select the System key, and then click Tree ⇛ Expand.
4. Select CurrentControlSet subkey, and then click Tree ⇛ Expand.
5. Select the Services subkey, and then click Tree ⇛ Expand.
6. Scroll through the list and you will see the Proxy Server subkeys, such as the W3Pcache, W3Proxy, and so forth.
7. Select the W3Proxy subkey, and then click Tree ⇛ Expand.
8. Select the Parameters subkey. A listing of settings appears in the right column. Click Tree ⇛ Expand.
9. Select the ReverseProxy subkey. Information appears in the right pane concerning default local hosts, Reverse Proxy name, and so forth.
10. Click through the other keys and explore the registry settings, as you desire. Make certain that you do not alter any of the settings.
11. Once you are finished exploring, click Close.

APPENDIX C

Answers to Instant Assessment and Critical Thinking Labs

Chapter One: Introduction to Proxy Server 2.0

Answers to Instant Assessment

1. *A and B. Security and Caching.* Proxy Server 2.0 is a hybrid product that provides advanced caching as well as firewall functions. This combination provides superior performance and security.
2. *D. Firewall.* A firewall is a piece of software or hardware that prevents intrusion from the Internet into the LAN. Proxy Server 2.0 provides firewall capabilities.
3. *A. Local storage of Internet objects.* Content caching stores URLs and Internet objects locally on the Proxy Server in a preconfigured cache drive. This functionality provides superior retrieval performance for Proxy clients.
4. *C. Performance.* The primary benefit of content caching is the superior performance it provides to clients. Cached objects are returned to clients much more quickly than standard retrieval from the Internet.

5. *B. Typical WWW services.* The Web Proxy Service provides typical Web services such as retrieval of HTML documents, URLs, and related Internet objects.
6. *C. Winsock application service.* The Winsock Proxy Service provides functionality for Winsock applications.
7. *A. WS-FTP.* Winsock FTP is an example of a Winsock application.
8. *B. Socks client support.* The Socks Proxy Service provides support for Socket applications used by Socks clients, such as UNIX and Macintosh.
9. *B. Reverse proxying.* Proxy Server can redirect Internet traffic to an internal Web server through reverse proxying.
10. *B. Site filtering.* Site filtering enables an administrator to restrict the sites users can access by domain.

Chapter Two: TCP/IP: The Language of the Internet

Answers to Instant Assessment

1. *C. ARPA.* TCP/IP was originally developed by ARPA as a way to link government and research institutions.
2. *B. TCP/IP contains multiple protocols.* TCP/IP is a protocol suite because it is made up of multiple protocols, such as TCP, IP, UDP, SMTP, and many others.
3. *A and D. SMTP and NNTP.* SMTP, Simple Mail Transfer Protocol, and NNTP, Network News Transfer Protocol, are two of the many protocols in the TCP/IP protocol suite.
4. *C. Port.* A port is a logical connection TCP/IP uses to establish connections among TCP/IP protocols.
5. *C. 20.* FTP uses Port 20 for logical TCP connections.
6. *B. 128–191.* Class B addresses contain beginning addresses of 128 to 191.
7. *A. Default Gateway.* To configure TCP/IP, you need the IP address, at least a default subnet mask, and often a default gateway.

8. *C. 131.107.2.200.* 131.107.2.200 is the binary representation of 10000011 01101011 00000010 11001000.
9. *B. Subnet Mask.* The subnet mask is used to mask, or hide, a portion of the network address.
10. *C. 255.255.255.0.* 255.255.255.0 is the default subnet mask of Class C networks and can support up to 254 hosts.
11. *A. Default Gateway.* The default gateway redirects traffic out of the local subnet to other subnets.
12. *A. WINS.* WINS, Windows Internet Naming Service, provides dynamic resolution of NetBIOS names, or computer names, to IP addresses.
13. *C. DNS.* DNS, Domain Name Service, provides resolution of domain names, such as `www.microsoft.com`, to IP addresses.
14. *B. `ping 127.0.0.1`.* The ping command can be used to perform a loopback test, or a self-test for connectivity, by using 127.0.0.1.
15. *C. Nbtstat.* The command nbtstat can be used to view statistical information concerning NetBIOS over TCP/IP.
16. *D. `/all`.* To get a complete listing of TCP/IP configuration for a given machine, use the ipconfig command with the `/all` switch.

Answers to Critical Thinking Labs

Lab 2.1 *Connectivity tests*

In this scenario, you need to test for connectivity. You can first test the connectivity of your own machine by typing **ping 127.0.0.1** at the command line. If this test is successful, you should ping the server you are trying to contact. Since WINS is enabled, you can simply ping the server name by typing **ping corpserverd** at the command line.

Lab 2.2 *IP address classes*

Class A addresses contain IP address numbers from 1 to 126, can contain 16, 387,064 hosts, and have a default subnet mask of 255.0.0.0. Class B addresses contain address numbers from 128 to 191, can contain 64, 516 hosts, and have a default subnet mask of 255.255.0.0. Class C addresses contain IP address numbers from 192 to 233, can contain 254 hosts, and have a default subnet mask of 255.255.255.0.

Lab 2.3 *Subnet masks*

Some networks use a different subnet mask other than their actual class address. This configuration provides more subnets per network and enables you to further subdivide the network.

Chapter Three: Before You Install Proxy Server

Answers to Instant Assessment

1. *B. Pentium 133.* Microsoft recommends you install Proxy Server on a computer with at least a 133MHz Pentium processor. Higher speeds are recommended for suitable performance, however.
2. *B. 32MB.* Microsoft recommends that you install Proxy Server on a computer that has at least 32MB of RAM. For faster performance, at least 64MB is recommended.
3. *D. NTFS.* Proxy Server 2.0 can only use cache drives formatted with NTFS. Proxy Server 1.0 can use FAT drives, but Proxy Server 2.0 does not support this format.
4. *B. A computer with two NICs.* A multi-homed computer has two NICs — one for the internal network and one for an interface to the Internet.
5. *A. 337MB.* To calculate the needed space for a cache drive, use the formula 100MB + (*Number of clients* x 0.5MB). In this case, because there are 475 clients, the calculation would be 100MB + (475 x 0.5) = 337MB.
6. *B. 3.0 or higher.* Proxy Server requires Internet Information Server 3.0 or higher to be installed.
7. *A. Local Address Table.* The Local Address Table contains all the internal IP addresses for the network.

8. A. *Internal IP addresses only.* Only the internal IP addresses of a network should be included in the LAT. Including external addresses is a serious security breach.
9. B. *Network Monitor.* Network Monitor is the tool you should use to gather statistical information about network performance.
10. A. *Performance Monitor.* To watch server component performance, use Performance Monitor.
11. C. *During normal traffic times.* You should establish a baseline of performance during normal network traffic hours. This gives you an accurate look at the performance of your server.
12. B. *56Kbps.* The maximum modem speed over analog lines is 56Kbps. This speed is actually slightly lower because of overhead.
13. C. *128Kbps.* An ISDN line is made up of two 64Kbps channels for a total of 128Kbps.
14. B. *1.54MB.* A T1 provides a bandwidth of 1.54Mbps.

Answers to Critical Thinking Labs

Lab 3.5 *Configuring the network*

Since the Lewis Manufacturing Company has 1,000 employees, they need to use a Proxy Server cache drive of 600MB to service the 1,000 clients. This is calculated using the Proxy Cache size formula of 100MB + (1,000 × 0.5MB) = 600MB. Considering the size of this organization, the best connectivity option would be a T1 or a fractional T1. This will provide the best performance for the number of clients on the network.

Lab 3.6 *Internet connectivity*

When making your arguments concerning an ISDN line or a T1 line, there are two major components: cost and performance. Obviously, the T1 line would provide the best performance, but the monthly lease expense may be too great. ISDN provides significantly lower throughput than a T1 line and may not provide the desired reliability and performance. So, if the budget will permit, the best choice is a T1 line.

Lab 3.7 *Establishing a baseline*

You should establish a baseline of performance during normal traffic and demand time on a network. This gives you an accurate reflection of how well the server or network is performing under normal conditions. To establish a baseline of performance for the server, use Performance Monitor. For the network, use Network Monitor to capture a typical traffic time.

Lab 3.8 *Needs assessment*

Although there are a number of questions and analyses you should perform as the consultant, two of your major questions should be expense and performance. What does the company expect to spend to gain with Internet connectivity for their clients, and what performance do they expect? These two questions and the answers the company provides will drive the other decisions that are made.

Chapter Four: Internet Information Server Overview

Answers to Instant Assessment

1. *C. Internet Explorer 4.01 or higher.* IIS 4.0 requires IE 4.01 or higher to be installed.
2. *B. Certificate Server.* Certificate Server is an add-on component of IIS that can used to generate and authenticate certificates.
3. *C. Index Server.* Index Server is an add-on component of IIS that provides keyword searches within Web sites.
4. *A. Transaction Server.* Transaction Server is an add-on component of IIS that provides secure transactions.
5. *B. MMC.* IIS uses the MMC, Microsoft Management Console.
6. *A and C. ActiveX and Jscript.* ASP supports a number of scripting languages such as ActiveX, Jscript, VBscript, and a number of others.
7. *B. Content Analyzer.* Site Server Express provides some of the functionality of the full product. The Express version provides a content analyzer, report writer, usage import and other basic functionality.

8. *B. Secure Sockets Layer.* SSL provides for secure transmissions.
9. *C. Snap-in.* Use snap-ins to customize the MMC to the application that is it.
10. *D. INETPUB.* IIS installs a directory called INETPUB where WWWROOT, FTPROOT, and GOPHPUB are stored.
11. *C. IUSER_username.* The default guest user account installed by IIS is IUSER_*username.*
12. *C. Key Manager.* Key Manager enables you to create and manage security keys.

Answers to Critical Thinking Labs

Lab 4.11 *IIS features*

IIS provides full Web services for hosting Web sites both on the Internet and the intranet, including support for FrontPage 98 Web sites. IIS also contains a number of additional components for full Internet functionality, such as Transaction Server, Index Server, Certificate Server, and full scripting and security functions.

Lab 4.12 *Securing transactions*

To send secure records over the Internet, the best choice is to use IIS's Transaction Server. This software enables you to transmit data with no corruption or alterations.

Lab 4.13 *Multiple administrators*

IIS enables you to assign Web administrative privileges to selected users on your network. This permits system administrators to share the workload with other capable employees.

Lab 4.14 *Checking FrontPage Extensions*

You can easily manage FrontPage Server Extensions by using the FrontPage Server Extensions interface. You can check and repair Extensions using the appropriate button within the interface.

Chapter Five: Installing Proxy Server

Answers to Instant Assessment

1. *D. Service Advertisement Packet.* SAP is used to advertise a server's presence and services, normally used in NetWare or NetWare-and-NT combination networks.
2. *C. 100MB + (number of users × 0.5MB).*
3. *B. Internal IP addresses.* The LAT is established during a Proxy Server installation and contains the internal IP addresses.
4. *C. External IP addresses.* The LAT should not contain the IP addresses of the external NICs or other adapters. This is a serious security breach.
5. *C. MSPCLNT.* The client directory is called MSPCLNT and contains files needed by the Proxy clients.
6. *A. `Msplat.txt`.* The `msplat.txt` file is the client file that resides on the clients and is updated periodically by the Proxy Server.
7. *C. `Locallat.txt`.* The `locallat.txt` file is a file stored on the Proxy clients that is not updated by the Proxy Server.
8. *B. Format the drives with NTFS.* Proxy Server 2.0 does not support cache drives formatted with FAT. All cache drives have to be formatted with NTFS.
9. *B. The drives are formatted as FAT.* If the cache drives are grayed out during Proxy Server installation, the drives are formatted with FAT. The drives must be formatted with NTFS before cache drive configuration can take place.

Answers to Critical Thinking Labs

Lab 5.18 *NWLink and Proxy*

Proxy Server provides IPX to IP translation for Internet connectivity, so clients on the network do not need to have TCP/IP installed to function with Proxy Server. This configuration actually provides additional security benefits against the network being compromised by Internet intruders.

Lab 5.19 *Building the LAT*

The LAT should contain all IP addresses within the network. This information can be entered manually, a private class address can be assigned, or Proxy Server can obtain this information from routing tables. However, the administrator should make certain that the IP addresses of external NICs or adapters are not included in the LAT. This could make the network visible to Internet intruders.

Lab 5.20 *Troubleshooting Setup*

LAT error messages received during Setup should be examined carefully because they may point to the fact that external NIC addresses may have been accidentally included.

Lab 5.21 *Proxy Licensing*

Proxy Server licensing is very simple. Each server must have a license, but clients are not required to have a license. Also, the Proxy server software may be sold, as long as you do not keep any copies. This makes the administration of Proxy Server easy.

Chapter Six: Proxy Server Architecture

Answers to Instant Assessment

1. *C. CERN.* Browsers that are used with Proxy Server must be CERN-compliant. Most major browsers today, such as Microsoft Internet Explorer and Netscape Navigator, are CERN-compliant.
2. *A.* `get`. The `get` and `post` commands are the most common Web commands. The `get` command is used to retrieve Internet objects.
3. *B.* `post`. The `post` command is used to send information to a Web site and post the data on the site.
4. *B and C. ISAPI Filter and ISAPI Application.* The two ISAPI components are the ISAPI Filter and the ISAPI Application.
5. *B. Passive caching.* Passive caching reacts to client requests and updates objects based on the request and the TTL.

6. *A. Active caching.* Active caching examines client requests based on the object's popularity and the TTL, and updates the cache accordingly.
7. *C. UNIX.* The Winsock API originated with Sockets, an API developed for UNIX based systems.
8. *B and D. RealAudio and RealVideo.* RealAudio and RealVideo are both examples of UDP transmissions, which are connectionless.
9. *A. `winsock32.dll`.* The Winsock Proxy client consists of two DLLs: `Winsock32.dll` and `Winsock.dll`.
10. *D. Control channel.* Proxy Server uses a control channel to manage the connection between the client and the server.

Answers to Critical Thinking Labs

Lab 6.23 *Proxy Server clients*

Your company does not have to worry. As long as the Macintosh clients are using a CERN-compliant browser such as Microsoft Internet Explorer or Netscape Navigator, they will be able to access the Internet through Microsoft's Proxy Server without any problems.

Lab 6.24 *Wsock32.dll file*

The `Winsock32.dll` file is required for communication with Proxy Server in Winsock Applications. This DLL replaces the normal Winsock DLL to redirect Winsock requests to the Proxy Server.

Lab 6.25 *Active and passive caching*

Passive caching responds to user requests for Web objects. If the object can be cached, Proxy Server caches the objects and assigns them a TTL. In this sense, Proxy Server is passive — it only responds to requests from clients. Active caching, on the other hand, enables Proxy Server to take an active role in caching. Proxy Server decides which URLs are most popular and automatically updates and creates new TTLs for those objects.

Lab 6.26 *Proxy Server services*

The Web Proxy Service provides typical Internet service regardless of the platform. As long as a CERN-compliant browser is used, the Web Proxy Service can fulfill Web requests, if those requests are permitted on the network. The Winsock Proxy Service provides service for Winsock applications, such as WS-FTP. The Socks Proxy Service provides service for Socket applications typically used by UNIX and Macintosh clients.

Chapter Seven: The Proxy Server Interface

Answers to Instant Assessment

1. *C. Service.* The Service tab contains services applicable to all three Proxy Server services and is shared by all services.
2. *A. Local Address Table button on the Service Tab.* The LAT is configured during Proxy Server installation, but changes to LAT can be made at any time by clicking the button on the Service tab.
3. *C.* `mspYYYYMMDD.mpc`. The default backup file records the year, month, and date the back was performed.
4. *B. Clients can access anything on the Internet.* Access control enables the administrator to control what clients access on the Internet. If this check box is not selected, clients can access anything they choose.
5. *D. Verbose.* Verbose logging records all information and can be used for detailed analysis, although verbose logging takes up more disk space.
6. *B. Unlimited Access on the Protocols tab.* The unlimited access selection on the protocols tab enables you to assign all protocol permissions to Winsock clients.
7. *A and D. Permit and Deny.* Socks permissions can be either permitted or not through the permit or deny permission.
8. *B. EQ.* The EQ, or equal to, selection enables you to require the port connection to equal the specified port.

Answers to Critical Thinking Labs

Lab 7.27 *Denying access in the Winsock Proxy Service*

To deny access to the Archie protocol in Winsock, access the Winsock properties page and select the Permissions tab. Because you want to deny access to Archie for certain groups, select Archie from the drop-down menu and click Edit. The Archie Permissions screen appears. Click Add. User Manager for Domains appears, and you can now select which users or groups you want to deny access for. Add the appropriate users, and then click the Type of Access drop-down menu. Click Deny. If you want to deny access to everyone, the easiest method is to select Archie from the Protocols tab of the Winsock Properties page and remove the protocol from this available list.

Lab 7.28 *Assigning and managing Proxy Server permissions*

Proxy Server permissions are easy to administer if users are organized into groups that receive certain rights or permissions to use Protocols.

Lab 7.29 *Monitoring users*

The current session button will enable you to view how long Mary is staying connected to the Internet. This information can be used to determine if Mary is abusing Internet privileges.

Chapter Eight: Configuring the Proxy Client

Answers to Instant Assessment

1. *D. All of the above.* The Winsock client software can be installed through a browser, at the command line, and by executing `setup.exe` in the MSPCLNT directory.
2. *A and C.* `mspclnt.ini` *and* `msplat.txt`. Both files reside on the client and are overwritten and updated periodically.
3. *A. Windows.* Only Windows clients can use Winsock.

4. *D. Any CERN-compliant browser.* Any CERN-compliant browser on any platform can use the Web Proxy Service.
5. *D. All of the above.* Any platform can use the Web Proxy Service as long as that platform uses a CERN-compliant browser.
6. *B.* `C:\MSP\Clients`. The default installation script is located in the MSP directory in the Clients subdirectory.
7. *D. WAIS.* WAIS is an older Internet search protocol that was primarily used in education institutions.

Answers to Critical Thinking Labs

Lab 8.34 *Configuring Proxy Server*

Because you need to configure 400 client computers, a script installation would be your best choice. By using a script, you avoid having to configure the browsers manually.

Lab 8.35 *Avoiding Web Proxy Server problems*

Because the Macintosh clients have only been communicating with each other, they are using the AppleTalk protocol and may not have TCP/IP installed. To avoid delays and problems, first check the machines for TCP/IP and general connectivity.

Lab 8.36 *Proxy Server administration*

Changes made to the Proxy Server that affect clients are automatically updated to the clients through `mspclnt.ini`, which is overwritten and updated by the server periodically. This way, configuration changes will be automatically made on each client machine without manual configuration.

Lab 8.37 *Netscape Proxy configuration*

You need to configure Netscape Navigator for the Proxy Server manually by clicking the Manual proxy configuration button and then clicking View. Once you do this, a dialog box that is similar to the one in IE 4.01 appears.

Lab 8.38 *UNIX clients*

Assuming the UNIX clients are using TCP/IP, you simply need to configure the browser to contact the Proxy Server for service. Any SOCKS applications have to be configured manually to point to the Proxy Server for service as well.

Lab 8.39 *NWLink clients*

The Winsock Proxy client software supports clients using the IPX/SPX compatible protocol, NWLink. The client has to be a Windows operating system, and a CERN-compliant browser must be used. Beyond that, the Winsock Proxy client software acts as an NWLink to TCP/IP gateway to the Proxy Server. Note that the Winsock Proxy client software for NWLink does not support Windows 3.*x* clients.

Lab 8.40 *Using JavaScript*

A default script is created from the client configuration option selected during Setup. Using JavaScript, a custom script can be configured and used in place of the default script. Each time the browser is opened, the script is downloaded from the Proxy Server to configure the browser to gain Web access from the Proxy Server.

Lab 8.41 *Editing mspclnt.ini*

You can make changes to the `mspclnt.ini` file with any text editor. To change the name of the server, you need to edit the Configuration URL line. After changing the computer name to ProxyCorpD, the line would read as follows:

```
Configuration Url=http://PROXYCORPD:80/
array.dll?Get.Routing.Script
```

Chapter Nine: Creating a Secure Environment

Answers to Instant Assessment

1. C. *Verbose.* Verbose logging records all information and data.
2. C. `C:\winnt\system32\msplogs`. Log files for Proxy Server are stored in the Winnt directory in the subdirectory Msplogs.

3. *C.* `Fpyymmdd.log`. This is the default packet filter log where *yymmdd* indicates the year, month, and date of the log.
4. *C. ODBC.* Open Database Connectivity is a standard API for developing platform independent databases.
5. *D. In TCP/IP Properties.* IP forwarding can be enabled or disabled in TCP/IP properties.
6. *B. They can be read and intercepted.* SMBs should not be used on the Internet because they can be read and intercepted by Internet users.
7. *A. To create tighter security.* Any services that are not needed on the external adapter, such as WINS, should be disabled to create tighter security against Internet intruders.
8. *A, B, C, and D. Minimum lengths, combinations of letters and numbers, account lockout options for failed password attempts, and password expirations.* All of these actions are good tactics for passwords to help keep security high.
9. *B. Through Winsock Proxy Protocol options.* Access to Winsock protocols, such as IRC (Internet Relay Chat), be granted or restricted through the Winsock Proxy service protocols tab.
10. *B. Administrators.* It is usually best to assign unlimited Winsock access only to administrators.
11. *A. UNIX.* Socks clients can be given a temporary identity and IP address by using IdentD
12. *D. This cannot be done.* Domain filters apply to all clients. They cannot be assigned to particular users or groups.

Answers to Critical Thinking Labs

Lab 9.44 *Password parameters*

Passwords are often overlooked as a means of making a network more secure. The best password policy is to make users use passwords that have minimum lengths and contain numbers and letters. Also, the server should only permit three password attempts before locking an account, and users should be forced to change their passwords every couple of months.

Lab 9.45 *Configuring filters*

Some protocols, such as PPTP, require permissions to be assigned to more than one protocol. In the case of the PPTP Call filter, the VPN requires the use of a PPTP Receive filter as well.

Lab 9.46 *Restricting protocol access*

The best way to configure protocols is to make certain users are organized in groups. This way, appropriate protocols can be assigned to appropriate groups with minimal administrative overhead.

Lab 9.47 *Restricting anonymous access*

To disable the default anonymous account, double-click the computer name under the WWW service in the Internet Service Manager. Clear the Allow Anonymous checkbox and apply the changes.

Lab 9.48 *Windows NT Security parameters*

When setting Windows NT security parameters, there are a number if issues you should consider. First, requirements for user names and passwords should be clearly established to protect the network. Also, you should discuss what type of Windows NT security will be implemented, such as basic authentication, clear text, or Windows NT Challenge/Response. The answers to these questions will depend on the needs of the individual environment.

Chapter Ten: Caching with Proxy Server

Answers to Instant Assessment

1. *B. Active.* Active caching enables the Proxy Server to update object TTLs automatically, based on popularity and other server factors.
2. *C. Reconfigure cache drives.* The Cache Size button enables you to reconfigure the size of the cache drive or add new cache drives if needed.

3. *B. Object popularity.* In active caching, an object's popularity is a big factor Proxy Server considers when updating objects and TTLs.
4. *D. 1,440.* The default maximum TTL is 1,440 minutes.
5. *A. Updates are more important.* The Updates are more important option enables Proxy Server to perform more pre-fetching so, objects are more current.
6. *A. Objects are pre-fetched and updated often.* Users get faster cache response.
7. *C. Only the domain and path would be cached.* Because there is no wildcard used in `www.microsoft.com/mcp`, only that specific domain and path would be cached.
8. *D. The domain, path, and all subtrees would be cached.* Because the wildcard character is used, `www.microsoft.com/mcp` and every sub-tree under `/mcp` would be cached.
9. *D. Any domain and path would be cached including www, ftp, and so forth.* The wildcard character can be used to permit any domain type, such as www, ftp, mail and so forth.
10. *A. An exception is made to another cache filter.* Cache filter exceptions can be used to create an exception rule to a particular filter. For example, if everything at a given site is cached, but you want to not cache a certain path, you can create an exception to the filter.

Answers to Critical Thinking Labs

Lab 10.52 *Active caching*

Active caching enables Proxy Server to take an active role in the caching process by determining which URLs or Internet objects are most popular. Proxy Server then caches and updates these objects without commands from clients. You can set the caching options so there is more or less pre-fetching, or so that fetching is equal.

Lab 10.53 *Cache filters*

The filter can be configured in the caching tab. Entering the URL and assigning it the property of never cache can create the filter. This way, the filter is created and the URL will never be cached.

Lab 10.54 *Cache filter exceptions*

Adding a filter for `www.microsoft.com/technet` and setting the filter to never cache can easily configure the exception. This creates an exception to previous filter that caches everything at `www.microsoft.com`.

Chapter Eleven: Proxy Server in the Enterprise

Answers to Instant Assessment

1. *D. All of the Above.* Proxy Server arrays provide superior performance, fault tolerance, and ease of administration. These benefits make arrays very practical and useful.
2. *A. Only Proxy Server 2.0 servers can be array members.* Because Proxy Server creates a logical cache across the servers, which each use NTFS partitions, only Proxy Server 2.0 servers can be array members.
3. *B. Hash.* A hash is a mathematical formula used by CARP to determine the location of stored URLs.
4. *B. Choose the Refresh option.* If another administrator makes changes to an array member before your changes are saved, you should choose the refresh option to maintain array synchronization, although this option will not save any changes you have made.
5. *D. ICP.* CARP replaced ICP, which used a query method to determine the location of URLs. ICP did not function well in large environments due to the query method.
6. *A.* `http://servername/array.dll?Get.Info.v1`. Any array member's membership table can be viewed from a browser by using this URL with the appropriate server name.

7. *D. 80.* Communication with an array uses a default port of 80, which is the same port used for HTTP traffic.
8. *C. RemotMSP.* RemotMSP is a command-line utility that can be used to gather array membership tables in lieu of a browser.
9. *B. Create a CNAME alias in DNS for all array members.* To make certain load balancing occurs with array members, a CNAME alias should be created with each members IP address assigned to the same name. DNS will take a round-robin approach to fulfill requests. This way, all array members receive equal traffic.
10. *D. Basic Text and NTCR.* For logon options, Basic Text and NT Challenge Response are both available choices.
11. *B. Reverse Hosting.* Reverse Hosting is the process for sending Internet requests to multiple Web servers within the network. This makes the Web servers appear as one server to Internet users.

Answers to Critical Thinking Labs

Lab 11.57 *Primary and backup routes*

Because the Denver and San Diego offices both have direct Internet connections and are both described as large environments, you should configure the primary route at the Atlanta site to the closest site, which is Denver in this case. San Diego should be the backup route.

Lab 11.58 *CARP*

CARP enables Proxy Server arrays to create logical cache drives among the servers. CARP uses a hash algorithm to place and find URLs within the logical cache. CARP provides superior performance, and is a big improvement over ICP, which used a query method to determine the location of URLs.

Lab 11.59 *Using DNS*

DNS can be used to load-balance Proxy Server access in environments with multiple Proxy Servers. Various records can be created, but mostly DNS A and CNAME records can be used so that DNS will use a round-robin approach to contacting the Proxy Servers. This way, all Proxy Servers receive an equal load of requests.

Lab 11.60 *Multiple Proxy administrators*

Because of the problems associated with synchronization, it is best for only one administrator to make configuration changes to an array member at a time. This avoids synchronization conflicts or a loss of configuration changes. Maintenance schedules can alleviate this problem and prevent two network administrators from making changes to two array members at the same time.

Lab 11.61 *Proxy Server and an intranet*

Proxy Server can be useful in an environment where there is no Internet access, but there is a company intranet. One of the big advantages is caching: Proxy Server can cache intranet content just as it would Internet content. This reduces the load on the Web server and speeds the retrieval of Web pages. Also, IPX environments see a benefit because Proxy Server can handle IPX-to-TCP traffic.

Lab 11.62 *IPX environments*

Proxy Server can function as an IPX/SPX-to-TCP/IP gateway. This way, your network can use IPX while still having the functionality of the Internet, which only uses TCP/IP. However, load balancing requires a little more work. In order to communicate with the array, the IPX addresses of the member servers in the array must be used. This information is found in the `LOCAL-ADDR.DUMP` file located in the C:\MSP\Clients directory on each Proxy Server in the array. This data from each server must be merged together and placed in the Servers IPX Addresses sections of the `mspclnt.ini` file. This creates a merged file, which can then be copied to the other members of the array so load balancing can be performed.

Lab 11.63 *WINS Servers*

The WINS Manager should be used to create a static mapping for the Proxy Servers. This ensures that proper load balancing occurs by providing a search order so a Proxy request is sent to a Proxy Server on the local subnet first, before using a Proxy Server on another subnet.

Chapter Twelve: Proxy Server and RAS

Answers to Instant Assessment

1. *B. HCL.* The Hardware Compatibility List (HCL) is a list of compatible hardware for use with Windows NT. The HCL can be viewed and downloaded at `www.microsoft.com`.
2. *B. Dial out.* Although Proxy Server can be configured to allow dial in and dial out, only dial out is recommended to reduce the possibility of authorized access.
3. *B. This computer only.* By restricting dial-in access to This Computer Only, access to the entire network is restricted. Permitting dial-in clients to access the entire network will enable IP forwarding, which is a serious security breach.
4. *C. Unbind WINS from the external adapter.* In order to preserve the security of your NetBIOS names, WINS should be unbound from the external adapter.
5. *D. PPTP.* The Point to Point Tunneling protocol is used to communicate via a Virtual Private Network.
6. *B. `Net start spsvc`.* To start the Socks Proxy Service via the command line, you should use the `net start spsvc` command.

Answers to Critical Thinking Labs

Lab 12.67 *Unbinding WINS*

WINS should be unbound from the external network adapter so the NetBIOS names of your network will not be compromised by Internet intruders.

Lab 12.68 *Auto Dial setup*

To correct this problem, a phonebook entry for the ISP must be configured in RAS before configuring Auto Dial. After the phonebook entry is configured, it will appear in the Credentials tab.

Lab 12.69 *Using RRAS*

Although Proxy Server supports the use of PPTP to establish VPNs, Microsoft does not recommended that Proxy Server be used for this purpose. This could enable more security breaches and affect the performance of the server. It is best to use another server for PPTP communications.

Chapter Thirteen: Proxy Server Performance

Answer to Instant Assessment

1. *B. Frames Dropped due to Protocol Violations.* This counter enables you to view information about the number of frames that have been dropped because of violations in protocol. This could give you a clue as to potential attacks from the Internet if the number is high.
2. *D. URLs in Cache.* This counter can be used to determine how many URLs are currently stored in the cache.
3. *B. Active Refresh Bytes/sec.* Use this counter to determine now much active caching is being performed.
4. *C. Current Average Milliseconds/Request.* This counter should be used to determine the speed of transmission from the clients to the Proxy Server and vice versa.
5. *D. Page Faults/sec.* To determine if a system needs more RAM, this counter should be monitored. If excessive paging is occurring, the system needs more RAM.

Answers to Critical Thinking Labs

Lab 13.72 *Performance Monitor and Active Caching*

If you want to gain information about active caching, the best counters to view are Active Refresh Bytes/sec, Max Bytes Cached, Total Actively Refreshed URLs, and URLs in Cache. These counters will give you a clear picture of the active caching functions on your server.

Lab 13.73 *Performance Monitor and processor speed*

To determine the effectiveness of a system processor, you should view the % Processor Time counter to determine the percentage of the time the processor is busy.

Lab 13.74 *Performance Monitor and client utilization*

To view counters for the Winsock Proxy Service, use Active Sessions and Active TCP Connections and Active UDP Connections. These counters will give you a good idea of how clients are utilizing the Winsock Proxy Service. For the Socks Proxy Service, view the Total Failed Socks Sessions and Total Socks Sessions counters.

Lab 13.75 *Performance Monitor Logs*

You can use Performance Monitor to create log files, which you can use to help determine problems and identify configuration changes that you need to make. To add a log, simply click the Log button on the toolbar, and then click the + button on the toolbar to add components to the log file.

Lab 13.76 *Internet Traffic*

To monitor any network traffic, the best tool to use is Network Monitor. By using Network Monitor, you can capture a portion of the network traffic for the desired time period, and then analyze the results of the capture.

Chapter 14: Troubleshooting Proxy Server

Answers to Instant Assessment

1. *A. Stop.* Stop events are displayed in red in Event Viewer.
2. *D. HKEY_LOCAL_MACHINE.* HKEY_LOCAL_MACHINE stores configuration information about the system device configurations, so modems would be included in this subtree.
3. *B. HKEY_CLASSES_ROOT.* HKEY_CLASSES_ROOT contains software configuration information.

4. *A. HKEY_CURRENT_USER.* HKEY_CURRENT_USER contains information about the policies and configuration for the current user.
5. *B. CHKWSP.* CHKWSP is a utility included with Proxy Server that enables you to view information about Winsock connections.

Answers to Critical Thinking Labs

Lab 14.79 *Client setup troubleshooting*

This error message occurs if the `msplat.txt` file is not present on the computer. You should make certain that your logon credentials are accurate and that you have enough disk space available.

Lab 14.80 *Troubleshooting the cache*

When you receive this error, you need to reset the default settings. Stop the Web Proxy Service. On the Caching tab, click the Advanced button, and then click Reset Defaults. Restart the Web Proxy Service.

Lab 14.81 *Troubleshooting the Winsock Proxy Service*

When you receive this error message, you need to modify the LAT to include the internal adapter's IP address.

APPENDIX

D

Exam Preparation Tips

The Microsoft Certified Professional Exams are not easy, and they require a great deal of preparation. The exam questions measure real-world skills. Your ability to answer these questions correctly will be enhanced by as much hands-on experience with the product as you can get.

Although the Exam Objectives in Appendix A were current when this book was published, you may want to ensure that you have the most current version of the exam objectives by accessing the Microsoft Training and Certification Web site at `www.microsoft.com/train_cert`.

About the Exams

An important aspect of passing the MCP Certification Exams is understanding the big picture. This includes understanding how the exams are developed and scored.

Every job function requires different levels of cognitive skills, from memorization of facts and definitions to the comprehensive ability to analyze scenarios, design solutions, and evaluate options. To make the exams relevant in the real world, Microsoft Certified Professional exams test the specific cognitive skills needed for the job functions being tested. These exams go beyond testing rote knowledge—you need to *apply* your knowledge, analyze technic-solutions, solve problems, and make decisions—just as you would on the job.

Exam Items and Scoring

Microsoft certification exams consist of four types of items: multiple-choice, multiple-rating, enhanced, and simulation. The way you indicate your answer and the number of points you receive differ depending on the type of item.

Multiple-choice item

A traditional multiple-choice item presents a problem and asks you to select either the best answer (single response) or the best set of answers (multiple response) to the given item from a list of possible answers.

For a multiple-choice item, your response is scored as either correct or incorrect. A correct answer receives a score of 1 point and an incorrect answer receives a score of 0 points.

In the case of a multiple-choice, multiple-response item (for which the correct response consists of more than one answer), the item is scored as being correct only if all the correct answers are selected. No partial credit is given for a response that does not include all the correct answers for the item.

For consistency purposes, the question in a multiple-choice, multiple-response item is always presented in singular form, regardless of how many answers are correct. Always follow the instructions displayed at the bottom of the window.

Multiple-rating item

A multiple-rating item presents a task similar to those presented in multiple-choice items. In a multiple-choice item, you are asked to select the best answer or answers from a selection of several potential answers. In contrast, a multiple-rating item presents a task, along with a proposed solution. Each time the task is presented, a different solution is proposed. In each multiple-rating item, you are asked to choose the answer that best describes the results produced by one proposed solution.

Enhanced item

An enhanced item is similar to a multiple-choice item because it asks you to select your response from a number of possible responses. However, unlike the traditional multiple-choice item that presents you with a list of possible answers from which to choose, an enhanced item may ask you to indicate your answer in one of the following three ways:

- Type the correct response, such as a command name.
- Review an exhibit (such as a screen shot, a network configuration drawing, or a code sample), and then use the mouse to select the area of the exhibit that represents the correct response.
- Review an exhibit, and then select the correct response from the list of possible responses.

As with a multiple-choice item, your response to an enhanced item is scored as either correct or incorrect. A correct answer receives full credit of 1 point, and an incorrect answer receives a score of 0 points.

Simulation item

A simulation imitates the functionality of product components or environments, complete with error messages and dialog boxes. You are given a scenario and one or more tasks to complete by using that simulation. A simulation item's goal is to determine if you know how to complete a given task. Just as with the other item types, the simulation is scored when you complete the exam. A simulation item may ask you to indicate your answer in one of the following ways:

- Review an exhibit (such as a screen shot, a network configuration drawing, or a code sample), and then use the GUI simulation to resolve, configure or otherwise complete the assigned task.
- Based on information in the exam scenario, resolve, configure, or otherwise complete the assigned task.

As with the other item types, you receive credit for a correct answer only if all of the requested criteria are met by your actions in the scenario. There is no partial credit for a incomplete simulation item.

Exam Formats

Microsoft uses two different exam formats to determine how many questions are going to be presented on the exam. The majority of Microsoft exams have historically used fixed length exam, with between 50 and 100 questions per exam. Each time you take the exam, you are presented with a different set of questions, but still comprising an equal number of questions. Recently, Microsoft has attempted to increase the reliability of its testing procedures, and has implemented new strategies to that end. The newest format is called *computer adaptive testing*. A computer adaptive test (CAT) is tailored to the individual exam taker. You start with an easy-to-moderate question; if you answer the question incorrectly, you get follow-up questions on the same topic.

This process continues only until the CAT determines your ability. As a result, you may have an exam that is only 15 questions, but contains extremely difficult questions. Alternately, you may have an exam that contains 50 moderately difficult questions.

Preparing for a Microsoft Certified Professional Exam

The best way to prepare for an exam is to study, learn, and master the job function on which you'll be tested. For any certification exam, you should follow these important preparation steps:

1. Identify the objectives on which you'll be tested.
2. Assess your current mastery of those objectives.
3. Practice the tasks and study the areas you haven't mastered.

This section describes tools and techniques that may be helpful as you perform these steps to prepare for the exam.

Exam Preparation Guides

For each certification exam, an Exam Preparation Guide provides important, specific information about what you'll be tested on and how best to prepare. These guides are essential tools for preparing to take certification exams. You'll find the following types of valuable information in the exam preparation guides:

- **Tasks you should master:** Outlines the overall job function tasks you should master
- **Exam objectives:** Lists the specific skills and abilities on which you should expect to be measured
- **Product resources:** Tells you the products and technologies with which you should be experienced
- **Suggested reading:** Points you to specific reference materials and other publications that discuss one or more of the exam objectives
- **Suggested curriculum:** Provides a specific list of instructor-led and self-paced courses relating to the job function tasks and topics in the exam

You'll also find pointers to additional information that may help you prepare for the exams, such as *Microsoft TechNet*, *Microsoft Developer Network* (MSDN), online forums, and other sources.

By paying attention to the verbs used in the "Exam Objectives" section of the Exam Preparation Guide, you will get an idea of the level at which you'll be tested on that objective.

To view the most recent version of the Exam Preparation Guides, which include the exam's objectives, check out Microsoft's Training and Certification Web site at www.microsoft.com/train_cert. For further reading on MCSE study tips, please refer to my book, *MCSE Study Tips For Dummies*, published by IDG Books Worldwide.

Assessment Exams

When preparing for the exams, take lots of assessment exams. Assessment exams are self-paced exams that you take at your own computer. When you complete an assessment exam, you receive instant score feedback so you can determine areas in which additional study may be helpful before you take the certification exam. Although your score on an assessment exam doesn't necessarily indicate what your score will be on the certification exam, assessment exams give you the opportunity to answer items that are similar to those on the certification exams. The assessment exams also use the same computer-based testing tool as the certification exams, so you don't have to learn the tool on exam day.

An assessment exam exists for almost every certification exam.

Taking a Microsoft Certified Professional Exam

This section contains information about registering for and taking a Microsoft Certified Professional exam, including what to expect when you arrive at the testing center to take the exam.

How to Register for an Exam

Candidates may take exams at any of more than 700 Sylvan Prometric testing centers around the world. For the location of a Sylvan Prometric testing center near you, call (800) 755-EXAM (755-3926). Outside the United States and Canada, contact your local Sylvan Prometric Registration Center.

You can also take exams at any of the over 160 different Virtual University Enterprises (VUE) testing centers around the world. To register for an exam at a VUE testing center in your area, call (888) 837-8616. Outside the United States and Canada, contact your local Virtual University Enterprises Registration Center.

Sylvan Prometric offers online registration for Microsoft exams at its Microsoft registration website — `https://www.slspro.com/msreg/ micros of.asp`. You can also register for an exam at a VUE testing center by visiting `http://www.vue.com/ms`.

To register for a Microsoft Certified Professional exam:

1. Determine which exam you want to take and note the exam number.
2. Call the Sylvan Prometric or VUE Registration Center nearest to you. If you haven't register with them before, you will be asked to provide information to the Registration Center.
3. You can then schedule your exam at your choice of locations. One the exam is scheduled, you will be asked to provide payment for the exam. Both of the testing centers take major credit cards and offer pre-payment options for purchasing exam certificates for future or corporate use.

When you schedule the exam, you'll be provided instructions regarding the appointment, cancellation procedures, and ID requirements, as well as information about the testing center location.

Exams must be taken within one year of payment. You can schedule exams up to six weeks in advance, or as late as one working day prior to the date of the exam. You can cancel or reschedule your exam if you contact the testing center at least one working day prior to the exam.

Although subject to space availability, same-day registration is available in some locations. Where same-day registration is available, you must register a minimum of two hours before test time.

What to Expect at the Testing Center

As you prepare for your certification exam, it may be helpful to know what to expect when you arrive at the testing center on the day of your exam. The following information gives you a preview of the general procedure you'll go through at the testing center:

- You will be asked to sign the log book upon arrival and departure.
- You will be required to show two forms of identification, including one photo ID (such as a driver's license or company security ID), before you may take the exam.
- The test administrator will give you a Testing Center Regulations form that explains the rules you will be expected to comply with during the test. You will be asked to sign the form, indicating that you understand the regulations and will comply.
- The test administrator will show you to your test computer and will handle any preparations necessary to start the testing tool and display the exam on the computer.
- You will be provided a set amount of scratch paper for use during the exam. All scratch paper will be collected from you at the end of the exam. Some testing centers might give you an erasable board to use as scratch paper. You can ask for scratch paper instead.
- The exams are all closed-book. You may not use a laptop computer or have any notes or printed material with you during the exam session.
- Some exams may include additional materials, or exhibits. If any exhibits are required for your exam, the test administrator will provide you with them before you begin the exam and collect them from you at the end of the exam.

- Before you begin the exam, the test administrator will tell you what to do when you complete the exam. If the test administrator doesn't explain this to you, or if you are unclear about what you should do, ask the administrator before beginning the exam.
- The number of items on each exam varies, as does the amount of time allotted for each exam. Generally, certification exams consist of about 50 to 100 items (unless you are taking a CAT exam) and have durations of 60 to 90 minutes. You can verify the number of items and time allotted for your exam when you register.

Because you'll be given a specific amount of time to complete the exam once you begin, if you have any questions or concerns, don't hesitate to ask the test administrator before the exam begins.

As an exam candidate, you are entitled to the best support and environment possible for your exam. In particular, you are entitled to the following:

- A quiet, uncluttered test environment
- Scratch paper
- The tutorial for using the online testing tools, and time to take the tutorial
- A knowledgeable and professional test administrator
- The opportunity to submit comments about the testing center and staff, or the test itself

The Certification Development Team will investigate any problems or issues you raise and make every effort to resolve them quickly.

Your Exam Results

Once you have completed an exam, you will be given immediate, online notification of your pass or fail status. You will also receive a printed Examination Score Report indicating your pass or fail status and your exam results by section. (The test administrator will give you the printed score report.) Test scores are automatically forwarded to Microsoft within five working days after you take the test. You do not need to send your score to Microsoft.

If you pass the exam, you will receive confirmation from Microsoft, typically within two to four weeks.

If You Don't Receive a Passing Score

If you do not pass a certification exam, you may call the testing center to schedule a time to retake the exam. Before retaking the exam, you should review the appropriate Exam Preparation Guide and focus additional study on the topic areas where your exam results could be improved. Please note that you must pay again for each exam retake.

One way to determine areas where additional study may be helpful is to review your individual section scores carefully. The section titles in your score report generally correlate to specific groups of exam objectives listed in the Exam Preparation Guide.

Here are some specific ways you can prepare to retake an exam:

- Go over the section-by-section scores on your exam results, noting objective areas where your score could be improved.
- Review the Exam Preparation Guide for the exam, with a special focus on the tasks and objective areas that correspond to the exam sections where your score could be improved.
- Increase your real-world, hands-on experience and practice performing the listed job tasks with the relevant products and technologies.
- Consider taking or retaking one or more of the suggested courses listed in the Exam Preparation Guide.
- Review the suggested readings listed in the Exam Preparation Guide.
- After you review the materials, retake the corresponding Assessment Exam.

For More Information

To find out more about Microsoft Education and Certification materials and programs, to register with a testing center, or to get other useful information, check the following resources. Outside the United States or Canada, contact your local Microsoft office or testing center.

- **Microsoft Certified Professional Program: (800) 636-7544.** Call for information about the Microsoft Certified Professional program and exams, and to order the *Microsoft Certified Professional Program Exam Study Guide* or the Microsoft Train_Cert Offline CD-ROM.

- **Sylvan Prometric Testing Centers: (800) 755-EXAM.** Call to register to take a Microsoft Certified Professional exam at any of more than 700 Sylvan Prometric testing centers around the world, or to order the *Microsoft Certified Professional Program Exam Study Guide*.
- **Virtual University Enterprises Testing Centers:** (888) 837-8616. Call to register to take a Microsoft Certified Professional exam at any of the over 160 different Virtual University Enterprises testing centers around the world.
- **Microsoft Sales Fax Service: (800) 727-3351.** Call for Microsoft Certified Professional Exam Preparation Guides, Microsoft Official Curriculum course descriptions and schedules, or the *Microsoft Certified Professional Program Exam Study Guide.*
- **Education Program and Course Information: (800) SOLPROV.** Call for information about Microsoft Official Curriculum courses, Microsoft education products, and the Microsoft Solution Provider Authorized Technical Education Center (ATEC) program, where you can attend a Microsoft Official Curriculum course, or to order the *Microsoft Certified Professional Program Exam Study Guide.*
- **Microsoft Certification Development Team: Fax (425) 936-1311.** Use this fax number to volunteer for participation in one or more exam development phases or to report a problem with an exam. Address written correspondence to: Certification Development Team, Microsoft Education and Certification, One Microsoft Way, Redmond, WA 98052.
- **Microsoft TechNet Technical Information Network: (800) 344-2121.** Call for support professionals and system administrators. Outside the United States and Canada, call your local Microsoft subsidiary for information.
- **Microsoft Developer Network (MSDN): (800) 759-5474.** MSDN is the official source for software development kits, device driver kits, operating systems, and information about developing applications for Microsoft Windows and Windows NT.
- **Online Services: (800) 936-3500.** Call for information about Microsoft Connection on CompuServe, Microsoft Knowledge Base, Microsoft Software Library, Microsoft Download Service, and Internet.

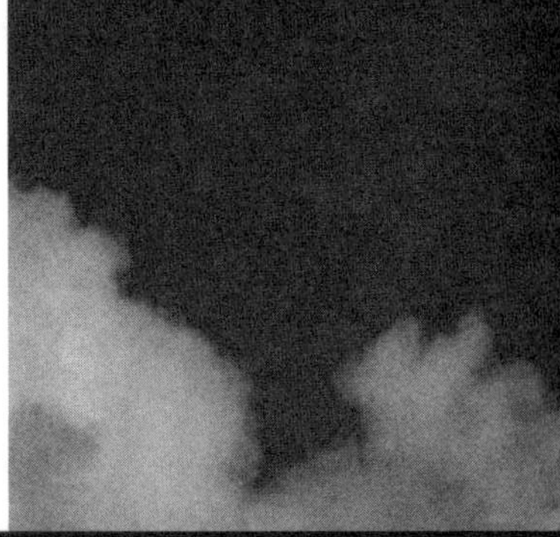

APPENDIX E

Well-Known TCP Ports

As I explained in Chapter 2, TCP/IP communicates using its various protocols through ports. Port numbers are assigned by the Internet Assigned Numbers Authority (IANA) and range from 0 to 1023. The following is a reference list of all well-known TCP ports.

Port	Port Number	Protocol	Explanation
	0	tcp	Reserved
	0	udp	Reserved
tcpmux	1	tcp	TCP Port Service Multiplexer
compressnet	2	tcp	Management Utility
compressnet	3	tcp	Compression Process
rje	5	tcp	Remote Job Entry
echo	7	tcp	Echo
echo	7	udp	Echo
discard	9	tcp	Discard
discard	9	udp	Discard
systat	11	tcp	Active Users
daytime	13	tcp	Daytime
daytime	13	udp	Daytime
qotd	17	tcp	Quote of the Day
qotd	17	udp	Quote of the Day
rwrite	18	tcp	RWP rwrite
rwrite	18	udp	RWP rwrite
msp	18	tcp	Message Send Protocol
msp	18	udp	Message Send Protocol
chargen	19	tcp	Character Generator
chargen	19	udp	Character Generator
ftp-data	20	tcp	File Transfer [Default Data]
ftp	21	tcp	File Transfer [Control]
telnet	23	tcp	Telnet
	24	tcp	any private mail system
	24	udp	any private mail system
smtp	25	tcp	Simple Mail Transfer
nsw-fe	27	tcp	NSW User System FE
nsw-fe	27	udp	NSW User System FE
msg-icp	29	tcp	MSG ICP
msg-icp	29	udp	MSG ICP

Port	Port Number	Protocol	Explanation
msg-auth	31	tcp	MSG Authentication
msg-auth	31	udp	MSG Authentication
dsp	33	tcp	Display Support Protocol
dsp	33	udp	Display Support Protocol
	35	tcp	any private printer server
	35	udp	any private printer server
time	37	tcp	Time
time	37	udp	Time
rap	38	tcp	Route Access Protocol
rap	38	udp	Route Access Protocol
rlp	39	udp	Resource Location Protocol
graphics	41	tcp	Graphics
graphics	41	udp	Graphics
nameserver	42	udp	Host Name Server
nicname	43	tcp	Who Is
mpm-flags	44	tcp	MPM FLAGS Protocol
mpm	45	tcp	Message Processing Module [recv]
mpm-snd	46	tcp	MPM [default send]
ni-ftp	47	tcp	NI FTP
ni-ftp	47	udp	NI FTP
auditd	48	tcp	Digital Audit Daemon
auditd	48	udp	Digital Audit Daemon
login	49	tcp	Login Host Protocol
re-mail-ck	50	tcp	Remote Mail Checking Protocol
re-mail-ck	50	udp	Remote Mail Checking Protocol
la-maint	51	udp	IMP Logical Address Maintenance
xns-time	52	tcp	XNS Time Protocol
xns-time	52	udp	XNS Time Protocol
domain	53	tcp	Domain Name Server
domain	53	udp	Domain Name Server

continued

Port	Port Number	Protocol	Explanation
xns-ch	54	tcp	XNS Clearinghouse
xns-ch	54	udp	XNS Clearinghouse
isi-gl	55	tcp	ISI Graphics Language
isi-gl	55	udp	ISI Graphics Language
xns-auth	56	tcp	XNS Authentication
xns-auth	56	udp	XNS Authentication
	57	tcp	any private terminal access
	57	udp	any private terminal access
xns-mail	58	tcp	XNS Mail
xns-mail	58	udp	XNS Mail
	59	tcp	any private file service
	59	udp	any private file service
	60	tcp	Unassigned
	60	udp	Unassigned
ni-mail	61	tcp	NI MAIL
ni-mail	61	udp	NI MAIL
acas	62	tcp	ACA Services
covia	64	tcp	Communications Integrator (CI)
tacacs-ds	65	tcp	TACACS-Database Service
sql*net	66	tcp	Oracle SQL*NET
bootps	67	udp	Bootstrap Protocol Server
bootpc	68	udp	Bootstrap Protocol Client
tftp	69	udp	Trivial File Transfer
gopher	70	tcp	Gopher
netrjs-1	71	tcp	Remote Job Service
netrjs-1	71	udp	Remote Job Service
netrjs-2	72	tcp	Remote Job Service
netrjs-2	72	udp	Remote Job Service
netrjs-3	73	tcp	Remote Job Service
netrjs-3	73	udp	Remote Job Service
netrjs-4	74	tcp	Remote Job Service

PORT	PORT NUMBER	PROTOCOL	EXPLANATION
netrjs-4	74	udp	Remote Job Service
	75	tcp	any private dial out service
	75	udp	any private dial out service
deos	76	tcp	Distributed External Object Store
deos	76	udp	Distributed External Object Store
	77	tcp	any private RJE service
	77	udp	any private RJE service
vettcp	78	tcp	vettcp
vettcp	78	udp	vettcp
http	80	tcp	World Wide Web HTTP
www-http	80	tcp	World Wide Web HTTP
hosts2-ns	81	tcp	HOSTS2 Name Server
hosts2-ns	81	udp	HOSTS2 Name Server
xfer	82	tcp	XFER Utility
xfer	82	udp	XFER Utility
mit-ml-dev	83	tcp	MIT ML Device
mit-ml-dev	83	udp	MIT ML Device
ctf	84	tcp	Common Trace Facility
ctf	84	udp	Common Trace Facility
mit-ml-dev	85	tcp	MIT ML Device
mit-ml-dev	85	udp	MIT ML Device
mfcobol	86	tcp	Micro Focus Cobol
	87	tcp	any private terminal link
	87	udp	any private terminal link
kerberos	88	tcp	Kerberos
su-mit-tg	89	tcp	SU/MIT Telnet Gateway
dnsix	90	tcp	DNSIX Securit Attribute Token Map
mit-dov	91	tcp	MIT Dover Spooler
npp	92	tcp	Network Printing Protocol
npp	92	udp	Network Printing Protocol

continued

Port	Port Number	Protocol	Explanation
dcp	93	tcp	Device Control Protocol
dcp	93	udp	Device Control Protocol
objcall	94	tcp	Tivoli Object Dispatcher
objcall	94	udp	Tivoli Object Dispatcher
supdup	95	tcp	SUPDUP
supdup	95	udp	SUPDUP
dixie	96	tcp	DIXIE Protocol Specification
swift-rvf	97	tcp	Swift Remote Virtural File Protocol
swift-rvf	97	udp	Swift Remote Virtual File Protocol
tacnews	98	tcp	TAC News
tacnews	98	udp	TAC News
metagram	99	tcp	Metagram Relay
metagram	99	udp	Metagram Relay
newacct	100	tcp	unauthorized use
hostname	101	tcp	NIC Host Name Server
hostname	101	udp	NIC Host Name Server
iso-tsap	102	tcp	ISO-TSAP Class 0
iso-tsap	102	udp	ISO-TSAP Class 0
gppitnp	103	tcp	Genesis Point-to-Point Trans Net
gppitnp	103	udp	Genesis Point-to-Point Trans Net
acr-nema	104	tcp	ACR-NEMA Digital Image
csnet-ns	105	tcp	Mailbox Name Nameserver
csnet-ns	105	udp	Mailbox Name Nameserver
3com-tsmux	106	tcp	3COM-TSMUX
3com-tsmux	106	udp	3COM-TSMUX
poppassd	106	tcp	Password Server
rtelnet	107	tcp	Remote Telnet Service
snagas	108	tcp	SNA Gateway Access Server
pop2	109	tcp	Post Office Protocol - Version 2
pop3	110	tcp	Post Office Protocol - Version 3
sunrpc	111	tcp	SUN Remote Procedure Call

PORT	PORT NUMBER	PROTOCOL	EXPLANATION
sunrpc	111	udp	SUN Remote Procedure Call
mcidas	112	tcp	McIDAS Data Transmission
auth	113	tcp	Authentication Service
audionews	114	tcp	Audio News Multicast
audionews	114	udp	Audio News Multicast
sftp	115	tcp	Simple File Transfer Protocol
sftp	115	udp	Simple File Transfer Protocol
ansanotify	116	tcp	ANSA REX Notify
ansanotify	116	udp	ANSA REX Notify
uucp-path	117	tcp	UUCP Path Service
sqlserv	118	tcp	SQL Services
sqlserv	118	udp	SQL Services
nntp	119	tcp	Network News Transfer Protocol
cfdptkt	120	tcp	CFDPTKT
cfdptkt	120	udp	CFDPTKT
erpc	121	tcp	Encore Expedited Remote Pro.Call
erpc	121	udp	Encore Expedited Remote Pro.Call
smakynet	122	tcp	SMAKYNET
smakynet	122	udp	SMAKYNET
ntp	123	tcp	Network Time Protocol
ntp	123	udp	Network Time Protocol
ansatrader	124	tcp	ANSA REX Trader
ansatrader	124	udp	ANSA REX Trader
locus-map	125	tcp	Locus PC-Interface Net Map Ser
unitary	126	tcp	Unisys Unitary Login
unitary	126	udp	Unisys Unitary Login
locus-con	127	tcp	Locus PC-Interface Conn Server
gss-xlicen	128	tcp	GSS X License Verification
gss-xlicen	128	udp	GSS X License Verification
pwdgen	129	tcp	Password Generator Protocol

continued

Port	Port Number	Protocol	Explanation
pwdgen	129	udp	Password Generator Protocol
cisco-fna	130	tcp	cisco FNATIVE
cisco-fna	130	udp	cisco FNATIVE
cisco-tna	131	tcp	cisco TNATIVE
cisco-tna	131	udp	cisco TNATIVE
cisco-sys	132	tcp	cisco SYSMAINT
cisco-sys	132	udp	cisco SYSMAINT
statsrv	133	tcp	Statistics Service
statsrv	133	udp	Statistics Service
ingres-net	134	tcp	INGRES-NET Service
loc-srv	135	tcp	Location Service
loc-srv	135	udp	Location Service
profile	136	tcp	PROFILE Naming System
netbios-ns	137	tcp	NETBIOS Name Service
netbios-ns	137	udp	NETBIOS Name Service
netbios-dgm	138	tcp	NETBIOS Datagram Service
netbios-dgm	138	udp	NETBIOS Datagram Service
netbios-ssn	139	tcp	NETBIOS Session Service
netbios-ssn	139	udp	NETBIOS Session Service
emfis-data	140	tcp	EMFIS Data Service
emfis-data	140	udp	EMFIS Data Service
emfis-cntl	141	tcp	EMFIS Control Service
emfis-cntl	141	udp	EMFIS Control Service
bl-idm	142	tcp	Britton-Lee IDM
bl-idm	142	udp	Britton-Lee IDM
imap2	143	tcp	Interactive Mail Access Protocol v2
news	144	tcp	NewS
news	144	udp	NewS
uaac	145	tcp	UAAC Protocol
uaac	145	udp	UAAC Protocol
iso-tp0	146	tcp	ISO-IP0

Port	Port Number	Protocol	Explanation
iso-tp0	146	udp	ISO-IP0
iso-ip	147	tcp	ISO-IP
iso-ip	147	udp	ISO-IP
cronus	148	tcp	CRONUS-SUPPORT
cronus	148	udp	CRONUS-SUPPORT
aed-512	149	tcp	AED 512 Emulation Service
aed-512	149	udp	AED 512 Emulation Service
sql-net	150	tcp	SQL-NET
sql-net	150	udp	SQL-NET
hems	151	tcp	HEMS
bftp	152	tcp	Background File Transfer Program
bftp	152	udp	Background File Transfer Program
sgmp	153	tcp	SGMP
sgmp	153	udp	SGMP
netsc-prod	154	tcp	NETSC
netsc-prod	154	udp	NETSC
netsc-dev	155	tcp	NETSC
netsc-dev	155	udp	NETSC
sqlsrv	156	tcp	SQL Service
knet-cmp	157	tcp	KNET/VM Command/Message
pcmail-srv	158	tcp	PCMail Server
nss-routing	159	tcp	NSS-Routing
nss-routing	159	udp	NSS-Routing
sgmp-traps	160	tcp	SGMP-TRAPS
sgmp-traps	160	udp	SGMP-TRAPS
snmp	161	udp	SNMP
snmptrap	162	udp	SNMPTRAP
cmip-man	163	tcp	CMIP/TCP Manager
cmip-man	16	udp	CMIP/TCP Manager
cmip-agent	164	tcp	CMIP/TCP Agent

continued

Port	Port Number	Protocol	Explanation
smip-agent	164	udp	CMIP/TCP Agent
xns-courier	165	tcp	Xerox
xns-courier	165	udp	Xerox
s-net	166	tcp	Sirius Systems
s-net	166	udp	Sirius Systems
namp	167	tcp	NAMP
namp	167	udp	NAMP
rsvd	168	tcp	RSVD
rsvd	168	udp	RSVD
send	169	tcp	SEND
send	169	udp	SEND
print-srv	170	tcp	Network PostScript
print-srv	170	udp	Network PostScript
multiplex	171	tcp	Network Innovations Multiplex
multiplex	171	udp	Network Innovations Multiplex
cl/1	172	tcp	Network Innovations CL/1
cl/1	172	udp	Network Innovations CL/1
xyplex-mux	173	tcp	Xyplex
xyplex-mux	173	udp	Xyplex
mailq	174	tcp	MAILQ
mailq	174	udp	MAILQ
vmnet	175	tcp	VMNET
vmnet	175	udp	VMNET
genrad-mux	176	tcp	GENRAD-MUX
genrad-mux	176	udp	GENRAD-MUX
xdmcp	177	udp	X Display Manager Control Protocol
nextstep	178	tcp	NextStep Window Server
NextStep	178	udp	NextStep Window Server
bgp	179	tcp	Border Gateway Protocol
ris	180	tcp	Intergraph
ris	180	udp	Intergraph

Port	Port Number	Protocol	Explanation
unify	181	tcp	Unify
unify	181	udp	Unify
audit	182	tcp	Unisys Audit SITP
audit	182	udp	Unisys Audit SITP
ocbinder	183	tcp	OCBinder
ocbinder	183	udp	OCBinder
ocserver	184	tcp	OCServer
ocserver	184	udp	OCServer
remote-kis	185	tcp	Remote-KIS
remote-kis	185	udp	Remote-KIS
kis	186	tcp	KIS Protocol
kis	186	udp	KIS Protocol
aci	187	tcp	Application Comm. Interface
aci	187	udp	Application Comm. Interface
mumps	188	tcp	Plus Five's MUMPS
mumps	188	udp	Plus Five's MUMPS
qft	189	tcp	Queued File Transport
gacp	190	tcp	Gateway Access Control Protocol
cacp	190	udp	Gateway Access Control Protocol
prospero	191	tcp	Prospero Directory Service
osu-nms	192	tcp	OSU Network Monitoring System
osu-nms	192	udp	OSU Network Monitoring System
srmp	193	tcp	Spider Remote Monitoring Protocol
srmp	193	udp	Spider Remote Monitoring Protocol
irc	194	udp	Internet Relay Chat Protocol
dn6-nlm-aud	195	tcp	DNSIX Network Level Mod. Audit
dn6-smm-red	196	tcp	DNSIX Session Mgt Mod.Aud.Redir
dls	197	tcp	Directory Location Service
dls	197	udp	Directory Location Service
dls-mon	198	tcp	Directory Location Service Monitor

continued

PORT	PORT NUMBER	PROTOCOL	EXPLANATION
dls-mon	198	udp	Directory Location Service Monitor
smux	199	tcp	SMUX
smux	199	udp	SMUX
src	200	tcp	IBM System Resource Controller
src	200	udp	IBM System Resource Controller
at-rtmp	201	tcp	AppleTalk Routing Maintenance
at-rtmp	201	udp	AppleTalk Routing Maintenance
at-nbp	202	tcp	AppleTalk Name Binding
at-nbp	202	udp	AppleTalk Name Binding
at-3	203	tcp	AppleTalk Unused
at-3	203	udp	AppleTalk Unused
at-echo	204	tcp	AppleTalk Echo
at-echo	204	udp	AppleTalk Echo
at-5	205	tcp	AppleTalk Unused
at-5	205	udp	AppleTalk Unused
at-zis	206	tcp	AppleTalk Zone Information
at-zis	206	udp	AppleTalk Zone Information
at-7	207	tcp	AppleTalk Unused
at-7	207	udp	AppleTalk Unused
at-8	208	tcp	AppleTalk Unused
at-8	208	udp	AppleTalk Unused
tam	209	tcp	Trivial Authenticated Mail Protocol
tam	209	udp	Trivial Authenticated Mail Protocol
z39.50	210	tcp	ANSI Z39.50
z39.50	210	udp	ANSI Z39.50
914c/g	211	tcp	Texas Instruments 914C/G Terminal
914c/g	211	udp	Texas Instruments 914C/G Terminal
anet	212	tcp	ATEXSSTR
anet	212	udp	ATEXSSTR
ipx	213	tcp	IPX
ipx	213	udp	IPX

PORT	PORT NUMBER	PROTOCOL	EXPLANATION
vmpwscs	214	tcp	VM PWSCS
vmpwscs	214	udp	VM PWSCS
softpc	215	tcp	Insignia Solutions
softpc	215	udp	Insignia Solutions
atls	216	tcp	Access Technology License Server
dbase	217	tcp	dBASE Unix
dbase	217	udp	dBASE Unix
mpp	218	tcp	Netix Message Posting Protocol
mpp	218	udp	Netix Message Posting Protocol
uarps	219	tcp	Unisys ARPs
uarps	219	udp	Unisys ARPs
imap3	220	tcp	Interactive Mail Access Protocol v3
fln-spx	221	tcp	Berkeley rlogind with SPX auth
fln-spx	221	udp	Berkeley rlogind with SPX auth
rsh-spx	222	tcp	Berkeley rshd with SPX auth
rsh-spx	222	udp	Berkeley rshd with SPX auth
cdc	223	tcp	Certificate Distribution Center
cdc	223	udp	Certificate Distribution Center
sur-meas	243	tcp	Survey Measurement
sur-meas	243	udp	Survey Measurement
link	245	tcp	LINK
link	245	udp	LINK
dsp3270	246	tcp	Display Systems Protocol
dsp3270	246	udp	Display Systems Protocol
pdap	344	tcp	Prospero Data Access Protocol
pawserv	345	tcp	Perf Analysis Workbench
pawserv	345	udp	Perf Analysis Workbench
zserv	346	tcp	Zebra server
fatserv	347	tcp	Fatmen Server
csi-sgwp	348	tcp	Cabletron Management Protocol

continued

PORT	PORT NUMBER	PROTOCOL	EXPLANATION
csi-sgwp	348	udp	Cabletron Management Protocol
clearcase	371	tcp	Clearcase
clearcase	371	udp	Clearcase
ulistserv	372	tcp	Unix Listserv
ulistserv	372	udp	Unix Listserv
legent-1	373	tcp	Legent Corporation
legent-1	373	udp	Legent Corporation
legent-2	374	tcp	Legent Corporation
legent-2	374	udp	Legent Corporation
hassle	375	tcp	Hassle
hassle	375	udp	Hassle
nip	376	tcp	Amiga Envoy Network Inquiry Proto
nip	376	udp	Amiga Envoy Network Inquiry Proto
tnETOS	377	tcp	NEC Corporation
tnETOS	377	udp	NEC Corporation
dsETOS	378	tcp	NEC Corporation
dsETOS	378	udp	NEC Corporation
is99c	379	tcp	TIA/EIA/IS-99 modem client
is99s	380	tcp	TIA/EIA/IS-99 modem server
hp-collector	381	tcp	hp performance data collector
hp-collector	381	udp	hp performance data collector
hp-managed-node	382	tcp	hp performance data managed node
hp-managed-node	382	udp	hp performance data managed node
hp-alarm-mgr	383	tcp	hp performance data alarm manager
hp-alarm-mgr	383	udp	hp performance data alarm manager
arns	384	tcp	A Remote Network Server System
arns	384	udp	A Remote Network Server System
ibm-app	385	tcp	IBM Application
ibm-app	385	tcp	IBM Application
asa	386	tcp	ASA Message Router Object Def.

PORT	PORT NUMBER	PROTOCOL	EXPLANATION
asa	386	udp	ASA Message Router Object Def.
aurp	387	tcp	Appletalk Update-Based Routing
aurp	387	udp	Appletalk Update-Based Routing
unidata-ldm	388	tcp	Unidata LDM Version 4
unidata-ldm	388	udp	Unidata LDM Version 4
ldap	389	tcp	LDAP
uis	390	tcp	UIS
uis	390	udp	UIS
synotics-relay	391	tcp	SynOptics SNMP Relay Port
synotics-relay	391	udp	SynOptics SNMP Relay Port
synotics-broker	392	tcp	SynOptics Port Broker Port
synotics-broker	392	udp	SynOptics Port Broker Port
dis	393	tcp	Data Interpretation System
dis	393	udp	Data Interpretation System
embl-ndt	394	tcp	EMBL Nucleic Data Transfer
embl-ndt	394	udp	EMBL Nucleic Data Transfer
netcp	395	tcp	NETscout Control Protocol
netcp	395	udp	NETscout Control Protocol
netware-ip	396	tcp	Novell Netware over IP
netware-ip	396	udp	Novell Netware over IP
mptn	397	tcp	Multi Protocol Trans. Net.
mptn	397	udp	Multi Protocol Trans. Net.
kryptolan	398	tcp	Kryptolan
kryptolan	398	udp	Kryptolan
iso-tsap-c2	399	tcp	ISO-TSAP Class 2
iso-tsap-c2	399	udp	ISO-TSAP Class 2
work-sol	400	tcp	Workstation Solutions
work-sol	400	udp	Workstation Solutions
ups	401	udp	Uninterruptible Power Supply
genie	402	tcp	Genie Protocol

continued

Port	Port Number	Protocol	Explanation
genie	402	udp	Genie Protocol
decap	403	tcp	decap
decap	403	udp	decap
nced	404	tcp	nced
nced	404	udp	nced
ncld	405	tcp	ncld
ncld	405	udp	ncld
imsp	406	tcp	Interactive Mail Support Protocol
imsp	406	udp	Interactive Mail Support Protocol
timbuktu	407	tcp	Timbuktu
prm-sm	408	tcp	Prospero Resource Man. Sys. Man.
prm-nm	409	tcp	Prospero Resource Man. Node Man.
decladebug	410	udp	DECLadebug Remote Debug
rmt	411	tcp	Remote MT Protocol
rmt	411	udp	Remote MT Protocol
synoptics-trap	412	tcp	Trap Convention Port
synoptics-trap	412	udp	Trap Convention Port
smsp	413	tcp	SMSP
smsp	413	udp	SMSP
infoseek	414	tcp	InfoSeek
infoseek	414	udp	InfoSeek
bnet	415	tcp	BNet
bnet	415	udp	BNet
silverplatter	416	tcp	Silverplatter
silverplatter	416	udp	Silverplatter
onmux	417	tcp	Onmux
onmux	417	udp	Onmux
hyper-g	418	tcp	Hyper-G
ariel1	419	tcp	Ariel
smpte	420	udp	SMPTE
ariel2	421	tcp	Ariel

PORT	PORT NUMBER	PROTOCOL	EXPLANATION
ariel3	422	tcp	Ariel
opc-job-start	423	tcp	IBM Ops Planning and Control Start
opc-job-track	424	tcp	IBM Ops Planning and Cntrl Track
icad-el	425	tcp	ICAD
smartsdp	426	tcp	smartsdp
smartsdp	426	udp	smartsdp
svrloc	427	udp	Server Location
svrloc	427	udp	Server Location
ocs_cmu	428	tcp	OCS_CMU
ocs_cmu	428	udp	OCS_CMU
ocs_amu	429	tcp	OCS_AMU
ocs_amu	429	udp	OCS_AMU
utmpsd	430	tcp	UTMPSD
utmpsd	430	udp	UTMPSD
utmpcd	431	tcp	UTMPCD
utmpcd	431	udp	UTMPCD
iasd	432	tcp	IASD
iasd	432	udp	IASD
nnsp	433	tcp	NNSP
nnsp	433	udp	NNSP
mobileip-agent	434	tcp	MobileIP-Agent
mobilip-mn	435	tcp	MobilIP-MN
dna-cml	436	tcp	DNA-CML
dna-cml	436	udp	DNA-CML
comscm	437	tcp	comscm
comscm	437	udp	comscm
dsfgw	438	tcp	dsfgw
dsfgw	438	udp	dsfgw
dasp	439	tcp	dasp Thomas Obermair
dasp	439	udp	dasp tommy@inlab.m.eunet.de

continued

Port	Port Number	Protocol	Explanation
sgcp	440	tcp	sgcp
sgcp	440	udp	sgcp
decvms-sysmgt	441	tcp	decvms-sysmgt
cvc_hostd	442	tcp	cvc_hostd
cvc_hostd	442	udp	cvc_hostd
https	443	tcp	https MCom
snpp	444	tcp	Simple Network Paging Protocol
snpp	444	udp	Simple Network Paging Protocol
microsoft-ds	445	udp	Microsoft-DS
ddm-rdb	446	tcp	DDM-RDB
ddm-rdb	446	udp	DDM-RDB
ddm-dfm	447	tcp	DDM-RFM
ddm-dfm	447	udp	DDM-RFM
ddm-byte	448	tcp	DDM-BYTE
ddm-byte	448	udp	DDM-BYTE
as-servermap	449	tcp	AS Server Mapper
as-servermap	449	udp	AS Server Mapper
tserver	450	tcp	TServer
sfs-smp-net	451	tcp	Cray Network Semaphore server
sfs-smp-net	451	udp	Cray Network Semaphore server
sfs-config	452	tcp	Cray SFS config server
sfs-config	452	udp	Cray SFS config server
creativeserver	453	tcp	CreativeServer
creativeserver	453	udp	CreativeServer
contentserver	454	tcp	ContentServer
contentserver	454	udp	ContentServer
creativepartnr	455	tcp	CreativePartnr
creativepartnr	455	udp	CreativePartnr
macon-tcp	456	tcp	macon-tcp
macon-udp	456	udp	macon-udp
scohelp	457	tcp	scohelp

Port	Port Number	Protocol	Explanation
scohelp	457	udp	scohelp
appleqtc	458	tcp	apple quick time
appleqtc	458	udp	apple quick time
ampr-rcmd	459	tcp	ampr-rcmd
ampr-rcmd	459	udp	ampr-rcmd
skronk	460	tcp	skronk
skronk	460	udp	skronk
exec	512	tcp	remote process execution
biff	512	udp	used by mail system to notify users
login	513	tcp	remote login a la telnet
who	513	udp	maintains data bases showing who's
cmd	514	tcp	like exec, but automatic
syslog	514	udp	
printer	515	tcp	spooler
talk	517	udp	
ntalk	518	tcp	
utime	519	tcp	unixtime
utime	519	udp	unixtime
efs	520	tcp	extended file name server
router	520	udp	local routing process
timed	525	tcp	timeserver
timed	525	udp	timeserver
tempo	526	tcp	newdate
tempo	526	udp	newdate
courier	530	tcp	rpc
courier	530	udp	rpc
conference	531	tcp	chat
conference	531	udp	chat
netnews	532	tcp	readnews
netnews	532	udp	readnews

continued

Port	Port Number	Protocol	Explanation
netwall	533	tcp	emergency broadcasts
netwall	533	udp	emergency broadcasts
apertus-ldp	539	tcp	Apertus Tech. Load Determination
apertus-ldp	539	udp	Apertus Tech. Load Determination
uucp	540	tcp	uucpd
uucp-rlogin	541	tcp	uucp-rlogin
uucp-rlogin	541	udp	uucp-rlogin
klogin	543	tcp	
klogin	543	udp	
kshell	544	tcp	krcmd
kshell	544	udp	krcmd
appleqtcsrvr	545	tcp	appleqtcsrvr
appleqtcsrvr	545	udp	appleqtcsrvr
new-rwho	550	tcp	new-who
new-rwho	550	udp	new-who
dsf	555	tcp	
dsf	555	udp	
remotefs	556	tcp	rfs server
remotefs	556	udp	rfs server
openvms-sysipc	557	tcp	openvms-sysipc
openvms-sysipc	557	udp	openvms-sysipc
sdnskmp	558	tcp	SDNSKMP
sdnskmp	558	udp	SDNSKMP
teedtap	559	tcp	TEEDTAP
teedtap	559	udp	TEEDTAP
rmonitor	560	tcp	rmonitord
rmonitor	560	udp	rmonitord
monitor	561	tcp	
monitor	561	udp	
chshell	562	tcp	chcmd
chshell	562	udp	chcmd

Port	Port Number	Protocol	Explanation
9pfs	564	tcp	plan 9 file service
9pfs	564	udp	plan 9 file service
whoami	565	tcp	whoami
whoami	565	udp	whoami
meter	570	tcp	demon
meter	570	udp	demon
meter	571	tcp	udemon
meter	571	udp	udemon
ipcserver	600	tcp	Sun IPC server
ipcserver	600	udp	Sun IPC server
nqs	607	tcp	nqs
nqs	607	udp	nqs
urm	606	tcp	Cray Unified Resource Manager
urm	606	udp	Cray Unified Resource Manager
sift-uft	608	tcp	Sender-Initiated/Unsol. File Transfer
npmp-trap	609	tcp	npmp-trap
npmp-trap	609	udp	npmp-trap
npmp-local	610	tcp	npmp-local
npmp-local	610	udp	npmp-local
npmp-gui	611	tcp	npmp-gui
npmp-gui	611	udp	npmp-gui
ginad	634	tcp	ginad
ginad	634	udp	ginad
mdqs	666	tcp	
mdqs	666	udp	
doom	666	tcp	doom Id Software
elcsd	704	tcp	errlog copy/server daemon
elcsd	704	udp	errlog copy/server daemon
flexlm	744	tcp	Flexible License Manager
flexlm	744	udp	Flexible License Manager

continued

Port	Port Number	Protocol	Explanation
fujitsu-dev	747	tcp	Fujitsu Device Control
fujitsu-dev	747	udp	Fujitsu Device Control
ris-cm	748	tcp	Russell Info Sci Calendar Manager
ris-cm	748	udp	Russell Info Sci Calendar Manager
kerberos-adm	749	tcp	kerberos administration
rfile	750	tcp	
loadav	750	udp	
pump	751	tcp	
pump	751	udp	
qrh	752	tcp	
qrh	752	udp	
rrh	753	tcp	
rrh	753	udp	
tell	754	tcp	send
tell	754	udp	send
nlogin	758	tcp	
nlogin	758	udp	
con	759	tcp	
con	759	udp	
ns	760	tcp	
ns	760	udp	
rxe	761	tcp	
rxe	761	udp	
quotad	762	tcp	
quotad	762	udp	
cycleserv	763	tcp	
cycleserv	763	udp	
omserv	764	tcp	
omserv	764	udp	
webster	765	tcp	
webster	765	udp	

PORT	PORT NUMBER	PROTOCOL	EXPLANATION
phonebook	767	tcp	phone
phonebook	767	udp	phone
vid	769	tcp	
vid	769	udp	
cadlock	770	tcp	
cadlock	770	udp	
rtip	771	tcp	
rtip	771	udp	
cycleserv2	772	tcp	
cycleserv2	772	udp	
submit	773	tcp	
notify	773	udp	
rpasswd	774	tcp	
acmaint_dbd	774	udp	
entomb	775	tcp	
acmaint_transd	775	udp	
wpages	776	tcp	
wpages	776	udp	
wpgs	780	tcp	
wpgs	780	udp	
concert	786	tcp	Concert
concert	786	udp	Concert
mdbs_daemon	800	tcp	
mdbs_daemon	800	udp	
device	801	tcp	
device	801	udp	
accessbuilder	888	tcp	AccessBuilder
accessbuilder	888	udp	AccessBuilder
xtreelic	996	tcp	Central Point Software
xtreelic	996	udp	Central Point Software

continued

PORT	PORT NUMBER	PROTOCOL	EXPLANATION
maitrd	997	tcp	
maitrd	997	udp	
busboy	998	tcp	
puparp	998	udp	
garcon	999	tcp	
applix	999	udp	Applix ac
puprouter	999	tcp	
puprouter	999	udp	
cadlock	1000	tcp	
ock	1000	udp	
	1023	tcp	Reserved
	1024	udp	Reserved

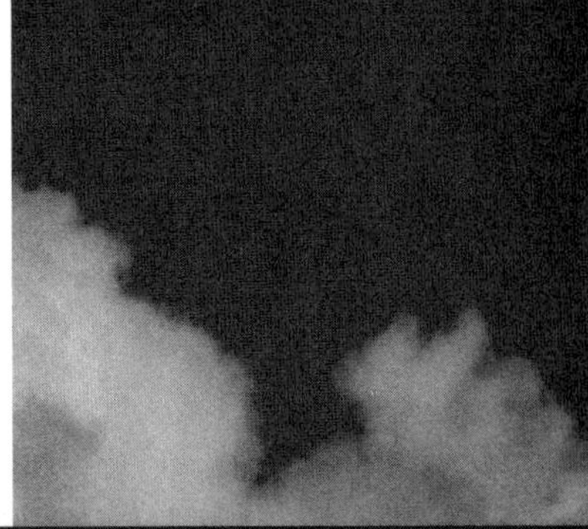

APPENDIX

F

What's on the CD-ROMs?

CD-ROM Contents

The CD-ROM included with this book contains the following materials:

- Microsoft Proxy Server 2.0 30-day Trial
- Adobe Acrobat Reader
- An electronic version of this book, *Microsoft Proxy Server 2.0 MCSE Study Guide,* in `.pdf` format
- BeachFront Quizzer test simulation software
- Microsoft Internet Explorer
- *Micro House Technical Library* (evaluation copy)
- Microsoft TechNet (trial version)

Installing and Using Items on the CD-ROM

The following sections describe each product and include detailed instructions for installation and use.

Microsoft Proxy Server 2.0 30-day Trial

A 30-day trial version of the Microsoft Proxy Server 2.0 software is included on the CD-ROM. As you study for the Proxy Server 2.0 exam, there is no substitute for hands-on experience with the product.

To install Proxy Server software, follow these steps:

1. You must install Proxy Server 2.0 on a Windows NT Server 4.0 computer. Start Windows NT Explorer and open the MSProxy folder on the CD-ROM.
2. Double-click the setup icon to begin the Proxy Server 2.0 installation.
3. When Setup prompts you for the CD Key, type 111-1111111.

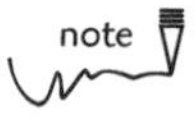

Your computer must meet certain hardware and software requirements before you can install Proxy Server 2.0. Read Chapters 3, 4, and 5 before attempting to install the software.

The Adobe Acrobat Reader Version of *Microsoft Proxy Server 2.0 MCSE Study Guide*

Adobe's Acrobat Reader is a helpful program that will enable you to view the electronic version of this book in the same page format as the actual book.

To install and run Adobe's Acrobat Reader and view the electronic version of this book, follow these steps:

1. Start Windows Explorer (if you're using Windows 95/98) or Windows NT Explorer (if you're using Windows NT), and then open the `Acrobat` folder on the CD-ROM.
2. In the `Acrobat` folder, double-click `ar32e30.exe` and follow the instructions presented onscreen for installing Adobe Acrobat Reader.
3. To view the electronic version of this book after you have installed Adobe's Acrobat Reader, start Windows Explorer (if you're using Windows 95) or Windows NT Explorer (if you're using Windows NT), and then open the `Books\MCSE Proxy Server 2.0` folder on the CD-ROM.
4. In the `MCSE Proxy Server 2.0` folder, double-click the chapter or appendix file you want to view. All documents in this folder end with a `.pdf` extension.

BeachFront Quizzer

The BeachFront Quizzer test simulation included on the CD gives you an opportunity to test your knowledge by taking simulated exams. The BeachFront Quizzer product has many valuable features, including:

- Study session
- Standard exam
- Adaptive exam
- New exam every time
- Historical analysis

If you want more simulation questions, you can purchase the full retail version of the BeachFront Quizzer software from BeachFront Quizzer. See the BeachFront Quizzer ad at the back of the book.

To install and run BeachFront Quizzer, follow these steps:

1. View the contents of the BeachFront folder
2. Execute `ExamName.exe`, whereas `ExamName` is the name of the exam you wish to practice.
3. Follow the directions for installation.

Microsoft Internet Explorer

A complete copy of Microsoft Internet Explorer is included on the CD-ROM. You can use Internet Explorer to browse the Internet if you have an Internet connection.

To install and run Microsoft Internet Explorer, follow these steps:

1. Start Windows Explorer (if you're using Windows 95/98) or Windows NT Explorer (if you're using Windows NT), and then open the `\Msie` folder on the CD-ROM.
2. In the `\Msie` folder, double-click `Setup.exe` and follow the instructions presented onscreen for installing Microsoft Internet Explorer.
3. To run Microsoft Internet Explorer, double-click the Internet Explorer icon on the desktop.

Micro House Technical Library (Evaluation Copy)

Micro House Technical Library is a useful CD-ROM-based set of encyclopedias that contains hardware-configuration information. This evaluation copy of *Micro House Technical Library* includes only the Encyclopedia of I/O cards. Use this evaluation copy to determine whether or not you want to purchase the full version of the *Micro House Technical Library*.

To install and access the *Micro House Technical Library*, follow these steps:

1. Start Windows Explorer (if you're using Windows 95/98) or Windows NT Explorer (if you're using Windows NT), and then open the `Micro House` folder on the CD-ROM.
2. In the `Micro House` folder, double-click `Install.exe` and follow the instructions presented onscreen for installing the *Micro House Technical Library*.

   To run the *Micro House Technical Library*, select Start ⇒ Programs ⇒ MH Tech Library ⇒ MTL Demo Edition.

Microsoft TechNet (Trial Version)

The Microsoft TechNet CD subscription product delivers the most complete and current source of Microsoft technical information right to your desktop. A one-year subscription includes an initial shipment of more than 20 CDs; thereafter a minimum of three CD updates are sent monthly. That's a total of more than 50 CDs included with a one-year subscription.

The trial version of TechNet located on this CD is a 30-day evaluation copy of the January 1999 Technical Information CD, one of the 50+ CDs a one-year TechNet subscription delivers. Check out the trial version to evaluate a portion of the content TechNet CD subscribers receive monthly.

Annual subscribers receive:

- The complete Microsoft Knowledge Base, the same database of technical support information developed and used by Microsoft support engineers
- Troubleshooting tips, workarounds, and technical notes
- Microsoft Resource Kits, deployment guides, and compatibility lists

- Current service packs, drivers and patches, utilities, and 3rd party tools
- Strategy and white papers, case studies, and training materials
- And much more

A subscription is a must-have for any IT professional who evaluates, deploys or supports Microsoft products. To subscribe in the United States or Canada, call (800) 344-2121 ext. 3442 or click to `http://www.microsoft.com/technet/cd/`.

System requirements include:

- PC with a 386DX/33 MHz or higher processor
- Microsoft Windows 3.1 or later operating system or Windows NT Workstation operating system version 3.51 or later
- 8MB of RAM for Windows 95 or Windows 3.1; 16MB for Windows 98 or Windows NT Workstation 3.51 or later operating system
- 2MB of available hard-disk space
- CD-ROM drive compatible with MPC Level 1 specifications
- Microsoft Compact Disc Extensions (MSCDEX) version 2.2 or later and compatible CD-ROM driver
- VGA or higher-resolution video adapter
- Microsoft Mouse or compatible pointing device

To install and access TechNet from Windows 95, Windows 98, or Windows NT Workstation 4.0, TechNet Setup will start automatically when the CD is inserted into the CD-ROM drive.

To install and access TechNet from Windows 3.1, Windows for Workgroups version 3.11, or Windows NT Workstation 3.51:

1. Insert the CD into the CD-ROM drive.
2. Start File Manager.
3. In File manager, select the CD-ROM drive, double-click `SETUP.EXE`, and follow the directions that appear on the screen.

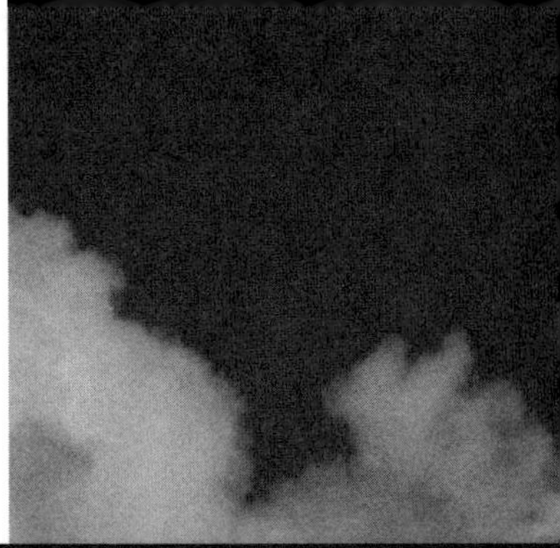

Glossary

Active Server Pages (ASP): A feature that enables plain HTML pages to be combined with other programming languages to create pages that are active in terms of the processes they perform and how they interact with the user.

Address Resolution Protocol (ARP): A protocol that assists in the translation of IP addresses to MAC addresses.

Advanced Research Projects Agency (ARPA): The organization that developed the TCP/IP protocol.

ARP: *See* Address Resolution Protocol.

ARPA: *See* Advanced Research Projects Agency.

Array: A Proxy Server configuration that connects multiple Proxy Servers together to form one logical cache. This design improves performance and stability.

ASP: *See* Active Server Pages.

Asynchronous Transfer Mode (ATM): A WAN connectivity solution that offers speeds from 155Mbps to over 2Gbps (theoretically). ATM sends data in fixed-sized cells and can transmit voice, data, and real-time audio or video.

ATM: *See* Asynchronous Transfer Mode.

Bandwidth throttling: An IIS feature that enables an administrator to assign more or less bandwidth to sites as needed.

BootP: A protocol used by diskless workstations to obtain a boot program from the server. Also called Boot Protocol.

Cache Array Routing Protocol (CARP): A protocol used in Proxy Server arrays to configure the location of URLs across the logical array cache. This is done through a hash calculation so all servers know where URLs are stored.

Cache drive formula: Cache drives for Proxy Server should be configured according to the formula 100MB + (Number of users × 0.5MB).

CARP: *See* Cache Array Routing Protocol.

CERN: A European company that developed HTTP. Proxy Server supports CERN-compliant browsers.

Chain: A Proxy Server configuration that links Proxy Servers, Proxy Server arrays, and even third-party products. The computer closest to the Internet is known as the *upstream server*, and the computer closest to the clients and known as the *downstream server*.

Content caching: The act of storing URLs and Internet objects on the proxy server.

Control channel: Proxy Server uses a control channel to manage the connection between Proxy clients and the Proxy Server to help reduce transmission problems associated with UDP.

Default Gateway: A gateway that provides a path for packets to take to get off of the local subnet and be routed to a remote subnet.

DHCP: *See* Dynamic Host Configuration Protocol.

Downstream server: The computer closest to the clients in a Proxy Server chain configuration.

Dynamic Host Configuration Protocol (DHCP): A protocol provides automatic assignment of IP addresses to network hosts. DHCP leases an IP address to each host for a specified period of time.

File Transfer Protocol (FTP): A protocol used to retrieve documents and files over the Internet.

Filter: A device used by Proxy Server to restrict both in-bound and out-bound traffic by domain, protocol, or IP address.

Firewall: Software or hardware that protects an environment against intrusion from Internet users.

Frame relay: A digital packet-switching technology used in WAN connectivity solutions.

FTP: *See* File Transfer Protocol.

Hash: A mathematical formula used by CARP to place URLs in a Proxy Server logical array cache.

HOSTS File: A static file on a local machine that contains domain name to IP address mappings.

HTML: *See* Hypertext Markup Language.

HTTP: *See* Hypertext Transfer Protocol.

Hypertext Markup Language (HTML): The language used to develop web pages. HTML pages are retrieved by using HTTP

Hypertext Transfer Protocol (HTTP): The standard protocol for retrieving HTML documents from the Internet.

ICMP: *See* Internet Control Message Protocol.

Integrated Services Digital Network (ISDN): A type of wiring consisting of lines that contain two 64Kbps for a maximum throughput of 128Kbps.

Internet Control Message Protocol (ICMP): A protocol used by TCP/IP utilities to request certain information from network components.

Internet Protocol (IP): A portion of the TCP/IP protocol suite concerned with addresses and network identity.

Internet Server Application Programming Interface (ISAPI): A standard programming interface made up of the ISAPI Filter and the ISAPI Application.

Internet Service Provider (ISP): A company that sells Internet connectivity to organizations or individuals.

IP: *See* Internet Protocol

IP Address: A network address composed of 32 bits represented as 4 bytes, often called an octect. A typical IP address is 131.107.2.200.

ISAPI: *See* Internet Server Application Programming Interface.

ISDN: *See* Integrated Services Digital Network

ISP: *See* Internet Service Provider.

LAT: *See* Local Address Table.

LMHOSTS File: A static file that maps NetBIOS names to IP addresses.

Local Address Table (LAT): A table created during Proxy Server installation that lists all the internal IP addresses of the network.

locallat.txt: A local LAT stored on the client computers that contains additional information not stored by the Proxy Server. This file is not overwritten on a periodic basis, as `msplat.txt` is.

mspclnt.ini: The local `ini` file that is stored on the client computers and updated periodically by the Proxy Server.

msplat.txt: The local client LAT, which is stored on the client computer and updated periodically by the Proxy Server.

Multi-homed Computer: A computer with two NICs, or a combination of a NIC and a modem/ISDN connection, if dial-out is used with Proxy Server.

Network Monitor: A Windows NT program that enables the monitoring of network components and network traffic. Network Monitor can be accessed in the Administrative Tools.

NTCR: *See* Windows NT Challenge/Response

ODBC: *See* Open Database Connectivity.

Open Database Connectivity (ODBC): A standard API used to construct open platform databases.

Open Systems Interconnect (OSI): A reference model that defines how computers process network data. The OSI model was developed by the International Standards Organization in 1978, and is the de facto standard for the development of networking applications and components.

OSI: *See* Open Systems Interconnect.

Performance Monitor: A Windows NT program that enables the monitoring of server components. Performance Monitor can be accessed in the Administrative Tools.

Point to Point Protocol (PPP): A protocol used to provide connection-oriented transmission of data over the Internet.

Point to Point Tunneling Protocol (PPTP): A protocol that enables a LAN to transmit LAN data securely over the Internet using a non-Internet protocol, such as NetBEUI.

PPP: *See* Point to Point Protocol

PPTP: *See* Point to Point Tunneling Protocol.

Proxy: Someone or something that stands in the place of another person or thing, as in proxy voting. Proxy Server stands in the place of network clients that request information from the Internet.

RAS: *See* Remote Access Service.

Remote Access Service (RAS): A part of Windows NT that enables clients to access a network remotely through a dial-up connection.

RemotMSP: A command-line utility used to view array information.

Reverse hosting: A Proxy Server feature that can forward Internet traffic to multiple servers within the LAN. This enables multiple servers to host a Web site that appears as one server to Internet users.

Reverse proxy: A Proxy Server feature that can forward Internet traffic to specified servers within the LAN through reverse proxy functions.

RIP: *See* Routing Information Protocol.

Routing and Remote Access Service (RRAS): An add-on product to RAS that enables the creation of Virtual Private Networks using the PPTP protocol.

Routing Information Protocol (RIP): A protocol that maintains and shares routing information for the network by using a distance vector algorithm.

RRAS: *See* Routing and Remote Access Service.

Secure Sockets Layer (SSL): A protocol that provides for secure transmissions via the SSL tunnel.

Serial Line Internet Protocol (SLIP): An older connectivity protocol that has been widely replaced by PPP.

Simple Mail Transport Protocol (SMTP): A protocol that provides messaging services and is a part of the TCP/IP protocol suite.

Simple Network Management Protocol (SNMP): A protocol that enables the monitoring of network devices and server components that use SNMP.

SLIP: *See* Serial Line Internet Protocol.

SMTP: *See* Simple Mail Transport Protocol.

SNMP: *See* Simple Network Management Protocol.

Socket: A set of rules originally developed to establish IP connections in UNIX computers.

Socks Proxy Service: A Proxy Server feature that provides support for Socket applications and Socks clients.

SSL: *See* Secure Sockets Layer.

Subnet mask: A number that hides a portion of the network ID in order to determine what portion of the IP address is the host ID and which portion is the network ID.

T1: A digital link that provides a bandwidth of 1.54Mbps.

T3: A digital link that is equal to 28 T1 lines, for a bandwidth of 44.736Mbps.

TCP: *See* Transmission Control Protocol.

Telnet: An application that provides terminal emulation for remote connections.

Time to Live (TTL): An attribute assigned to cached objects to indicate how long they should be stored in the cache.

Transmission Control Protocol (TCP): A protocol that handles data transmissions, error control, and ensures that data arrives intact. TCP is a connection-oriented protocol.

TTL: *See* Time to Live.

UDP: *See* User Datagram Protocol.

Upstream: The computer closest to the Internet in a Proxy Server chain.

User Datagram Protocol (UDP): A protocol that provides connectionless communication similar to TCP.

Virtual Private Network (VPN): A network that is created to send secure data over the Internet using the PPTP protocol.

VPN: *See* Virtual Private Network.

Web Proxy Service: A Proxy Server feature that provides typical Web service for any CERN-complaint browser on any platform.

Windows NT Challenge/Response (NTCR): The most secure authentication method offered in NT.

Winsock API: A standard API for the development of Windows sockets applications.

Winsock Proxy Service: A Proxy Server feature that provides functionality for Winsock clients and Winsock applications.

WWW: A common name for the World Wide Web. WWW is usually used in conjunction with HTTP and HTML documents.

X Window: A standard used to define a protocol for the writing of graphical client/server applications.

Index

A

D

E

F

G

H

I

(continued)

J

K

L

M

N

R

S

T

U

V

W

X

IDG BOOKS WORLDWIDE, INC. END-USER LICENSE AGREEMENT

terms and conditions of this Agreement and you retain no copies. If the Software is an update or has been updated, any transfer must include the most recent update and all prior versions.

4. Restrictions On Use of Individual Programs. You must follow the individual requirements and restrictions detailed for each individual program in Appendix F, "What's on the CD-ROM?" of this Book. These limitations are also contained in the individual license agreements recorded on the Software Media. These limitations may include a requirement that after using the program for a specified period of time, the user must pay a registration fee or discontinue use. By opening the Software packet(s), you will be agreein g to abide by the licenses and restrictions for these individual programs that are detailed in Appendix F, "What's on the CD-ROM?" and on the Software Media. None of the material on this Software Media or listed in this Book may ever be redistributed, in original or modified form, for commercial purposes.

5. Limited Warranty.

   (a) IDGB warrants that the Software and Software Media are free from defects in materials and workmanship under normal use for a period of sixty (60) days from the date of purchase of this Book. If IDGB receives notification within the warranty period of defects in materials or workmanship, IDGB will replace the defective Software Media.

   (b) IDGB AND THE AUTHOR OF THE BOOK DISCLAIM ALL OTHER WARRANTIES, EXPRESS OR IMPLIED, INCLUDING WITHOUT LIMITATION IMPLIED WARRANTIES OF MERCHANTABILITY AND FITNESS FOR A PARTICULAR PURPOSE, WITH RESPECT TO THE SOFTWARE, THE PROGRAMS, THE SOURCE CODE CONTAINED THEREIN, AND/OR THE TECHNIQUES DESCRIBED IN THIS BOOK. IDGB DOES NOT WARRANT THAT THE FUNCTIONS CONTAINED IN THE SOFTWARE WILL MEET YOUR REQUIREMENTS OR THAT THE OPERATION OF THE SOFTWARE WILL BE ERROR FREE.

   (c) This limited warranty gives you specific legal rights, and you may have other rights that vary from jurisdiction to jurisdiction.

6. Remedies.

   (a) IDGB's entire liability and your exclusive remedy for defects in materials and workmanship shall be limited to replacement of the

Software Media, which may be returned to IDGB with a copy of your receipt at the following address: Software Media Fulfillment Department, Attn.: *Microsoft Proxy Server 2.0 MCSE Study Guide*, IDG Books Worldwide, Inc., 7260 Shadeland Station, Ste. 100, Indianapolis, IN 46256, or call 1-800-762-2974. Please allow three to four weeks for delivery. This Limited Warranty is void if failure of the Software Media has resulted from accident, abuse, or misapplication. Any replacement Software Media will be warranted for the remainder of the original warranty period or thirty (30) days, whichever is longer.

(b) In no event shall IDGB or the author be liable for any damages whatsoever (including without limitation damages for loss of business profits, business interruption, loss of business information, or any other pecuniary loss) arising from the use of or inability to use the Book or the Software, even if IDGB has been advised of the possibility of such damages.

(c) Because some jurisdictions do not allow the exclusion or limitation of liability for consequential or incidental damages, the above limitation or exclusion may not apply to you.

7. U.S. Government Restricted Rights. Use, duplication, or disclosure of the Software by the U.S. Government is subject to restrictions stated in paragraph (c)(1)(ii) of the Rights in Technical Data and Computer Software clause of DFARS 252.227-7013, and in subparagraphs (a) through (d) of the Commercial Computer—Restricted Rights clause at FAR 52.227-19, and in similar clauses in the NASA FAR supplement, when applicable.

8. General. This Agreement constitutes the entire understanding of the parties and revokes and supersedes all prior agreements, oral or written, between them and may not be modified or amended except in a writing signed by both parties hereto that specifically refers to this Agreement. This Agreement shall take precedence over any other documents that may be in conflict herewith. If any one or more provisions contained in this Agreement are held by any court or tribunal to be invalid, illegal, or otherwise unenforceable, each and every other provision shall remain in full force and effect.

CD Installation Instructions

Each software item on the *Microsoft Proxy Server 2.0 MCSE Study Guide* CD-ROM is located in its own folder. To install a particular piece of software, open its folder with My Computer or Internet Explorer. What you do next depends on what you find in the software's folder:

1. First, look for a `ReadMe.txt` file or a `.doc` or `.htm` document. If this is present, it should contain installation instructions and other useful information.
2. If the folder contains an executable (`.exe`) file, this is usually an installation program. Often it will be called `Setup.exe` or `Install.exe`, but in some cases the filename reflects an abbreviated version of the software's name and version number. Run the `.exe` file to start the installation process.
3. In the case of some simple software, the `.exe` file probably is the software — no real installation step is required. You can run the software from the CD to try it out. If you like it, copy it to your hard disk and create a Start menu shortcut for it.

The `ReadMe.txt` file in the CD-ROM's root directory may contain additional installation information, so be sure to check it.

For a listing of the software on the CD-ROM, see Appendix F.

Microsoft Product Warranty and Support Disclaimer